D1491165

Uneasy Compromise

Studies of Government Finance: Second Series

TITLES PUBLISHED

Uneasy Compromise
Problems of a Hybrid
Income-Consumption Tax

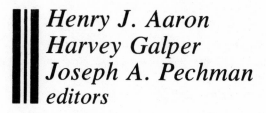

Henry J. Aaron
Harvey Galper
Joseph A. Pechman
editors

Studies of Government Finance

THE BROOKINGS INSTITUTION
WASHINGTON, D.C.

Copyright © 1988 by
THE BROOKINGS INSTITUTION
1775 Massachusetts Avenue, N.W., Washington, D.C. 20036

Library of Congress Cataloging-in-Publication data
Uneasy compromise : problems of a hybrid income-
consumption tax / Henry J. Aaron, Harvey Galper, Joseph
A. Pechman, editors.
    p.   cm.—(Studies of government finance. Second
series)
  Includes index.
  ISBN 0-8157-0046-6   ISBN 0-8157-0045-8 (pbk.)
  1. Income tax—United States. 2. Spendings tax—
United States.   I. Aaron, Henry J. II. Galper, Harvey,
1937–   . III. Pechman, Joseph A., 1918–   .
IV. Series.
HJ4652.U55 1988   336.2'00973—dc19   88-464
                                          CIP

9 8 7 6 5 4 3 2 1

THE BROOKINGS INSTITUTION is an independent organization devoted to nonpartisan research, education, and publication in economics, government, foreign policy, and the social sciences generally. Its principal purposes are to aid in the development of sound public policies and to promote public understanding of issues of national importance.

The Institution was founded on December 8, 1927, to merge the activities of the Institute for Government Research, founded in 1916, the Institute of Economics, founded in 1922, and the Robert Brookings Graduate School of Economics and Government, founded in 1924.

The Board of Trustees is responsible for the general administration of the Institution, while the immediate direction of the policies, program, and staff is vested in the President, assisted by an advisory committee of the officers and staff. The by-laws of the Institution state: "It is the function of the Trustees to make possible the conduct of scientific research, and publication, under the most favorable conditions, and to safeguard the independence of the research staff in the pursuit of their studies and in the publication of the results of such studies. It is not a part of their function to determine, control, or influence the conduct of particular investigations or the conclusions reached."

The President bears final responsibility for the decision to publish a manuscript as a Brookings book. In reaching his judgment on the competence, accuracy, and objectivity of each study, the President is advised by the director of the appropriate research program and weighs the views of a panel of expert outside readers who report to him in confidence on the quality of the work. Publication of a work signifies that it is deemed a competent treatment worthy of public consideration but does not imply endorsement of conclusions or recommendations.

The Institution maintains its position of neutrality on issues of public policy in order to safeguard the intellectual freedom of the staff. Hence interpretations or conclusions in Brookings publications should be understood to be solely those of the authors and should not be attributed to the Institution, to its trustees, officers, or other staff members, or to the organizations that support its research.

Foreword

Passage of the Tax Reform Act of 1986, though widely hailed as a major legislative achievement, did not resolve all the structural issues in income taxation. The compromises required to move the bill through Congress left the tax system with major problems, largely because the individual and corporation income taxes still contain elements of both income and consumption taxation. This book is intended to help policymakers understand the problems inherent in such a hybrid system and to suggest alternative methods of resolving them.

The papers in this volume were presented at a research conference held at the Brookings Institution in October 1986. The topics are divided into two categories. The first consists of conceptual issues that would be important under any tax system. The second consists of issues that arise because the current U.S. tax system reflects conflicting tax principles, some derived from the precept that all income should be taxed, some from the precept that saving should be exempted and only consumed income should be taxed, and some that are consistent with neither precept.

The editors are particularly grateful to Nancy D. Davidson, who directed the editing of the volume; individual chapters were edited by Barbara de Boinville, Martha V. Gottron, and James McEuen. Kathleen M. Bucholz, Richard Rice, and Kathleen Elliott Yinug provided secretarial assistance for the project. Victor M. Alfaro and Almaz S. Zelleke reviewed the tables and text for accuracy. Susan Woollen coded the manuscript for typesetting, and Florence Robinson prepared the index.

Henry J. Aaron and Joseph A. Pechman are senior fellows in the Economic Studies program at Brookings, and Aaron is also professor of economics at the University of Maryland. Harvey Galper is a former senior fellow in the Brookings Economic Studies program and is associate national director for tax analysis at Peat Marwick Main & Co.

This volume is the twenty-fourth publication in the Brookings Studies in Government Finance second series, which is devoted to examining issues in taxation and public expenditure policy. The research conference and this volume were supported by grants from the Arthur Young Foundation, Coopers and Lybrand, Deloitte, Haskins and Sells, and Peat Marwick Main & Co.

The views expressed in this volume are those of the authors and the conference participants and should not be ascribed to the trustees, officers, or other staff members of the Brookings Institution or to the organizations contributing to the support of the project.

BRUCE K. MAC LAURY
President

February 1988
Washington, DC

Contents

ix

Tables

Figures

Uneasy Compromise

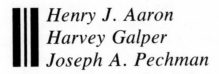
Henry J. Aaron
Harvey Galper
Joseph A. Pechman

Introduction

FOR DECADES U.S. tax experts have been debating whether the nation would be better served by an income tax or by a consumption tax. Both taxes apply to total household resources and both taxes can be levied at graduated rates. The essential difference is that the consumption tax exempts saving, while an income tax does not. In practice, all tax systems are mixed or "hybrid" systems that contain both income tax and consumption tax features. Although legislators have reasons for enacting such mixtures, they result in inequities, inefficiencies, and abuse. This book deals with the difficult issues raised by a hybrid tax system and the solutions to those problems.

The Hybrid Tax System

Analysts have recognized that despite their names, neither the "personal income tax" nor the "corporation income tax" is a true income tax. For a variety of reasons, practical and political, Congress has repeatedly shied away from any attempt to tax such major elements of income as accrued but unrealized capital gains. It has also exempted such important elements of both income and consumption as employer-financed health insurance and term life insurance. And certain elements of the personal income tax—notably the treatment of qualified pensions, individual retirement accounts, Keogh plans, and other tax-sheltered saving—resemble the rules that would apply under a consumption tax. In addition, Congress on its own initiative and with the consent of successive administrations has enacted a host of special-purpose credits, deductions, and allowances for reasons that had no basis in the principles of either income or consumption taxation.

In combination, these provisions drastically narrowed the tax base.

1

In 1986, the year before the Tax Reform Act of 1986 became effective, total personal income was $3,534 billion and total consumption was $2,800 billion; but total taxable personal income was only about $1,650 billion. An important cumulative consequence of separate decisions that narrowed the tax base—few of which were justifiable on grounds of equity or economic efficiency—was to increase substantially the tax rates needed to raise any given amount of revenue.

Accordingly, the administration and Congress faced a choice in 1986 when they considered the options for comprehensive tax reform. They could have affirmed the principles of income taxation or they could have moved decisively to convert the hybrid tax to a true consumption tax. In many respects they chose the former course. Congress repealed a number of provisions that are inconsistent with income taxation, particularly the capital gains preference, and it considerably broadened both the personal and corporation tax bases in other respects. But Congress barely considered a number of other measures that would have further strengthened the income tax. Lawmakers clearly were not prepared, among other things, to tax accrued but unrealized capital gains, to deny longstanding tax benefits to pension and retirement saving, or to include in the tax base imputed income from owner-occupied housing and the value of employer-financed nonpension fringe benefits. Congress was also not prepared to require either that businesses deduct annually only the actual decline in the value of depreciable equipment and structures or that all capital income should be adjusted for the distortions introduced by inflation.

Alternatively, if the administration and Congress had elected to shift the tax base to consumption, a number of highly controversial steps would have been required. Among them would have been the inclusion in the personal tax base of the value of all employer-financed consumer-type fringe benefits, such as health insurance, term life insurance, and child-care allowances. Also, because there is no rationale under a consumption tax for imposing a corporation income tax, it would have been necessary either to repeal the corporation income tax or to allow businesses to take immediate deductions for all capital expenditures and to pay refunds for resulting losses. And, although the tax benefits to retirement saving could be continued, consumption tax rules would either deny all interest deductions or require borrowers to take into their tax bases the net value of loans received. Neither Congress nor the president was willing to take any of these steps. Whatever merits academic economists and lawyers might find in the consumption tax, it was clear that the U.S. political system was not ready to embrace it.

By the actions it did not take, as much as by those it did, Congress confirmed that the U.S. tax system would remain à hybrid system composed in part of elements consistent with the principles of income taxation, in part of elements consistent with the principles of consumption taxation, and in part of provisions consistent with neither. The United States, it has become clear, will continue the effort to tax some income from capital, as required by the canons of income taxation. But it will also continue to allow income to accumulate tax free in qualified pensions and various tax-sheltered savings instruments, and it will continue not to tax appreciation of assets not sold during the tax year, as required by the principles of consumption taxation. At least for the time being, the United States will also continue to permit fringe benefits to go untaxed, in contravention of the principles of both income and consumption taxation. In short, Congress and the administration have affirmed that the United States will continue to maintain a hybrid tax system, altered in significant ways by the Tax Reform Act of 1986, but still a vexing and at times confusing amalgam to those who yearn for the pure and consistent implementation of one form of ideal tax or another.

Problems of a Hybrid Tax System

This political consensus to maintain the hybrid tax system is important not because it offends the esthetic sensibilities of some economists and lawyers, but because the coexistence of provisions reflecting conflicting principles of taxation, or no principles at all, creates problems for the achievement of the goals of tax reform. An improvement in fairness, economic efficiency, and simplicity is much more difficult to achieve under a hybrid system than it would be under either a pure income or a pure consumption tax.

For example, the decision to permit businesses to take depreciation deductions greater than the true decline in the value of assets creates artificial tax losses that can be used to shelter real income. In extreme cases, large and profitable businesses might show no taxable income whatsoever, a situation widely regarded as unfair. The congressional response was to introduce in 1969 and to strengthen greatly in 1986 the minimum taxes on corporations and individuals.

4 HENRY AARON, HARVEY GALPER, AND JOSEPH PECHMAN

Many of the other provisions of the Tax Reform Act of 1986 and of other recent tax legislation were fashioned to prevent taxpayers from achieving unintended reductions in tax liabilities by combining transactions—some taxed according to income tax principles and some according to consumption tax principles. The act, for example, divides interest deductions into several categories, each with its own rules and limitations. These categories include interest on up to two mortgages secured by residences, plus interest on loans for home improvements and for qualified medical or educational expenses, all of which may be deducted; interest payments associated with passive investments, which may not be deducted currently if the investments generate losses above stipulated limits on this category of investment; personal interest, which after a phase-in period will no longer be deductible at all; investment interest, which is deductible only up to the amount of net investment income; and business interest, which is fully deductible if the taxpayer has a bona fide trade or business. These distinctions, which add greatly to complexity, are designed to prevent groups of transactions—say, personal loans to finance the purchase of mutual fund shares—through which taxpayers could generate both currently deductible interest payments and income in the form of capital gains that would be taxable only in the distant future, if at all.

Whether the new restrictions will prove to be administratively workable or effective in curbing abuses is unclear. What is beyond dispute is that taxpayers will find in the inconsistencies of a hybrid system legal ways to avoid taxes and that policymakers will then consider whether additional changes are needed to prevent tax avoidance. The tax legislation of 1986 should be regarded as another skirmish in a long and continuing contest.

This book contains a series of papers that examine the state of debate about tax reform in the wake of the Tax Reform Act of 1986. The authors were asked to focus on two types of issues. First, how much is known about the effects of tax policy? Are current models and analytical techniques adequate to answer the questions that policy officials ask? If further progress is to be made on tax reform, tax theorists and practitioners must outline targets at which Congress should be aiming. Second, what are the special problems for tax policy that arise within a hybrid tax system, and how can they be resolved? It is not sufficient, for example, to urge that interest income or interest expenses be treated uniformly if Congress has made clear, emphatically and repeatedly, that it wishes to distinguish between special accounts labeled as "retirement saving," income from which is exempt, from current taxation, and other forms of interest income, which are taxed as earned. As long as the hybrid system continues to exist, tax reformers must specify the restrictions that should be placed on these patently inconsistent rules to minimize unintended taxpayer manipulation and tax avoidance. Similar problems arise with respect to business losses, rental activities, capital gains, and investment incentives.

Major Issues

The book is divided into four main parts. The first part is devoted to the application of general equilibrium models to tax analysis. The second is concerned with the transmission of the effect of tax legislation through capital markets. The third deals with the taxation of saving and investment. The fourth considers how to resolve two major structural issues in a hybrid tax system: how to correct the distortions that arise from the taxation of nominal rather than real incomes and how to deal with the ability of some high-income individuals and corporations to pay little or no tax.

General Equilibrium Models

Unlike smaller-scale or partial equilibrium analyses, general equilibrium models use an analytical framework that divides the entire economy into its component factor and product markets. Such models have important advantages over analyses limited to one market. Many tax policies have effects far removed from the person, business, or market where the tax is imposed. In some cases the ultimate effects differ in essential ways from the direct consequences.

A quarter-century ago, Arnold Harberger pointed out that the effects of capital income taxes levied in only part of the economy produced economywide effects on the allocation of capital and on the rate of return. The effects spread because owners of capital, he assumed, seek the highest net rate of return. If taxation of capital in one sector of the economy is increased, capital will move from that sector to other sectors, changing the before-tax rate of return everywhere. Harberger concluded that the corporation income tax reduces net income of all owners of capital—not just of owners of corporations—and that the total burden of the tax on owners of capital approximates total collections.

Harberger's seminal contribution inspired several economists—notably, John Shoven, John Whalley, and their collaborators—to develop empirical general equilibrium models. Typically, these models contain mathematical representations of two or more production sectors, a variety of households, and several commodities. The mathematical values in the equations are selected to approximate actual values of the corresponding real economic activities.

A critical question for policymakers concerns what to make of this large and highly technical branch of research. John Whalley surveys this field in the first chapter. He points out that such models are finding increasing application in several branches of economic analysis, including international trade, economic development, and public finance.

According to Whalley, general equilibrium models have advanced the understanding of tax policy in two important ways. First, these models can educate policymakers about tax issues within a framework that encompasses the interrelationships of various product and factor markets. Although the models do not yet produce reliable empirical estimates, they do generate fresh insights and perspectives about the implications of tax policy for resource allocation and income redistribution. In general, these models have persuaded many economists that public policy should increase the attention paid to the effects of taxes on economic efficiency, because taxes have been shown to generate costly distortions in investment, risk taking, and labor supply.

The second kind of benefit from general equilibrium models has resulted from their application to specific problems. Whalley points out that general equilibrium models have challenged the traditional conclusion of economic literature that sales taxes levied on the producer have the same effects on international trade as do sales taxes levied on the consumer. General equilibrium modeling shows that because of variations in the structure of sales taxation and the patterns of trade for specific commodities, the traditional conclusion may be far off the mark. Whalley also points out the major weaknesses of general equilibrium models, both statistical deficiencies for particular policy applications and more narrowly defined technical shortcomings.

Harberger and his successors made a number of assumptions that simplified analysis but also excluded important elements of economic decisionmaking. For example, they assumed that all assets are perfect substitutes in household portfolios. Harvey Galper, Robert Lucke, and Eric Toder use an approach in the spirit of Harberger's, but consider specifically the role of household portfolio choice in general equilibrium modeling. They examine how differences in the tax status of individuals, the taxation of various assets, and the riskiness of these assets influence the incidence of capital income taxation. Galper, Lucke, and Toder divide assets by their risk and tax characteristics and distinguish households on the basis of tax rates and willingness to bear risk. Their model highlights the link between the taxation of capital income at the household level and the cost of capital to firms that issue the assets households purchase.

Galper, Lucke, and Toder simulate the effects of the Tax Reform Act of 1986 on household portfolios, relative before-tax returns of various assets, costs of capital among economic sectors, and the welfare of households in various income classes. Changes in risk bearing account for an important part of the change in welfare, especially among high-income taxpayers, who benefit greatly under the new law from both increased after-tax incomes and reduced portfolio risk.

In his original work, Harberger also ignored international trade and capital movements. Joel Slemrod drops this assumption and finds that doing so transforms standard conclusions about the incidence of capital income taxes. Much or most of the burden of some capital taxes, he reports, will be borne by workers, rather than by owners of capital. This startling reversal of the normal result arises if domestic owners of capital have the option of shifting capital abroad to earn the prevailing world rate of return. By reducing the domestic capital stock, these capital movements cut the amount of capital available to each domestic worker, reduce productivity, and lower the wage rate.

The degree to which such shifting of capital taxes to labor occurs depends on a number of factors, including the nature of the capital tax (does it fall on all income generated within the taxing country, all income received by residents of the taxing country, or in some other fashion?); whether the taxing country is a capital importer or a capital exporter; the degree to which foreign assets are substitutes for domestic assets; the role of riskiness and of portfolio diversification; the nature of foreign tax systems; and the rules for offsetting foreign tax payments against domestic liabilities. The principal general conclusion of Slemrod's paper is that in a world of economically interdependent nations, analysis of the incidence and effects of taxes that ignores these interdependencies is likely to be highly misleading.

Financial Decisions

Sophisticated investors hold portfolios designed to maximize returns for a given level of risk. Because capital markets have become so highly developed and interrelated, such portfolios typically contain many different assets and are constructed so that investors are roughly indifferent at the margin to change in the composition of asset holdings. Accordingly, changes in tax rules affecting only a part of the portfolio will cause investors to reallocate their holdings, generating changes in prices and yields of all or many different assets. Only by taking the full range of such effects into account can one understand the consequences of tax legislation.

The two papers in this section develop this theme. Myron Scholes and Mark Wolfson argue persuasively for maintaining a very broad perspective in analyzing the effects of tax rules on corporate financial behavior. In their view, what are widely regarded as puzzles of corporate finance—such as why companies with high tax rates issue very little debt—may well be resolved in the context of the overall tax planning strategy of the corporation. In this context, tax planning includes not only the decision about how much debt of various maturities and how much stock of various classes and types to issue, but also the decisions about whether to buy or to lease assets, whether to buy physical capital or invest in research and development, whether to pay current or deferred compensation to employees, and what forms of deferred compensation to provide. These decisions are influenced not only by current tax law, but also by other tax rules that Congress might plausibly adopt. In addition, each company has a unique tax history; while its current capital structure may not be the one that managers would pick if they could change it costlessly or could start with a clean slate, adjusting the structure also generates costs that prevent quick responses.

The scope of tax planning is vast because tax rates vary by industry, asset, and form of organization, by company history, and over time. Traditional economic models usually fail to capture the richness of tax rules, expectations regarding future changes, and the other sources of variations in tax rates. Scholes and Wolfson draw together these various elements that must be part of any reasonably accurate predictive theory.

Alan Auerbach dramatizes these effects with an extended numerical exercise that illustrates the distributional effects of first allowing tax-payers to borrow to acquire tax-preferred assets and then limiting this privilege. In either case, the ability to borrow creates dramatic and surprising effects on relative and absolute tax liabilities and after-tax incomes of various groups in the economy. The key to the results is what happens to the before-tax returns on particular assets under alternative scenarios. When unrestricted borrowing is allowed, for example, the before-tax return on tax-preferred assets may fall to the point that high-income borrowers are actually worse off than they would be if borrowing were restricted. This result applies in a world of certainty. If assets are regarded as risky, this paradoxical outcome may be somewhat muted but is qualitatively unchanged. Auerbach's message is that policymakers should keep their eyes on the real effects of borrowing limits on after-tax incomes rather than on the cosmetics of tax avoidance.

Saving and Investment

The differences between income and consumption taxes are centered on the treatment of saving and investment. Recent tax debates have also been particularly intense in this area. Should the government offer incentives for certain types of investment, such as capital investment or research and development? How sensitive is household saving to tax rules affecting saving? Given the diverse rules governing the taxation of various kinds of saving and investment, how should transactions be restricted to prevent abuse? The most exotic changes of the Tax Reform Act of 1986—such as the limits on "passive" losses, the classification of interest into several different categories with separate rules, and the minimum taxes—affect this area of taxation. Critical questions remain concerning the ability of tax authorities to design rules that taxpayers cannot effectively circumvent and the willingness of elected officials to stick by such rules.

David Starrett reviews what is known about the sensitivity of saving to changes in the taxation of capital income. Because taxes can directly change the net return to savers, this question is part of the broader issue of how sensitive saving is to any change in the net rate of return. Two recent articles have had considerable influence among economists on these issues. Michael Boskin estimated that an increase in net income to savers of 10 percent—say, from 6 percent to 6.6 percent—would increase saving by about 4 percent—say, from 5 percent of income to 5.2 percent of income. Lawrence Summers developed a simulation model that suggested cuts in taxes on capital income might increase saving much more than suggested by previous theoretical or empirical estimates, such as Boskin's. Starrett reports the generally accepted point that economic theory gives no indication whether a reduction in taxes on capital income will increase or decrease saving, in either the short run or the long run. He presents a variety of simulations that lead to the conclusion that cuts in taxes on capital income might plausibly increase saving, but by less than either Summers or Boskin suggests, or might even reduce saving. Without considerable additional research, Starrett concludes, there is simply no way to predict the effect on saving of a cut in capital income taxes.

William Andrews and David Bradford examine the role and purpose of savings incentives in an income tax. They point out that the very concept of savings "incentives" presumes that income, rather than consumption, is the correct base for taxation. On the other hand, if the tax system is acknowledged to be a hybrid, why should rules that differ from those required for a pure income tax be regarded as incentives? If a good model existed of what a hybrid tax should be, the treatment of saving should be evaluated against this standard; but none exists.

Andrews and Bradford review the features of the current hybrid system and then define savings incentives as provisions that tend to increase after-tax returns to saving. They leave to others the question of how saving responds to these incentives.

They point out that whether a particular savings incentive actually increases after-tax rates of return on the margin is often unclear. If capital markets permit households to borrow and lend as much as they want at a given before-tax interest rate, tax incentives for saving are unlikely to increase after-tax rates of return, although they will change the forms in which savings are held. Taxpayers will simply borrow to buy the tax-preferred asset, with no marginal increase in after-tax returns. Savings incentives may, however, affect other measures of economic performance. For example, if rules limit the use of savings incentives to a certain fraction of earnings, as in the case of individual retirement accounts, people may increase labor supply in order to be able to divert saving to such instruments.

If capital markets do not permit households to borrow and lend as much as they want at a single interest rate, savings incentives can have direct effects on household savings behavior. Furthermore, rules against deducting interest on loans taken to finance investments in tax-sheltered accounts help to ensure that savings incentives increase the returns of saving to taxpayers. Andrews and Bradford devote particular attention to the largest savings incentive in current law, the collection of preferential rules governing retirement saving.

Charles Hulten and Robert Klayman examine a striking paradox between the implications of recent contributions to economic theory for optimal tax structures and the character of recommendations for tax reform. According to economic theory, the optimum tax structure should consist of a mixture of commodity taxes at different rates and of taxes at different rates on labor and capital income. Tax reform plans, however, typically exclude such variations in tax rates in favor of uniformity. How can this inconsistency be reconciled? Hulten and Klayman do not challenge the analytical correctness of recent theoretical advances, but suggest a number of practical reasons why they should not be applied. Uniformity and simplicity of business taxation should remain centerpieces of desirable reforms because the complexity of the theoretical analysis makes it susceptible to manipulation by clever model builders and difficult for the general public to understand. At the same time, the informational requirements for determining the various tax rates suggested by the theory are prohibitively burdensome.

Structural Features of a Hybrid Tax

The final section of the book examines the functioning of the tax system when external forces or internal manipulations lead to outcomes that legislators did not anticipate. Daniel Halperin and Eugene Steuerle consider the question of whether the income taxes should be levied on real income or, as is now done, on nominal income. In 1984 the Treasury Department proposed adjustments in the calculations of capital gains, interest income and deductions, depreciation, and costs of goods sold from inventories that would have moved the tax system toward the goal of taxing real, rather than nominal, income. This was the plan that became known as "Treasury I." The White House rejected most of these suggestions and Congress rejected the rest. Because the threat of inflation remains credible and the distortions in tax liabilities that it generates are large, Halperin and Steuerle examine whether it is possible to design a relatively simple and fair set of inflation adjustments. They demonstrate that full taxation of all nominal income would impose unacceptably high tax rates on real capital income, even at modest rates of inflation. But almost all forms of capital income receive some special treatment, which is then justified in part as a substitute for indexing. As a result, the effective rates of tax on different types of capital income varied greatly under the pre-1986 law—from outright subsidies in some cases to rates exceeding 50 percent in others. The 1986 law eliminated most, if not all, of the subsidies and narrowed the differences in tax rates. However, the effective tax rates on capital income would rise precipitously if inflation were to accelerate.

Halperin and Steuerle conclude that the proper solution to this problem is to adjust capital income for inflation. In the case of capital gains, depreciation, and inventory costs, the remedy is to adjust the cost of assets for price changes and then calculate the taxable quantity with the inflation-adjusted basis. Adjustment of interest payments (for both debtors and creditors) is more difficult, but the authors believe that a suitable method can be devised to make the adjustments in a fair and practicable way.

Whether inflation or its tax-related distortions are ended, some taxpayers will continue to manipulate the inconsistent rules of a hybrid system to reduce their tax liabilities more than Congress intended. This problem can be handled in a variety of ways. The most elegant is to revise the underlying rules so that taxes fall on all economic income and almost no one can avoid these taxes to an undesired extent. A less elegant approach is to enact a minimum tax as a backstop to the regular income tax to prevent businesses and households from completely escaping their tax-paying responsibilities.

The tax reform plan submitted by the Treasury Department in November 1984 came close to meeting the first standard. It included in the tax base all income receipts except interest on state and local securities and eliminated most, but not all, unnecessary personal deductions. It would also have adjusted all elements of capital income for inflation. With these elements in place, the Treasury concluded that it could call for the repeal of the minimum tax on both individuals and corporations. In the end, Congress changed the tax code far less than the Treasury had initially suggested and therefore felt impelled to strengthen the individual and corporate minimum taxes to prevent the abuse that would still be possible. These minimum taxes are highly complex. Some critics claim that they are unfair and doubt that they can be administered.

Michael Graetz and Emil Sunley examine the desirability and likely effects of the minimum taxes. Despite the complexities, they conclude that equity justifies a minimum tax for both the individual and the corporate income taxes. Their preferred approach would apply one-half of the regular income tax rates to all of the taxpayer's income—including a comprehensive list of tax preferences

The papers in this book do not add up to a call for either an income tax or a consumption tax. They are inspired by the realization that while advocates of either pure approach to taxation may pave the way for a superior tax system sometime in the distant future, the tax debate today and in the years immediately ahead will address how to balance conflicting tax principles, drawn in part from the norms of income taxation, in part from the norms of consumption taxation, and in part from concerns over nontax problems. Tax analysts interested in contributing to that debate must come to terms with this fact. They should recognize that recommendations for perfecting pure forms of taxation may well be inferior advice for improving a hybrid tax system. Of equal importance, they may be politically irrelevant.

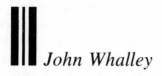 *John Whalley*

Lessons from General Equilibrium Models

THIS PAPER reviews experience with general equilibrium models, reflecting on what has been learned and how these models can best be used in the policy process. People in both the policy and academic communities are impressed by the technical sophistication of recent general equilibrium tax policy models, since they capture interactions among many different markets in the economy and contain a rich array of preference and technology parameters. But there is a degree of skepticism in both communities when it actually comes to using their results to formulate policy.

It is widely believed that these models, even if structurally complex, remain overly simple in their treatment of a variety of features, such as time, market structure, foreign trade, public expenditures, and especially the intricacies of the taxes being studied. Also, the specifications used are not tested in any meaningful sense, and model simulations are based on imperfect and sometimes grossly unreliable data. Therefore policymakers are tempted to dismiss results from general equilibrium tax policy models as both naive and too remote from the practicalities of day-to-day policymaking to be useful.

I find this view of recent modeling experience a little too negative. While it may be true that there have been unrealistic models, this is by no means true of them all. Moreover, while their results are perhaps still found largely in the professional journals rather than in the folklore of the policy community, these models have already contributed a surprisingly large amount of direct relevance and enduring value to tax policy design. Their major contribution lies in providing broad-ranging insights,

I am grateful to Debbie Fretz for research assistance and to Mervyn King, Charles McLure, and conference participants for comments on an earlier version.

15

many of which challenge existing perceptions as to the ways in which tax policies affect the economy, rather than in providing precise estimates of the effects of this or that tax policy. Many of the most important contributions are in the form of background work that contributes to a general climate of opinion in which policy decisions are made. These models thus need to be seen in a quite different light from the macro forecasting models of the 1960s. They are best thought of as attempts to use numerical versions of existing theoretical models with specific functional forms and parameter values. This added structure is then used to investigate model behavior under alternative policy changes.

Also, one has to evaluate experience with these models relative to the other options available to policymakers. It is the effects of taxes on resource allocation and income distribution that usually dominate debates on tax structure. But when it actually comes to making decisions, time horizons are short, reliable data are frequently unavailable, and decisions are often based on the hunches and firmly held beliefs of a small group of advisers. If policymakers want input from economywide numerical models that deal with both of these key dimensions of tax effects and are based on a solid theoretical framework, there really are few alternatives to using some form of numerical general equilibrium model.

Applied General Equilibrium Policy Analysis

Most existing general equilibrium tax policy models are based on the well-known Arrow-Debreu model, which has become the centerpiece of modern economics since its introduction in 1954.[1] This model appears in the literature in many different forms. Its original formal statement by Arrow and Debreu was at an abstract level. It appears in diagrammatic form in the well-known two-sector treatment associated with Johnson and Meade.[2] It is also to be found in the formalizations of market-clearing equilibrium that are now popular in modern macroeconomics.[3]

1. Kenneth J. Arrow and Gerard Debreu, "Existence of an Equilibrium for a Competitive Economy," *Econometrica*, vol. 22 (July 1954), pp. 265–90.

2. Harry G. Johnson, "The Gains from Freer Trade with Europe: An Estimate," *Manchester School of Economic and Social Studies*, vol. 26 (September 1958), pp. 247–55; and James E. Meade, *The Theory of International Economic Policy*, vol. 2: *Trade and Welfare* (London: Oxford University Press, 1955).

3. Thomas J. Sargent, "A Classical Macroeconometric Model for the United States," *Journal of Political Economy*, vol. 84 (April 1976), pp. 207–37.

The structure of the basic model is both simple and easy to understand. Consumers have preferences and maximize utility subject to their budget constraints. This maximization leads to consumer demand functions, which, when aggregated across households, yield market demand functions. The economy also has a specification of technological possibilities, through which commodities can be used to produce other commodities. All commodities are owned by consumers, and when sold yield income, which finances demands. Commodities and technology jointly define the production possibilities set for the economy. Producers decide what to produce and how to produce it to maximize profits. An equilibrium occurs when relative commodity prices are such that all markets clear simultaneously. In equilibrium, market demands (consumer demands plus business demands for inputs) equal market supplies (endowments plus production), and no above-normal profits are made by any producer.

Over the years, many economists have applied and reapplied this basic model to tax analysis. In the 1950s Johnson and others used it to analyze tax incidence questions theoretically. Harberger, using various approximation devices, investigated functional incidence questions and the efficiency effects of taxes.[4] In the early 1970s Shoven and Whalley and others used this model, together with general equilibrium computational techniques, to analyze the combined efficiency and distributional effects of a variety of taxes.[5] This work led to larger-scale applied general equilibrium tax models based on representative data sets and parameter values for particular economies, such as Piggott and Whalley's model of the United Kingdom; the Ballard, Fullerton, Shoven, and Whalley model of the United States; Kehoe and Serra-Puche's model of Mexico; Keller's model of Holland; Piggott's model of Australia; and Kehoe and others' model of Spain.[6]

4. Arnold C. Harberger, "The Incidence of the Corporation Income Tax," *Journal of Political Economy*, vol. 70 (June 1962), pp. 215–40.

5. John B. Shoven and John Whalley, "A General Equilibrium Calculation of the Effects of Differential Taxation of Income from Capital in the U.S.," *Journal of Public Economics*, vol. 1 (November 1972), pp. 281–321.

6. John Piggott and John Whalley, "General Equilibrium Investigation of U.K. Tax-Subsidy Policy," in Michael J. Artis and A. Robert Nobay, eds., *Studies in Modern Economic Analysis* (Oxford: Blackwell, 1977), pp. 259–95; John Piggott and John Whalley, *U.K. Tax Policy and Applied General Equilibrium Analysis* (Cambridge University Press, 1985); Charles L. Ballard and others, *A General Equilibrium Model for Tax Policy Evaluation* (University of Chicago Press, 1985); Timothy J. Kehoe and Jaime Serra-Puche, "A Computational General Equilibrium Model with Endogenous Unemployment: An Analysis of the 1980 Fiscal Reform in Mexico," *Journal of Public*

Clearly, in building such models there are many elements of model design to be dealt with, even before one confronts the issue of how taxes are to be analyzed using such an approach. The dimensionality of the model in terms of goods and numbers of households needs to be decided upon. The treatment of time, foreign trade, and a series of other issues has to be resolved. Functional forms must be selected, and parameter values representative of the economy being studied must be chosen.

Functional forms are typically restricted to the family of "convenient" forms (Cobb-Douglas, CES, LES), in part to simplify computation, and static or simple dynamic models are used.[7] Taxes typically are represented as ad valorem distortions between buyers' and sellers' prices, which affect the allocation of resources and redistribute income.

In conducting policy analysis with the applied general equilibrium approach, the procedure that has come to be widely used is counterfactual equilibrium analysis.[8] This approach first involves calibration of a general equilibrium model to a data observation deemed representative of an original equilibrium. This is based on the strong assumption that the economy in question is in equilibrium under the existing tax policies. Policy changes are then considered as counterfactual experiments, with a new equilibrium computed for each alternative policy. A comparison between any computed counterfactual equilibrium and the original (or benchmark) equilibrium provides the basis for an evaluation of the consequences of the policy change. Counterfactual analysis using these techniques therefore offers a capability for analysis of the effects of a variety of hypothetical tax alternatives.

The current widespread use of model calibration is due, in part, to the

---

Economics, vol. 22 (October 1983), pp. 1–26; Wouter J. Keller, *Tax Incidence: A General Equilibrium Approach* (Amsterdam: North-Holland, 1980); John Piggott, "A General Equilibrium Evaluation of Australian Tax Policy" (Ph.D. dissertation, University of London, 1980); and Timothy J. Kehoe and others, "A General Equilibrium Analysis of the Indirect Tax Reform in Spain," Working Paper 66.86 (Universidad Autonoma de Barcelona, Department of Economics, 1986).

7. CES refers to "constant elasticity of substitution functions," and LES to the "linear expenditure system." Both of these are extensions of the familiar Cobb-Douglas functions, which, in the CES case, allow for nonunitary (but constant) substitution elasticities in preferences or production, and in the LES case, nonhomothetic preferences. The latter allow for cases in which the income elasticities of demand for commodities are different from unity.

8. Ahsan Mansur and John Whalley, "Numerical Specification of Applied General Equilibrium Models: Estimation, Calibration and Data," in Herbert E. Scarf and John B. Shoven, eds., *Applied General Equilibrium Analysis* (Cambridge University Press, 1984), pp. 69–127.

difficulties encountered in some of the larger-scale models developed in the early 1970s. At that time, the thinking was that one could simply go to the literature and extract estimates for production functions, demand functions, and other model parameters and use them directly in numerical general equilibrium models. However, models based on such estimates predicted unrealistic behavior with aggregate results unlike that summarized in national income accounts.

Because of this experience, calibration now requires the choice of behavioral relations that lead to realistic aggregate behavior even if the parameters and coefficients differ from those reported in the economic literature. This, in turn, means that applied models are typically not estimated, but only calibrated to a benchmark equilibrium data observation. Any additional parameter values required in this process, such as elasticities, are exogenously specified. Computation of equilibrium is thus undertaken only when the effects of a hypothetical policy change are to be considered, and at this point any one of a variety of computational methods can be applied.

Extending the Basic General Equilibrium Model

The basic general equilibrium model is static, assumes a competitive market structure, and ignores risk. In its simplest form it also ignores international trade by assuming a closed economy. There is no time dimension specified for the economy to adjust from one equilibrium to another, nor is any intertemporal optimization explicitly introduced. Because of these deficiencies, in extending general equilibrium models to incorporate tax effects and in building models to represent actual economies, this basic structure has had to be elaborated on in a variety of ways.

Incorporating Taxes

Early on, Shoven and Whalley showed how a variety of taxes can be simultaneously incorporated into the basic general equilibrium approach.[9] These include income taxes, modeled as taxes on personal

9. Shoven and Whalley, "A General Equilibrium Calculation of the Effects of Differential Taxation"; and John B. Shoven and John Whalley, "General Equilibrium with Taxes: A Computational Procedure and an Existence Proof," *Review of Economic Studies,* vol. 40 (October 1973), pp. 475–89.

incomes at progressive rates; corporate taxes, modeled as taxes on inputs of capital by industry; property taxes, also modeled as taxes on factor inputs; social security taxes, modeled as payroll taxes; and sales and excise taxes, modeled as either output taxes by industry or consumption taxes by households.

Shoven and Whalley indicated a fundamental difference in equilibrium structure that taxes introduce into the original Arrow-Debreu general equilibrium formulation. It arises from the endogeneity of tax revenues. They showed how the traditional N dimensional equilibrium problem becomes an $N + 1$ dimensional problem in models incorporating taxes. This is because tax revenues have to be fully incorporated as part of the equilibrium structure, accruing either to the government or to households through government redistribution. This creates a simultaneity: until revenues are known, it is not possible to calculate household demands, but tax revenues depend upon demands. Shoven and Whalley developed an approach to deal with these features, and showed that it is possible to have both a traditional Arrow-Debreu proof of the existence of a competitive equilibrium in the presence of taxes and a constructive proof based on Scarf's algorithm.[10]

They also demonstrated how it is possible to move beyond small-dimensional illustrative examples and build computational general equilibrium models representative of actual economies. An early example was Whalley's general equilibrium tax model of the United Kingdom, designed to analyze the effects of several tax changes occurring at the time of British entry into the European Economic Community.[11]

Subsequently, however, the adequate treatment of various taxes has become a central issue in model design. Inevitably, any attempt to capture the full complexity of modern tax systems in a single all-embracing model will miss some of the distortion generated by taxes, and most of the taxes analyzed raise difficulties in modeling. In the case of the corporate tax, for instance, modern public finance treats the tax as one financing instrument available to firms. These models, however,

10. John B. Shoven, "A Proof of the Existence of a General Equilibrium with *ad valorem* Commodity Taxes," *Journal of Economic Theory,* vol. 8 (May 1974), pp. 1–25; and Shoven and Whalley, "General Equilibrium with Taxes." See also Herbert Scarf, "On the Computation of Equilibrium Prices," in *Ten Economic Studies in the Tradition of Irving Fisher* (Wiley, 1967), pp. 207–30; and Herbert E. Scarf with Terje Hausen, *The Computation of Economic Equilibria* (Yale University Press, 1973).

11. John Whalley, "A Numerical Assessment of the April 1973 U. K. Tax Reforms" (Ph.D. dissertation, Yale University, 1973).

largely continue to treat it as a tax on the use of capital service inputs at different rates across industries. The full variety of differences in tax treatment across assets, financing vehicles, and sectors, stressed by King and Fullerton, is not captured.[12] Social security schemes are frequently modeled as payroll taxes and transfer schemes, without the intertemporal structure stressed in recent literature. Marginal distortions in personal taxes in such areas as housing, charitable giving, and debt financing of asset accumulation are not well captured.

Modeling Time

To incorporate time more fully, a number of the general equilibrium tax models have used dynamic equilibrium specifications in which sequences of equilibria are computed. An important strand of this literature initiated by Summers and taken further by Auerbach, Kotlikoff, and Skinner has used an overlapping-generations life-cycle structure to model numerically the intertemporal effects of taxes.[13] Their dynamic sequencing approach involves utility-maximizing behavior subject to lifetime wealth constraints. Summers's original work, based on a comparison between steady states, suggested large welfare effects from moving from an existing income tax to a consumption tax, and it attracted a lot of attention when it appeared because of the size of the results. Subsequent work suggested, however, that these effects are considerably smaller once the transition to a new balanced growth path is also included.[14]

In related work, Ballard and others have also developed a tax policy model for the U.S. economy with an intertemporal structure in which

12. Mervyn A. King and Don Fullerton, *The Taxation of Income from Capital: A Comparative Study of the United States, the United Kingdom, Sweden, and West Germany* (University of Chicago Press for National Bureau of Economic Research, Institut für Wirtschaftsforschung, and Industriens Utredningsinstitut, 1984).

13. Lawrence H. Summers, "Capital Taxation and Accumulation in a Life Cycle Growth Model," *American Economic Review*, vol. 71 (September 1981), pp. 533–44; and Alan J. Auerbach, Laurence J. Kotlikoff, and Jonathan Skinner, "The Efficiency Gains from Dynamic Tax Reform," *International Economic Review*, vol. 24 (February 1983), pp. 81–100.

14. Alan J. Auerbach and Laurence J. Kotlikoff, "National Savings, Economic Welfare, and the Structure of Taxation," in Martin Feldstein, ed., *Behavioral Simulation Methods in Tax Policy Analysis* (University of Chicago Press for National Bureau of Economic Research, 1983), pp. 459–98; and Auerbach, Kotlikoff, and Skinner, "The Efficiency Gains from Dynamic Tax Reform."

savings depend upon expected rates of return facing investors.[15] Savings reflect household intertemporal utility-maximizing behavior, with the utility function of households defined over current consumption and expected future consumption. Consumers are infinitely lived, and in each period they maximize utility subject to current income rather than lifetime wealth constraints.

In these models, the economy is specified as having a capital stock at an initial given point in time, which subsequently changes through time to reflect savings behavior. A change in tax policy, such as a move from an income to a consumption tax, has the effect of instantaneously increasing saving, which increases the capital stock but decreases consumption. This reduction in consumption leads to an immediate decrease in welfare, but the higher capital stock eventually generates higher output and thus higher consumption. At some point the consumption profile under the new tax regime will cross the consumption profile associated with the original tax regime. The welfare effects of changing from one tax regime to another can then be assessed by comparing these consumption profiles.

Treating Trade and Factor Flows

Elaborations on the basic general equilibrium model have also incorporated foreign trade and factor flows. These elaborations raise important modeling issues for tax policy models, particularly when they are used to analyze the effects of taxes on small open economies.[16]

A number of different approaches have been used. Trade in goods has been incorporated through a net trade function for the foreign country with which the single country being modeled trades. This can involve a foreign offer curve, as used by Goulder, Shoven, and Whalley.[17] Typically these net trade functions are specified in constant-elasticity

15. Ballard and others, *A General Equilibrium Model for Tax Policy Evaluation.*

16. See John Whalley and Bernard Yeung, "External Sector 'Closing' Rules in Applied General Equilibrium Models," *Journal of International Economics,* vol. 16 (February 1984), pp. 123–38; and Bob Hamilton and John Whalley, "General Equilibrium Tax Policy Modeling for Small Open Economies" (University of Western Ontario, Department of Economics, 1986).

17. Lawrence H. Goulder, John B. Shoven, and John Whalley, "Domestic Tax Policy and the Foreign Sector: The Importance of Alternative Foreign Sector Formulations to Results from a General Equilibrium Tax Analysis Model," in Feldstein, ed., *Behavioral Simulation Methods in Tax Policy Analysis,* pp. 333–64.

form, which in the simple two-good case degenerates to a constant-elasticity offer curve. In this case, through the trade balance restriction, the elasticity of the offer curve simultaneously implies both an elasticity for export demand and an elasticity of import supply for the country being modeled.

Other approaches, however, can be taken to closure of the external sector. One involves explicitly incorporating price-taking behavior for the economy whose tax policies are being investigated.[18] This allows use of the fixed world prices and full employment conditions for domestic factors to determine endogenously both zero-profit factor prices and outputs of domestic industries. For smaller economies, such as Canada, this form of treatment may be more appropriate than assuming foreign export demand and import supply functions.

Other modeling issues arise with the treatment of international factor flows. The traditional general equilibrium model assumes fixed endowments of factors by country, yet tax policy toward inward and outward capital flows can be important, especially in smaller economies. In their elaborations of the basic U.S. tax model, Goulder, Shoven, and Whalley have shown not only how this model can be extended to incorporate factor flows, but also that the extension significantly affects the analysis of tax policies.[19] (Slemrod also explores these issues in his paper in this book.)

Modeling Risk

Another elaboration of the basic Arrow-Debreu model incorporates risk. This is somewhat more complex than modifications to include time, but Slemrod and Galper, Lucke, and Toder have taken important strides in this direction.[20] In Slemrod's model, for instance, household behavior

18. Hamilton and Whalley, "General Equilibrium Tax Policy Modeling."

19. Goulder, Shoven, and Whalley, "Domestic Tax Policy and the Foreign Sector."

20. Joel Slemrod, "A General Equilibrium Model of Taxation with Endogenous Financial Behavior," in Feldstein, ed., *Behavioral Simulation Methods in Tax Policy Analysis,* pp. 427–54; Joel Slemrod, "A General Equilibrium Model of Taxation That Uses Micro-Unit Data: With an Application to the Impact of Instituting a Flat-Rate Income Tax," in John Piggott and John Whalley, eds., *New Developments in Applied General Equilibrium Analysis* (Cambridge University Press, 1985), pp. 221–52; and Harvey Galper, Robert Lucke, and Eric Toder, "Taxation, Portfolio Choice, and the Allocation of Capital: A General Equilibrium Approach," Brookings Discussion Papers in Economics, March 1986.

toward risk is reflected in utility functions that include a constant coefficient of relative risk aversion. Before they decide how much to consume, households decide the amount of risk they wish to bear. In turn, firms supply both risky and riskless assets, with their supply decisions reflecting relative tax costs of these financing instruments and elasticity of substitution parameters among them. As Slemrod shows, the treatment of risk can also make a substantial difference to the behavior of general equilibrium tax models.

Incorporating Market Structure

Market structure is another area that invites elaboration on the basic Arrow-Debreu model. The basic general equilibrium model uses a strong assumption of competitive pricing, but in some of the other policy areas where applied general equilibrium models have been used, it has become apparent how important these market structure assumptions are. This is most notable in the trade area, where the work of Harris has emphasized how a change in assumption from competitive behavior to collusive pricing, along with increasing returns to scale, can dramatically change the welfare effects associated with changes in trade policy, such as trade liberalization.[21] Although similar modifications have not yet been made in the tax policy area, their potential importance seems clear from the work in trade.

The discussion above thus gives some idea as to how the basic Arrow-Debreu general equilibrium approach has been adapted and extended when applied to numerical general equilibrium tax policy modeling. These variations on the basic approach offer a rich modeling capability for tax policy analysts, but also a perplexing range of choices for the policymaker wishing to obtain definitive answers as to the likely effects of any proposed policy changes. The particular model variant used, along with the choice of numerical specification, can substantially affect the results that these models yield. Anyone familiar with the way economic theory has evolved over the last ten or fifteen years will be well aware that there are many different variants of theoretical models that each give widely differing analyses of policy issues, and the proliferation of variants of the basic Arrow-Debreu model in applied work is in part a reflection of this.

21. Richard G. Harris with David Cox, *Trade, Industrial Policy, and Canadian Manufacturing* (Toronto: Ontario Economic Council, 1984).

Some Examples of Applied General Equilibrium Tax Models

To get a more complete picture of the general equilibrium approach to tax policy modeling, it may help to delve more deeply into individual models to see how they have been constructed, to what issues they have been applied, and what the main findings have been. I briefly summarize seven recent modeling efforts, representing a variety of approaches. Two are larger-scale, multipurpose models aiming to capture the major distorting effects of complete tax systems. Two are smaller-scale, more issue-specific modeling efforts focused respectively on tax issues associated with risk taking and intertemporal allocation. The final three are more recent work, indicative of the evolution of the field into new areas. Tables 1 and 2 summarize some of the main features and policy implications of results of each of these models, as well as four additional models for other countries.

Large Multipurpose Models

Piggott and Whalley use a large-scale model developed in the mid-1970s to evaluate the distorting effects of the tax and subsidy system in operation in the United Kingdom at the time.[22] This model is calibrated to a data set from 1973, a year in which major changes were made in the U.K. system, including the introduction of a value-added tax.

Production functions in the model allow for substitution between factors according to CES value-added functions. Joint production and intermediate use of goods in production are incorporated using a fixed-coefficient structure. Literature sources are used to select a central set of production function elasticity values, around which sensitivity analysis is conducted.

Counterfactual experiments performed with the model involve cases in which the entire existing tax and subsidy system is removed, as well as cases in which only specific taxes are abolished or modified. Each of these counterfactual policy changes is made under substitution of yield-preserving, broadly based taxes or subsidies that keep the size of the public sector constant in the model. This procedure is necessary because

22. Piggott and Whalley, "General Equilibrium Investigation of U.K. Tax Subsidy Policy"; and Piggott and Whalley, *U.K. Tax Policy and Applied General Equilibrium Analysis*.

Table 1. *Main Characteristics of Eleven Tax Policy Models*

Model	Economy studied	Base year for data	General-purpose or issue-specific	Dimensionality	Taxes covered	Functional forms
Piggott and Whalley	United Kingdom	1973	General-purpose	33 industries, 100 household groups	All major taxes and subsidies	Nested CES-LES
Ballard and others	United States	1973	General-purpose	19 industries, 15 consumer goods, 12 household classes	All major federal, state, and local taxes	Nested CES-fixed coefficient (production); nested CES-Cobb-Douglas (consumption)
Slemrod	United States	1977	Issue-specific: capital income	9 income classes, 4 goods, 6 assets	Personal and corporate income taxes, property taxes	Cobb-Douglas (consumption)
Summers	United States	No historical data used (rough approximation)	Issue-specific: capital taxation	1 good, 1 household sector	Capital taxes	Constant elasticity with constant rate of discount (utility)
Goulder and Summers	United States	1973	Issue-specific: asset prices and investment	5 industries, 15 consumer goods, 1 household	Major federal, state, and local taxes	CES-fixed factor (production); fixed expenditure shares (consumption)
Galper, Lucke, and Toder	United States	1983	Issue-specific: capital stock allocation	3 suppliers of capital, 400 representative households, 5 assets	Statutory corporate tax, entire schedule of personal taxes	Unit-elastic demand for capital

Author	Country	Year (data)	Purpose	Dimensions	Taxes	Functional forms
Jorgenson and Yun	United States	1955–80 (econometric estimation)	Issue-specific: efficiency effects of taxes on capital allocation	1 consumer, 3 sectors, 4 commodity groups	Sales tax on consumer and investment goods, income tax on capital and labor services, property taxes	Intertemporal logarithmic utility function; translog price functions with two-stage allocation process (production)
Piggott	Australia	1972–73	General-purpose	12 household groups, 18 domestic and 14 foreign industries	All major taxes and subsidies	Nested CES (demand); CES value-added (production)
Keller	Netherlands	1973	General-purpose	4 demand sectors, 4 industries	Taxes on consumer goods and services, on capital goods, imports, labor capital and corporate income; lump-sum taxes	Nested CES (demand and production)
Kehoe and Serra-Puche	Mexico	1977	General-purpose	35 goods (including 14 production goods), 12 consumer groups	All major taxes including sector-specific taxes	Fixed coefficient-Cobb-Douglas (production); Cobb-Douglas (demand)
Kehoe and others	Spain	1980	General-purpose	12 production sectors, 27 goods, 8 households, 2 foreign sectors	Major taxes including turnover tax on production, social security taxes, taxes on foreign trade	Cobb-Douglas (demand and production)

Sources: See footnotes in text.

Table 2. *Policy Implications of Model Results*

Model	Policy implications
Piggott and Whalley	Distortionary effects of tax-subsidy system higher than conventionally assumed (6–9 percent of NDP); major sources of welfare loss are housing subsidies, excise taxes, capital income taxes.
Ballard and others	Integration of corporate and personal taxes yields significant welfare gains; introduction of progressive consumption tax yields similar gains; both policies can be Pareto-improving for income classes modeled.
Slemrod	Indexing of tax system leads to efficiency gains; lowest income classes slightly worse off, highest income classes substantially better off.
Summers	Increase in output and welfare from shift from capital taxation to consumption taxation much larger than previously thought; increase in welfare for representative consumer equivalent to approximately six years' income.
Goulder and Summers	Reduction of corporate income tax from 46 to 34 percent raises firm values significantly in all industries modeled (15 to 21 percent); reduction of investment tax credit reduces capital stock and productivity of capital; a combination of these policies reduces aggregate capital stock over the longer term.
Galper, Lucke, and Toder	Introduction of flat tax rates and integration of corporate and personal taxes each lead to expansion of corporate sector in the absence of portfolio effects; inclusion of portfolio effects weakens and in some cases reverses this result.
Jorgenson and Yun	Tax reform of 1981–82 increased potential economic welfare by 3.5 to 4 percent of 1980 private national wealth; neutralizing treatment of assets between corporate and noncorporate sectors leads to welfare losses, while shifting from direct taxation of income from capital to indirect consumption taxation leads to large gains.
Piggott	Replacement of all taxes and subsidies with an equal-yield export tax leads to a total welfare gain of 3.5 percent of NDP.
Keller	Efficiency effects of most taxes are small (about 10 percent of the induced changes in public consumption); an increase in corporate income tax generates a positive excess burden that is twice the resulting change in consumption, with only a moderate burden borne by suppliers of capital.
Kehoe and Serra-Puche	Goal of stimulating activity in agriculture and foodstuffs by exempting these sectors from taxation appears plausible; all model scenarios estimate that the lowest- and highest-income households will benefit more from the tax changes considered than will the middle-income groups.
Kehoe and others	Introduction of value-added tax reduces consumer welfare by 2–3 percent on average, with the high-income group experiencing greater reductions than the low-income group; retention of the value-added tax accompanied by a reduction in social security contributions paid by employers leads to an overall improvement in welfare.

changes in the relative size of the public and private sectors in tax models can give misleading estimates of gains or losses from tax changes, especially where the focus of the analysis is on the distorting effects of particular taxes and subsidies.

Piggott and Whalley estimate that the U.K. tax and subsidy system accounted for annual welfare losses of 6 to 9 percent of net domestic product in 1973, an estimate that at the time was higher than that conventionally used for such distortions. They find the principal sources of these losses to be capital income taxes, excise taxes, and local authority housing subsidies, which jointly account for approximately 80 percent of the distorting costs of the combined tax and subsidy system. They also find the effects of inflation (in the absence of indexing) yield another significant source of distorting loss.

They also evaluate the income redistribution effects of the tax and subsidy system. In welfare terms, they find that a removal of all tax and subsidy policies and a replacement by a yield-preserving single-rate commodity tax inflict a welfare loss on the poorest decile of households equivalent to around 20 percent of their income (in part due to the removal of local authority housing subsidies), while the top decile gains about the same amount (in part through the removal of the income tax). This picture is different from the conventional view of the redistributive effects of the tax system based on incidence calculations, which are taken by many to suggest that the tax system has almost no effect on the household income distribution.[23]

Ballard and his colleagues also use a large-scale model, but of the U.S. economy rather than the U.K. economy, and have as their major focus intertemporal aspects of tax policy.[24] Like Piggott and Whalley, their elasticity estimates are also derived from literature sources, and they perform sensitivity analyses for the more important of these parameters, principally elasticities of labor supply and saving.

Ballard and colleagues focus on a dynamic equilibrium structure. They calculate a sequence of single-period static equilibria, in which savings decisions change the time profile of the economy's capital stock. Myopic expectations regarding the return on savings are assumed in order to simplify their computations, although in related work Ballard

23. See Joseph A. Pechman and Benjamin A. Okner, *Who Bears the Tax Burden?* (Brookings, 1974).

24. Ballard and others, *A General Equilibrium Model for Tax Policy Evaluation.*

and Goulder have found that a different treatment of expectations has little effect on results.[25]

They use their model for a series of policy analyses. The first of these evaluates four plans for corporate and personal income tax integration. They also consider replacing the federal personal income tax with a progressive consumption tax. In this model application, eight different plans are evaluated, differing in the fraction of savings treated as deductible, the fraction of dividends that are taxable, the fraction of nominal capital gains taxable at personal level, and the elimination or inclusion of preferential treatment of housing and changes in the corporate tax.

Ballard and colleagues also use their model to investigate, among other things, the relationship between tax rates and government revenue and the effects of changes in tax treatment of foreign income. They plot the relationship between tax rates and revenue for a range of values of labor supply elasticities, for instance, and find that reasonable estimates of the appropriate parameters suggest that broad-based cuts in labor tax rates would not increase tax revenues.

Small Issue-Specific Models

In contrast to the above two models, Slemrod uses a general equilibrium model to analyze U.S. capital income taxation issues, allowing for adjustments in the financial behavior of households and firms in response to tax changes.[26]

A number of features distinguish Slemrod's from other general equilibrium tax models. The most important is the explicit treatment of risk. Capital owners are not affected identically by tax changes in the model because they hold different portfolios. This is because a risk-aversion parameter enters preferences and utility-maximizing behavior determines behavior toward risk, as well as commodity demands. In this treatment household tax rates are endogenous, tax-exempt bonds can be held in household portfolios, and rental and owner-occupied housing

25. Charles L. Ballard and Lawrence H. Goulder, "Consumption Taxes, Foresight, and Welfare: A Computable General Equilibrium Analysis," in Piggott and Whalley, eds., *New Developments in Applied General Equilibrium Analysis*, pp. 253–82.

26. Slemrod, "A General Equilibrium Model of Taxation with Endogenous Financial Behavior"; and Slemrod, "A General Equilibrium Model of Taxation That Uses Micro-Unit Data."

are separately distinguished. Changes in corporate financial policy are accommodated by the model through response on the supply side of financial asset markets to the different costs of issuance of financial assets, including taxes, with exogenous elasticity parameters determining these supply-side effects.

In one of the first intertemporal equilibrium tax models, Summers evaluates the welfare effects of capital income taxation using a numerical overlapping-generations life-cycle model, crudely specified to be representative of the U.S. economy.[27] Only one sector is assumed, and the richness of the model lies in its intertemporal specification.

One of the most important features of his model is the high interest elasticity of household savings that it generates. He argues that the commonly used two-period formulation of savings behavior underestimates the interest elasticity because it ignores the wealth effect associated with changes in interest rates. He finds, for almost any plausible formulation of the life-cycle hypothesis, much greater implied interest elasticities of savings than conventionally thought to be the case.

Summers uses his model to evaluate alternatives to existing capital income taxation, specifically taxation of labor income or of consumption. Through a comparison across steady states, Summers estimates that replacing the capital income tax with a wage tax will increase income by 14 percent, and replacing it with a consumption tax, by 18 percent. These results reflect the high interest elasticity of savings in the model, as this leads to a substantial increase in capital formation.

Replacing an income tax with a wage tax would increase welfare by nearly 5 percent of lifetime earnings; replacing it with a consumption tax would increase welfare by approximately 12 percent, the equivalent of nearly five years' income for the economy. Summers attributes the greater gains estimated under consumption taxes to increased capital formation. He concludes from his results that the costs of capital income taxation are much higher than had previously been believed.

More Recent Models

In subsequent work, Goulder and Summers have formulated a tax model of the United States in which they treat investment demand explicitly, rather than assume that it is determined by savings, as in

27. Summers, "Capital Taxation and Accumulation."

Summers's earlier work.[28] They also explicitly incorporate the adjust-ment costs faced under any reallocation of capital between industries in response to capital income tax changes, using a quadratic adjustment cost formulation related to that used by Treadway.[29] As a result, capitalization effects of tax policies enter their analysis.

Goulder and Summers evaluate a number of tax policy changes, first assuming that these changes are unanticipated. They calculate equilibria for their policy experiments at one-year intervals over a seventy-five-year period, with personal taxes being scaled to yield equal tax revenue under all simulations. Goulder and Summers conclude that the effects of tax changes shown by their policy simulations, while consistent with economic theory, would not have resulted from models with perfect intersectoral mobility of capital or static expectations. They also point out the importance for their results of the distinction in their model between new and existing capital.

A further recent modeling effort is by Galper, Lucke, and Toder, who extend previous work on the interactions of behavior toward risk and taxes.[30] They examine the effects of tax policy changes on the allocation of physical capital by industry in a model that incorporates firm and household portfolio choice under uncertainty. The model contains an explicit treatment of risk and uncertainty. It also differs from traditional Harberger-type general equilibrium tax models by including an optimiz-ing equation for corporate debt-equity decisionmaking instead of assum-ing it is fixed, and their model allows asset demands to differ among households.

The policy changes they examine include the introduction of a flat-rate tax for corporate and personal income and the full integration of corporate and personal taxes. In implementing their experiments, Gal-per, Lucke, and Toder compare their model with Harberger-type simu-lations, which are achieved by replacing the demand for risky assets in the full version of their model with a specification that equalizes risk-adjusted returns for the representative asset holder and by fixing the corporate debt-equity ratio at its initial value.

28. Lawrence H. Goulder and Lawrence H. Summers, "Tax Policy, Asset Prices, and Growth: A General Equilibrium Analysis," National Bureau of Economic Research Working Paper 2128 (Cambridge, Mass.: NBER, Janaury 1987).

29. A. B. Treadway, "On Rational Entrepreneurial Behaviour and the Demand for Investment," *Review of Economic Studies*, vol. 36 (April 1969), pp. 227–39.

30. Galper, Lucke, and Toder, "Taxation, Portfolio Choice, and the Allocation of Capital."

There are great differences in the results from the two model specifications. The estimated effects of tax policy changes in the Harberger-type model are in some cases opposite in sign to those from the full specification of the model. Galper, Lucke, and Toder conclude that the way in which financial behavior is modeled is an important determinant of the effects of tax changes on physical capital stock allocation among industries.

Jorgenson and Yun use an intertemporal general equilibrium model for the United States to analyze the impact of tax policies on capital allocation.[31] Their analysis of tax issues concentrates on the provisions of U.S. tax law applicable to income from capital. Their work is distinguished by the use of econometric methods for estimating model parameters. Their estimation involves the construction of a system of accounts for the United States for 1955–80 that includes income and expenditure accounts for the business and household sectors.

Jorgenson and Yun's simulations indicate that policies with effective tax rates of zero for all assets dominate other tax reforms. Expensing of investment expenditures and elimination of sales taxes on investment goods yield the greatest potential gains: $3.6 trillion (in 1980 dollars) under a lump-sum revenue adjustment, or 43 percent of 1980 private national wealth. Under increases in labor income taxes or sales taxes, these gains are reduced to $1.9 trillion and $1.7 trillion, respectively, because of offsetting distortions.

Lessons from General Equilibrium Tax Modeling

The previous section briefly describes only a small subset of the general equilibrium tax models that have been built over the last ten or so years. All the models in this area differ substantially in structure, but most yield important (and at times contradictory) indications as to the ways in which tax policies affect the economy and the ways in which components of the tax system interact with one another.

What one draws from these results inevitably remains highly subjective. Some policymakers are convinced by some of them, while others are more skeptical. Some like some of the features of any given model,

31. Dale Jorgenson and Kun-Young Yun, "Tax Policy and Capital Allocation," Discussion Paper 1107 (Harvard Institute of Economics Research, November 1984).

but find other features disturbing and often attach only limited credibility to model results. Results can often reveal as much about the model structure and the key role of particular parameter values as about the economy being modeled. But fresh insights emerge that are frequently provocative and stimulate debate. They can support or contradict previously held positions or provide genuinely new perspectives (frequently where no received wisdom existed).

My view is that all of these contributions help the policy process, and I provide below some examples of relevant model-generated insights. These are largely drawn from work I have been involved with, but I hope they serve to highlight how general equilibrium models can constructively contribute to policy debate.

Taxes and the Equity-Efficiency Trade-off

One of the more prominent themes emerging from the general equilibrium tax modeling work thus far concerns broad-ranging implications for the equity and efficiency effects of taxes. The importance of model results has to be seen relative to the perspectives on the equity-efficiency trade-off that prevailed before the current round of modeling. In the early 1960s beliefs about efficiency effects of taxes were largely based on Harberger's pioneering work.[32] Harberger had estimated that the efficiency costs of the corporate tax were perhaps one-half to three-quarters of 1 percent of GNP, and in a famous paper in 1964 he extended his work to a wider analysis of the efficiency effects of the whole tax system.

His conclusion was that the major efficiency costs of distorting taxes lay in the corporate tax area, and that the combined efficiency costs of all major taxes were perhaps 1 percent of GNP. At the time, many people interpreted these estimates not in the same sense as Harberger. Rather than demonstrating that welfare gains could be realized through major

32. Arnold C. Harberger, "The Corporation Income Tax: An Empirical Appraisal," in House Committee on Ways and Means, *Tax Revision Compendium*, vol. 1, Committee Print, 86 Cong. 1 sess. (Government Printing Office, 1959), pp. 231–50; Arnold C. Harberger, "Taxation, Resource Allocation and Welfare," in *The Role of Direct and Indirect Taxes in the Federal Revenue System*, a conference report of the National Bureau of Economic Research and the Brookings Institution (Princeton University Press for National Bureau of Economic Research and the Brookings Institution, 1964), pp. 25–80; and Arnold C. Harberger, "Efficiency Effects of Taxes on Income from Capital," in Marian Krzyzaniak, ed., *Effects of Corporation Income Tax* (Wayne State University Press, 1966), pp. 107–17.

tax reform, they were instead regarded as evidence that the efficiency costs of taxes were small.

Perceptions of distributional effects of taxes have long been based on tax incidence calculations that have their origins in the work of Bowley, Stamp, and Clark, and even earlier, of Gregory King. From the more recent work by Pechman and Okner on tax burdens in the United States, the picture that has emerged is that the tax system does little to redistribute income.[33] Their analysis suggests that the progression that operates under the income tax (which is perhaps less in practice than might appear on paper) is offset by regression elsewhere in the tax system, such as in sales and excise taxes and payroll taxes.

In the 1960s and 1970s the belief among economists, in part influenced by these studies, seems to have been that while the tax system had repeatedly been changed in an attempt to make the tax system more redistributive, little of this change had proved successful. Since the efficiency costs of the additional interventions associated with changed tax policies appeared to be small, the direction suggested for tax policy seemed to be to continue with attempts to make the tax system more redistributive, in the hope that substantive redistribution would eventually be achieved. Meanwhile, social costs through any induced misallocation of resources would not be a major factor.

This view of the tax system has clearly been challenged by the results emerging from the general equilibrium tax policy models. The efficiency costs of taxes reported are generally much higher than those suggested by Harberger's work, especially the costs at the margin as extra revenues are raised from existing distorting taxes. In their work in the 1970s on the U.K. tax subsidy system, Piggott and Whalley suggest a range of between 6 and 9 percent of GNP per year for the annual welfare costs from distortions. In comparable work on the United States, Ballard, Shoven, and Whalley suggest an estimate in the region of 4–7 percent of GNP.[34] These models have also been used to calculate the efficiency costs of raising additional tax revenues by using existing distorting taxes. Ballard, Shoven, and Whalley, for instance, suggest efficiency costs for

33. Pechman and Okner, *Who Bears the Tax Burden?*; and Joseph A. Pechman, *Who Paid the Taxes, 1966–85?* (Brookings, 1985).

34. Charles L. Ballard, John B. Shoven, and John Whalley, "The Total Welfare Cost of the United States Tax System: A General Equilibrium Approach," *National Tax Journal*, vol. 38 (June 1985), pp. 125–40; and Piggott and Whalley, "General Equilibrium Investigation of U.K. Tax-Subsidy Policy."

the United States of around 35 cents per additional dollar of revenues collected.[35]

Model results have also suggested that the redistributive effects of taxes may be more significant than those portrayed by earlier incidence studies. In part, this reflects the added price endogeneity in these models. But as pointed out by Browning, fully allocating the burden of indirect taxes such as sales taxes and excises to purchasers of taxed commodities, as is done in most incidence calculations, tends to produce a less progressive pattern.[36] As mentioned above, the work on the United Kingdom by Piggott and Whalley suggests that a replacement of 1973 taxes and subsidies by a yield-preserving sales tax would benefit the top 10 percent of income recipients by around 20–25 percent of their original before-tax income and would cost the lower 10 percent of income recipients around 20–25 percent of income.

Thus, if one takes recent model results seriously, the perspective one should have on the equity-efficiency choice in the design of tax policy seems to change compared with earlier received wisdom. Efficiency costs of taxes appear more important than perhaps previously thought, and the tax system appears to be redistributing income to a more substantial degree. The implication is that a change in the weight attached to tax policy concerns may be merited, shifting more toward efficiency considerations and away from redistributive issues.

Intertemporal Effects of Taxes

Another important subject for general equilibrium tax policy models has been intertemporal distortions. In his work in the 1960s, Harberger suggested the intertemporal effects of taxes were small. This was largely

35. Charles L. Ballard, John B. Shoven, and John Whalley, "General Equilibrium Computations of the Marginal Welfare Costs of Taxes in the United States," *American Economic Review*, vol. 75 (March 1985), pp. 128–38. See also Charles L. Ballard, "The Marginal Efficiency Cost of Redistribution," working paper (Michigan State University, Department of Economics, November 1987), who evaluates the efficiency costs of redistribution through the tax system.

36. Edgar K. Browning, "The Burden of Taxation," *Journal of Political Economy*, vol. 86 (August 1978), pp. 649–72. Under this treatment, savings are effectively treated as free indirect taxes, a treatment inconsistent with the analysis of intertemporal tax distortions emphasized in recent consumption tax literature. See also Edgar K. Browning and William R. Johnson, *The Distribution of the Tax Burden* (Washington, D.C.: American Enterprise Institute for Public Policy Research, 1979); and John Whalley, "Regression or Progression: The Taxing Question of Incidence Analysis," *Canadian Journal of Economics*, vol. 17 (November 1984), pp. 654–82.

based on the belief that the elasticity of savings with respect to the real net of tax rate of return is small, with the implication that the associated Harberger triangles were also small.

This view was initially challenged in the 1970s by Feldstein's work, which pointed out a conceptual error in Harberger's analysis: namely, that a zero elasticity of savings with respect to the real (net of tax) rate of return does not necessarily imply a zero elasticity of intertemporal substitution in consumption.[37] A zero savings elasticity corresponds to constant expenditure shares, which, in terms of underlying preferences defined over present consumption and future consumption, implies a substitution elasticity of approximately one. This observation sparked a resurgence of interest in the effects of intertemporal tax distortions in the late 1970s and early 1980s.

A series of model-based papers followed, giving further emphasis to the view that intertemporal effects of taxes are more important than had previously been thought. Summers's work has been especially influential in this area, and the recent results of Jorgenson and Yun further emphasize the same theme.[38] As noted above, Summers uses an equilibrium structure to analyze the effects of capital taxation distortions in a life-cycle model, concluding that the welfare costs of intertemporal tax distortions under an income tax can be as large as 10 percent of GNP.

While Summers's calculation refers only to a comparison between steady states,[39] this strand of work has nonetheless been influential in reigniting concerns over the tax treatment of savings. Such concern has been instrumental in fostering support for a consumption tax, which in turn has injected new themes into tax reform debate in a number of countries. Nevertheless, recent reforms in the United States represent a turn toward taxation of income and not consumption.

Interasset versus Intertemporal Effects of Taxes

Important insights have also emerged from recent general equilibrium tax policy models concerning the relative importance of interasset and

37. Martin S. Feldstein, "The Welfare Cost of Capital Income Taxation," *Journal of Political Economy,* vol. 86 (April 1978, pt. 2), pp. S29–S51; and Feldstein, "The Rate of Return, Taxation, and Personal Savings," *Economic Journal,* vol. 88 (September 1978), pp. 482–87.

38. Summers, "Capital Taxation and Accumulation"; and Jorgenson and Yun, "Tax Policy and Capital Allocation."

39. When the transitional path is added in, these estimates are considerably reduced, as noted by Auerbach, Kotlikoff, and Skinner, "The Efficiency Gains from Dynamic Tax Reform."

intertemporal tax distortions. A recent paper by Hamilton and Whalley, for instance, highlights how a Haig-Simons approach toward tax reform stresses the need to fully include imputed housing income in the tax base on the ground that this is part of broadly based income.[40] However, when the issue of tax treatment of housing is approached from a consumption tax point of view, housing income appears to be appropriately taxed, and it is the income return to nonhousing assets that seems to be inappropriately treated.

But, as Hamilton and Whalley point out, tax breaks for housing occur only if owners of housing directly consume the services yielded by the asset. There is therefore both an intertemporal and an interasset distortion involved in evaluating the effects of the current tax treatment of housing.

They formulate an equilibrium model using 1972 data for Canada to simulate the effects of either removing taxes on other assets or including housing income in the tax base. They show that a move from the current tax treatment to either a pure income tax or a pure consumption tax is welfare improving. These results are consistent with the themes emerging from the work by King and Fullerton and others on effective tax rates, which has also stressed the importance of interasset tax distortions.[41] These results are important in that they suggest that the variance of tax treatment across assets is currently a more important source of distortion than conventional intertemporal tax distortions.

Border Tax Adjustments

An example of a more specific insight generated by a general equilibrium tax model is contained in a paper by Hamilton and Whalley on border tax adjustments.[42] They analyze the effect of changes between an origin basis and destination basis for sales taxes imposed by major U.S. trading partners. Currently the United States has no broadly based sales tax, whereas its major trading partners in Europe, Canada, and Japan all have broadly based sales taxes administered on a destination basis.

40. Bob Hamilton and John Whalley, "Tax Treatment of Housing in a Dynamic Sequenced General Equilibrium Model," *Journal of Public Economics*, vol. 27 (July 1985), pp. 157–75.

41. King and Fullerton, *The Taxation of Income from Capital*.

42. Bob Hamilton and John Whalley, "Border Tax Adjustments and U.S. Trade," *Journal of International Economics*, vol. 20 (May 1986), pp. 377–83.

Hamilton and Whalley note the differences between policy and academic literature on this issue. Over the years, there have been repeated calls from U.S. industry and other groups to offset the perceived effects of these foreign sales taxes on U.S. trade. One preferred option is that the United States also introduce an indirect tax administered on a destination basis. The belief is that because of the destination basis abroad, exports leaving the United States have to cross a tax barrier, whereas imports into the United States enter tax free. A similar U.S. tax would, in the current jargon, "level the playing field."

Academic literature has generally rebutted this argument, on the ground that for broadly based taxes any change between the origin and destination bases will be fully offset by a change in the exchange rate. In long-run equilibrium there will be no real effects on trade flows from such a change, and the choice between the origin and destination bases is a purely monetary issue, involving exchange rates only and with no real consequences.

However, as Hamilton and Whalley point out, the taxes by U.S. trading partners are not broadly based, they are discriminatory. In addition, higher tax rates apply on manufactured products than on nonmanufactures. Under such circumstances, if the country with which the United States is trading is a net exporter of manufactures, an origin-based tax operates akin to an export tax, while if the country in question is a net importer of manufactures, a tax on a destination basis operates largely as an import tax.

Hamilton and Whalley use a multicountry general equilibrium trade model that incorporates these sales tax effects. Their results show that if the United States were to persuade its three major trading partners to move to an origin-based tax, the United States would lose if Europe or Japan changed, but would gain if Canada did so. They emphasize that from a U.S. point of view it does not make sense to pursue a uniform approach with all countries on the border tax issue (contrary to current thinking in the United States), nor does it necessarily make sense to press foreign countries to use an origin basis. Instead, a pragmatic country-by-country approach should be taken, reflecting the bilateral balance of trade in taxed commodities. These results are a reflection of the underlying data, which show that Europe and Japan are net exporters of manufactures in their trade with the United States, but Canada is a net importer of manufactures in its U.S. trade.

Technical Shortcomings

The examples above illustrate the ability of general equilibrium tax
policy models to provide important insights into policy issues. Some
(such as the border tax example) are generated by applying an existing
model to an issue for which there were no previous results. Others (such
as tax policies' broad implications for equity and efficiency) reflect
insights from quantification in a general equilibrium framework capturing
price endogeneity. Although important insights have been generated,
there are technical shortcomings with existing models that both weaken
the impact of results and make some modelers cautious about promoting
these models too vigorously.

Taxes and Tax Rates

A central difficulty with these models is selecting the appropriate
treatment of the taxes to be studied. Any tax evaluated with a general
equilibrium model has to be represented in some model-equivalent form,
and a specification of tax rates is needed in order to complete the model.
It is clear that the formulation adopted has important implications for
the behavior of these models and, to a degree, predetermines results.

A number of examples serve to illustrate the ambiguity in theoretical
literature as to the appropriate way to represent any particular tax and
how this makes numerical modeling difficult. For instance, there has
been a debate for some years on whether the property tax is an excise
tax or a tax on factor incomes. There has been a series of different
treatments of the corporate tax since Harberger's original treatment of
it as a partial factor tax. Stiglitz suggested that the corporate tax should
be considered as a lump-sum tax.[43] More recent literature has focused
on the tax as applying to equity financing by firms. Recent work by King
and Fullerton and others has also emphasized how the effective tax rates
on corporations vary and have to be disaggregated to a very fine level to
capture their marginal effects, even the level at which project investment
decisions are made.[44] In their analysis, effective tax rates depend upon
the financing vehicle used, eligibility for investment tax credits, loss

43. Joseph E. Stiglitz, "Taxation, Corporate Financial Policy, and the Cost of
Capital," *Journal of Public Economics*, vol. 2 (February 1973), pp. 1–34.
44. King and Fullerton, *The Taxation of Income from Capital.*

carryforwards, and many other features. Fortin and Rousseau have also clearly demonstrated how modeling the implicit tax rates underlying transfer programs can affect tax policy analysis.[45]

Since all economic modeling involves choosing simplifications that capture the essence of the processes at issue, these problems should not be surprising, but the modeling of taxes and tax rates undoubtedly remains as a major difficulty. There is equally little doubt that current applied general equilibrium tax models do not always capture details in ways that are wholly satisfactory, especially to those involved in policymaking. The strength of general equilibrium models is their ability to capture interacting effects of different policy instruments among various markets within an overall framework representing the whole economy. Their weakness is their inability to deal simultaneously with large amounts of detail in many areas of the economy, and the detailed treatment of tax effects in particular is often less than satisfactory.

Elasticities

Elasticities also represent a difficult area, both for applied general equilibrium tax models and models used in other areas, in part because the empirical literature is not conclusive as to appropriate elasticity values. But the problem is more difficult than just selecting elasticity values, because the ways in which model parameters are generated from literature elasticities introduce many pitfalls.

In many areas there are very few elasticity estimates, and where elasticity estimates exist they vary widely. It is something of a "cheap shot" to place too much blame on the applied econometricians, in part because it is undoubtedly a difficult area, but it does seem that over the last ten or fifteen years a major focus has been on testing hypotheses rather than generating parameters.

Two of the more important sets of elasticities used in general equilibrium tax policy models illustrate the difficulties: elasticities of labor supply, and elasticities of savings with respect to the real net-of-tax rate of return on capital. In both cases there is substantial ambiguity in the

45. Bernard Fortin and Henri-Paul Rousseau, "The Marginal Welfare Cost of Taxes and Transfers in a Small Open Economy: A Multi-Household Applied General Equilibrium Approach," Working Paper 86-02 (Laval University, Department of Economics, 1986).

literature about the appropriate elasticity values. There are further difficulties involved in using literature estimates in model calibration.

An example is provided by the use of estimates of savings elasticities. In a model in which there are overlapping generations, for instance, there is no clear relationship between the aggregate elasticity of savings with respect to the real net-of-tax rate of return and the intertemporal substitution elasticities in individual preferences. There can be an economy in which there is always zero savings because the economy is in a steady state, but there may be either large or small elasticities of substitution in individual preferences. It is therefore difficult to base the selection of intertemporal substitution elasticities in general equilibrium tax models on estimated aggregate savings elasticities, even though this is something many modelers have attempted to do.

Aggregation

A further difficulty is in choosing the appropriate level of commodity and industry aggregation in a model. On the one hand, the level of aggregation should be kept small, both to generate clearer intuition as to the ways in which the model behaves, and to keep execution costs within manageable bounds. A crude level of aggregation also has the virtue of making the data requirements for any given model more modest. On the other hand, claims to realism and the pressures from the policy process will often dictate much larger levels of aggregation. The most detailed of the applied general equilibrium tax models currently in use has around thirty to forty commodities. But even this is hardly the level of detail with which tax policymakers typically operate in actually deciding upon appropriate tax treatment for individual industries and commodities. For household disaggregation, Slemrod's attempt to use micro unit data in general equilibrium tax models is the most ambitious attempt at disaggregation thus far, but, as Slemrod notes, this comes with a significant computational cost.[46]

Calibration

Another area of concern is the process through which models are calibrated. These methods involve calibrating a chosen model structure

46. Slemrod, "A General Equilibrium Model of Taxation That Uses Micro-Unit Data."

to a given benchmark equilibrium data set, in effect working from a constructed microconsistent equilibrium data set to the model parameters through a deterministic process that calculates parameters, not from a statistical process of estimation.

This method of parameter generation has caused a fair degree of discomfort, especially to econometricians. This is because under calibration the numerical specification produced for any given model is not tested in any meaningful statistical sense since a purely deterministic calculation procedure is employed to generate parameter values. Econometricians who would like to see calibration to more than a single data observation have suggested systemwide estimation of models.

The difficulties with this are, however, well known.[47] Overall systemwide estimation for a model with the large numbers of parameters used in the applied general equilibrium tax models would involve long time series.[48] Also, if one partitions models and separately estimates model subsystems, problems can arise when these parameters are reintroduced into the original model. The equilibrium computed by the model and meant to be representative of the state of the world before any given policy change occurs may in no way correspond to what is known from national accounts and related data sources. Calibration continues to be widely used, in part because of its relatively easy implementation and the difficulties of systemwide econometric estimation, but concerns persist.

Functional Forms

A further source of discomfort with the present stable of applied tax models is the widespread use of convenient functional forms such as Cobb-Douglas, CES, and LES. Recent econometric literature rejects the strong separability assumptions implicit in CES functions. Some have therefore suggested that more flexible functional forms should be used in these models, but as yet little work has been done using them. However, computational problems can result from using translog functions because some of these functions may not behave well for large changes.

47. See Mansur and Whalley, "Numerical Specification of Applied General Equilibrium Models."

48. The Piggott-Whalley model of the United Kingdom, for instance, has around 20,000 parameters, if one includes all the share parameters in demand and production functions.

Model Closure

All of the applied modelers who have dealt with tax policy issues have also confronted important issues of model closure, that is, the need to close off models in some way to features not central to the question being analyzed. The problem is that while a feature may not appear crucial for the issue under analysis, the closure treatment adopted may nonetheless have substantial effects on the behavior of the model.

One area where the issue of model closure has arisen is foreign trade. Should the model assume the economy is a taker of prices on world markets or a maker of prices? And if the economy is a maker of prices, how should one specify the behavior of trading partners? Another closure issue is the treatment of investment and savings, which has also been central in the applied general equilibrium development models. Yet another area is the treatment of government expenditures and public goods and transfers.

In all these areas, the experience that modelers have accumulated thus far suggests that model closure is both a delicate and difficult issue. As Whalley and Yeung have shown in the trade area, it is unfortunately all too easy to adopt innocent-looking ad hoc closure rules, only to find with hindsight that these can seriously influence the behavior of the model in unintended ways.[49] In the tax area, the same general message is almost certainly true.

Issue-Specific versus General-Purpose Modeling

A further difficult issue of model design concerns the balance between issue-specific and general-purpose modeling. In the early work done in the 1970s with general equilibrium tax models, the focus was very much on building general-purpose models that yielded the capability to analyze several different taxes simultaneously.

While these models have been helpful in providing an overall assessment of how tax systems operate, their weaknesses have increasingly become apparent as they have been used for specific policy analyses. Generally speaking, for the analysis of particular policy questions, model users often find that there are substantial amounts of superfluous detail

49. Whalley and Yeung, "External Sector 'Closing' Rules in Applied General Equilibrium Models."

in these models, yet the amount of detail relevant to the policy question at hand is never wholly satisfactory. Model users have often had to modify parts of existing models relevant to the policy questions being examined while carrying along significant amounts of excess baggage.

The reaction to this problem in the modeling work of the 1980s has been to focus on more issue-specific, targeted modeling. However, issue-specific models also have their weaknesses. It is easy to repeatedly reconstruct models that are so closely related that it is an inefficient exercise. Also, these models miss many of the policy and other interactions captured in a general-purpose model. While many of these effects are of secondary importance for the issue at hand, the difficulty is that, ex ante, it is never wholly apparent which of these effects are more important than others. One of the virtues of a large general-purpose model is that by taking a first cut at a policy issue within an overall multipurpose modeling framework one obtains some indication as to which feedback elements are important for subsequent further development.

A partial resolution of this issue in future work may be for policy questions to be analyzed through a range of models, so that general-purpose broad-ranging models can give one set of perspectives that can then be refined with more targeted issue-specific modeling.

Broadening the Range of Model Policy Analyses

Future work with these models will clearly benefit from being better focused in a number of ways. One is an improved policy focus in modeling.

Distributional Issues

The general equilibrium tax models have thus far largely concentrated on generating improved estimates of the efficiency costs of taxes. Less has been done on the effects of taxes on the distribution of income and the distribution of welfare among different household groups. In their model of the United Kingdom, Piggott and Whalley analyze the distributional effects of all U.K. tax and subsidy policies considered in combination on one hundred household groups stratified by income, family size, and occupation. Their results suggest that the distributional effects of taxes are different from those associated with conventional tax incidence calculations.[50]

While a few other models, such as Slemrod's, have focused on the detailed treatment of household income groups, the focus in most other modeling efforts has remained the efficiency effects of taxes. From tax policy debates, however, it is clear that distributional effects of taxes are often more important politically than efficiency effects. In discussions of the possibility of replacing the income tax by a consumption tax, for instance, it is the distributional effects that are usually given as the reason for not making such a change, rather than a perception that the efficiency effects are either too small to worry about or negative. Concerns over distribution follow directly from the observation that a large fraction of household savings (around 40–50 percent) is accounted for by a relatively small number of households (around 10 percent) in the top level of the income distribution.

Incorporating considerably more detail on the household side of models is therefore clearly central to adequately dealing with such concerns. However, it is also clear that more needs to be done in terms of underlying model structure, especially in analysis of capital income taxation. The perception that there is a sharp regressive effect of a move toward a consumption tax is likely to be radically altered by a life-cycle approach. Analyses performed by Davies, St-Hilaire, and Whalley suggest that the incidence effects of individual taxes can be significantly altered by moving to a life-cycle basis.[51] Because the fraction of lifetime savings accounted for by the top decile of recipients of lifetime resources is quite different from the fraction of annual savings accounted for by the top decile of recipients of annual income, the distributional effects of tax changes are likely to change when viewed on a lifetime basis.

Also, as Auerbach and Kotlikoff and others have pointed out, capital income tax changes create windfall gains or losses for owners of existing assets, and these can produce large intergenerational effects when taxes change.[52] A widened coverage of distributional effects of tax changes, particularly in existing dynamic models, would undoubtedly be a major advance.

50. Piggott and Whalley, *U.K. Tax Policy and Applied General Equilibrium Analysis*.
51. James B. Davies, France St-Hilaire, and John Whalley, "Some Calculations of Lifetime Tax Incidence," *American Economic Review*, vol. 74 (September 1984), pp. 633–50.
52. Auerbach and Kotlikoff, "National Savings, Economic Welfare, and the Structure of Taxation."

Taxes and National Debt

A further important area of policy concern, little investigated by existing general equilibrium tax models, is the relationship between taxes and national debt. In many OECD countries, the dominant concern underlying current tax policy is the public-sector deficit and the resulting need to raise revenue. In some countries these deficits are in the range of 6–8 percent of GNP.

Any analysis of tax changes that ignores outstanding debt can clearly be misleading. One has, for instance, to face the issue raised by Barro as to whether debt issuance is equivalent in present-value terms to raising future taxes.[53] In such circumstances household behavior can be affected by not only current taxes but also expectations of future taxes because of current debt. Thus future taxes that may result from current debt policies should be taken into account in analyses of tax changes. For instance, an analysis of the marginal welfare costs of current taxes when deficits are large could result in inappropriate cost estimates if it ignored expected future tax increases.

Thus far none of the applied general equilibrium tax models has tried to incorporate the effects of debt policy in an adequate way. All the models assume balanced government budgets, usually on an annual basis. In the current policy environment, one has to wonder about both the accuracy of such model calculations and also the desirability of continuing to use models with this structure.

Tax Transfer Programs

Another potential area for extending the application of existing models is the treatment of the expenditure side of government activity, in particular transfer programs. The small amount of work already done along these lines has yielded some intriguing results. Fortin and Rousseau have shown that because of the large implicit taxes involved in transfer programs, estimates of the marginal welfare costs of conventional taxes also have to take into account these implicit taxes. They have shown that estimates incorporating these effects are much higher than those estimated by Ballard, Shoven, and Whalley and others.[54]

53. Robert J. Barro, "Are Government Bonds Net Wealth?" *Journal of Political Economy*, vol. 82 (November–December 1974), pp. 1095–1117.

54. Fortin and Rousseau, "The Marginal Welfare Cost of Taxes and Transfers in a Small Open Economy"; and Ballard, Shoven, and Whalley, "General Equilibrium Computations of the Marginal Welfare Costs of Taxes in the United States."

In turn, Browning and Johnson have clearly shown that raising taxes to redistribute to the poor entails larger welfare costs than a general increase in taxes for all households.[55] Marginal welfare costs of raising additional taxes from the rich are larger because existing tax rates on the rich are higher. Thus the implicit tax rates involved and the large redistributive role played by transfer programs suggest that the existing models need to incorporate a fully integrated tax transfer system.

Taxes in the International Economy

The role of the international economy in analyses of the effects of taxes is another important area that has been considered only somewhat tangentially. Grubert and Mutti have provided one of the few numerical contributions that centrally analyzes these issues, which are also discussed in the paper by Slemrod in this book.[56] Goulder, Shoven, and Whalley have also shown how important the inclusion of the international economy can be in models used for analyzing domestic tax policies.[57]

For instance, in an economy that is a taker of rental rates on world capital markets, taxes on capital income cannot be borne by domestic owners of capital, simply because capital is internationally mobile. Therefore, an analysis of the incidence of such taxes that neglects the international economy may miss a central feature of the analysis.

In analyzing dynamic effects of taxes, many modelers have devoted substantial energy to determining the transitional path that the economy would follow from an initial to a new balanced growth path. In the open economy case, where capital is internationally mobile, the transition between balanced growth paths will occur instantaneously as international capital flows adjust. The complexity of modeling required to capture fully the changes in relative prices along the transitional path can be avoided by using this treatment. Issues such as the effect of foreign tax credits and the exploitation of deferral advantages for investments from source countries can also be important.

On the goods side, analyzing the effects of tax changes on relative

55. Edgar K. Browning and William R. Johnson, "The Trade-Off between Equality and Efficiency," *Journal of Political Economy*, vol. 92 (April 1984), pp. 175–203.

56. John Mutti and Harry Grubert, "The Domestic International Sales Corporation and Its Effects," in Robert E. Baldwin and Anne O. Krueger, eds., *The Structure and Evolution of Recent U.S. Trade Policy* (University of Chicago Press for National Bureau of Economic Research, 1984), pp. 279–320.

57. Goulder, Shoven, and Whalley, "Domestic Tax Policy and the Foreign Sector."

commodity prices is substantially simplified in the small open-economy case, since international prices are given. The effect of taxes is simply to raise domestic commodity prices paid by consumers by the full amount of the tax.

All of these international economy issues potentially change the results of models. The international dimensions of taxes appear to be growing in importance and thus merit considerable further attention in the models.

Surrogate Taxes

Most of the current models are also weak in their analysis of surrogate taxes associated with inflation, price controls, and government enterprise pricing. These can have a major effect on behavior and are central to analyses of tax reform.

As the high inflation of the late 1970s and the early 1980s has subsided, the importance of the inflation tax as a revenue-raising device has fallen. But higher inflation is still an ever-present threat. Also, in many economies government enterprises or government-owned or -controlled organizations operate a surrogate tax system through their pricing policies. For instance, in Canada the profits of liquor commissions are a major revenue source for provincial governments. In France the profits of the tobacco monopoly are an important source of tax activity.

It is therefore important that models analyzing the effects of tax policies be able to do so in a way that fully captures the distorting and distributional effects of the inflation tax and other surrogate taxes. Widening the coverage of models in the range of taxes covered would greatly enhance their power to contribute to policy debate.

Conclusions

From my own experiences with modeling projects in both tax policy and other areas, one of the striking features of current models is the difficulty they demonstrate of working simultaneously on many levels. Modelers need to have a good grasp of economic theory, a sense of the policy issues they are working on, familiarity with computers, an ability to interpret and communicate their results, and a full understanding of the data with which they are working. To me this suggests the need for modeling teams, as has been the direction taken in other areas, particularly the natural sciences. No doubt this is a direction research in the tax area will take as it focuses more fully on the policy questions of the day.

As a result of my own involvement in the policy process, I have also been made acutely aware of the difficulty of formulating modeling work in a way that is truly useful to policymakers. To be fully relevant, models have to be built close to the policy process and with a fair amount of communication with those involved in policymaking activity. The curse of the model builder is that to be realistic the model inevitably becomes complex, but in the process it increasingly takes on the guise of an impenetrable "black box." An acceptable simplification in theoretical work is often not acceptable in numerical work with a claim to realism, but realistic modeling is by necessity not simple. Simultaneously, those in policymaking positions have limited time and energy (and sometimes interest) to digest models or to participate in a dialogue with modelers. To develop models that are closer to, and thus more useful to, policymaking is a challenge for the future.

Comments by Mervyn King

Numerical general equilibrium modeling began in earnest in the early 1970s with the work of Scarf, Shoven, and Whalley. Within a few years it has spawned the new industry of applied general equilibrium modeling. The question is whether after surviving its infancy applied general equilibrium modeling is a sunrise or a smokestack industry. The papers by Whalley and by Galper, Lucke, and Toder provide us, in their different ways, with an opportunity to assess the state of general equilibrium modeling today.

The paper by John Whalley provides an excellent survey of work on applied general equilibrium modeling. It blends the general overview with the specific example and sets out clearly both the contributions of the approach and its problems. It should be required reading for anyone who wants a feel for both the technical issues that arise in such modeling as well as the motivation for this branch of research.

When general equilibrium modeling first came to prominence, much attention and a good deal of the glamour was associated with the algorithms that were used to compute the solutions. The cognoscenti debated the relative merits of Scarf's and Merrill's algorithms.[58] Speculation on the possibilities that might arise from improvements in computing power underestimated the extent of technical developments. It is striking, I think, that computational algorithms are hardly mentioned in either this paper or the one that follows. I welcome this shift in attention toward the economics of the specification of the model.

The principal strength of applied general equilibrium modeling is, of course, the emphasis on the need to consider tax policy in a general equilibrium setting. Although hardly novel, the imposition of a modeling framework ensures that this point is taken seriously. It imposes a consistency on the model that is crucial to the interpretation of the empirical results.

The Whalley paper provides an assessment of the main challenges that face research on general equilibrium modeling. He also describes previous work on the application of such modeling to taxation.

In my view there are five areas in which there are serious problems with the application of general equilibrium modeling to the analysis of policy changes, such as the recent U.S. tax reform. The first concerns the modeling of uncertainty and intertemporal behavior. In the absence of a complete set of Arrow-Debreu markets, the behavior of agents in the economy can be described by the relevant first-order equations corresponding to the stochastic dynamic programming problem facing those agents. Such models have been the basis of recent work on the Euler equation models of consumption and portfolio behavior. This sort of model is hard to embody in a general equilibrium framework because of the difficulty of finding explicit solutions to the optimization problem. The results are likely to be sensitive to the assumed market structure. Moreover, if uncertainty is modeled explicitly in terms of a joint distribution for asset prices, for example, the distribution is unlikely to be independent of policy parameters. Hence changes in the tax system will alter the distribution of shocks hitting the economy, and the covariance structure of returns is endogenous. There is no simple way to model dynamic behavior with uncertainty and incomplete markets,

58. The basis for the algorithms used in numerical general equilibrium modeling is described in Herbert Scarf, "An Example of An Algorithm for Calculating General Equilibrium Prices," *American Economic Review*, vol. 59 (September 1969), pp. 669–77. See also Scarf with Hausen, *The Computation of Economic Equilibria*; and Orin H. Merrill, "Applications and Extensions of an Algorithm That Computes Fixed Points of Certain Upper Semicontinuous Point to Set Mappings" (Ph.D. dissertation, University of Michigan, 1972).

but the results are likely to be sensitive to the assumptions made, and it is perhaps the single most important modeling problem.

The second point concerns the use of sensitivity analysis. Because general equilibrium models are usually calibrated rather than estimated econometrically, the need for sensitivity analysis is greater than would be the case with a conventional econometric model. The results may be sensitive to small changes in parameter values and it is not easy in a large numerical model to know how robust the conclusions are to the assumed parameter values. Nevertheless, it is important to know in which areas research will have the highest payoff.

The third point, which follows from the case for sensitivity analysis, is the need to find a more formal method of describing the mapping from parameter values to conclusions. How can beliefs about the accuracy of the assumed parameter values be mapped into a confidence interval for some of the key predictions about the effect of policy changes on the economy? The work of Leamer on the econometrics of model selection is directly relevant here.[59]

The fourth point concerns the incorporation of research findings on the microeconomic response of the behavior of households and firms to changes in taxes. Although general equilibrium modeling imposes an overall accounting framework that is essential to analyze the effect of changes in exogenous variables on the economy as a whole, the need to integrate microeconomic models of behavior with the overall model leads to the use of rather simplified models for individual responses. State-of-the-art research on microeconomic responses to taxes shows the importance of carefully modeling complex nonlinear budget constraints that may be either concave or convex at different points. These nonlinearities may have an important influence on individual responses. Numerical general equilibrium models usually assume linear budget constraints, and hence yield biased estimates of responses.

The fifth and final point concerns the presentation of results of this sort of modeling exercise. The basic question that arises from the simulation of a proposed or actual tax reform is "who gains and who loses from the reform?" In other words, one needs to model the vector of welfare levels of households in the economy. This might be either because of a concern with a traditional social welfare approach to taxation or because of an interest in a positive theory of which agents

59. See Edward E. Leamer, *Specification Searches: Ad Hoc Inference with Non-experimental Data* (Wiley, 1978).

benefited from the political process. To represent the effect of a tax reform in terms of a single summary statistic, such as change in deadweight loss, conceals most of the interesting results of the simulation. Although applied general equilibrium models deal with a highly disaggregated structure of production, to date few models have paid much attention to the need for disaggregating the household sector. Ideally, these models should be linked to a distributional policy model comprising a random sample of households taken from, for example, an expenditure survey. The next step in general equilibrium modeling would seem to be to try to link together the existing numerical general equilibrium models with the detailed models of households constructed by researchers interested in analyzing the distributional and efficiency consequences of tax reform. These distributional policy models typically comprise between 5,000 and 10,000 households. With rapid developments in computing power, the linkage of disaggregated models of production and detailed household expenditure surveys will become feasible.

The success of general equilibrium modeling will lie in its ability to avoid a "black box" approach to modeling that is characteristic of some macroeconometrical models. The insights from general equilibrium modeling have depended to a considerable extent on the skills of the individual researchers in blending together theory, a good feel for the data, computational techniques, and an understanding of which policy issues are important. The Whalley paper provides a valuable critique of the achievements of and potential for research in such modeling by one of its most successful practitioners.

Comments by Charles E. McLure, Jr.

As I reflect on my recent experience in the tax reform arena, I think of three ways in which general equilibrium tax models can contribute to the tax policy process. I would characterize these as offering background or insights, providing quantification of qualitatively expected results, and assisting in the selling of tax reform.

Background

One common hallmark of the tax reforms proposed in Treasury I, of the president's proposals, and of the Tax Reform Act of 1986 is the need to think in a general equilibrium mode if one is to understand their effects on the economy in terms of resource allocation and income distribution. Most economists would probably accept this statement as obvious, yet twenty-five years ago this probably would not have been the case. In the interim general equilibrium analysis has permeated economists' way of thinking about changes in tax policy, thanks to the contributions of Harberger, Shoven, and Whalley, along with an army of others. In short, we bring to the analysis of tax policy a different mind-set. In examining the effects of tax policy changes on a given industry we look not only at changes in the tax treatment of that industry, but also at how that industry will be affected by changes in the tax treatment of other industries.

To see the importance of this difference in outlook, it is instructive to compare the general equilibrium assessment of tax reform with that of those taking a partial equilibrium view on behalf of particular industries.

One of the earliest and loudest complaints about Treasury I was from those who claimed it had reneged on the president's promise to preserve the home mortgage interest deduction. Presumably the implicit complaint was that the reduction in marginal tax rates would reduce the value of the mortgage deduction, since it was much too vociferous to have involved only the elimination of the deduction for mortgage interest on second homes. I must admit that I was dumbfounded by an attack from this quarter; since owner-occupied housing was one of the few major sectors where tax benefits had been left essentially intact, it could be expected to be one of the primary beneficiaries of tax reform. Indeed, the real concern from a public policy point of view was that to leave housing preferences unscathed while attempting to rationalize the tax treatment of all other sources and uses of income would accentuate the uneconomical misallocation of capital into housing.

To some extent, complaints from the corporate sector about the effects of the 1986 act also reflect a partial equilibrium view of the world. That is, much is made about the increase in corporate taxes and the implied increase in the cost of capital, but there is little recognition (or at least little admission) that the corporate sector could benefit from reforms in other sectors. For example, the virtual elimination of benefits for unproductive tax shelter investments and curtailment of the tax benefits of borrowing should result in more funds for corporate invest-ment and lower interest rates. (The reduction of the tax rate paid by high-income taxpayers to well below that paid by corporations may, however, result even more in making these funds available to unincorporated businesses enjoying the nontax advantages of incorporation without the tax disadvantages, as argued by Myron Scholes and Mark Wolfson in their paper.)

Quantification

Quantification of the effects of tax reform is of obvious importance. Even if one knows that tax reform will increase welfare in the long run, it is important to know the size of expected welfare gains in deciding whether to expose the economy to the agony of tax reform. Moreover, there are times when economic intuition does not even reveal whether a particular change will improve welfare or worsen it.

Having said this, one must keep in mind several caveats implicit in John Whalley's paper. First, he notes that general equilibrium analysis produces "broad-ranging insights . . . rather than precise numbers." Even worse, "results can often reveal as much about the model structure and the key role of particular parameter values as about the economy being modeled." Given these concerns, the formulation of tax reform may inevitably involve more intuition than one would like. But that intuition is at least informed by a careful general equilibrium view of the world.

One of my primary concerns about general equilibrium modeling efforts has been that the model-specific ways in which many tax policies are simulated depart so radically from the way the taxes in question actually function that results may be misleading. In many instances this shortcoming is forced on the analyst by the structure of the model: if there is only one corporate (or noncorporate) sector or only one corporate asset, it is impossible to capture intracorporate or interasset distortions; and if there is only a rudimentary description of the financial sector, differential taxation of alternative investment vehicles cannot be captured.

Some defects in the modeling of tax provisions could, in principle, be remedied fairly easily; for example, the differences between exemptions and zero-rating under a credit-method value-added tax can be modeled, but not if the tax is treated as a retail sales tax. Similarly, it is a relatively simple matter to model the benefits accorded by industry-specific tax provisions such as percentage depletion and expensing of intangible drilling costs in the oil and gas industry and capital gains treatment of timber. On the other hand, some tax provisions may be inherently difficult to capture. For example, it appears to be much more difficult to model the effects of provisions that in principle affect the entire economy, such as the alternative minimum tax and limitations on deductions for passive losses and interest expense. Although these provisions have interindustry effects that are well known, they are not explicitly targeted at particular industries.

Selling Tax Reform

I regret that resources did not allow the development of a full-blown general equilibrium analysis of the economic effects of Treasury I. The regret does not stem from concern that such an analysis would have shown the proposals to be inappropriate; after all, the primary distortions involved in Treasury I were in the saving-consumption choice (partially offset by the proposals for IRAs and pensions), in the preferential treatment of owner-occupied housing, and in the continued exclusion of interest on general-purpose obligations of state and local governments—all issues on which deliberate choices were made or forced by political pressures, despite well-known objections on efficiency grounds.

Rather, I regret that those of us who were trying to sell Treasury I were placed at such an unfair advantage in the early stages of the war of public opinion relative to those who marshaled studies by the various macroeconomic forecasting groups predicting impending doom if tax reform became law. Fighting defensively in this war is essentially hopeless. The press and the public accord results of computer models far more credibility than they deserve. But for us to have said so would have been to no avail.

Nor did it do much good to explain that short-term macro models are not really suited to the task of appraising the costs and benefits of tax policy (aside from the short-term macro effects). We were eventually able to gain admission that macroeconomic models generally make no allowance for the improvements in the productivity of investment (and greater benefits of preferred consumption) that provided much of the rationale for tax reform. It was also acknowledged that some of the more outspoken critics of tax reform had made no allowance for the effects interest indexing would have in terms of lower interest rates and greater investment. But by then the damage had been done in the press.

Had we presented general equilibrium estimates of the improvements in economic welfare resulting from tax reform, we would have initially held the high ground in the war of economic estimates. It would have been far easier to defend our estimates, no matter how suspect, than to overcome the attacks we experienced.

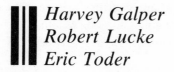

Harvey Galper
Robert Lucke
Eric Toder

A General Equilibrium Analysis of Tax Reform

BY ANY STANDARD the Tax Reform Act of 1986 was a comprehensive and far-reaching restructuring of the federal income tax. It lowered individual and corporate marginal tax rates, raised the personal exemption and standard deductions, and paid for these changes by reducing and eliminating many tax preferences in the individual and corporate income taxes. On balance, tax reform was estimated to be revenue neutral over a five-year period, with an increase in corporate tax revenues offsetting a reduction in individual revenues.

The lower and flatter tax rate schedule and the broader tax base under the new law have altered the incentives of households to hold particular assets in their portfolios. These tax-induced changes in asset demands, in turn, affect interest rates and costs of capital for different sectors of the economy, thus changing the allocation of the capital stock and real output among sectors.

We have developed a portfolio-based general equilibrium model to simulate the effects of the Tax Reform Act on interest rates, the allocation of the capital stock, and the distribution of household income. In particular, our model shows how the response of household portfolio behavior to changes in relative asset yields can affect the budgetary and distributional consequences of tax reform. Simulations performed with the model also illustrate the gains in welfare attributable to a more efficient allocation of risk bearing among households and a more efficient distribution of the ownership of housing and consumer durables.

Two of our most significant findings are that the Tax Reform Act could result in a somewhat lower federal budget deficit in the long run due to higher revenues and reduced debt service costs; and that the act will generate a welfare gain for high-income classes, but not other income

59

groups, after portfolio changes are made in response to the new tax law. Both findings result from portfolio shifts of wealthy households away from tax-preferred and risky assets in favor of less tax-preferred and less risky assets.

General Equilibrium Models

General equilibrium models represent the entire economy as a set of interconnected markets for goods and services (outputs) and factors of production (inputs).[1] Taxes enter such models as differences between prices paid by consumers and those received by sellers of final goods and services and as differences between prices paid by firms for factor inputs and net wage rates and rates of return of suppliers of labor and capital services. General equilibrium models can yield useful insights into the effects of policy changes because they capture interactions among behavioral responses of different agents and sectors in the economic system. Thus, for example, if corporate taxes are increased, a general equilibrium model will account for effects on prices of outputs, taxes paid, and before-tax returns on investment in all sectors of the economy, not just those of the corporate sector. The model will also maintain necessary identities between final spending of consumers and total revenues of producers; in effect, nothing is lost from the system.

The results of simulating any general equilibrium model depend heavily on the behavioral assumptions it uses. How demands for and supplies of various products and factors respond to a particular change in prices (that is, the price elasticities) is often uncertain and sometimes controversial. General equilibrium models cannot settle disagreements about those elasticities, that is, how demands for and supplies of products and factors will respond to changes in the tax law. They can, however, illustrate the implications of alternative behavioral assumptions for how the entire economic system will respond to policy changes.

1. Much of the most original work in computable general equilibrium modeling has been done by John Shoven and John Whalley and their colleagues. See, for example, Charles L. Ballard and others, *A General Equilibrium Model for Tax Policy Evaluation* (University of Chicago Press, 1985). For a further discussion of the use of general equilibrium models in tax analysis, see John B. Shoven and John Whalley, "Applied General-Equilibrium Models of Taxation and International Trade: An Introduction and Survey," *Journal of Economic Literature*, vol. 22 (September 1984), pp. 1007–51; and John Whalley's paper in this volume.

Description of GEMDAT

We have named our model the General Equilibrium Model of Differential Asset Taxation (GEMDAT). As its name implies, it is designed to capture the interaction between differential tax treatments among assets and differences in marginal tax rates among taxpayers. The particular assets each household holds in its portfolio will reflect its own tax status, the tax treatment of all available assets, and the riskiness of these assets.[2] At the same time, in making their portfolio choices households will affect market yields that in turn determine the costs of capital to each sector of the economy. These costs of capital determine real capital allocations and assets supplied to households. Thus the structure of GEMDAT emphasizes the simultaneous interaction among household portfolio choices, business financing, and real investment in physical capital.[3]

The Tax Reform Act of 1986 substantially changed the tax treatment of different assets and lowered and flattened the tax rate schedule faced by households. Because GEMDAT specifically incorporates both of

2. For earlier versions of this model, see Harvey Galper and Eric Toder, "Transfer Elements in the Taxation of Income from Capital," in Marilyn Moon, ed., *Economic Transfers in the United States* (University of Chicago Press for National Bureau of Economic Research, 1984), pp. 87–135; and Harvey Galper, Robert Lucke, and Eric Toder, "Taxation, Portfolio Choice, and the Allocation of Capital: A General Equilibrium Approach," Brookings Discussion Papers in Economics, March 1986. A similar model has been developed by Joel Slemrod. See Slemrod, "A General Equilibrium Model of Capital Income Taxation" (Ph.D. dissertation, Harvard University, 1980); "A General Equilibrium Model of Taxation with Endogenous Financial Behavior," in Martin Feldstein, ed., *Behavioral Simulation Methods in Tax Policy Analysis* (University of Chicago Press for National Bureau of Economic Research, 1983), pp. 427–58; and "A General Equilibrium Model of Taxation That Uses Micro-Unit Data: With an Application to the Impact of Instituting a Flat-Rate Income Tax," in John Piggott and John Whalley, eds., *New Developments in Applied General Equilibrium Analysis* (Cambridge University Press, 1985), pp. 221–52.

3. For a discussion of various theoretical issues relating to business and household portfolio behavior and general equilibrium modeling that incorporates such behavior, see Alan J. Auerbach and Mervyn A. King, "Taxation, Portfolio Choice, and Debt-Equity Ratios: A General Equilibrium Model," *Quarterly Journal of Economics,* vol. 98 (November 1983), pp. 587–609; J. Gregory Ballentine and Charles E. McLure, Jr., "Corporate Tax Integration: Incidence and Effects on Financial Structure," in U.S. Department of the Treasury, Office of Tax Analysis, *1978 Compendium of Tax Research* (Government Printing Office, 1978), pp. 243–80; Michael J. Brennan, "Taxes, Market Valuation and Corporate Financial Policy," *National Tax Journal,* vol. 23 (December 1970), pp. 417–27; and Edwin J. Elton and Martin J. Gruber, "Taxes and Portfolio Composition," *Journal of Financial Economics,* vol. 6 (December 1978), pp. 399–410.

these effects, it can yield useful insights on how tax reform can affect the distribution of income, the allocation of the capital stock, and economic efficiency.

A complete listing of the equations in GEMDAT is given in the Appendix, but the main features of the model are summarized here. GEMDAT has five capital-using sectors and production functions that make the demand for capital services in each sector inversely related to its real cost of capital. Household demands for each financial asset depend positively on the asset's expected rate of return and negatively on its riskiness as measured by the after-tax variance of the return. Aggregate supplies of capital (wealth) and labor are assumed to be fixed.

The five capital-using sectors are the corporate and noncorporate business sectors (both of which produce marketable goods and services), state and local governments, and two separate household "sectors" (which produce in-kind services from owner-occupied homes and from consumer durables). Each sector finances the capital it uses by issuing financial assets that households buy. The financial assets that households can acquire are taxable bonds, corporate equities, shares of noncorporate business, and tax-exempt bonds. Capital is also used directly in the household sector to produce services from owner-occupied homes and consumer durables.

The supply of financial assets issued to households depends on both the demand for capital services in each sector and the way in which the capital stock of that sector is financed. The sectoral demands for capital services, including capital services used directly in the household sector, are unit-elastic functions of the real costs of capital. The particular financial assets issued to households vary by sector. Corporations issue corporate equity, taxable bonds, and to a limited degree, tax-exempt bonds. Corporations choose their debt-equity ratio by balancing the net tax benefits of debt finance against leverage costs that increase with the share of capital that is debt financed.[4] Noncorporate enterprises issue

4. Thus both tax considerations and bankruptcy and other leverage costs influence the debt-equity decision. For a discussion of tax effects, see Merton H. Miller, "Debt and Taxes," *Journal of Finance,* vol. 32 (May 1977), pp. 261–75. For a discussion of bankruptcy and other leverage costs, see Roger H. Gordon and Burton G. Malkiel, "Corporation Finance," in Henry J. Aaron and Joseph A. Pechman, eds., *How Taxes Affect Economic Behavior* (Brookings, 1981), pp. 131–98. The literature on taxation and corporate financial policy is reviewed in Alan J. Auerbach, "Taxation, Corporate Financial Policy and the Cost of Capital," *Journal of Economic Literature,* vol. 21 (September 1983), pp. 905–40. The effects of the corporation income tax when returns

shares in unincorporated business, and state and local governments issue tax-exempt bonds. In addition, the federal government issues taxable bonds to finance a fixed level of national debt.

These financial assets are held by 400 sample households, weighted to represent the entire taxpaying population and disaggregated by labor income, capital income, tax-filing status (single or married), and itemizing status under current law. Households select their portfolios under uncertainty, allocating their fixed wealth among financial assets and household-sector capital (owner-occupied homes and consumer durables).[5] Demands for financial assets, as noted above, vary directly with their after-tax expected return and inversely with their after-tax variance. Demands for consumer durables and homes vary inversely with their opportunity costs (in most cases, the after-tax interest rate).[6]

The model contains a fairly detailed representation of the tax law. Each sample household confronts the actual schedule of tax rates; tax liabilities are computed directly based on these rates and on gross income flows, exclusions, excess itemized deductions (if positive), other adjustments to income (such as individual retirement account [IRA] and second-earner deductions), and personal exemptions. Taxable income includes all income from wages and taxable bonds, but excludes portions of the income from corporate equity and noncorporate capital. All the income from tax-exempt bonds, owner-occupied homes, and consumer durables is untaxed. The fractions of corporate equity income and noncorporate capital income included in the tax base are fixed and reflect the partial exclusion of capital gains, accelerated depreciation on rental housing, and other business preferences.

---

are uncertain have been the subject of a debate between Roger Gordon on one side and Jeremy Bulow and Lawrence Summers on the other. See Roger H. Gordon, "Taxation of Corporate Capital Income: Tax Revenues versus Tax Distortions," *Quarterly Journal of Economics,* vol. 100 (February 1985), pp. 1–27; and Jeremy I. Bulow and Lawrence H. Summers, "The Taxation of Risky Assets," *Journal of Political Economy,* vol. 92 (February 1984), pp. 20–39. The original analysis in this area is by Evsey D. Domar and Richard A. Musgrave, "Proportional Income Taxation and Risk-Taking," *Quarterly Journal of Economics,* vol. 58 (May 1944), pp. 388–422.

5. For analyses of household portfolio choice under uncertainty, see Irwin Friend and Marshall E. Blume, "The Demand for Risky Assets," *American Economic Review,* vol. 65 (December 1975), pp. 900–22; and William F. Sharpe, "Capital Asset Prices: A Theory of Market Equilibrium Under Conditions of Risk," *Journal of Finance,* vol. 19 (September 1964), pp. 425–42.

6. As explained in the Appendix, these demands are derived from a nested utility function that captures both the utility from the direct consumption of goods and services and the losses in utility from the variance of the real income stream.

The separate corporate-level tax, also represented in the model, affects the relationship between the before-tax rate of return on corporate capital and rates of return to individuals who hold debt and equity of corporations. The corporate income tax is described by two parameters: the statutory corporate tax rate (u) and the percentage of corporate economic income included in the tax base (a_c). The parameter a_c represents an estimate of the effect of the investment credit, accelerated depreciation, and other tax preferences in reducing the long-run, steady-state tax base. If all assets generating corporate income were immediately written off or expensed, a_c would be equal to zero; if all assets were allowed tax depreciation equal to economic depreciation (and there were no investment credit), a_c would equal one.

GEMDAT also takes some account of the effects of financial intermediaries on tax liabilities, although it lacks detailed modeling of the behavior of financial institutions. Each household is assigned a fixed amount of wealth in pensions and IRA accounts; the returns on assets held through these accounts are tax free. In addition, financial intermediaries (mostly commercial banks and property and casualty insurance companies) hold a fixed amount of tax-exempt bonds, which are financed by issuing taxable debt to households. Thus the model is designed to provide a roughly accurate representation of the supply of tax-exempt and taxable debt available for acquisition by individual households.

In equilibrium, the net amount of each asset demanded by households equals the amount supplied by capital-using sectors and the federal government. The model solves simultaneously for the value of physical capital in each productive sector, the share of corporate capital that is debt financed (debt-capital ratio), the composition of each household's portfolio of financial and physical assets, rates of return on all assets, and after-tax income and taxes paid by each household (including each household's allocated share of any corporate income taxes).

When the parameters that represent the tax law are changed, the model solves for a new configuration of total capital stocks, household portfolio holdings, and interest rates. In the new equilibrium, financial asset holdings and rates of return are again consistent with a single set of real capital stocks and costs of capital in each capital-using sector. The solution to a simulation also implies new values for each household in the model of before-tax income, taxes paid, after-tax income, and income adjusted for the riskiness of the household's portfolio. The model can thereby be used to assess the effect of the tax change on the distribution of income as well as on the efficiency of resource use.

GEMDAT is solved by a computer algorithm that searches for the set of rates of return on financial assets at which demands by households for each asset are equal to the amounts supplied by the capital-using sectors and by the federal government.

Advantages of GEMDAT

GEMDAT is particularly useful for modeling the distributional effects of the Tax Reform Act of 1986 because of its detailed representation of income flows and asset holdings among households and its emphasis on the differential taxation of various types of financial claims. Elimination and reduction of tax preferences either directly, or indirectly through the lowering of marginal tax rates, can be expected to alter relative yields among different types of assets. The effects of these changes in yields on the before-tax income of any household depend, in turn, on the mixture of real and financial assets held in that household's portfolio.

Because the composition of asset holdings differs systematically among households in different tax brackets, these changes in relative yields can have significant effects on the distribution of before-tax income. Thus GEMDAT provides a much fuller representation of the distributional incidence of tax reform than would a static model that assumes before-tax incomes are fixed and examines only the changes in individual taxes paid. Similarly, GEMDAT includes in its measure of incidence the effects of changes in corporate taxation—an important element of the 1986 act—because it solves for the effects of changes in the corporate tax on before-tax returns on different financial assets at the household level.

GEMDAT is also useful for assessing the effects of tax reform on economic efficiency. Since households in different tax brackets face different opportunity costs of housing and consumer durables, their marginal benefits from consuming additional services from these assets will also differ. As a result, efficiency gains can be achieved by reallocating household capital from high-bracket taxpayers (facing low opportunity costs) to low-bracket taxpayers (facing high opportunity costs). These "exchange efficiency" benefits are ignored in models that look only at the overall allocation of capital between household and business sectors but do not consider the portfolio behavior of individual households. The model also can illustrate analogous gains from the more efficient allocation of risk bearing that results from lower marginal tax rates and less preferential treatment of risky assets.[7]

On the other hand, GEMDAT is not designed to capture the full allocation gains from taxing different types of business-sector capital more equally. These gains are not measured because the model contains only two business sectors (corporate and noncorporate) and because each business sector uses only one composite capital asset. Thus the model does not fully account for possible gains from equalizing taxation of capital across industries accomplished by eliminating the investment credit and reducing accelerated depreciation on structures and other physical assets.

GEMDAT also does not capture any overall effects on economic growth, because it treats factor supplies of both labor and capital as fixed. In particular, the model does not measure intertemporal efficiency gains or losses from increasing or reducing the overall taxation of capital income. It can, however, be used to point out the likely direction of those intertemporal gains or losses by providing a first-round estimate, with fixed wealth, of the effects of tax reform on the after-tax returns to savers in different tax brackets.

The Base Case

In the base case, GEMDAT is calibrated to replicate interest rates and capital stocks at the end of 1985. Total capital stocks are those reported by the Federal Reserve Board.[8] The sample of households is

7. It should be noted that Slemrod specifically considers these sources of efficiency gain in his work. See his "Tax Effects on the Allocation of Capital Among Sectors and Among Individuals: A Portfolio Approach," National Bureau of Economic Research Working Paper 951 (Cambridge, Mass.: NBER, August 1982); and "A General Equilibrium Model of Taxation with Endogenous Financial Behavior."

8. See Board of Governors of the Federal Reserve System, *Balance Sheets for the U.S. Economy, 1946–85* (The Board, April 1986). Adjustments have been made to correct for inconsistencies in the measurement of asset values. In these data physical capital stocks are valued at replacement cost, debt held by households at acquisition cost, and corporate equity held by households and financial intermediaries at market value. In the case of nonfinancial corporations, net worth computed as the difference between the estimated replacement cost of assets and net financial liabilities is much greater than the market value of equity. For the purpose of this model, the physical capital stock of the corporate sector is taken as equal to the sum of the market value

selected from the public-use version of the 1983 Statistics of Income (SOI) computer tape produced by the Internal Revenue Service, with incomes and deductions adjusted to 1985 levels. Asset holdings are imputed to households based on capital income flows from the SOI and data from the computer tape of the 1982–83 Survey of Consumer Finances produced by the Federal Reserve Board. The parameters of each household's preference function, including those representing its degree of risk aversion, are chosen so as to replicate imputed portfolio holdings.

Table 1 displays before-tax rates of return, allocation of the physical capital stock, and total financial asset holdings in the 1985 base case and in simulations we discuss below. Before-tax rates of return vary among assets because of both tax and risk characteristics. Taxable bonds are riskless assets in the model. However, the yield on tax-exempt bonds is lower than that on taxable bonds, reflecting the fact that the greater riskiness of tax-exempts is more than offset in the market by the benefits of tax exemption. The relative yields of noncorporate capital and corporate equity illustrate just the opposite result. Noncorporate capital, despite its more favorable tax treatment, bears a higher before-tax return than corporate equity. In this case, the greater riskiness of noncorporate capital exerts the more important influence on market yields.

In the base case, over 40 percent of the physical capital stock is in owner-occupied housing and consumer durables, less than 30 percent is in corporate capital, and over 20 percent is in noncorporate capital. Total household wealth exceeds the physical capital stock by the amount of net federal debt held by the public ($1,280 billion in 1985). The financial assets issued by corporations, state and local governments, and the federal government ($4,955.8 billion in 1985) are held by households and pension funds, as shown in the third panel of table 1. A portion of the holdings of taxable bonds by households and pension funds, however, is issued by banks, which in turn hold some of the tax-exempt bonds

---

of equity and the acquisition value of net financial liabilities. For long-term bonds (but not all debt) the use of acquisition value will overstate the market value of debt to the extent interest rates have increased between the acquisition date and 1985.

The physical capital stock outside the corporate sector is reported by the Federal Reserve Board at its estimated replacement value. The capital stocks for the noncorporate and household sectors were derived by assuming that the ratio of market value to replacement costs of capital was the same as for the corporate sector and scaling down the reported replacement cost data accordingly. Other adjustments in the data have been made to reconcile estimated net taxable debt demanded by households and estimated net debt supplied by corporations, unincorporated enterprises, and the federal government.

Table 1. *Rates of Return and Capital Allocations before Tax Reform Act of 1986 (Base Case) and Simulated Effects after Tax Reform Act*

Rate of return and capital allocation	*Base case (1985)* (1)	*1986 act* (2)	*Change from base case* (3)	*Modified 1986 act* (4)	*Change from base case* (5)
Before-tax rates of return (percent)					
Taxable bonds[a]	8.00	7.07	−0.93	6.97	−1.03
Corporate equity[b]	11.28	10.60	−0.68	10.71	−0.57
Tax-exempt bonds[c]	6.00	6.30	0.30	6.32	0.32
Noncorporate capital[d]	16.48	16.68	0.20	16.67	0.19
Corporate capital[e]	12.65	12.74	0.09	12.63	−0.02
Capital stock (billions of dollars)					
Corporate capital	3,083.8	3,054.0	−29.8	3,091.2	7.4
Noncorporate capital	2,425.6	2,389.1	−36.5	2,390.6	−35.0
State and local capital	592.0	528.6	−63.4	524.6	−67.4
Housing	3,329.0	3,368.7	39.7	3,336.2	7.2
Consumer durables	1,395.2	1,485.2	90.0	1,483.2	88.0
Financial assets (billions of dollars)					
Held by households and pensions					
Net taxable bonds	2,519.8	2,224.8	−295.1	2,219.2	−300.6
Corporate equity	2,057.0	2,107.2	50.2	2,150.0	93.0
Tax-exempt bonds	379.0	530.5	151.5	526.3	147.3
Tax-exempt bonds held by banks	335.7	100.0	−235.7	100.0	−235.7
Corporate debt-equity ratio	0.499	0.449	−0.050	0.438	−0.061

a. Weighted average of long-term and short-term rates, based on approximations of each type of borrowing financing the capital stock and the federal debt.

b. Both the dividend yield and expected appreciation of equity, with dividends representing a fixed share of the total return. Spread between total return on corporate equity and taxable bonds computed from data on relative returns of the two assets between 1951 and 1984.

c. Estimated at 75 percent of taxable rate, about the spread between twenty-year high-grade corporate and municipal bonds in early 1980s.

d. Based on calculations from data in Roger G. Ibbotson and Rex A. Sinquefield, *Stocks, Bonds, Bills, and Inflation: The Past and the Future* (Charlottesville, Va.: Financial Analysts Research Foundation, 1982), on spread between returns to small corporations and those to large corporations. This spread is used as a proxy for the spread between returns to noncorporate capital and corporate equity.

e. Gross of corporate income tax; represents a weighted average of the costs of debt and equity.

Table 2. *Portfolio Holdings before Tax Reform Act of 1986 (Base Case), by Income Class*
Billions of dollars unless otherwise specified

Income class (thousands of dollars)[a]	Holdings						
	Net taxable bonds	Corporate equity	Non-corporate business	Tax-exempt bonds	Housing	Consumer durables	Wealth
0–5	17.5	6.5	15.4	0	7.8	4.9	52.1
5–10	− 78.9	13.6	69.4	0	212.8	180.8	397.8
10–15	86.7	20.5	95.3	0	64.3	56.6	323.4
15–20	87.1	50.7	103.3	0	272.2	159.5	672.8
20–30	153.7	70.0	139.8	10.7	370.0	161.0	905.2
30–50	− 11.3	145.3	308.6	13.3	804.9	325.5	1,586.4
50–100	387.3	367.0	515.9	57.2	796.0	302.2	2,425.8
100–200	106.7	307.1	419.5	45.9	386.0	88.3	1,353.4
200 and up	86.8	790.7	758.3	251.9	415.1	116.2	2,419.0
Direct household holdings	835.6	1,771.4	2,425.6	379.0	3,329.0	1,395.2	10,135.7
Pension funds	1,684.2	285.6	0	0	0	0	1,969.5
Total	2,519.8	2,057.0	2,425.6	379.0	3,329.0	1,395.2	12,105.5

a. Sum of labor income, interest income net of interest payments, and before-tax income from corporate equity, noncorporate capital, and tax-exempt bonds. Does not include in-kind return from holdings of housing and consumer durables. Measured in nominal terms and not adjusted for inflation.

issued by state and local governments and corporations ($335.7 billion). These bonds provide tax-exempt interest rates to issuers but taxable rates to households who are the ultimate suppliers of finance.

Table 2 shows the distribution of asset holdings by income class. Households are classified by a measure of income that approximates comprehensive before-tax cash income, although appreciation of equity values, as part of the total return to corporate equity, is also included. The return to corporate equity is gross of corporate income taxes so that the entire before-tax return earned by corporations is attributed to holders of corporate debt and equity. Although corporate taxes are thus distributed in proportion to ownership of corporate equity, this allocation does not imply any particular incidence of the corporate tax. The allocation in table 2 merely imputes both before-tax income and taxes to shareholders, holding after-tax returns constant as observed. The incidence of any tax is measured by how it changes after-tax returns.

Table 2 shows that ownership of corporate equity, noncorporate business, and tax-exempt bonds is highly concentrated among the top

Table 3. *Income and Taxes before Tax Reform Act of 1986 (Base Case), by Income Class*
Billions of dollars unless otherwise specified

Income class (thousands of dollars)	Before-tax income	Taxes			After-tax income
		Individual income taxes	Corporate income taxes	Subsidy to financial institutions	
0–5	6.5	0	0.2	0.1	6.4
5–10	227.5	7.2	0.8	0.4	219.9
10–15	69.7	0.9	0.8	0.6	68.6
15–20	297.0	22.5	2.2	1.1	273.4
20–30	393.3	36.0	3.0	1.7	356.0
30–50	816.0	88.9	6.9	2.0	722.3
50–100	776.8	99.9	13.4	3.6	667.1
100–200	357.3	58.0	10.3	1.4	290.5
200 and up	407.4	65.0	24.4	1.4	319.4
Total	3,351.6	378.4	62.0	12.4	2,923.5

income classes, while housing and consumer durables are owned more broadly and thus represent larger shares of the wealth of middle- and lower-income classes. Net taxable bond holdings may be positive or negative; that is, households may be net lenders or borrowers. No pattern of holdings is discernible. In terms of shares of wealth, households with incomes between $10,000 and $30,000 and between $50,000 and $100,000 are the largest net lenders; and households with incomes between $5,000 and $10,000 are the largest net borrowers.

Table 3 displays base-case data on before-tax income, taxes paid, and after-tax income by income class. Corporate taxes, as noted, are allocated to individuals according to stock holdings. The subsidy to financial institutions shown in table 3 is an offset to corporate tax collections and results from the mechanism discussed above for reconciling the volume of tax-exempt bonds issued by state and local governments (and to a much lesser extent by private corporations) with the volume held by individual households. Since financial institutions deduct virtually all the interest costs on borrowing incurred to hold tax-exempt bonds, the federal government pays them a subsidy in the form of net tax deductions on their debt-financed tax-exempt holdings. This subsidy is equal to the corporate tax rate times the taxable interest rate times the $335.7 billion of such borrowing.[9]

9. Although this subsidy is conveyed in a formal sense to banks, we have represented it as if it is paid directly to all holders of taxable bonds. In table 3, therefore, this

Representation of the Tax Reform Act of 1986

The Tax Reform Act of 1986 is represented in GEMDAT in a number of ways. Changes in the rate schedules for single and married taxpayers, personal exemptions, the standard deduction, itemized deductions other than interest, and second-earner and IRA deductions directly affect the computation of taxes paid by households. Similarly, the drop in the corporate tax rate is expressed by a reduction in the corporate tax parameter, u, from 46 percent to 34 percent.

In other cases, changes made by the act are incorporated indirectly by estimating their effects on parameters of the model. The removal of the investment credit, the reduction in business preferences, the imposition of an alternative minimum tax on corporations, the tightening of the individual minimum tax, the new passive-loss restrictions, and the elimination of the individual capital gains deduction are represented by increases in three parameters of the model: the share of pretax corporate economic income included in corporate taxable income (a_c) and the shares of the returns to noncorporate business and to corporate equity included in household taxable income.

The restrictions on new tax-exempt financing are represented by reductions in the share of corporate debt financed by tax-exempt bonds. Limits on the deductibility of interest used to finance tax-exempt bond holdings by banks and property and casualty insurance companies are represented by reductions in steady-state tax-exempt holdings by financial intermediaries. The long-run effects of restrictions on new contributions to IRAs and pension funds are represented by reducing individual holdings of assets in the form of IRAs and pensions and, under the assumption that the wealth of each household is fixed, offsetting these reductions with an equal increase in financial assets held directly in household portfolios and therefore subject to tax.

Restrictions on the deductibility of consumer interest, investment interest, and home equity loans require more complex treatment in GEMDAT. The model treats borrowing as fungible; that is, debt can be issued to finance any asset. Limits on interest deductibility are then modeled by limiting the amount of net debt (that is, debt greater than

subsidy has been allocated to households according to their holdings of taxable bonds, and the before-subsidy (before-tax) income of such households has been correspondingly reduced.

taxable bond holdings) on which interest can be deducted to 80 percent of the value of owner-occupied homes plus the full value of other financial assets that give rise to taxable income.[10] Only households that borrow above this debt limit confront the before-tax interest rate as the opportunity cost of holding consumer durables and tax-exempt bonds. Households owning houses or income-earning assets of sufficient value can finance additional holdings of durables by borrowing against these assets; for these households the opportunity cost of consumer durables remains the after-tax interest rate, despite the elimination of the consumer interest deduction.

Overall, the initial representation of the Tax Reform Act is designed to be revenue neutral, before allowance is made for portfolio behavior. Revenue neutrality has been accomplished by adjusting the model parameters in order to hit the base-case level of revenue.

Simulation Results

When the tax law changes, households discover that their current portfolio holdings are no longer optimal under the new rules. Their portfolio reallocations trigger market responses that ultimately change rates of return, the cost of capital across sectors, real capital allocations, income flows, and government revenues. The total budgetary effects of tax reform can be viewed as made up of two separate components: first, the effects of changes in the tax rules given the before-tax returns, portfolio holdings, and the allocation of the capital stock in the base case; and second, the effects of changes in before-tax returns, portfolio holdings, and capital stock allocations under the new tax rules. The first effect—under prereform conditions—may be termed the *static budget-*

10. New provisions of the 1986 act, together with the rules of prior law, give rise to several different restrictions on the deductibility of interest expense. Interest on borrowing incurred to hold tax-exempt bonds is not deductible; other investment interest expense is deductible, but only to the extent of investment income. Personal interest, such as on consumer installment loans, is not deductible (after a phase-in period). Mortgage interest on first and second homes is deductible, but only on loans no greater than the cost of the property. Because of the fungibility of money, we have combined these various limits into a single overall limit, as noted in the text, which determines the total amount of borrowing the household may undertake before interest is no longer deductible. At the rates of return on the various assets prevailing in the model, this borrowing limit also approximates the investment interest limitation of current law based on flows of investment income and interest expense.

ary effect. The combination of both effects yields the *full equilibrium response* to tax reform.

In our simulation, the Tax Reform Act lowers the taxable interest rate, increases the corporate cost of capital, and reallocates capital from the business and state and local sectors to the household sector. These changes and the associated portfolio reallocations by income class increase tax revenues relative to the static estimates and lower debt service payments because of the decline in the taxable interest rate. On both counts, the deficit decreases once the system has fully adjusted to the new tax rules.

We then performed a second simulation to identify the distributional effects of the Tax Reform Act. Because the model is not designed to evaluate changes in government expenditures or deficits, we simulated a modified version of the Tax Reform Act that is revenue neutral after behavioral adjustments, although the static simulation shows a revenue loss. This modified tax reform law has the same tax base as the actual Tax Reform Act, but individual and corporate tax rates are 5.4 percent lower. In the modified simulation, aggregate after-tax income is unchanged, but total welfare increases because of efficiency gains. The largest increases in both after-tax income and welfare are received by the highest income classes, especially taxpayers with annual income greater than $200,000.

Capital Stocks and Rates of Return

Table 1 shows the effects of the 1986 act on rates of return, the allocation of the capital stock, and aggregate holdings of financial assets (see page 68). The reduction in individual tax rates, the removal of preferences on noncorporate business and corporate equity, and the increase in corporate taxes all combine to make taxable bonds more attractive than other financial assets at the initial set of before-tax returns. As a result, to restore equilibrium, the yield on taxable bonds falls by almost a full percentage point from 8.00 percent to 7.07 percent. The tax-exempt yield rises moderately, but the yield spread between taxable and tax-exempt bonds declines substantially, from 25 percent of the taxable yield to 11 percent. This decline in the yield spread occurs because the cut in marginal tax rates reduces the value of tax exemption. Portfolio adjustments also raise the yield on noncorporate capital.

The increase in corporate taxes causes the rate of return on corporate equity to fall to 10.32 percent, but portfolio adjustments cause the return to rebound to 10.6 percent, leaving it 68 basis points below the base case. The increase in corporate taxes raises the cost of capital to corporations, but the decline in yields to holders of corporate debt and equity lowers it. The net effect is a slight increase in the cost of corporate capital to 12.74 percent.

The corporate debt-equity ratio falls slightly because of tax reform. This drop reflects two offsetting effects. The decline in the corporate tax rate by itself reduces the debt-equity ratio by lowering the marginal tax advantage to debt caused by the double taxation of corporate equity income. The reduction in the preferential taxation of equity relative to debt, at the shareholder level, brought about by the increase in the capital gains tax and lower individual marginal tax rates, largely offsets this effect.[11]

Associated with these changes in before-tax returns are reallocations of the physical capital stock. The quantity of capital in corporations, unincorporated business, and the state and local sectors declines, while that in housing and consumer durables increases. The changes in the stocks of housing and durables are the net result of offsetting movements in the opportunity costs of holding these assets for higher- and lower-income households. Because the opportunity cost of housing equals the real after-tax return on taxable debt, households with different marginal tax rates face different opportunity costs. The Tax Reform Act lowers this opportunity cost for low-income households and raises it for high-income households.

This reallocation of the physical capital stock changes the composition of financial assets issued by firms and governments and held by households either directly or indirectly through pension funds. Households and pension funds hold fewer taxable bonds for two reasons. The main reason for this decline is a shift of tax-exempt holdings from banks to individuals, also shown in the table. Recall that this shift results from the loss of interest deductibility for banks on debt allocable to the holding of tax-exempt bonds. The second reason for lower holdings of taxable bonds is the reduction in debt issued by corporations.

---

11. In contrast to this result, Scholes and Wolfson argue in this volume that the 1986 act will increase the corporate debt-equity ratio. We do, however, share their view that one cannot predict the structure of corporate finance solely by reference to the corporate tax rate. Rather, it is necessary to look at both individual and corporate tax changes.

Portfolio Adjustments by Income Class

Behind these aggregate changes in asset holdings are substantially different portfolio adjustments among taxpayers. These adjustments occur in response to changes in relative after-tax returns, which in turn reflect changes in both the tax law and in before-tax yields.

Table 4 presents the static and full equilibrium effects of the Tax Reform Act on after-tax returns. The static effect is calculated by holding all before-tax returns fixed at their base-case rates and allowing only the new tax rules to affect after-tax returns. The full equilibrium effect is calculated by allowing both the new before-tax returns (see table 1) and the new tax rules to affect after-tax returns. The first three columns of table 4 show after-tax returns on taxable bonds. The remaining columns display yield spreads—the difference between the after-tax returns on taxable bonds and those on corporate equity, noncorporate capital, and tax-exempt bonds. Changes in after-tax yield spreads show the changes in incentives to hold each risky asset.

With before-tax yields fixed, the reduction in individual tax rates increases the after-tax return on taxable bonds in all but the lowest income classes. For three reasons, the after-tax return on other financial assets declines relative to the after-tax return on taxable bonds for all income classes. First, lower marginal tax rates raise the after-tax return by less on the three risky financial assets than on taxable bonds because all or part of the income from tax-exempt bonds, corporate equity, and noncorporate capital is exempt from tax. Second, the preferences for corporate equity and noncorporate capital are reduced, offsetting wholly or in part the higher after-tax returns on those assets from lower marginal tax rates. Third, the increase in corporate-level taxes lowers the yield before individual tax on corporate equity.

These changes in after-tax yields disturb the initial equilibrium. At the base-case before-tax yields, households hold too few taxable bonds (or issue too much debt) and hold too large a share of their wealth in risky financial assets, housing, and consumer durables. (Recall that the after-tax return on taxable bonds is the opportunity cost of household capital.) Their attempts to reallocate their wealth lower the before-tax yield on taxable bonds and raise before-tax yields on other financial assets, as noted above.

In full equilibrium, after-tax yields on taxable bonds and relative after-tax yields on other financial assets increase for some income classes and

Table 4. *Effects of Tax Reform Act of 1986 on After-Tax Returns on Financial Assets: Base Case, Static Effect, and Full Equilibrium, by Income Class*
Percent unless otherwise specified

Income class (thousands of dollars)[a]	Taxable bonds			Corporate equity minus taxable bonds			Noncorporate minus taxable bonds			Tax-exempt bonds minus taxable bonds		
	Base case	Static effect[b]	Full equilibrium[c]	Base case	Static effect[b]	Full equilibrium[c]	Base case	Static effect[b]	Full equilibrium[c]	Base case	Static effect[b]	Full equilibrium[c]
0–5	8.00	8.00	7.07	3.28	2.32	3.53	8.48	8.48	9.61	-2.00	-2.00	-0.77
5–10	6.96	6.90	6.09	3.59	2.43	3.48	9.09	8.45	9.43	-0.96	-0.90	0.21
10–15	7.07	7.39	6.58	3.55	2.38	3.51	9.03	8.46	9.52	-1.07	-1.39	-0.28
15–20	6.68	6.82	6.03	3.67	2.43	3.48	9.26	8.44	9.42	-0.68	-0.82	0.27
20–30	6.46	6.52	5.88	3.73	2.46	3.47	9.38	8.44	9.40	-0.46	-0.52	0.42
30–50	5.97	6.26	5.68	3.88	2.49	3.46	9.67	8.43	9.36	0.03	-0.26	0.62
50–100	5.26	5.70	5.10	4.09	2.54	3.43	10.09	8.41	9.26	0.74	0.30	1.20
100–200	4.58	5.40	4.79	4.29	2.57	3.42	10.49	8.40	9.20	1.42	0.60	1.51
200 and up	4.05	5.66	5.06	4.45	2.55	3.43	10.80	8.41	9.25	1.95	0.34	1.24

a. See table 2 for definition.
b. Shows effect of only new tax rules with before-tax returns held fixed.
c. Shows effect of both new before-tax returns and new tax rules.

Table 5. *Full Equilibrium Effects of Tax Reform Act of 1986 on Portfolio Holdings, by Income Class*[a]
Billions of dollars unless otherwise specified

Income class (thousands of dollars)[b]	Holdings						
	Net taxable bonds	Corporate equity	Non-corporate business	Tax-exempt bonds	Housing	Consumer durables	Wealth
0–5	−6.1	1.3	1.7	0	2.0	1.3	0.2
5–10	−111.6	4.0	−1.6	0	60.9	51.1	2.8
10–15	−28.0	2.6	4.0	0.9	11.5	10.3	1.2
15–20	−83.4	8.7	−1.6	1.4	51.0	28.4	4.6
20–30	−81.5	6.1	−4.8	38.2	31.5	16.2	5.8
30–50	−255.0	−7.2	−14.2	95.7	155.8	41.9	17.2
50–100	−175.0	11.5	10.4	78.4	61.2	29.7	16.2
100–200	63.7	7.0	8.5	10.0	−66.8	−15.6	6.9
200 and up	497.2	−40.1	−38.9	−73.1	−267.5	−73.4	4.2
Direct household holdings	−179.6	−6.1	−36.4	151.5	39.7	105.9	59.1
Pension funds	−115.5	56.4	0	0	0	0	−59.1
Total	−295.1	50.2	−36.4	151.5	39.7	105.9	0

a. Changes from base-case holdings shown in table 2.
b. See table 2 for definition.

fall for others. The after-tax return on taxable bonds increases beyond the base case for the top two income classes because lower marginal tax rates more than compensate them for the decline in the before-tax yield. For all other income classes, the after-tax return on taxable bonds (and thus the opportunity cost of housing and consumer durables) declines. The result, as shown in table 5, is that the top two income classes reduce their holdings of owner-occupied housing and consumer durables, and all other income classes increase such holdings.

Incentives to hold risky financial assets change in a direction similar, though not identical, to incentives to hold housing and consumer durables. In general, in full equilibrium, relative after-tax returns on risky financial assets increase for lower-income classes and pension funds (that is, those investors with low marginal tax rates) and decline for the highest income classes (see table 4). Relative after-tax returns on corporate equity increase only for the lowest income class and pension funds and decline for all other income classes. Relative returns on noncorporate capital increase for income classes under $30,000 and

Table 6. *Budgetary Effects of Tax Reform Act of 1986*
Billions of dollars

Effect	Changes from base case	
	Static effect[a]	Full equilibrium[a]
Change in individual taxes	−28.4	−25.0
Change in corporate taxes	19.5	23.9
Change in tax subsidy to financial institutions	−9.6	−9.9
Change in all taxes (net of subsidy)	0.8	8.9
Change in federal interest payments	0	−11.9
Change in budget	0.8	20.8

a. See table 4 for definition.

decline for all other classes. Finally, the relative after-tax yield on tax-exempt bonds increases for all classes except the highest one.

The portfolio movements shown in table 5 generally reflect these changes in relative after-tax yields.[12] High-income households reduce holdings of both equity and tax-exempt bonds. Households with incomes between $20,000 and $200,000 absorb most of the tax-exempt bonds released by the highest income group, as well as the holdings released by financial institutions. Almost all households other than those in the highest income class increase their equity holdings moderately. Pension funds, as zero tax-bracket investors, exhibit somewhat greater shifts of their assets into equity and away from debt.

Budgetary Effects

The effects of behavioral responses on taxes paid and federal interest costs are shown in table 6. The Tax Reform Act, as we estimate it in our model, is virtually revenue neutral in static terms (an increase in taxes of $0.8 billion). This static revenue estimate is based on the before-tax rates of return prevailing in the base case. Induced portfolio responses and the resulting changes in before-tax rates of return are not taken into account.[13]

12. They are also influenced by changes in the taxation of variance of returns and changes in the covariance between returns on the risky assets and the level of government revenues.

13. Even so-called static revenue estimates involve some assumed behavioral responses such as the direct shift of funds by households into or out of IRAs as their availability is liberalized or restricted or the switch of bank portfolios out of tax-exempt bonds when the deductibility of interest is denied on borrowing to hold such bonds. For

As shown in the second column of table 6, portfolio responses have significant budgetary consequences in the simulation. Revenue increases account for about 40 percent of the net change in the budget. In the full equilibrium, revenues are $8.9 billion higher than base-case revenues and $8.1 billion higher than the static estimate. Individual taxes fall by about $3 billion less than the static tax cut. The decline in the tax base caused by the reduction in the taxable interest rate is more than offset by increases in the average tax rate, as higher-income taxpayers shift from tax-preferred into fully taxed assets. Corporate taxes increase by over $4 billion more than in the static estimate, because reduced corporate reliance on debt, combined with lower interest rates, leads to smaller interest deductions, resulting in greater corporate taxable income.

The change in federal interest payments accounts for the remaining 60 percent of the reduction in the deficit. Because the taxable interest rate declines almost one full percentage point, debt service payments of the federal government fall by about $12 billion. The net reduction in the deficit is $20 billion when all behavioral effects are taken into account.

This shift in the budget represents a net transfer of resources from individuals to the federal government, and this transfer reduces aggregate household utility. Our model does not allow for any offsetting increase in household utility resulting from the government's use of these resources because household utility functions are not affected by direct spending programs. Therefore the simulation presented above cannot be used to compute net welfare effects of the tax change.

Budget-Neutral Simulations and Distributional Effects

To make calculations of the distributional or welfare consequences of the Tax Reform Act, we simulated a modified version of the act with slightly lower tax rates but no changes in other provisions. The tax rates are 5.4 percent below those in the 1986 legislation—14.2 percent, 26.5 percent, and 31.2 percent for individuals (compared with actual rates of

---

a discussion of various types of behavior associated with changes in tax rules and of the behavior usually incorporated into "static" revenue estimates, see Harvey Galper, Robert Lucke, and Eric Toder, "Revenue Effects and Portfolio Behavior: A Simulation of the Tax Reform Act of 1986," National Tax Association–Tax Institute of America, *Proceedings of the Seventy-Ninth Annual Conference* (Columbus, Ohio: NTA–TIA, 1987), pp. 225–33.

Table 7. *Budgetary Effects of Modified Tax Reform Act of 1986*
Billions of dollars

Effect	Changes from base case	
	Static effect[a]	Full equilibrium[a]
Change in individual taxes	−47.7	−42.9
Change in corporate taxes	15.1	19.9
Change in tax subsidy to financial institutions	−9.8	−10.1
Change in all taxes (net of subsidy)	−22.9	−12.8
Change in federal interest payments	0	−13.2
Change in budget surplus	−22.9	0.4

a. See table 4 for definition.

15 percent, 28 percent, and 33 percent) and 32.2 percent for corporations (compared with an actual rate of 34 percent). We chose these rates to keep the budget surplus or deficit constant in the model simulation after all behavioral responses are taken into account.

Table 7 presents the budgetary effects of this modified Tax Reform Act in the static case and for the full equilibrium. The lower rates (compared with those in the actual legislation) cause a revenue loss of $22.9 billion in the static case, but behavioral responses increase net tax revenues by $10 billion and reduce federal interest payments by $13 billion. Thus, after the economy has adjusted, a budget-neutral outcome is achieved.

Table 1 shows the effects of the modified act on rates of return, the capital stock, and financial asset holdings (see page 68). A comparison of the original simulation results with the results of modifying the act (columns 3 and 5) reveals that the lower tax rates under the modified act do not change the results to any substantial degree. With lower individual tax rates, the taxable bond rate falls by somewhat more. The lower cost of debt finance and the reduced corporate taxes on equity finance yield a very slight reduction in the cost of corporate capital in contrast to the original slight increase. Consequently, where the corporate capital stock in the previous simulation contracted somewhat, it expands marginally in the simulation of the modified act. The primary offsetting effect is that the housing stock expands by less with reduced rates than it did with the rates in the Tax Reform Act. The reduced tax rates cause an increase in holdings of corporate equity and a reduced corporate debt-equity ratio. The changes in portfolio holdings by income class (not shown) closely resemble those shown in table 5.

Table 8 presents the changes in income and taxes paid under the modified act. In the static case, the net tax reduction of about $23 billion translates directly into a corresponding increase in after-tax incomes because aggregate before-tax incomes are held fixed. However, the pattern of tax changes varies by income class. All classes benefit from individual tax cuts and all must bear their allocated share of corporate tax increases. Only for two classes—the very bottom income class (with no reduction in individual income taxes) and the $10,000–$15,000 income class—do taxes increase on balance. Despite the substantial corporate tax increase attributed to the very highest income class ($200,000 and over), the individual tax cut outweighs it, resulting in a net tax reduction.

The right-hand columns of table 8 show the changes in the full equilibrium. In the aggregate, the $13 billion drop in before-tax incomes is exactly equal to the decline in government interest payments.[14] As shown in table 7, individual income taxes increase by about $5 billion over the static simulation, while corporate tax payments, net of the subsidy to financial intermediaries that hold tax-exempt bonds, rise by another $5 billion. Thus the total change in after-tax income—from the static case to the full equilibrium—has three separate components: a $13 billion decline in before-tax income, a $5 billion increase in individual taxes, and a $5 billion rise in corporate taxes. Consequently, total after-tax income, instead of increasing by $23 billion, changes negligibly (− $0.4 billion). This result is the mirror image of the constant federal budget deficit shown in table 7.

The distribution among households of these tax and income changes in the full equilibrium is complex and depends on changes in the pattern of yields and household portfolio allocations. Behavioral responses of high-income households (those with incomes above $100,000) transmute the individual tax cut of $16.6 billion in the static case to a tax cut of only $2.1 billion in the full simulation. This smaller tax cut is due to an increase in the taxable income of high-income households in the full simulation, which occurs for two reasons. First, because high-income taxpayers initially hold a larger share of their portfolios in risky assets, the increase in yields on such assets raises taxable income more than the decline in the taxable interest rate lowers it. Second, the portfolio shift of these households toward taxable bonds and away from tax-preferred assets

14. Factor incomes generated from production (national income) must remain unchanged, whatever the allocation of the capital stock, because the model assumes Cobb-Douglas production functions.

Table 8. *Changes in Income and Taxes under Modified Tax Reform Act of 1986, by Income Class*
Billions of dollars unless otherwise specified

Income class (thousands of dollars)[a]	Static effect			Full equilibrium			
	Individual income taxes	Corporate taxes and subsidy to financial institutions[b]	After-tax income	Before-tax income	Individual income taxes	Corporate taxes and subsidy to financial institutions[b]	After-tax income
0–5	0	0.1	-0.1	*	0	0.2	-0.2
5–10	-3.2	0.3	2.9	-3.5	-3.8	1.0	-0.7
10–15	-0.2	0.4	-0.2	-1.0	-0.4	0.9	-1.5
15–20	-3.2	0.9	2.3	-3.5	-4.0	2.3	-1.8
20–30	-5.5	1.4	4.1	-3.4	-6.8	2.8	0.6
30–50	-12.3	2.5	9.8	-10.5	-16.8	4.5	1.8
50–100	-6.7	5.3	1.4	-5.7	-9.1	8.0	-4.6
100–200	-5.1	3.6	1.6	4.2	-2.4	4.4	2.1
200 and up	-11.5	10.3	1.1	10.2	0.3	5.9	4.0
Total	-47.7	24.8	22.9	-13.2	-42.9	30.1	-0.4

* Less than $50 million.
a. See table 2 for definition.
b. Includes the effects of corporations issuing taxable bonds rather than tax-exempt industrial development bonds and the attendant shifts in income from corporate shareholders to bondholders.

increases taxable income. The change in before-tax returns increases the before-tax incomes of this upper-income group by $14.4 billion, leading to an overall increase in after-tax income of $6.1 billion—$3.4 billion greater than the static increase.

Middle-income households (between $20,000 and $50,000), in contrast, experience a large static individual tax cut of $17.8 billion and an even larger reduction in individual tax payments of $23.6 billion in the full-model simulation. This reduction in individual taxes occurs in part because before-tax income declines substantially (−$13.9 billion), reflecting both a lower return on taxable bonds and reduced holdings of such bonds in favor of housing, consumer durables, and other tax-preferred assets. The net result is a small increase in after-tax income for this middle-income group.

Taxpayers in the $50,000–$100,000 income class are literally caught in the middle. First, they receive a smaller initial individual tax cut of $6.7 billion. Second, as major beneficiaries of pension fund holdings, they are adversely affected by the decline in the taxable interest rate. Third, the phaseout of the first-bracket rate and personal exemptions in the 1986 act puts many households in this group in the highest marginal tax bracket.[15] The after-tax return on every financial asset except tax-exempt bonds declines for this income class. Portfolio reallocations help, but only to a limited extent. The result is a reduction of almost $5 billion in after-tax income.

The changes in after-tax income shown in table 8 do not directly measure the welfare gains and losses by income class. In addition to income changes, individual well-being can change for two other reasons: first, because the riskiness of each household's portfolio may change (a source of welfare gain or loss), and second, because the relative prices of goods and services change, thus allowing consumers to reach a higher or lower level of satisfaction with any given income.

Table 9 reports estimates of the total change in household utility resulting from the modified Tax Reform Act after behavioral responses have occurred. The utility change for each household is measured as the dollar payment the household would have to receive (or to make) in the base case, with base-period prices and incomes, to be as well off as under the new rules.[16] The sum of all household net payments is the

15. Under the modified Tax Reform Act, this highest marginal rate is 94.6 percent of 33 percent, or 31.2 percent.
16. This payment is termed the *equivalent variation*. A positive value of the equiv-

Table 9. *Changes in Welfare under Modified Tax Reform Act of 1986,*
by Income Class
Billions of dollars unless otherwise specified

Income class (thousands of dollars)[a]	Components of welfare change				Total welfare	Percent of base-case after-tax income
	After-tax income	Risk	Relative prices	Interaction[b]		
0–5	−0.2	−0.4	0.1	*	−0.6	−9.9
5–10	−0.7	−2.1	3.6	−0.1	0.7	0.3
10–15	−1.5	−1.4	0.4	−0.1	−2.5	−3.7
15–20	−1.8	−3.0	1.9	−0.1	−3.0	−1.1
20–30	0.6	−3.1	0.2	−0.1	−2.5	−0.7
30–50	1.8	−5.5	2.2	−0.1	−1.5	−0.2
50–100	−4.6	−2.7	−0.2	−0.1	−7.7	−1.2
100–200	2.1	3.8	−0.8	−0.1	5.0	1.7
200 and up	4.0	21.7	0.2	−0.7	25.2	7.9
Total	−0.4	7.3	7.5	−1.5	13.0	0.4

* Less than $50 million.
a. See table 2 for definition.
b. Needed because utility is a nonlinear function of income, relative prices, and risk bearing.

total welfare gain for the society. This aggregate welfare gain is equal to $13.0 billion, less than one-half of 1 percent of after-tax income in the base case.

The welfare gains are concentrated overwhelmingly in the top income classes. Welfare gains of households with incomes of $100,000 or more are over twice the total increase in social welfare; this finding means that households with incomes under $100,000 are on balance net losers (over $17 billion), although the losses relative to income are generally not large.[17] For the top income class of $200,000 and above, the welfare gain is equal to a cash grant of about 8 percent of base-period income. In our model, therefore, the Tax Reform Act is highly regressive in its distributional effects, as measured by changes in welfare among households. This effect arises primarily from the reallocation of risk bearing.

Table 9 also decomposes the total welfare change into the following

alent variation means that households must receive a cash payment in the base case to achieve the same level of satisfaction as in the new equilibrium (and hence they are better off in the new equilibrium). A negative value means that households are worse off; that is, they would be willing to make a cash payment to remain in the base-case situation.

17. The bottom income class appears to lose the equivalent of almost 10 percent of its base-period income, but the absolute numbers are so small in this class as to render this calculation unreliable.

four components: changes in after-tax income, changes in risk bearing, changes in relative prices, and a term reflecting the interaction among the first three components. The change in after-tax income is taken directly from table 8. As noted in the earlier discussion, the gains in after-tax income are also concentrated at the top of the income distribution, as are the gains in welfare, but the numbers are not as large.

The change in relative prices is somewhat more important in increasing aggregate welfare than is the increase in utility resulting from reduced risk bearing. The reallocation of risk bearing, however, is a much more important influence on the distribution of total welfare, since high-income taxpayers are the only beneficiaries and they benefit handsomely. Almost 85 percent of the welfare gain for taxpayers with incomes above $100,000 can be attributed to the benefits of reduced risk bearing.[18]

The reason for this large welfare gain for the rich from reduced risk taking is that the tax system before reform encouraged highly inefficient portfolio choices by these taxpayers. Portions of income from certain assets—corporate equity, noncorporate capital, and tax-exempt bonds—were excluded from taxable income. Risky assets therefore enjoyed large tax advantages over fully taxable assets. Since the relative advantages of tax-favored assets rise with the marginal tax rate, the incentive to hold risky, tax-favored assets is greater for high-bracket investors than for low-bracket investors and pension funds.

Under the prior tax law, high marginal-rate taxpayers had to sacrifice more expected return to obtain secure income than did low-bracket taxpayers. Consequently, the marginal disutility—the amount of expected income an investor would sacrifice for risk reduction—was greater for those in high tax brackets. Total utility can be increased by changing the price of risk avoidance to encourage the reallocation of risky assets from high-bracket investors to low-bracket investors and

18. In our model, government taxation of the return on risky assets cannot cause risk to disappear from the private sector. Taxation of the return on such risky assets as noncorporate business or corporate capital increases the variance of the government's revenue stream and reduces the after-tax variance of private portfolios. But this is not the end of the story. We then assume that as the federal revenue stream becomes more risky, this risk is returned to individuals in the form of a "transfer asset" that is distributed among households according to labor income. This transfer asset has a mean equal to zero and a variance equal to the variance of the federal revenue stream. Thus government taxation of risky capital does not change the aggregate risk borne by the private sector. This is the same approach as that followed by Joel Slemrod, "A General Equilibrium Model of Taxation That Uses Micro-Unit Data." See the Appendix for further details.

pension funds. Because tax reform will increase the fraction of income from previously favored assets that is subject to tax, as well as flatten the tax rate schedule, the incentives for high-bracket investors to hold risky assets will decrease substantially. As a result, utility of high-income investors will rise under the Tax Reform Act, because the reduction in riskiness of their investments will more than compensate them for any reduction in after-tax income they may have to accept. The resulting gain to high-income investors from lower risk is greater than the loss to low-income investors from increasing their holdings of risky assets.

The third column of table 9 shows the gain in welfare from changes in relative prices among sectors, the traditional efficiency gain resulting from eliminating tax-induced misallocations of resources—"leveling the playing field" in current jargon. In our model, these gains come from two sources. First, capital is allocated more efficiently among sectors. The tax-preferred state and local and noncorporate sectors shrink as their cost of capital increases and the more heavily taxed corporate sector expands slightly. Second, although there is an increase in capital devoted to two currently untaxed sectors—housing and particularly consumer durables—the reallocation of this capital among households, away from higher-income households and toward lower-income households, raises welfare.

To summarize briefly, table 9 shows that the Tax Reform Act of 1986 increases net welfare by both increasing the efficiency of allocation of the physical capital stock and reducing tax-induced distortions in holdings of financial assets. Furthermore, the welfare gain in the top two income classes—those with income over $100,000—greatly exceeds the total welfare gain for the entire population. Static simulations that hold before-tax returns fixed do not reveal these gains. The main reason for the large welfare gains in the top income classes is that the act raises the after-tax return they receive on taxable bonds and causes them to hold less risky portfolios.

Qualifications

As noted above, the results of simulating any general equilibrium model can be highly sensitive to how equations in the model are specified. GEMDAT assumes specific functional forms for production functions and for demand functions for goods and assets, and it treats labor supply and saving of all households as fixed. Changing these assumptions could dramatically alter the simulated incidence of the Tax Reform Act. Thus one should regard our results as illustrative rather than definitive, although they do provide important insights on how the act might alter the distribution of income.

CLOSED- VERSUS OPEN-ECONOMY MODELS. In considering how different assumptions might affect the results, two aspects of GEMDAT deserve special emphasis. The first is the assumption of a closed economy.[19] If domestically issued taxable bonds and corporate equity could be held by foreign as well as domestic savers and U.S. savers could hold similar claims issued by foreign governments and corporations, U.S. tax policy would change before-tax yields to all asset holders much less than the results shown here suggest. In particular, the simulated decline in the taxable interest rate would be much smaller in an open-economy model than the 1 percentage point change we estimate. In the extreme case of a small country with an open economy, the taxable interest rate would be determined exogenously in a world capital market and would not be changed at all by domestic tax reform.

If tax reform changed the taxable interest rate little or not at all, the simulated allocational and distributional effects of the act would be substantially different. The after-tax costs of owner-occupied housing and consumer durables would then rise for all households, and stocks of these assets would decline. The corporate capital stock would fall by a larger amount than in the simulation because no decline in the taxable interest rate would moderate the effects of higher corporate-level taxes. Because of foreign lending and borrowing in such a model, domestic saving would not have to equal investment and the total domestic capital stock could fall.

Some of the qualitative results from analysis based on an open-economy model would probably be similar to those we derived. High-income investors would switch to taxable bonds, perhaps to an even greater degree, because the taxable rate would not fall. As a result, before-tax returns on preferentially taxed assets used to support domes-

19. For discussions of capital income taxation in an open economy, see Lawrence Goulder, John B. Shoven, and John Whalley, "Domestic Tax Policy and the Foreign Sector: The Importance of Alternative Foreign Sector Formulations to Results from a General Equilibrium Tax Analysis Model," in Feldstein, ed., *Behavioral Simulation Methods in Tax Policy Analysis*, pp. 333–67; John Mutti and Harry Grubert, "The Taxation of Capital Income in an Open Economy: The Importance of Resident-Nonresident Tax Treatment," *Journal of Public Economics*, vol. 27 (August 1985), pp. 291–309; and Joel Slemrod's paper in this volume.

tic capital, such as noncorporate equity and tax-exempt bonds, would have to rise. Reductions in holdings of tax-preferred assets would also cause revenues to be higher in the full equilibrium than in the static case, but the increased revenues would be attributed more to larger individual income tax revenues than we found in a closed-economy model.

UTILITY FUNCTION. The choice of a utility function affects household asset demands. Because the substitutions among assets in response to tax policy changes are the major source of difference between the distributional results in the full model and in the static simulations, the preferences that influence those substitutions are a critical feature of the model.[20]

In the model used in this paper, households balance after-tax returns and risk based on a utility function that produces demand curves for risky assets that are linearly related to the difference between the after-tax return on the risky asset and the after-tax return on taxable bonds. This higher return on risky assets is a "compensating differential" required to induce households to hold these assets. One consequence of this particular form of the utility function is that the required compensating differential increases in proportion to holdings of the risky asset in the household's portfolio.

An alternative way of modeling asset demands within the same general utility framework would be to treat a portion of the compensating differential not as a "slope" factor such that the required differential increases with the asset's share in the portfolio, but as an "intercept" or "shift" factor that maintains a constant required differential of the returns on risky assets over that on riskless taxable bonds. Such an alternative utility function would generate much larger elasticities of substitution among assets with respect to changes in expected after-tax returns than does our model. The reason is that much smaller changes in yields, only enough to change the after-tax return relative to the constant differential initially required, will cause households to shift out of or into risky assets.[21]

20. In contrast to GEMDAT, the Harberger model of the incidence of the corporation income tax and models in the Harberger tradition treat all assets as perfect substitutes in household portfolios by assuming that investors must receive the same after-tax return on all assets. The implied utility function is one in which utility depends only on after-tax income, but not on risk. See Arnold C. Harberger, "The Incidence of the Corporation Income Tax," *Journal of Political Economy*, vol. 70 (June 1962), pp. 215–40; and Ballard and others, *A General Equilibrium Model for Tax Policy Evaluation*.

21. Simulations of an earlier version of this model with this alternative utility function

Conclusions

The simulation results shown in this paper illustrate some important consequences of the Tax Reform Act of 1986. The act is shown to reduce the taxable interest rate, increase before-tax returns on tax-preferred financial assets, raise the cost of capital to noncorporate business and state and local governments, and leave essentially unchanged the cost of capital to corporations. As a result, it reallocates capital away from noncorporate business and government uses and toward owner-occupied housing and consumer durables.

The aggregate effects on capital allocation mask some significant shifts in portfolio holdings among households. High-income households reduce their direct holdings of corporate equity, other risky financial assets, and owner-occupied housing and consumer durables. Pension funds and low- and middle-income households generally increase their holdings of these assets. These portfolio shifts occur because lower and flatter marginal tax rates, the elimination of the capital gains deduction, and the reduction in other tax shelter opportunities reduce the incentive for high-income households to hold tax-preferred assets.

The simulation results indicate that the Tax Reform Act could lower the federal deficit in the long run even though it is estimated to be revenue neutral without considering portfolio changes. Reductions in outlays and increases in revenues both contribute to a lower deficit. The fall in taxable interest rates reduces federal debt service costs. Revenues increase because portfolio shifts among individuals increase individual taxes. High-income taxpayers substitute taxable bonds for tax-preferred assets and low-income households move in the opposite direction. These portfolio shifts increase the average tax rate on income from capital. Also, a reduction in the corporate debt-equity ratio leads to higher revenues from corporate taxes.

The most interesting insights from the simulations relate to distributional effects. While tax reform is shown to be approximately neutral with fixed before-tax returns and portfolio holdings, the distributional results change dramatically when behavioral responses are taken into account. The big gainers are the top two income classes comprising

---

generated portfolio shifts that were too large to be believed. The results are not reported here.

taxpayers with annual incomes above $100,000. These income classes pay higher taxes (individual and corporate) after behavioral responses, but also receive higher after-tax income because their before-tax incomes rise. In addition, they experience a substantial gain in welfare from a reduction in portfolio risk. In fact, the Tax Reform Act is estimated to generate a welfare gain for the top two income classes of more than double the aggregate welfare gain. All other income classes experience welfare losses.

The distributional results can be given a simple intuitive explanation. Tax reform is a trade-off of lower rates for a broader tax base. The highest income groups enjoy the largest rate reductions. They also experience the biggest loss in tax preferences. Under prior law, high-income taxpayers avoided some of the effects of steeply progressive rates by holding preferentially taxed assets. Households avoided tax by accepting higher portfolio risks, lower marginal utility from the services of housing and consumer durables, and lower before-tax returns on some assets (notably tax-exempt bonds). Lowering rates and broadening the tax base in a way that holds fixed the tax payments of each income class when incomes do not change benefits high-income groups by reducing the costs they must incur to avoid taxes. As a result, high-income taxpayers are the major beneficiaries of tax reform, even though their tax payments increase.[22]

It should again be emphasized that these results depend heavily on behavior that is assumed, not empirically estimated. The main advantage of general equilibrium models is not the precise numerical results, but their capacity to illustrate potential interactions among sectors of the economy that are not revealed by partial analysis. In particular, the simulations in this paper suggest three main insights from using a portfolio-based general equilibrium model. First, tax reform may lower taxable interest rates, thus offsetting to some degree the adverse effects on corporate investment estimated by models that assume interest rates are fixed. Second, tax reform may improve efficiency by reallocating household capital and consumer durables from high-bracket to low-bracket taxpayers, even though the overall increase in holdings of these assets at the expense of business capital lowers efficiency. Finally, even when account is taken of the effects of higher corporate taxes, tax reform

22. A similar point is made by James M. Buchanan, "Tax Reform as Political Choice," *Journal of Economic Perspectives*, vol. 1 (Summer 1987), pp. 29–35.

is much more favorable to the highest income groups than would be shown by static estimates of changes in individual tax liability.

Appendix

This appendix gives a formal presentation of GEMDAT. Considered in order are the supplies of assets held in household portfolios (derived from the demand for the services of physical capital by the capital-using sectors), the household demand for assets (derived from household utility-maximizing considerations), the determination of the optimum corporate debt-capital ratio, the treatment of financial intermediaries in the model, and the derivation of sectoral capital stocks from production functions.

Demand for Capital and Supplies of Assets

The demand for capital financed by each of the five sectors can be expressed as a unit-elastic function of the cost of capital net of depreciation (that is, the real before-tax return on capital):

(1.1)–(1.5) $$K_i = K_{i0}/(r_i - \pi), i = 1 \ldots 5,$$

where K_i = capital financed respectively by corporations, noncorporate business, state and local governments, and households (owner-occupied housing and consumer durables), K_{i0} = a set of constants, r_i = the nominal before-tax return on capital financed by sector i, and π = the annual inflation rate. The values of the constant terms, $K_{i0}, i = 1 \ldots 5$, depend on production relationships and the value of output in each sector and are derived at the end of this appendix.

The net cost of capital in each sector is determined by before-tax rates of return on financial assets supplied to households (and corporate taxes for the corporate sector). These before-tax returns differ among assets for three reasons. First, the financial assets issued by different producing sectors are taxed differentially at the household level. Second, assets differ in their attractiveness to households, per dollar of after-tax return, because of risk and other factors. Third, corporate equity alone is subject to an extra income tax at the entity level.

Corporations supply taxable bonds, tax-exempt bonds (industrial development bonds), and corporate equity to households. The volume of tax-exempt bonds that corporations are allowed to issue is assumed to be a fixed, predetermined share of total corporate borrowing. Payments to lenders, but not returns to equity holders, are deductible in computing taxable corporate income. In addition, only a_1 per dollar of corporate economic income is included in the tax base.[23] Finally, corporations incur leverage costs of debt finance that vary with the debt-equity ratio. This is modeled by assuming that lenders to corporations extract a premium per unit of capital (Z) that rises with leverage.[24] The particular function chosen to represent this "leverage premium" is:

$$(2) \qquad\qquad Z = zf_1^2/(1 - f_1),$$

where Z = leverage cost per unit of capital, f_1 = the corporate debt-capital ratio, and z = a calibrated constant. The value of z is selected so as to replicate the observed debt-equity ratio of the corporate sector. The procedure for optimizing the debt-equity ratio is described below. In equation 2, $Z'(f_1) > 0, Z''(f_1) > 0, Z(0) = 0, Z'(0) = 0$, and Z approaches infinity as f_1 approaches one. This means that the average and marginal leverage premiums are zero when there is no debt finance, but increase

23. The value of a_1 is less than one, reflecting accelerated depreciation, the investment credit, and other corporate preferences. In principle, if corporations had sufficient taxable income to offset all depreciation deductions and if there were no investment credit or other tax subsidies, then the value of a_1 would equal one if economic and tax depreciation were equal and zero if all capital assets were expensed. In simulating the model, the value of a_1 was set equal to 0.48 so as to approximate long-run revenue from the taxation of income of nonfinancial corporations at 1985 levels. This value reflects the facts that losses cannot be deducted immediately and that investment credits in any year are limited to 85 percent of before-tax credit tax liability. Also, in theory, the value of a_1 should be affected by changes in the discount rate of corporations; as a first approximation we held a_1 constant in simulations of the model.

24. The "leverage premium" is to be thought of as a contingency reserve that must be set aside to pay off creditors in the event a corporation cannot meet its debt payments. The earnings used for this reserve are not used to pay dividends to shareholders and do not give rise to increases in share values because shareholders view them as required to satisfy this contingent liability. Therefore, this premium is not deductible against the corporate income tax and is also not taxable to shareholders.

This indirect procedure for providing protection to creditors for leverage-related risks increases the cost of debt finance to the corporation. A more direct way to model this component of borrowing cost would be to assume that creditors require a higher interest rate to compensate them for the increased risk of default when the debt-equity ratio rises. This latter approach would be more complicated because it would require adding another risky asset—corporate debt—to the model and would therefore necessitate the determination of the amount of risky and riskless taxable debt held in each household's portfolio.

as the corporation increases its debt-equity ratio, ultimately offsetting the tax advantage to debt finance.[25]

The nominal before-tax return on corporate capital can be expressed as a weighted average of payments to owners and creditors (including retained earnings) plus leverage costs, gross of corporate taxes:

$$(3.1) \quad r_1 = [1/(1 - ua_1)] \{f_1[ei_e + (1 - e)i_f] (1 - u) \\ + (1 - f_1)i_c + [zf_1^2/(1 - f_1)]\}.$$

In equation 3.1, r_1 = the nominal before-tax return on capital used by the corporate sector, u = the corporate tax rate, a_1 = the percentage of corporate economic income included in the tax base, e = the share of corporate debt financed by tax-exempt bonds, i_e = the tax-exempt interest rate, i_f = the before-tax interest rate on taxable bonds, and i_c = the rate of return (before individual taxes) on corporate equity.[26]

Noncorporate enterprises supply "shares" of noncorporate capital to individuals. Because there is no entity-level tax, the before-tax return on noncorporate capital is equal to the return on shares of noncorporate capital received by households. This return to households, denoted as i_b, reflects a premium that compensates individual investors for the

25. The tax advantage to debt finance results because corporations can deduct interest, but not the return to equity. See Merton H. Miller, "Debt and Taxes," *Journal of Finance*, vol. 32 (May 1977), pp. 261–75. As Miller points out, there is an offsetting tax advantage to equity finance because appreciation of corporate stock is tax preferred at the individual level, while interest income is generally fully taxable to individuals. In the model, corporations optimize their debt-equity ratio when an additional dollar of debt finance results in corporate tax savings just equal to the sum of marginal interest premium costs and the increases in before-tax payments required to compensate individuals who finance corporate capital for the higher individual income taxes applied to debt finance.

26. Equation 3.1 is a simplification of the standard formulation of the cost of capital developed by Hall and Jorgenson and used in many studies of how tax burdens vary among industries, including Gravelle and Auerbach, among others. See Robert E. Hall and Dale W. Jorgenson, "Tax Policy and Investment Behavior," *American Economic Review*, vol. 57 (June 1967), pp. 391–414; Jane G. Gravelle, "Effects of the 1981 Depreciation Revisions on the Taxation of Income from Business Capital," *National Tax Journal*, vol. 35 (March 1982), pp. 1–20; and Alan J. Auerbach, "Corporate Taxation in the United States," *Brookings Papers on Economic Activity, 2:1983*, pp. 451–505. The major differences with the standard formulation are that: (1) the cost of capital is expressed net of depreciation; (2) the discount rate is expressed as a weighted average of after-tax payments to equity owners and holders of taxable and tax-exempt bonds, rather than as a single after-tax rate, and (3) the effects of the investment credit and tax depreciation are reflected in a single value, a_1, that approximates the percentage of corporate economic income included in the corporate tax base.

greater riskiness and other disadvantages of noncorporate capital relative to taxable bonds.

State and local government capital is taken as financed by tax-exempt bonds. Therefore, $r_3 = i_e$, the interest rate received by holders of tax-exempt bonds.

Capital in owner-occupied housing and consumer durables is supplied by households to themselves. The before-tax returns on these assets, $r_4{}^j$ and $r_5{}^j$, reflect the marginal productivity of capital in producing the services of housing and durables for each household j. The payment for these capital services is in the form of imputed rent instead of cash income. Because each household's utility function (see discussion below) implies a diminishing marginal utility for all goods and services, the before-tax return on the capital each household supplies for owner-occupied homes and consumer durables also declines as the quantity of capital increases. In equilibrium, each household equates its before-tax return on these assets to its opportunity cost. For households who are itemizers, and for nonitemizers who are net lenders, this opportunity cost equals the after-tax interest rate on fully taxed securities, $i_f(1 - t^j)$, where t^j is the marginal tax rate of household j. For households who are nonitemizers and net borrowers, the opportunity cost of homes and durables is i_f because interest payments are not deductible at the margin.

Summarizing, the nominal before-tax returns for capital used in sectors two through five (noncorporate business, state and local governments, owner-occupied housing, and consumer durables) can be expressed as:

(3.2) $$r_2 = i_b;$$

(3.3) $$r_3 = i_e;$$

(3.4a) $$r_4 = i_f(1 - t^j)$$

for all itemizers and nonitemizers who are net lenders;

(3.4b) $$r_4 = i_f$$

for nonitemizers who are net borrowers;

(3.5a) $$r_5 = i_f(1 - t^j)$$

for all itemizers and nonitemizers who are net lenders;

(3.5b) $$r_5 = i_f$$

for nonitemizers who are net borrowers.

The total supplies of the four financial assets to households can be derived directly from the capital stocks in the noncorporate business and state and local sectors and the corporate debt-equity ratio by these equations:

(4.1) $$F = f_1(1 - e)K_1 + G + TTE,$$

(4.2) $$C = (1 - f_1)K_1,$$

(4.3) $$B = K_2,$$

(4.4) $$E = K_3 + f_1eK_1 - TTE,$$

where F = net taxable bonds supplied to households, G = federal debt, C = corporate equity supplied to households, B = noncorporate business capital supplied to households, E = tax-exempt bonds supplied to households, and TTE = tax-exempt bonds held by financial intermediaries. Within both the taxable and tax-exempt bond categories, the bonds of different issuers are treated as perfect substitutes by households.

TTE is exogenously determined in the model. The inclusion of TTE reflects the fact that financial institutions (mostly commercial banks and property and casualty insurance companies) hold almost half of the outstanding stock of tax-exempt bonds, which causes the supply of tax-exempts available to households to be much lower than the amount issued by borrowers. Institutions that hold tax-exempt bonds are assumed to finance these holdings by issuing an equal amount of taxable debt to households. The resulting difference between the taxable interest rate received by the ultimate lenders (households) and the tax-exempt rate paid by borrowers can be regarded as a subsidy to state and local borrowing (and some corporate borrowing) that is conveyed indirectly by means of a reduction in the taxes paid by the financial institutions holding tax-exempt bonds.[27]

Household Utility Maximization and Asset Demands

In the model, assets are demanded by 400 representative households and by pension funds. The representative households are chosen by subdividing the tax-filing population into four groups—joint itemizers, joint nonitemizers, single itemizers, and single nonitemizers. Each of

27. The role of financial intermediaries in the model is discussed further below.

the four groups is then further disaggregated into a matrix of 100 cells of 10 labor income and 10 capital income classes. Pension funds have a separate decision function for portfolio allocation that is independent of the utility functions of households who hold pension fund claims. (Households, however, take the portfolio decision made on their behalf by pension funds into account in choosing their optimal portfolios.) Each household has the average value for its cell of labor income, itemized deductions (other than for interest paid), second-earner deductions, personal exemptions, and IRA and Keogh contributions. Furthermore, each household confronts the tax rate schedule applicable to its filing status. In the simulations, the marginal tax rate and the decision to itemize are endogenous.

Households hold owner-occupied housing and consumer durables, which they "rent" to themselves, and allocate their remaining wealth among four financial assets: taxable bonds, corporate equity, noncorporate capital, and tax-exempt bonds. Household-sector capital (owner-occupied housing and consumer durables) and taxable bonds are treated as riskless in the model, while the other three assets have varying degrees of taxability and risk.

The interest income from taxable bonds is fully includable in the taxable income of households, while interest paid is fully deductible to itemizers. The return from corporate equity is treated as partially taxable (with an inclusion rate of 50 percent), reflecting the deferral of accrued capital gains, the exemption of gains passed on at death, and the exclusion of 60 percent of realized gains. The return from noncorporate capital is also treated as partially taxable, but with a lower inclusion rate of 20 percent, reflecting business tax preferences passed directly through to individuals and nonreporting of much of this type of income. The returns from both tax-exempt bonds and household-sector capital are not included in taxable income.

Households are not allowed to hold negative amounts of corporate equity, noncorporate business capital, tax-exempt bonds, or household-sector capital, but may hold either positive or negative amounts of taxable bonds. Changes in the amount of debt issued by any household are not tied directly to any particular asset in its portfolio; instead, debt is treated as fungible. In contrast, pension funds hold only corporate equity and debt and are not allowed negative holdings of either asset.

Each household is also assigned a fixed amount of wealth in IRAs and Keogh plans, based on imputations from the Survey of Consumer

Finances. IRA and Keogh wealth is assumed to be invested in taxable bonds.[28]

Households maximize a utility function of the form:

(5) $$U = m_0(1 - e^{-m_1 V}), m_0, m_1 > 0,$$

where V is a Cobb-Douglas function of outputs financed by the corporate, noncorporate, and state and local sectors and the two outputs financed by households (the services of owner-occupied housing and consumer durables); m_0 is a constant, and m_1 is a parameter that represents the household's degree of risk aversion. Maximizing U first requires maximizing V subject to the constraint that expenditures on the outputs must equal total after-tax income. This can be expressed as maximization of:

(6) $$V = \prod_{i=1}^{5} X_i^{v_i}, \quad \sum_{i=1}^{5} v_i = 1,$$

subject to:

(7) $$Y = \sum_{i=1}^{5} P_i X_i,$$

where Y = the household's after-tax income and the P_i and X_i are the prices and quantities of the outputs. For owner-occupied housing and durables, the "prices" are rental values per unit of service.

Solving equations 6 and 7 gives the familiar result with a Cobb-Douglas function:

(8) $$X_i = v_i Y/P_i \text{ for } i = 1, \ldots 5.;$$

that is, the expenditure on each good, $P_i X_i$, is a fixed share (v_i) of the household's total income.

---

28. Because there are no limits on borrowing in the model and because households are allowed to deduct interest paid, it pays for them to hold taxable bonds within IRAs and preferentially taxed assets outside IRAs. This is because the tax exemption on income earned within an IRA is wasted if it is applied to an asset that is otherwise tax preferred; even if households want to hold 100 percent of their net wealth in preferentially taxed assets such as corporate shares, they can do so without adding to risk by borrowing to finance their corporate shares outside IRAs and offsetting the borrowing with holdings of taxable bonds inside an IRA. Of course, given restrictions on the ability to leverage purchases of equity and barriers to the effective use of IRAs as collateral for loans, households are not observed to hold all of their IRA and Keogh wealth in the form of taxable securities. This simplifying assumption approximates observed data, however. In 1985 households held about 85 percent of IRA wealth in financial institutions in which the primary asset was taxable securities.

Substituting equation 8 into equation 6 produces an indirect utility function in terms of prices and after-tax income of the form:

(9) $$V = m_2 Y,$$

where $$m_2 = \prod_{i=1}^{5}(v_i/P_i)^{v_i}.$$

Substituting equation 9 into equation 5 produces a general utility function of the form:

(10) $$U = m_0(1 - e^{-m_1 m_2 Y}).$$

Let $E(\cdot)$ represent the expectations operator. Then, if Y is normally distributed with mean $E(Y)$ and variance σ_Y^2, it can be shown that maximizing $E(U)$ is equivalent to maximizing the expression $[E(Y) - (m_1 m_2 \sigma_Y^2/2)]$. That is, expected utility is positively related to the expected value of income and negatively related to the product of the variance of income, a term m_1 that represents the degree of risk aversion, and a term m_2 that represents an index of utility per dollar of expected consumption.

Thus, to choose the optimal financial portfolio, each household j allocates the amount of its wealth not held in the form of owner-occupied housing and durables among financial assets so as to maximize:

(11) $$E(U^j) = E(Y^j) - m_1^j m_2^j \sigma_{Y^j}^2/2$$

subject to:

(11.1) $$W^j - X_4^j - X_5^j = F^j + C^j + B^j + E^j$$

(11.2) $$C^j, B^j, E^j, X_4^j, X_5^j \geq 0.$$

The constraints 11.1 and 11.2 state that the sum of all financial assets must equal household j's total wealth (W^j) minus wealth used to supply services of owner-occupied housing and consumer durables; and that households cannot hold negative amounts of corporate equity (C), noncorporate business capital (B), tax-exempt bonds (E), owner-occupied housing (X_4), and consumer durables (X_5). Households can hold negative amounts of taxable bonds (F); that is, they can issue debt.

The expected value of household j's after-tax income (other than imputed income from services of housing and durables), $E(Y^j)$, is equal to:

$$(12) \quad E(Y^j) = L^j(1 - t^j) + Y^j_{inf} + W^j\{i_f(1 - t^j)f^j + E(i_e)e^j$$
$$+ E(i_b)(1 - a_b t^j)b^j + E(i_c)(1 - a_c t^j)c^j$$
$$+ [i_f F_{pen} + E(i_c)C_{pen}]pen^j$$
$$+ i_f ira^j\},$$

where L^j = labor income of household j; t^j = marginal tax rate of household j; Y^j_{inf} = inframarginal income of household j attributable to fact that the average tax rate is below the marginal tax rate; W^j = total wealth of household j; $E(i_e)$, $E(i_b)$, and $E(i_c)$ = expected returns to households (including expected capital appreciation) on tax-exempt bonds, noncorporate business capital, and corporate equity; a_b and a_c = percentages of noncorporate business income and income from corporate equity holdings (after corporate taxes) included in the individual income tax base; f^j, e^j, b^j, and c^j = shares of the household's wealth in taxable bonds, tax-exempt bonds, noncorporate business, and corporate equity held outside of pensions, IRAs, and Keogh plans; F_{pen} and C_{pen} are shares of pension fund and life insurance wealth in taxable bonds and corporate equity; pen^j = share of wealth of household j in pensions and life insurance; and ira^j = share of wealth of household j in IRA and Keogh plans (assumed held in taxable bonds).

The variance of after-tax income is taken to be the sum of the variances of the after-tax returns on each risky asset. It is assumed that the covariances among the risky assets are zero.[29] In computing the after-

---

29. This assumption, along with the assumption that taxable bonds have zero variance, was made mainly for computational tractability. In examining historical data on annual variances and covariances of total returns to assets, we did find that the correlations between returns on taxable bonds and common stocks and between returns on tax-exempt bonds and common stocks were both insignificantly different from zero. We also found that the variance on common stocks was greater than the variance on tax-exempt bonds, which in turn was greater than the variance on taxable bonds. No data on noncorporate business returns were available, but we suspect they have a higher variance than any of the other assets and a positive covariance with common stocks. The method we used to compute total rates of return was similar to that used by Ibbotson and Sinquefield. See Roger G. Ibbotson and Rex A. Sinquefield, *Stocks, Bonds, Bills, and Inflation: The Past and the Future* (Charlottesville, Va.: Financial Analysts Research Foundation, 1982).

In the model, we assume a before-tax variance of 0.08 for noncorporate business

tax variance on any asset, the tax rate on the asset is not generally the same as the tax rate on expected income from the asset. Variability of year-to-year returns to individuals is mostly in the form of capital gains, not ordinary income; therefore the effective tax rate on variance is approximated by the product of the individual's marginal tax rate and the percentage of annual nominal capital gains included in the tax base. Under current law, this rate is taken to be equal to 20 percent, based on the 60 percent deduction for long-term capital gains and an assumption that realized gains are roughly 50 percent of accrued gains.[30] At the corporate-entity level, however, the inclusion rate on variance is taken to be equal to the inclusion rate on expected income, a_1.

The variance of the individual's income also includes a term that reflects the variance of the government's revenue stream. When part of the government's revenue is raised from taxation of the income from risky assets, the government's revenue is itself uncertain. In the model, we hold the level of public services fixed and investigate only the effects of changes in the tax structure. Therefore, if federal revenue is higher or lower than expected, this difference must be distributed back in some way to households. Put another way, any variance in federal revenue must result in an equal amount of aggregate variance in the net after-tax and after-transfer income of private individuals.

GEMDAT takes account of this variance feedback by creating an additional asset, government transfers (*TRANS*), with an expected value of zero and a total variance equal to the variance of the government revenue stream.[31] Each household is assigned a fixed share of *TRANS*

capital, 0.03 for corporate equity, 0.01 for tax-exempt bonds, and 0 for taxable bonds. These numbers probably accurately reflect the rank-ordering of the variances of these four assets and, for corporate equity and tax-exempt bonds, accurately reflect the relative magnitude of the variances.

Any attempt to incorporate covariances among assets into the model would greatly complicate the analysis. The current model does have the advantage of resulting in diversified portfolios that respond in the expected direction to relative changes in after-tax yields. Nonetheless, one should recognize that the asset substitutions occurring in GEMDAT should be taken as only rough approximations of real-world portfolio choices.

30. The inclusion rate on the variance of corporate equity at the household level is assumed to be 25 percent, slightly higher than the 20 percent inclusion rate used for capital gains alone, because a small share of the variance of the total return on equity is attributable to the variance of dividends, which are fully taxable. In addition, it is worth noting that the variance on tax-exempt bonds is also subject to tax, with an inclusion rate of 20 percent, because capital gains on sales of tax-exempt securities are taxable and capital losses can be deducted from gains on other assets.

31. This approach follows Slemrod. See Slemrod, "A General Equilibrium Model of Taxation That Uses Micro-Unit Data."

equal to lump sum transfers that it will receive, or taxes it will pay, if government revenue exceeds or falls short of expectations. The total variance of the government revenue stream, in turn, depends on the total stock of risky assets in the economy, the before-tax variance of those risky assets, and the tax rate applied to returns above or below expected returns.

The amount of the government transfer received by household j can be expressed as:

$$(13) \quad TRANS^j = S^j \left(\{[i_e - E(i_e)]\, a_e^* t_e E\} + \{[i_b - E(i_b)] a_b^* t_b B\} \right.$$
$$\left. + \{[i_c - E(i_c)]\, t_k C\} \right),$$

where S^j = the share of the total government transfer received by household j; $t_k = ua_1^* + a_c^* t_c\,(1 - ua_1^*)$, the combined average marginal tax rate (individual plus corporate) on equity-financed corporate capital; a_e^*, a_b^*, and a_c^* = the share of the variances of tax-exempt bonds, noncorporate business income, and corporate equity income received by households that is included in taxable income; t_e, t_b, and t_c = weighted average marginal tax rates of households, where the weights are the proportionate holdings of tax-exempt bonds, noncorporate business capital, and corporate equity; and E, B, and C = total household holdings of tax-exempt bonds, noncorporate business capital, and corporate equity.

The variance of after-tax income of household j, adjusted for j's asset-specific risk preferences, can then be written as:

$$(14) \quad \sigma_y^{2j} = [(1 - a_e^* t^j) e^j W^j + a_e^* t_e E S^j]^2 m_e^j \sigma_e^2$$
$$+ [(1 - a_b^* t^j) b^j W^j + a_b^* t_b B S^j]^2 m_b^j \sigma_b^2$$
$$+ [(1 - a_c^* t^j) c^j W^j + t_k C S^j + C_{pen} pen^j W^j]^2 m_c^j\, \sigma_c^2.$$

The terms m_e^j, m_b^j, and m_c^j are asset-specific adjustment factors for each household. These adjustment factors represent compensating differentials in the form of higher required returns that vary directly with the amount of the asset in the household's portfolio.

Substituting equations 12 and 14 into equation 11, differentiating with respect to household j's shares of the risky assets, e^j, b^j, and c^j, and setting the results equal to zero, produces share-demand equations for the three risky assets: tax-exempt bonds, shares of noncorporate business capital, and corporate equity. They are:

$$(15.1) \quad e^j = [E(i_e)(1 - a_e t^j) - i_f(1 - t^j) - m_1^j m_2^j m_e^j a_e^* t_e(1 - a_e^* t^j) S^j E \sigma_e^2]$$

$$/ [m_1^j m_2^j m_e^j (1 - a_e^* t^j)^2 \sigma_e^2 W^j].$$

$$(15.2) \quad b^j = [E(i_b)(1 - a_b t^j) - i_f(1 - t^j) - m_1^j m_2^j m_b^j a_b^* t_b(1 - a_b^* t^j) S^j B \sigma_b^2]$$

$$/ [m_1^j m_2^j m_b^j (1 - a_b^* t^j)^2 \sigma_b^2 W^j].$$

$$(15.3) \quad c^j = [E(i_c)(1 - a_c t^j)] - i_f(1 - t^j)$$

$$- m_1^j m_2^j m_c^j (1 - a_c^* t^j)(t_k S^j C + C_{pen} pen^j W^j) \sigma_c^2]$$

$$/ [m_1^j m_2^j m_c^j (1 - a_c^* t^j)^2 \sigma_c^2 W^j].$$

The demand for each risky asset as a share of household j's wealth is seen to be positively related to the difference between its expected after-tax return and the after-tax return on taxable bonds, less a term representing the covariance of return on the asset with the return on $TRANS^j$, and inversely related to the product of the after-tax variance on the asset and constants representing household j's general degree of risk aversion, utility per dollar of expected consumption, and an adjustment factor for the specific risky asset.

To calibrate the demand equations, the variances of the risky assets and the before-tax returns are estimated from actual data, and, as noted above, household asset holdings are imputed from tax return data and data from the Survey of Consumer Finances. Each sample household is also assigned amounts of labor income, itemized deductions (other than interest), personal exemptions, IRA deductions, and second-earner deductions based on computations from tax return data. These data can be used to calculate the initial marginal tax rate for all households.

Given this observed and imputed data, equations 15.1 through 15.3 can be used to calibrate the values of m_1^j and two of the three asset-specific adjustment factors (m_e^j, m_b^j, and m_c^j) for all households, given the differences between the after-tax returns on the three risky assets, at tax rate t^j, and the after-tax return on taxable bonds. For each household, the coefficient representing the general disutility of variance (m_1^j) is chosen so as to make the asset-specific adjustment factor equal to 1 for one of the risky assets and positive for the other two. Thus m_e^j, m_b^j, and m_c^j represent relative degrees of disutility experienced by each household among the three assets.

With these demand equations, households will tend to hold diversified portfolios, with optimum portfolio shares responding to changes in before-tax returns, the relative degree of taxability of different assets, the structure of marginal tax rates, and the extent to which the variance of assets is subject to tax.

Optimal Corporate Debt-Capital Ratio

The optimal corporate debt-capital ratio, f_1^*, is calculated using the equations on both the demand and supply sides of the model. The corporate sector chooses the value of f_1 that maximizes $C/(1-f_1)$, the demand for corporate sector capital by households, for a given r_1, the before-tax return on corporate-sector capital. This is equivalent to minimizing r_1 for a given capital stock.

Taking the expected value of equation 3.1 and rearranging terms, we can express the expected return on corporate equity before individual taxes as a function of the expected before-tax return on corporate-sector capital:

$$(16) \qquad \mathbf{E}(i_c) = \{[(1 - ua_1)\mathbf{E}(r_1) - f_1 INT(1 - u)]$$
$$/(1 - f_1)\} - [zf_1^2/(1 - f_1)^2],$$

where INT = the average interest rate paid by corporations = $ei_e + (1 - e)i_f$.

The variance of the return on corporate equity can also be expressed as a function of the variance of the before-tax return on corporate capital:

$$(17) \qquad \sigma_c^2 = (1 - ua_1^*)^2 \, \sigma_{r_1}^2/(1 - f_1)^2,$$

where ua_1^* = the tax rate on the variance of corporate before-tax returns at the corporate level and $\sigma_{r_1}^2$ = the variance of corporate before-tax returns.

Substituting equations 16 and 17 into equation 15.3, the demand for corporate equity by each household, and dividing by $(1 - f_1)$, produces:

$$(18) \quad c^j/(1 - f_1) = \{[\mathbf{E}(r_1)(1 - ua_1) - f_1 INT (1 - u)$$
$$- zf_1^2/(1 - f_1)] (1 - a_c t^j) - i_f(1 - t^j)(1 - f_1)$$
$$- m_1^j m_2^j m_c^j (1 - a_c^* t^j)(t_k S^j C + C_{pen} pen^j W^j)$$
$$(1 - ua_1^*)^2 \, \sigma_{r_1}^2/(1 - f_1)\}$$
$$/[m_1^j m_2^j m_c^j (1 - a_c^* t^j)^2(1 - ua_1^*)^2 \sigma_{r_1}^2 W^j].$$

Summing equation 18 over all households, differentiating with respect to f_1, and setting the resulting expression equal to zero, we obtain the optimal debt-capital ratio, f_1^*. The optimal debt-equity ratio minimizes the corporate cost of capital, given the interest rate, the corporate tax rate, and the parameters of individual demand schedules for corporate equity. It can be expressed as:

$$(19) \quad f_1^* = 1 - \bigg([z(N + SUM_1) - SUM_3]$$

$$/\{SUM_2 + Ni_f - (SUM_1 + N)[INT(1 - u) + z]\} \bigg)^{\frac{1}{2}},$$

where

$$N = \sum_{j=1}^{400} pen^j W^j \, / \, [2(1 - ua_1)^2 \, \sigma_{r_1}^2 m_1^p]$$

$$SUM_1 = \sum_{j=1}^{400} \{[(1 - a_c t^j)W^j]$$

$$/[m_1^j m_2^j m_c^j (1 - ua_1)^2 (1 - a_c t^j)^2 \sigma_{r_1}^2]\}$$

$$SUM_2 = \sum_{j=1}^{400} \{[(1 - t^j)i_f W^j]$$

$$/[m_1^j m_2^j m_c^j (1 - ua_1)^2 (1 - a_c t^j)^2 \sigma_{r_1}^2]\}$$

$$SUM_3 = \sum_{j=1}^{400} [(t_k CS^j + C_{pen} pen^j W^j)/(1 - a_c t^j)]$$

and m_1^p = risk-aversion parameter of pension fund managers.

The need for the summation terms in equation 19 results from the differential value among individuals and between individuals and pensions funds of preferential treatment of corporate equity and from the effects of changes in the variance of the government revenue stream on risks borne by households.

Treatment of Financial Intermediaries

Financial intermediaries are generally outside the scope of the model; financial assets supplied by capital-using sectors are linked directly to assets held by households. Thus, for example, household bank deposits that banks use for mortgages and corporate loans are treated as if the mortgages and corporate bonds were held directly by households.

The few exceptions noted above where financial intermediaries directly enter the model were made to prevent gross misrepresentation of the tax status of assets held by households. For example, wealth held by households in the form of pension funds and life insurance claims (referred to as pension wealth) is treated as tax exempt at the household level. Each household is assigned a fixed amount of pension wealth; pension funds then use a simple function of expected income and variance to choose the shares of their portfolio held in taxable bonds and corporate equity. In effect, pension funds behave as would a zero-bracket household that is required to divide its entire portfolio between the two assets and is not allowed to hold negative amounts of either one. (Unlike corporations, pension funds' portfolio behavior does not take direct account of the preferences of households on whose behalf they hold assets.) Households are also assigned fixed amounts of wealth in IRAs, all of which, as noted above, is invested in taxable bonds.

Financial intermediaries also enter the model as institutions that hold a given amount of tax-exempt bonds, which are financed by issuing taxable bonds to households. (About half the outstanding stock of tax-exempt bonds is held by these intermediaries—mainly commercial banks and property and casualty insurance companies.) These "taxable tax-exempt bonds," which are tax exempt to the issuer but taxable to the holder, are introduced into the model to avoid what would otherwise be a substantial overstatement of tax-exempt bonds available for household portfolios. Tax-exempt bonds held by financial intermediaries are treated as exogenous variables in the simulations; that is, there is no explicit equation for the portfolio behavior of institutions that hold them.

Derivation of Capital Stocks from Production Functions

The production functions for corporate goods, noncorporate goods, and state and local capital services are assumed to be Cobb-Douglas functions of labor and the flow of capital services, with the same production coefficients (gross shares) for labor (A) and capital services ($1 - A$) in all three sectors. Rental services of owner-occupied housing and consumer durables are produced only with the services of capital and require no direct labor input. These direct production functions are expressed as follows:

(20.1) $$X_1 = L_1^A M_1^{1-A},$$

(20.2) $$X_2 = L_2^A M_2^{1-A},$$

(20.3) $$X_3 = L_3^A M_3^{1-A},$$

(20.4) $$X_4 = M_4,$$

(20.5) $$X_5 = M_5.$$

In these equations, $X_1 \ldots X_5$ are total physical units of outputs produced by corporations, noncorporate business, and state and local governments, and the services of owner-occupied housing and consumer durables; $L_1 \ldots L_3$ are direct labor inputs to corporate, noncorporate business, and state and local production; and $M_1 \ldots M_5$ are the flow of services of capital goods in the five sectors.

Capital services used in the production functions are in turn produced by two inputs: permanent savings (or capital) and replacement production that is required to maintain the flow of capital services. This required replacement production offsets the annual depreciation in each sector's capital. Replacement production for capital in all sectors is assumed to be done in the corporate sector. The production functions for capital services are also taken to be Cobb-Douglas functions and can be written as:

(21.1)–(21.5) $$M_i = K_i^{B_i} X_{1i}^{1-B_i} \qquad i = 1 \ldots 5,$$

where M_i = the flow of capital services used in sector i, K_i = the direct input of capital in producing capital services in sector i, B_i = the share of the annual rental cost of capital services used in i that represents a return to direct suppliers of capital to sector i, X_{1i} = the annual amount of corporate-sector product used to maintain the flow of capital services in sector i, and $(1 - B_i)$ = the share of the rental cost of capital services represented by this replacement production or depreciation. Thus the two coefficients in the production of capital services can be expressed as $B_i = (r_i - \pi)/(r_i - \pi + d_i)$; and $(1 - B_i) = d_i/(r_i - \pi + d_i)$, where $r_i - \pi$ = the real before-tax return to capital used directly in sector i and d_i = the annual depreciation rate of capital used in sector i.

The form of the production function used in equations 21.1 through 21.5 results in constant shares of gross product to direct capital inputs and replacement corporate production for sector i. Because each B_i is a constant, however, the rate of depreciation (d_i) of capital used in each sector varies with changes in the real before-tax return so as to keep real before-tax returns and depreciation as constant fractions of the gross rental cost of capital services. This means that, as the real before-tax return to capital $(r_i - \pi)$ increases, d_i also increases so that producers not only substitute labor for capital services in the production of output, but also substitute "depreciation" for capital in the production of capital services by using shorter-lived capital goods.

Combining equations 20.1 through 20.5 with equations 21.1 through 21.5, we can eliminate the equations for intermediate production and express final output in each sector as a function of total direct and indirect labor and capital inputs:

$$(22.1)–(22.5) \qquad X_i = L^{A_{Li}} K_i^{A_{Kii}} K_i^{A_{Kli}}, \qquad i = 1 \ldots 5,$$

where A_{Li} = labor's share in output of sector i, A_{Kii} = the share of own capital used in sector i, A_{Kli} = the share of corporate capital in the output of sectors 2–5, and $A_{Li} + A_{Kii} + A_{Kli} = 1$ for all i. In equations 22.1 through 22.5:

$$A_{L1} = A/[A + B_1(1 - A)], \quad A_{K11} = B_1(1 - A)/[A + B_1(1 - A)];$$

$$A_{L2} = A + A_{L1}(1 - B_2)(1 - A), \quad A_{K22} = B_2(1 - A),$$
$$A_{K12} = (1 - A_{L1})(1 - B_2)(1 - A);$$

$$A_{L3} = A + A_{L1}(1 - B_3)(1 - A), \quad A_{K33} = B_3(1 - A),$$
$$A_{K13} = (1 - A_{L1})(1 - B_3)(1 - A);$$

$$A_{L4} = A_{L1}(1 - B_4), \quad A_{K44} = B_4, \quad A_{K14} = (1 - A_{L1})(1 - B_4);$$

$$A_{L5} = A_{L1}(1 - B_5), \quad A_{K55} = B_5, \text{ and } A_{K15} = (1 - A_{L1})(1 - B_5).$$

Recall again that A is the direct share of labor in the production of corporate goods and services and that $B_1 \ldots B_5$ are the shares of the total rental cost of capital services accounted for by the before-tax return to capital in sectors 1–5.

Differentiating the production functions in equations 22.1 through 22.5 and setting the resulting marginal revenue products equal to the cost of capital produces the demand equations for capital stocks shown as equations 1.1 through 1.5.

The constant term in the demand equation for capital financed by the corporate sector, K_{10}, is equal to:

$$(23.1) \qquad\qquad K_{10} = \sum_{i=1}^{5} A_{k1i} P_i X_i$$

where A_{k1i} = corporate capital's share in the output of sector i, X_i = the output of sector i, and P_i = the price of output in sector i.

The constant terms in the demand equations for capital financed by the other four sectors—noncorporate business, state and local governments, the services of owner-occupied housing, and the services of consumer durables—are equal to:

$$(23.2)\text{–}(23.5) \qquad\qquad K_{i0} = A_{kii} P_i X_i \qquad i = 2 \ldots 5,$$

where A_{kii} = the shares of production of final output in sector i paid to capital financed by sector i.

Because the production functions and consumer demand functions for goods and services in GEMDAT are assumed to be Cobb-Douglas, total expenditures on output and shares of each sector's capital in the production of output are fixed. When the tax rules are revised, the model solves for a new set of interest rates at which demands and supplies for financial and physical assets are equilibrated. The resulting new capital stocks are then substituted into equations 22.1 through 22.5 to obtain levels of real outputs of $X_1 \ldots X_5$ corresponding to the new capital market equilibrium. These outputs are then divided into the fixed expenditure levels to obtain the new prices of outputs.

Comments by Mervyn King

Many of the general points made by Whalley are illustrated by the specific application of general equilibrium modeling in the paper by Galper, Lucke, and Toder. This is an ambitious paper that attempts to model the financial structure of the economy and the changes in corporate and personal financial decisions that might result from the 1986 Tax Reform Act. It focuses on one of the weakest areas in previous applications of general equilibrium modeling, but one that is surely crucial to an assessment of tax reform, namely the link between financial behavior and the real economy. Their attempt to model household marginal tax rates as endogenous is encouraging.

Inevitably Galper and colleagues make some heroic assumptions (of which more later), but the justification is the focus on the question central to any analysis of investment: what is the cost of capital to the corporate sector? In a world with only one financial instrument, equity, for example, and complete information, the answer to this question is the traditional Hall-Jorgenson cost of capital. With several alternative methods of financing investment, the cost of capital is not well defined until there is a theory explaining how the different marginal costs of finance are brought into equality. One possibility is to model the trade-off between the tax advantages of certain financial instruments (such as debt) on the one hand and other offsetting costs (such as bankruptcy) on the other. Broadly speaking, this trade-off view is the approach adopted by Galper, Lucke, and Toder. A second approach would be to focus on the implications of nonlinearities in the budget constraint facing households, but the paper does not make clear the extent to which the results depend upon a trade-off view of the determinants of corporate debt-equity ratios or upon the joint distribution of household wealth and marginal tax rates, which is crucial in such a Miller equilibrium.

The view one takes of the appropriate model of financial equilibrium is crucial to an assessment of the 1986 Tax Reform Act. It is, therefore, understandable that the paper focuses on the financial side of the model. It solves for the set of equilibrium rates of return on a range of financial assets that must be offered to persuade the household sector to hold the supplies of assets that are forthcoming at those rates of return.

The solution for the level of interest rates is central to the model and plays a crucial role in determining the responses to the changes in the tax system. A specific example makes this point clear. One of the main empirical findings of the paper is that the 1986 Tax Reform Act might lead to a small federal budget deficit. This is because in the model the reform lowers the general level of interest rates and hence the cost of financing outstanding government debt.

Three assumptions, in particular, are crucial for this result to follow. The first is that the total level of both capital and labor are fixed in aggregate. The tax system can change their allocation among sectors, but total amounts of capital and labor are held constant. But if the 1986 Tax Reform Act raises the tax component of the cost of capital, as the authors show is the case, then one might expect that the capital stock would fall in the long run, thus leading to an increase in rates of return that would help to offset the lower level of interest rates predicted by the model.

The second critical assumption is that the U.S. economy is closed. In recent years international capital mobility has been a major factor both in financing the federal deficit and in determining the level of U.S. interest rates. The assumptions either of a closed economy or of the United States as a small country facing a large world capital market are both implausible. But the level of interest rates does not seem to be determined solely by domestic factors. International capital mobility may be an important determinant of the effects of tax reform.

The third assumption concerns the way in which interest deductibility is modeled. The Tax Reform Act introduces some restrictions on interest deductibility, but mortgage interest deductibility is retained. In the model mortgage interest deductibility is granted at a fraction of 80 percent of the interest payments. This is an attempt to proxy the fact that there is some restriction on interest deductibility and that increases in house prices will not enable purchasers to increase their leverage automatically. But when borrowing in the form of mortgages becomes the only or main source of interest deductibility, then mortgage loans may be increased in order to finance expenditure elsewhere. Experience in the United Kingdom, where mortgages are the only form of tax-deductible borrowing for households, illustrates clearly that when interest rates are high borrowing for home purchase may often exceed total expenditure on owner-occupied housing, implying some leakage for borrowing for other types of expenditure or saving. This illustrates the difficulty of modeling financial behavior. Nevertheless, the authors are to be congratulated on making their assumptions clear at each stage.

One of the novel features of the paper is the attempt to model a large number of households. There are 400 representative households chosen to proxy four different types of taxpayers according to their tax-filing status. Within each group 100 households comprise a joint distribution across 10 classes of earnings and 10 classes of capital income. As I indicated in my comments on Whalley's paper, it would be interesting to extend this part of the model to link directly to a sample of households from an expenditure survey.

Within the authors' framework there are several specific features of their modeling that merit comment. The first is that the authors need to introduce unmeasured costs of holding financial assets in order to reconcile observed data on household portfolio composition with the model's predictions of expected utility-maximizing behavior. Rational investors would exploit comparative tax advantages in order to sort investments among different types of financial assets (a "Miller equilibrium"). This is contradicted by the data used in the model. Hence the authors introduce the holding costs in order to equalize the marginal after-tax return on each asset, including both risk and the holding costs. The values of the holding costs vary among households. The problem with this approach is that in the absence of any information on the plausibility of the values used for the holding costs, the underlying portfolio model may simply be a very poor description of how households choose their portfolios. Since the holding costs are used to reconcile the assumed expected utility-maximizing model with the observable data, a check on their plausibility seems crucial. Previous work suggests that the existence of holding costs is necessary to explain the diversification of household portfolios, but there is no empirical measurement of these costs in the authors' work. Again, the basic question is, is this a satisfactory model of household savings and portfolio behavior?

A second modeling issue concerns the cost of capital. The model has a single parameter for each sector that measures the proportion of economic income included in the tax base for that sector. In principle, it would not be difficult to model these parameters in terms of the underlying tax code, and this surely should include the inflation rate, a point that is not discussed explicitly in the paper.

A third factor is the treatment of pension funds. The paper does not discuss in detail the important difference between defined benefit plans and defined contribution plans. If the pension fund is providing a defined benefit plan, then it is in essence a savings account for the company. The liability for the pension and the risk of the investment fall on the shareholders of the company. Hence the structure of the pension fund should be related to the capital structure of the company. In this case, it is the *shareholders* of companies who will be concerned with the composition of the portfolio of the pension fund. In contrast, in a defined contribution plan it is the *pension recipients* themselves who will take into account the composition and size of the pension fund. The paper states that households take portfolio decisions made by pension funds into account by choosing their optimum portfolios, but the nature of the plan should determine whether it is future pension recipients or current shareholders who are concerned with the composition of the pension fund's investments.

Finally, there are some minor issues concerning the model of taxation that deserve some elaboration. These include the treatment of passive losses from tax shelter partnerships, the assumption in the paper that investment in IRA-Keogh plans will be cut back by 50 percent following the Tax Reform Act (which seems rather high), and the omission of the corporate minimum tax in the model for the cost of capital. In the paper, these are all treated as affecting the parameters for the inclusion of economic income in the tax base. This does not seem to be a satisfactory treatment.

I draw three conclusions from the paper. First, the authors should be congratulated for focusing attention on the crucial issue of the interaction between financial decisions and real savings and investment decisions. Even a concept as apparently straightforward as the cost of capital can be interpreted empirically in many ways according to the nature of the financial equilibrium assumed. Second, in the construction of a satisfactory equilibrium for financial behavior, the authors were forced to introduce holding costs in order to reconcile conventional portfolio models with the observed data. Unless these holding costs can be interpreted and estimated satisfactorily, there is clearly a lacuna in the theory of household portfolio behavior. Finally, some of the assumptions are crucial to the particular simulation results. In particular, the result that the federal deficit may fall following the passage of the Tax Reform Act depends on several critical assumptions that imply a reduction in interest rates. The authors' approach to general equilibrium modeling with differential asset taxation achieves one of its major objectives of focusing attention on some of these critical issues. But it cannot be said yet—and here the authors are very honest—to represent a set of conclusions that are a robust guide to the effects of the 1986 Tax Reform Act.

Comments by Charles E. McLure, Jr.

As John Whalley indicates in his survey, general equilibrium analysis has been extended in a number of ways since the pioneering efforts by Harberger. One of the most important has been the attempt to provide a description of financial structures that allows analysis of the tax treatment accorded various techniques of financing business. Galper, Lucke, and Toder continue the extension of prior work by Slemrod and others in order to provide an assessment of the Tax Reform Act of 1986. Rather than comment in detail on the way they have modeled the economy and financial decisions, I want to confine myself primarily to a few remarks about some limitations of the analysis and some policy conclusions.

First, it is unfortunate that the effects of all provisions affecting taxation of the corporate and noncorporate sectors (aside from rates) are lumped together, since one loses the ability to examine the inter-industry and interasset distortions that can be so important and that motivated tax reform. Of course, that is an accepted price for the degree of aggregation found in this paper. But given this model structure, I was surprised that the authors did not use the model to examine the single issue that generated the most controversy in the tax reform debate: the relative benefits of rate reductions (especially for corporations) and investment incentives. The structure of the model lends itself naturally to addressing this important issue.

I was also disappointed that no more attention was paid to the importance of inflation assumptions, since inflation played such an important role in undermining the neutrality and equity of the tax system during the 1970s, would have been neutralized under the proposals of Treasury I, and will presumably again wreak havoc on the unindexed system resulting from the 1986 act. It would have been interesting to see some analysis of the sensitivity of the simulation results to variations in the rate of inflation. The adequate analysis of inflation is made difficult by the use of a single parameter to capture all corporate (and noncorpor-ate) tax provisions.

One of the important contributions of the type of analysis presented here is attention to the taxation of variance in income. But I believe that even this analysis falls short of its potential because of the failure to include more variation in the inflation scenario, since the failure to provide indexing in the measurement of taxable income accentuates variance in after-tax incomes.

Even though they must be considered illustrative and tentative, the results of the Galper, Lucke, and Toder analysis tell a fascinating story. Because the opportunities for high-income taxpayers to shelter income are reduced, this group shifts into taxable investments, and those in lower-income groups move into tax-preferred investments. As a result, interest rates on taxable securities drop, and corporate investment actually increases slightly. Moreover, housing investment and the stock of consumer durables increase, despite cuts in tax rates on investment income. Not surprisingly, the largest absolute decline is in noncorporate investment—the model's name for tax-sheltered investment.

While this is a believable story, one must be a bit uneasy about believing it. First, as the authors readily admit, it may be quite dependent on two features of their model: the closed-economy assumption that allows interest rates to drop, rather than being determined in world capital markets, and the high elasticity of portfolio response to differences in tax treatment of alternative investments. The second of these points the way to an important line of future research, attempting to identify the factors that determine these elasticities and quantify their importance.

Second, much important detail is lost by including in one noncorporate sector both activities that are conducted in noncorporate form for tax shelter reasons and the regular business activities of proprietorships and partnerships. As Scholes and Wolfson note and Galper, Lucke, and Toder suggest, the former will shrink as a result of the 1986 act, but use of the noncorporate form for other than tax shelter purposes is likely to expand at the expense of use of the traditional corporate form.

The discussion of alternative measures of changes in economic well-being highlights an important issue that goes well beyond whether progressivity should be measured in terms of tax reduction or increase in income. Galper, Lucke, and Toder note that the high-income groups that invest in tax shelters under current law will benefit from being able to incur less risk under a tax regime that does not encourage investment in risky shelters in order to beat the tax man. That is a story about tax reform that should not be lost in the blizzard of estimates of tax savings at various income levels.

 *Joel Slemrod*

Effect of Taxation
with International Capital Mobility

INTERNATIONAL TRADE and capital movements are vital to contemporary economies. Nevertheless, most analyses of taxation ignore such flows and proceed as if each country had no economic contact with any other. This blinkered approach is critical because changing from a closed-economy to an open-economy view of the world dramatically changes some familiar propositions about the burdens and economic effects of capital income taxation. This paper summarizes and integrates some of the new implications, problems, and propositions that present themselves when international economic relations are incorporated into tax analysis. It also suggests directions for future research.

The focus is on long-run implications of capital income taxation in an open economy. Of course the transition from the status quo to a new economic reality may be neither immediate nor direct. But emphasis on the long-run effects of tax changes is necessary and proper because policymakers too frequently pursue short-run objectives with little awareness of the consequences of their acts. I do not treat the strategic aspects of setting tax policy in an international context or the role of policy coordination, but assume instead that the tax policies of other countries are fixed and, in particular, unresponsive to domestic policy changes. This perspective prevents consideration of the possibility that policies that are beneficial if passively accepted by other countries may be harmful if other countries retaliate against them. Although important, the problems traceable to strategic interaction among governments are complex and cannot be treated in the space allotted here. It is assumed

Helpful comments on an earlier version were received from Avinash Dixit, Dan Frisch, Roger Gordon, Jack Mintz, and participants in the National Bureau of Economic Research Summer Institute Tax Workshop.

in what follows that the objective of policy is to improve the welfare of domestic residents only. Thus an increase in domestic welfare, even at the expense of foreigners, is optimal, and an increase in national income, however distributed, improves welfare.

This paper adopts a stylized treatment of international tax rules and ignores many complications that arise in actual tax systems. The issues raised by multinational corporations (and the intricacies of their tax treatment), those raised by the differential tax treatment of debt and equity, and the incentives for a particular financial structure created by the tax system are not analyzed. Although the details of the tax system applicable to corporations and individuals are important to understanding their economic effects, I take a more general approach to highlight fundamental issues.[1]

The goal is to reorient discussions about tax policy from a closed-economy to an open-economy framework for three issues: the incidence of capital income taxation, the implications of such taxation for efficiency, and the optimal mix of taxation on labor and capital income. The chapter begins with a brief statement of the standard propositions about capital income taxation in a closed economy and then turns to a simple graphical exposition of taxation in an open economy. Several differences from the closed-economy analysis emerge. Foreign capital markets provide domestic wealth owners with a choice between investing at home and investing abroad. As a result, they can avoid the burden of taxes levied only on domestically located capital. Taxes that depend on the location of capital (for example, that fall only on capital located abroad or on domestically located capital) reduce economic efficiency. Policymakers anxious to maximize the welfare of domestic residents must also consider how the domestic economy can gain at the expense of foreigners. For that reason I next consider the rationale for trying to tax income from the domestic investments of foreigners, a policy that captures some of the revenue that would otherwise accrue to the foreign country. In particular, I show how a country can take advantage of its prominence in world capital markets by manipulating prices in its favor.

I then examine recent evidence that seems to suggest that the international mobility of capital is limited. An Appendix discusses several dynamic models of capital income taxation, which indicate that, in the

---

1. Unfortunately, "the most striking feature of the existing [foreign] tax system is its complexity," as stated in C. Fred Bergsten, Thomas Horst, and Theodore H. Moran, *American Multinationals and American Interests* (Brookings, 1978), p. 195.

absence of foreign tax or large-country considerations, an optimal tax system should never cause an inefficient domestic capital stock. This proposition implies that domestic investment by foreigners should not be taxed, and that investment by domestic wealth owners should be taxed the same regardless of location. This strong conclusion must be modified when foreign tax credit systems exist or the home country is large enough to influence rates of return in its favor.

Some Propositions about Capital Income Taxation in a Closed Economy

Mainstream views about the incidence, efficiency, and optimal taxation of capital income in a closed economy hold that a general tax on capital income is borne entirely by capital owners, if the total capital stock is fixed in supply.[2] Such a tax has no real effect on the economy and does not reduce economic efficiency. If labor supply varies with the wage rate but the supply of capital is fixed, a general tax on capital is superior, on efficiency grounds, to a general tax on labor.

If capital accumulation depends on the rate of return, the incidence of a tax on capital income depends on the effect of the tax on capital accumulation and on the substitutability of capital and labor. The optimal mix of labor and capital taxes depends on how much each distorts individuals' lifetime consumption decisions and on the relative efficacy of these taxes in moving the economy toward the capital-labor ratio that generates the highest level of welfare across generations. Whether a capital income tax is imposed at the point of the real investment or on the saver is irrelevant in most analyses because the difference between before-tax and after-tax returns depends only on the amount of tax, not on whom it is imposed.

2. "General" here means that all sources of capital income are taxed equally. A tax on capital income in some but not all sectors will be borne by capital owners or labor depending on the relative factor intensity of the taxed and untaxed sectors, the elasticities of substitution in production, and the elasticities of demand. Unequal capital income taxation also causes an inefficient allocation of capital because, in equilibrium, the marginal product of capital used in highly taxed sectors will exceed the marginal product of capital in the relatively lightly taxed sectors.

Figure 1. *Capital Market Equilibrium in a Small Open Economy,*
with No Taxation

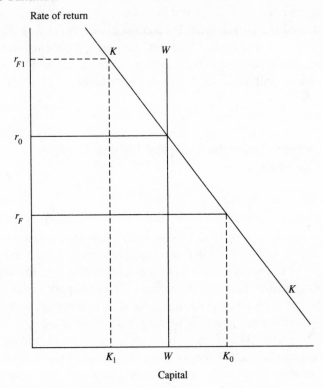

Static Models of an Open Economy

Figures 1–4 illustrate the standard graphical analysis of capital income
taxation in an open economy.[3] The domestic country's wealth is shown
by the *WW* schedule (see figure 1). The demand for capital is shown by
the schedule *KK*, whose height is equal to the net marginal product of
capital. The intersection of these two schedules yields the rate of return
that will prevail in the absence of capital mobility. In the absence of
taxation, that return is r_0.

If capital in all other countries earns a lower rate of return, r_F, capital

3. This analysis dates back at least to Sir Donald MacDougall, "The Benefits and
Costs of Private Investment Abroad: A Theoretical Approach," *Economic Record*, vol.
36 (March 1960), pp. 13–35.

will move into the domestic country.[4] The inflow will continue until the domestic capital stock has risen to K_0 and the marginal product of capital and the domestic interest rate become r_F.

If the foreign rate of return exceeds r_0—that is, r_{F1} in figure 1—capital would be exported until the marginal product of domestic capital rises to r_{F1}; the amount of capital exported would be $W - K_1$.

In either case the small country benefits from the movement of capital—either because the inflow of capital produces output that exceeds the return that must be paid to the foreign owners, or because the capital flowing out of the country earns more than it could within the country.[5]

Alternative Capital Income Taxes

In an open economy various taxes imposed by the home country can be distinguished.[6] The tax rate on domestic wealth owners' investment in domestically located capital is t_{DD}. The tax rate on domestic wealth

4. "Move" requires some explanation. The exercises described in this section all compare the characteristics of two equilibria and ignore the transition between the two equilibria, that is, the performance of the economies when out of equilibrium. In response to a change in taxes, physical capital goods need not be physically transported across borders. Alternatively, depreciation combined with zero or small gross investment may reduce one country's net capital stock, whereas positive net investment increases another country's capital stock.

5. Capital movement does not necessarily occur when an economy is opened. It is likely to occur in a one-good model because it is improbable that capital would earn the same rate of return in all countries if all economies were closed. In a model with two or more goods, free trade in goods is sufficient to ensure that factor returns will be equalized across countries under certain conditions. See Richard E. Caves and Ronald W. Jones, *World Trade and Payments: An Introduction,* 2d ed. (Little, Brown, 1977), pp. 154–58. With two countries, two goods, two factors, and a common world technology, this result will obtain as long as neither country produces only one good or levies tariffs. The idea is that when both countries' firms face the same world prices of goods, only one common set of factor prices will ensure that there are no economic profits earned in any activity. If factor prices in the two countries are identical, then capital will not move even if there are no barriers to such mobility.

6. More complications are possible. For example, the tax system may differentiate between capital income earned by corporations and that earned directly by individuals, or it may differentiate between the income earned on foreign portfolio investment and that earned on foreign direct investment (that is, when ownership exceeds some fraction of the firm's equity). The tax system may also distinguish between the income earned on equity securities and that earned on debt securities, or between capital gains on foreign exchange and other forms of income. These dimensions of tax policy are ignored in the paper.

Figure 2. *Capital Market Equilibrium in a Small Open Economy,*
with Source-Based Capital Income Tax by Capital-Importing Country

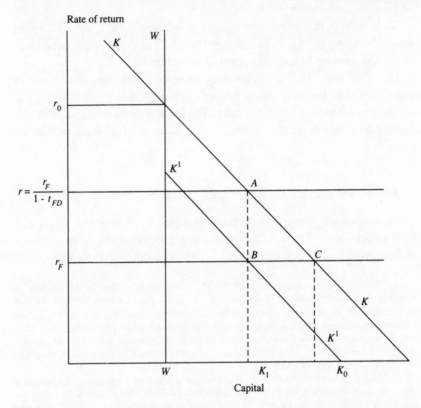

owners' investment in capital abroad is t_{DF}, and t_{FD} denotes the tax rate
on foreign wealth owners' investment in domestically located capital.

   Figure 2 portrays the effect of a source-based tax imposed by a capital-
importing country on capital income flowing to both domestic and foreign
owners of domestically located capital ($t_{DD} = t_{FD}$). No tax is imposed on
the capital of domestic owners that is located abroad ($t_{DF} = 0$). Because
foreign owners must earn at least the world rate of return, r_F, the taxation
of income from their domestically located assets ($t_{FD} > 0$) forces the
domestic rate of return, r, to rise until it equals $r_F/(1 - t_{FD})$. The *net*
return to foreigners is unchanged. Because domestic and foreign wealth
holders receive the same before-tax return on their domestic assets and
pay the same tax ($t_{FD} = t_{DD}$), the tax leaves net returns to domestic
wealth owners unchanged. Although the tax does not affect net rates of

return, it does reduce domestically located capital from K_0 to K_1, because it is profitable for foreigners to invest only up to the point at which the marginal product after the newly imposed tax equals r_F. Here, as in all subsequent figures, the K^1K^1 curve represents the after-tax marginal product of domestic capital received by the marginal investor, who is a foreign resident in the capital-importing situation and a domestic resident in the capital-exporting situation. Owners of immobile factors such as land and labor will earn a lower return as long as the factors are complementary to capital in production. The economy suffers a welfare loss, represented by the area ABC, because of forgone domestic investment, the marginal product of which exceeds the world rate of return.[7]

Figure 3 depicts the effect in a capital-exporting country of imposing a tax on domestic wealth owners, regardless of the location of the capital ($t_{DD} = t_{DF} > 0$). In this case no tax is imposed on income from domestic capital owned by foreigners ($t_{FD} = 0$). This combination of taxes represents a residence-based capital income tax. Because the same tax is imposed on income from both foreign and domestic investments, domestic wealth owners have no incentive to shift the location of their investments to avoid tax. In the new equilibrium the return earned by the domestic wealth owner falls by the amount of the tax from r_F to $r_F(1 - t_{DD}) = r_F(1 - t_{DF})$. The domestic capital stock is unchanged, as is the return to the immobile factors.

Figure 4 shows the effect in a capital-importing country of imposing a tax on the capital income paid on domestically located capital owned by foreigners ($t_{FD} > 0$). No tax is imposed on domestic wealth owners ($t_{DD} = t_{DF} = 0$). Because foreigners must earn at least as much as they receive abroad, r_F, the before-tax return on domestic investments must rise enough to permit them to pay the new tax and still net a return of r_F. Because all domestic capital receives the same rate of return regardless of ownership and domestic owners pay no tax, the before-tax and after-tax returns received by domestic wealth owners increase from r_F to $r_F/(1 - t_{FD})$. The before-tax return on domestically located capital increases as foreigners shift capital out of the country to avoid the tax.

7. Because capital generates output with a total value indicated by the area under the KK schedule in figure 2, the net gain in the no-tax case is represented by the area between KK and the income received by owners of capital, represented by the area under the horizontal line through r_F. When the quantity of capital falls from K_0 to K_1, the value of output represented by the area ACK_0K_1 is lost to the taxing economy, but payments to foreign owners fall by the amount BCK_0K_1. The difference, represented by the triangle ABC, is the net loss.

Figure 3. *Capital Market Equilibrium in a Small Open Economy,
with Tax on All Capital Income of Residents by Capital-Exporting
Country*

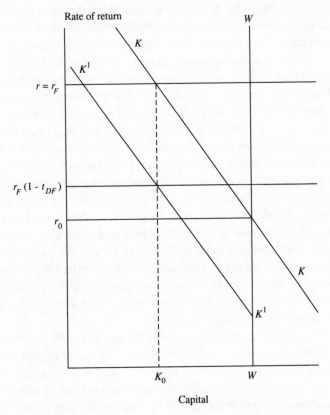

The result, as with the source-based tax, is a lower domestic capital
stock and a welfare loss. The tax actually enriches domestic wealth
owners, but it reduces the income of suppliers of immobile factors. Both
the tax on only foreign owners of domestically located capital and the
tax on both domestic and foreign owners lead to an increase in the
before-tax rate of return. The benefits to domestic wealth owners are
taxed away in the latter case, but not in the former.

Contrasts with Closed-Economy Analyses

These results clearly differ from the conclusions of a closed-economy
analysis. First, in an open economy one must state precisely to what and

Figure 4. *Capital Market Equilibrium in a Small Open Economy, with Tax on Income from Foreign-Owned Capital*

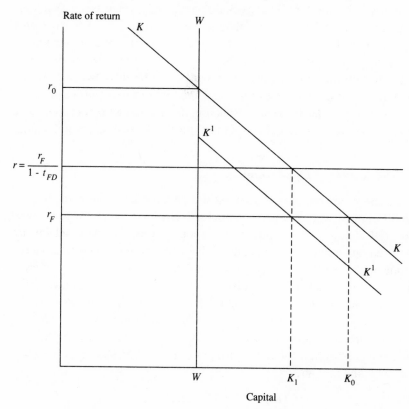

to whom a tax applies. In particular, taxes on domestic investment are not equivalent to taxes on the return to residents' saving. Second, although a general tax on capital by one country generates no efficiency cost if capital is internationally immobile, a tax that differentiates on the basis of the international location of the capital does generate an efficiency cost in an open economy. Finally, capital owners bear the burden of a general tax on capital if capital is internationally immobile. This conclusion holds in an open economy only for taxes on domestically owned capital that are imposed at the same rate wherever the capital is located. Taxes levied only on domestically located capital, including that part owned by foreigners, will not be borne by domestic capital owners.

These results all depend on strong implicit assumptions. The analysis of the effect of a source-based capital income tax in a capital-importing country ($t_{DD} = t_{FD} > 0$) assumes that in equilibrium the foreign wealth owner will be indifferent between domestic and foreign assets that yield the same rate of return and that domestic wealth owners own only domestically located assets. For a residence-based capital income tax in a capital-exporting country ($t_{DD} = t_{DF} > 0$), it is assumed that in equilibrium domestic wealth owners will be indifferent between domestic and foreign assets with the same yield and that foreign wealth owners do not own any domestic assets. Relaxing these assumptions represents a step toward realism and changes the nature of the resultant equilibrium.

The Nature of Equilibrium

Equilibrium requires that domestic and foreign wealth owners be indifferent between investing in domestically located capital and capital located abroad.[8] If considerations such as risk and nationalism are ignored, such indifference requires that each owner of capital earn the same after-tax rate of return on both foreign and domestic investments. If g_D and g_F equal, respectively, the marginal product of domestically located capital, K_D, and foreign-located capital, K_F; t_{ij} denotes the domestic government's tax on ith-owned, jth-located capital; and W_D and W_F are domestic and foreign wealth, then domestic wealth owners are in equilibrium if the net return per dollar of investment is the same at home and abroad,

(1a) $$g_D(K_D)(1 - t_{DD}) = g_F(1 - t_{DF}).$$

Equilibrium for foreign wealth owners requires that

(1b) $$g_D(K_D)(1 - t_{FD}) = g_F.$$

A final condition is expressed by the identity equating the sum of capital in both countries to the sum of wealth,

(1c) $$K_D + K_F = W_D + W_F.$$

These relations ignore any taxes imposed by foreign governments. Although the marginal product of domestically located capital, g_D,

---

8. Throughout the remainder of this paper, the analysis proceeds from the standpoint of a "domestic" country, indicated by the letter D. "Foreign" always refers to a country other than country D and is denoted by F. "A domestic tax on foreign wealth holders" refers to a tax by the government of country D on owners who reside in F.

depends on the amount of such capital, K_D, the marginal product of foreign-located capital, g_F, is treated as a constant because the domestic country is assumed to be small enough that movements of capital do not significantly affect the world rate of return.[9] Equations 1a and 1b are simultaneously satisfied if and only if

(2) $$(1 - t_{DD}) / (1 - t_{FD}) = (1 - t_{DF}).$$

If this condition is not satisfied, the domestic or foreign wealth owner, or both, will face different after-tax rates of return on the two alternative investments. Whenever investors face such a situation, they have the incentive to engage in arbitrage, selling short the asset with lower yield and buying the asset with higher yield.

In the absence of any foreign-imposed tax, the condition expressed by equation 2 is satisfied if residents are taxed equally on income from domestically and foreign-located capital ($t_{DD} = t_{DF}$) and foreigners are untaxed ($t_{FD} = 0$), as under a residence-based income tax. In this case $g_D = g_F$.[10] The condition in equation 2 is also satisfied if income from all domestically located capital, whether owned by residents or foreigners, is taxed equally ($t_{DD} = t_{FD}$), but income from foreign-located capital is untaxed ($t_{FD} = 0$), as under a source-based capital income tax. In this case, $g_D = g_F/(1 - t_{FD})$. In general, values of t_{DD}, t_{DF}, and t_{FD} will not satisfy condition 2. For example, if the only tax is one on domestically owned, domestically located capital ($t_{DD} > 0$, $t_{DF} = t_{FD} = 0$), either domestic or foreign wealth owners, or both, will have an incentive to own only the capital of the other country and, moreover, to sell short (hold negative quantities of) their own country's capital.

9. The marginal products of capital, g_D and g_F, equal the rates of return, r_D and r_F, in the previous section.

10. See, however, Maurice D. Levi, "Taxation and 'Abnormal' International Capital Flows," *Journal of Political Economy*, vol. 85 (June 1977), pp. 635–46. Levi suggests that condition 2 may fail to hold even if $t_{DD} = t_{DF} > 0$ and $t_{FD} = 0$. This can occur if exchange rate gains receive preferential capital gains taxation while interest is taxed as ordinary income. He shows that, when the forward sale price of domestic currency exceeds its spot price, there is a range of interest rates for which foreign wealth owners will wish to invest in domestic securities at the same time that domestic wealth owners will wish to invest in foreign issues. See also Roger H. Gordon, "Taxation of Investment and Savings in a World Economy," *American Economic Review*, vol. 76 (December 1986), pp. 1086–1102. Gordon also relies on the differential taxation of nominal interest and exchange rate gains, combined with the existence of various inflation rates of different currencies, to construct an equilibrium model in which residents sort themselves into asset-ownership classes and usually do not hold any domestic securities.

Table 1. *Portfolio Composition of Domestic and Foreign Wealth Owners When One Country Taxes Capital and Short Sales Are Prohibited*

Case	Portfolio of domestic wealth owners	Portfolio of foreign wealth owners	Conditions on equations 1a and 1b	
			Domestic wealth owners	Foreign wealth owners
1	All domestic assets and some foreign assets	Foreign assets only	$g_D(1 - t_{DD}) = g_F(1 - t_{DF})$	$g_D(1 - t_{FD}) < g_F$
2	All foreign assets and some domestic assets	Domestic assets only	$g_D(1 - t_{DD}) = g_F(1 - t_{DF})$	$g_D(1 - t_{FD}) > g_F$
3	Domestic assets only	All foreign assets and some domestic assets	$g_D(1 - t_{DD}) > g_F(1 - t_{DF})$	$g_D(1 - t_{FD}) = g_F$
4	Foreign assets only	All domestic assets and some foreign assets	$g_D(1 - t_{DD}) < g_F(1 - t_{DF})$	$g_D(1 - t_{FD}) = g_F$
5	Domestic assets only	Foreign assets only	$g_D(1 - t_{DD}) > g_F(1 - t_{DF})$	$g_D(1 - t_{FD}) < g_F$
6	Foreign assets only	Domestic assets only	$g_D(1 - t_{DD}) < g_F(1 - t_{DF})$	$g_D(1 - t_{FD}) > g_F$
7	Some of both assets[a]	Some of both assets[a]	$g_D(1 - t_{DD}) = g_F(1 - t_{DF})$	$g_D(1 - t_{FD}) = g_F$

a. In this case both wealth owners are indifferent to the choice between domestic and foreign assets, and the location of capital holdings is indeterminate.

Constraints on Portfolio Behavior

If the condition expressed by equation 2 does not hold—that is, if tax rates create opportunities for profitable arbitrage regardless of the before-tax rates of return to capital—an equilibrium can exist only if unlimited arbitrage is not possible (for example, through the prohibition or limitation of short sales). A wealth owner then responds to two different after-tax rates of return on the two assets by not holding the lower-yielding asset and investing only in the higher-yielding asset.

In this case the equilibrium will be one of seven possible types, depending on which wealth owners are faced with binding short-selling constraints (table 1).

The effect of changing tax policy may depend on the nature of the initial equilibrium. As an example, consider the case in which a country taxes equally all capital income originating within its borders or received from abroad by its residents ($t_{FD} = t_{DD} = t_{FD}$). With this combination of taxes, case 1 may arise. In that event, foreign and domestic before-tax returns are equal ($g_D = g_F$), domestic wealth owners hold both foreign and domestic assets, but foreign wealth owners hold only foreign assets, thereby avoiding the tax (t_{FD}) imposed by the domestic country on income paid to foreigners. A case-3 equilibrium is also possible, in which the before-tax return is higher domestically than abroad by the amount of the tax imposed on income paid to foreign wealth owners. In that event domestic wealth holders hold only domestic assets, whereas foreign wealth holders own both domestic and foreign assets. Also possible is a case-5 equilibrium, in which the domestic before-tax return is higher than abroad, but by less than the tax rate imposed on foreign wealth holders. Then foreign wealth owners prefer to hold their wealth in their own country, as do domestic wealth owners.

In case 1, domestic wealth must exceed the equilibrium domestic capital stock, so that the domestic country exports capital. In case 3, domestic wealth must be smaller than the domestic capital stock, so that the domestic country imports capital. In case 5, domestic wealth equals the domestic capital stock; there is no movement of capital across borders.

Now consider the effect of a policy that reduces taxes imposed on the income of domestic owners that issues from domestically located capital, t_{DD}—perhaps with the goal of encouraging domestic ownership of domestic capital. If a case-1 equilibrium exists, this policy will increase the domestic capital stock. All of the increased capital will be owned by domestic wealth owners. In case 3 or case 5, a small reduction in t_{DD} will not affect capital allocation or ownership but will merely increase the after-tax return earned by domestic wealth owners, as well as the premium they earn on domestic assets compared with foreign assets.[11]

Two lessons emerge from this analysis. First, the qualitative characteristics of equilibrium can differ, depending on the set of taxes in place. The effect of many policies depends on which type of equilibrium prevails. Second, the models presented so far imply that residents of many countries will not simultaneously hold part of their wealth in foreign assets and part in domestic assets.

But in actuality they do. This inconsistency between the implications of the models and observed behavior indicates that the models omit key elements of reality. The discrepancy can be traced in part to the failure so far to recognize that assets differ in risk characteristics and are not perfect substitutes even if they offer the same expected yield.

In addition, one country may try to enrich itself at the expense of other countries. I examine below two ways that taxes can be used for this purpose. First, a country can increase its own welfare by ensuring that tax revenues that could be claimed by other governments accrue to its own treasury. Second, a large country can use the capital income tax system to manipulate the terms of borrowing and lending in its favor, also at the expense of the rest of the world.

The Role of Foreign Tax Systems

The means by which the rest of the world taxes capital income and the interaction among tax systems have important effects on the influence and welfare implications of domestic tax policy, even if foreign tax systems are taken as given. If one recognizes the possibility that other countries may change their tax laws in response to domestic tax legislation, a subject I do not deal with here, the issues become even more complex.

---

11. Note that a decrease in t_{DD}, or any other tax change, could also cause a shift from one type of equilibrium to another. For example, under a case-1 equilibrium, if t_{DD} falls enough so that the domestic wealth owner puts all his wealth into domestically located assets, a case-5 equilibrium then prevails. Any further drop in t_{DD} will not increase the domestic capital stock but will merely increase the after-tax return to domestic wealth owners.

In general, the United States taxes capital income earned abroad by U.S. residents but allows a credit for most taxes paid to foreign governments as long as the foreign tax payments do not exceed the U.S. tax liability on the income. Portfolio investors in foreign equity, however, cannot claim a credit against foreign corporate taxes unless they have at least a 10 percent share in the equity. Most other countries impose a withholding tax on dividend and interest payments paid to nonresidents, which can be credited against U.S. tax liability.

Most major U.S. trading partners (including Canada, Japan, and the United Kingdom) have a foreign tax credit system similar to that of the United States. Some apply the credit on a country basis (Canada, United Kingdom), others on a global basis (Japan, United States). A few countries (for example, France and the Netherlands) exempt from taxation any income from foreign investment, although a foreign tax credit system may apply to portfolio investment.[12]

Another important feature of the U.S. system of international taxation (and, with some modifications, of most other countries with foreign tax credits) is that the earnings of foreign subsidiaries are subject to tax in the home country only when they are repatriated. At that time corporate taxes paid to the foreign governments are credited against the U.S. tax on those earnings. If foreign taxes are lower than U.S. taxes, this rule defers a portion of the U.S. tax liability beyond the time when income is earned.[13]

---

12. Mintz examines these rules in more detail. Jack M. Mintz, "Corporate Tax Design in an International Setting: Tax Competition and the Openness of the Economy" (Kingston, Ontario: Queens University, June 1986). Note that the size of U.S. capital transactions with a particular country does not necessarily measure the relative importance of that country's tax rules because investment may be channeled through conduit countries to gain the most advantageous tax treatment.

13. David Hartman has argued that this feature restores the influence of the source country's tax rate on the cost of capital to foreign investors. The argument, which depends on the constancy over time of the relevant tax rates, is as follows. For an investment to be financed by retained earnings of the subsidiary, the "patriation tax" (the excess of the home country's tax rate over the source country's tax rate) reduces the opportunity cost of the investment (in dividends paid to shareholders of the parent country) in the same proportion as it reduces the after-tax return on the investment. The marginal incentive to invest is thus unaffected. The tax imposed by the *source* country does, however, affect the return on an investment out of retained earnings. See David G. Hartman, "Tax Policy and Foreign Direct Investment," *Journal of Public Economics*, vol. 26 (January 1985), pp. 107–21. Scott Newlon also addresses these issues in "Tax Policy and the Firm's Incentive to Invest Abroad" (Princeton University, Department of Economics, July 1986). Note that this treatment does not apply to branch

The following analysis assumes that all countries use a foreign tax credit system similar to that in the United States. A superscript asterisk (*) indicates a tax imposed by a foreign government. In that case, domestic wealth holders are in equilibrium when the net return on domestic investment, $g_D(1 - t_{DD})$, equals the net return on foreign investment, $g_F[1 - \max(t_{DF}, t_{DF}^*)]$.[14] Similarly, foreign wealth holders are in equilibrium if the rates of return at home and abroad are the same, so that $g_D[1 - \max(t_{FD}^*, t_{FD})] = g_F(1 - t_{FF}^*)$. In both cases the tax relevant for wealth holders planning investments abroad is the larger of the tax rate in the wealth holders' country or the country in which they plan to invest. If these conditions hold simultaneously, then

$$(3) \quad (1 - t_{DD})/[1 - \max(t_{FD}^*, t_{FD})] = [1 - \max(t_{DF}, t_{DF}^*)]/(1 - t_{FF}^*),$$

a condition that is analogous to equation 2 but that takes the foreign tax system and the domestic tax credit for foreign income into account.

Many of the results presented earlier must now be modified. For example, consider an initial situation in which there are no domestic taxes and in which the capital-exporting foreign country imposes a residence-based capital income tax ($t_{FD}^* = t_{FF}^*$). In this case the before-tax rate of return to capital is the same in both countries. If the domestic country now imposes a small source-based capital income tax ($t_{DD} = t_{FD} < t_{FD}^*$), then equation 3 can no longer be satisfied. If the domestic country remains a capital importer, the resultant equilibrium will feature cross-ownership of capital with all domestic capital owned by foreigners, who incur no additional tax liability from the imposition of t_{FD}, because this tax is fully creditable against foreign tax. Domestic wealth owners would own foreign capital and would pay no tax because the foreign country taxes only its own residents and the domestic country taxes only income from domestic sources. The domestic tax causes no reduction in the domestic capital stock, and therefore no change in the equilibrium wage rate, but it does cause a change in the ownership of the domestic capital stock. The tax on foreign-owned, domestically located capital raises revenue from foreigners but does not reduce their rate of return after

---

income in the United States and many other countries with foreign tax credit systems, where branch income is subject to tax whether remitted or not and where the tax is creditable.

14. This formulation assumes that the U.S. foreign tax credit is refundable and ignores the effects of deferral.

taxes and credits. Foreign capital owners will accept a lower rate of return from the investment after domestic taxes because they receive additional tax credits from their own government. The cost of capital to the domestic country, net of taxes paid to the domestic government, falls.[15]

Because such a tax raises revenue from foreigners with no real allocational effect, it causes a first-order increase in domestic welfare. In other words, reducing t_{FD} below t_{FD}^* will cost a capital-importing country revenue but will not, if the capital-exporting country has a foreign tax credit, increase the domestic capital stock.[16]

The foreign tax credit may also have important welfare implications for a capital-exporting country. If the tax rates on income from domestic and foreign sources are equal (a residence-based tax, where $t_{DD} = t_{DF}$) and the foreign tax rate is positive but less than or equal to domestic taxes ($0 < t_{DF}^* \leq t_{DF}$), then the productivity of capital is the same at home and abroad, $g_D = g_F$.[17] Although the domestic wealth owner earns the same *after-tax* rate of return on domestic and foreign investments—that is, $g_D(1 - t_{DD}) = g_F[1 - \max(t_{DF}, t_{DF}^*)]$, the total return to the country on a domestic investment, g_D, is greater than the return to the country *net of foreign taxes* on a foreign investment, $g_F(1 - t_{DF}^*)$. From a domestic national standpoint, there is overinvestment in foreign capital because domestic wealth owners are indifferent about which government they pay taxes to, but only taxes paid to foreign governments represent a transfer away from domestic residents.[18]

15. Compare this scenario with the effect of a source-based income tax when the foreign government levies no taxes. In that case, a case-7 equilibrium prevails before and after the imposition of the tax. The tax causes the domestic capital stock to decrease, g_D to increase to $g_F/(1 - t_{DD})$, and the tax revenue raised from foreigners to offset exactly the increased payment that must be made to foreign capital owners.

16. Christopher Findlay suggests that a capital-importing country can preserve its ability to influence the size of the domestic capital stock by paying a subsidy to foreign-owned capital, which it conceals from the foreign tax authorities, and by collecting tax at a rate $t_{FD} = t_{FD}^*$. By this mechanism the credit system becomes equivalent to the exemption system. See Christopher C. Findlay, "Optimal Taxation of International Income Flows," *Economic Record*, vol. 62 (June 1986), pp. 208–14.

17. I ignore here the possibility that the domestic wealth owner is faced with a short-selling constraint.

18. From a global perspective, an unlimited foreign tax credit by all countries assures an efficient allocation of capital (where $g_D = g_F$). If the foreign tax credit is limited to the home country's tax on income from a foreign source, then an efficient allocation is

Figure 5. *Capital Market Equilibrium in an Open Economy, with Taxes by a Large Open Economy*

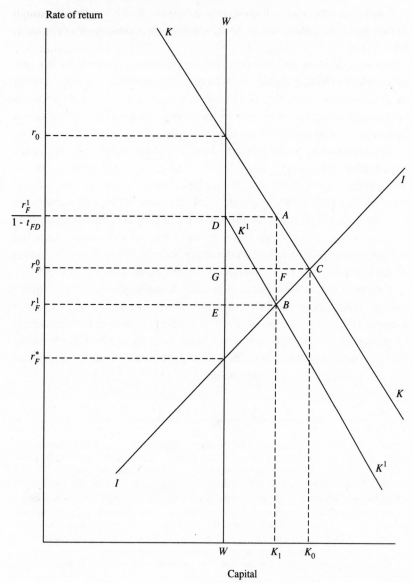

Taking Advantage of Size

Until now I have assumed that the domestic country is small enough so that its capital imports and exports do not change the rate of return in other countries. The U.S. economy is so large that this assumption may not hold, and I now investigate the effects of dropping it. In the interest of simplicity, I shall ignore both equilibria with cross-ownership of capital and foreign tax systems.

A country is defined as "large" if increasing (decreasing) its net export of capital drives down (up) the world rate of return by lowering (increasing) the marginal product of foreign-located capital. In other words, both the dependence of g_F on K_F and the equality $K_F = W_D + W_F - K_D$ are recognized. Largeness means that the supply of capital is not perfectly elastic at one rate of return. Rather, the rate of return that must be paid to foreign capital owners depends positively on how much capital is imported. Alternatively, if a large country exports capital, the rate of return its wealth owners can earn abroad declines the more capital that is exported.

A large country that is trying to maximize the welfare of its residents should tax international capital flows differently from the way in which a small country should do so. In particular, a large country should take advantage of its capacity to influence the world rate of return. In general, a large country can improve its welfare by imposing a tax that impedes the international flow of capital. If the country is a net exporter of capital, a tax on exported capital will reduce the quantity of capital on which it earns a higher rate of return than is domestically available, but it will increase the rate of return on all foreign investments that remain.[19] A large capital-importing country that imposes a tax on capital imports will forgo some investment that yields benefits, but it will also reduce the price it must pay for the capital it continues to import as the world rate of return declines.[20] Figure 5 illustrates this proposition. The capital import supply function is the schedule II; r_F^* is the foreign alternative return in the absence of any capital imports; and r_F^0 is the alternative

---

assured only if all countries levy the same tax rate. Allocation of capital will not be efficient, in general, if all countries allow deductibility.

19. The optimal tax on the income from capital exports can be written as ze, where z is the ratio of capital exports to foreign output and e is the (absolute value of the) elasticity of the marginal product of capital in the foreign country with respect to the quantity of such capital.

20. In this case the revenue collected from foreigners, $DABE$ in figure 5, is not fully

return that would prevail in equilibrium in the absence of taxes. Imposing a tax of t_{FD} decreases the domestic capital stock from K_0 to K_1. The rate of return earned by foreign wealth owners, net of taxes paid to the domestic government, however, falls from r_F^0 to r_F^1.

Whether a country is large or small, a tax on all domestically owned capital reduces the domestic wealth owners' rate of return but causes no capital movement. Although domestic capital owners in a small country bear none of the burden of a tax on all domestically located capital, such a tax by a large country reduces the world rate of return and thus does reduce the equilibrium after-tax return to all owners of capital, domestic and foreign.

How responsive the world rate of return will be to the movement of a given fraction of the capital stock of a large country such as the United States depends positively on how large the U.S. capital stock is relative to the world capital stock and negatively on the degree of substitutability between capital and other inputs in world production. The incidence of a source-based capital income tax depends on these factors plus the degree of factor substitutability in U.S. production. A rough approximation is that U.S. capital owners would bear about one-third of the burden of a source-based capital income tax.[21]

If a country is large enough so that its domestic policies can affect the world return to capital, its policies probably can affect the world prices

---

offset by the increase in the rental price paid for imported capital, *DAFG*. Note that these policies are necessarily optimal only in the absence of any retaliatory taxation by foreign countries. See Martin Feldstein and David Hartman, "The Optimal Taxation of Foreign Source Investment Income," *Quarterly Journal of Economics*, vol. 93 (November 1979), pp. 613–29.

21. The fraction of the tax borne by domestic capital owners will be $e^f/(e^f + fe^d)$, where e^f and e^d are the elasticities of the marginal product of capital in foreign and in domestic production, respectively, with respect to the quantity of capital, and f is the ratio of foreign-located capital to domestically located capital. The small-country case corresponds to $f = \infty$, so that the burden on domestic capital owners is zero. The autarky case is defined by $f = 0$. In that case capital owners bear the entire burden of a general tax on capital. Mutti and Grubert estimate the U.S. capital stock to be one-third of the world capital stock, so that $f \cong 2$. See John Mutti and Harry Grubert, "The Domestic International Sales Corporation and Its Effects," in Robert E. Baldwin and Anne O. Krueger, eds., *The Structure and Evolution of Recent Trade Policy* (University of Chicago Press for National Bureau of Economic Research, 1984), pp. 279–317. They base their estimate on Harry P. Bowen, "Changes in the International Pattern of Factor Abundance and the Composition of Trade," Economic Discussion Paper 8 (U.S. Department of Labor, Bureau of International Labor Affairs, 1980). If e^f is assumed to equal e^d, then U.S. capital owners would bear one-third of the burden of a source-based capital income tax.

of at least some of the goods that it imports and exports. Such a country can use tariffs to shift the terms of commodity trade in its favor. The capital income tax policies that maximize domestic welfare for such a country are likely to depend on the particular tariff policies it is pursuing.[22]

Perfect or Imperfect Capital Mobility?

Up to this point I have assumed that capital can flow across national borders without cost. But is this assumption valid? Martin Feldstein and Charles Horioka have recently raised questions about the degree of international capital mobility.[23] They analyze post-1960 data on domestic saving and investment rates from twenty-one members of the Organization for Economic Cooperation and Development and conclude that a sustained increase in a country's savings ratio caused an almost equal increase in the domestic investment ratio.[24] If international capital were perfectly mobile, one would expect a sustained increase in saving (wealth) in one country to be divided among investment in all countries in a way that depends on the relative size of each country's initial capital stock and the rate at which the productivity of investment falls as the

22. This statement holds even for a country that is a price taker in international capital markets. Only if tariffs are always set optimally can this interaction be ignored. In general, policies directed toward capital movements may exacerbate or alleviate the distortions present in goods markets. Ronald Jones demonstrates that in some cases it may even be optimal to subsidize foreign investment, if by doing so the terms of commodity trade are altered favorably. See Ronald W. Jones, "International Capital Movements and the Theory of Tariffs and Trade," *Quarterly Journal of Economics,* vol. 81 (February 1967), pp. 1–38.

23. See Martin Feldstein, "Domestic Saving and International Capital Movements in the Long Run and the Short Run," *European Economic Review,* vol. 21 (March–April 1983), pp. 129–51; and Martin Feldstein and Charles Horioka, "Domestic Savings and International Capital Flows," *Economic Journal,* vol. 90 (June 1980), pp. 314–29.

24. This finding has been corroborated by others—see Norman S. Fieleke, "National Saving and International Investment," in Federal Reserve Bank of Boston, *Saving and Government Policy* (FRBB, 1983); Maurice Obstfeld, "Capital Mobility in the World Economy: Theory and Measurement," National Bureau of Economic Research Working Paper 1692 (Cambridge, Mass.: NBER, August 1985); and Lawrence H. Summers, "Tax Policy and International Competitiveness," National Bureau of Economic Research Working Paper 2007 (Cambridge, Mass.: NBER, August 1986). Obstfeld finds that the association between saving and investment is weaker for small countries than it is for large countries.

quantity of capital increases.[25] Feldstein and Horioka rationalize the close relationship between national saving and investment rates on the basis of risk considerations, institutional barriers, and government policies that impede the flow of capital. But these are not the only possible explanations.

Fieleke and Summers suggest that governments actively seek to maintain external balance (because either net capital flows or current account imbalances are deemed undesirable), thereby minimizing deviations from capital account balance for all countries.[26] By this view capital would move freely but for offsetting government policies.

Identifying the exact causes of the close correlation of domestic saving and domestic investment rates is critical to understanding the effects of tax policy. The idea of "institutional barriers" seems closest to what is normally thought of as capital immobility. Such barriers could restore closed-economy results about taxation, but an explicit modeling of these barriers has not yet appeared (see the treatment of risk below).

Some recent papers have, however, explored the implications of linking the international allocation of capital to some function of relative after-tax rates of return. Mutti and Grubert and Goulder, Shoven, and Whalley, for example, assume that the equilibrium allocation of the world capital stock depends on relative after-tax rates of return.[27] In these formulations the domestic capital stock is positively related to the domestic interest rate and inversely related to the foreign interest rate, with a sensitivity depending on the value of some parameter. The domestic and foreign interest rates can differ in equilibrium.

This approach has effects similar to that of introducing a large-economy assumption. In both cases the supply of capital for the domestic economy becomes less than perfectly elastic. Some of the same results

25. Note, however, that in the simple model presented here a capital-importing country may invest all of a small increase in wealth entirely in domestic capital. In this case the capital-exporting country will spread new wealth among all countries' capital.

26. Fieleke, "National Saving and International Investment"; and Summers, "Tax Policy and International Competitiveness."

27. John Mutti and Harry Grubert, "The Taxation of Capital Income in an Open Economy: The Importance of Resident-Nonresident Tax Treatment," *Journal of Public Economics,* vol. 27 (August 1985), pp. 291–309; Lawrence H. Goulder, John B. Shoven, and John Whalley, "Domestic Tax Policy and the Foreign Sector: The Importance of Alternative Foreign Sector Formulations to Results from a General Equilibrium Tax Analysis Model," in Martin Feldstein, ed., *Behavioral Simulation Methods in Tax Policy Analysis* (University of Chicago Press for National Bureau of Economic Research, 1983), pp. 333–64.

follow. For example, in either case a capital-importing country gains from taxing capital imports. For a large country, such a tax causes a significant increase in the foreign capital stock, which lowers the foreign rate of return and thus lowers the interest rate that must be paid to foreign suppliers of capital. For a small country facing a less than perfectly elastic supply schedule, because the tax causes some foreign capital to be repatriated, it reduces the domestic return that the remaining capital importers are willing to accept. A small capital-exporting country in this situation, however, does not gain by taxing capital exports as a large country would. Because the foreign return is fixed, such a tax causes a shift of wealth toward domestic investment but does not improve the terms of foreign investment. The difference in the two cases is that the domestic country has monopoly power over capital located within its borders; only if it is a seller of this capital (that is, a capital importer) can it exploit this monopoly power. As in the large-country case, domestic capital owners bear part of a tax on domestically located investment in a capital-exporting country. In the new equilibrium domestic wealth owners are still willing to hold some domestic assets, even though they earn a lower after-tax return than that available on foreign assets.

Neither the Mutti-Grubert nor the Goulder-Shoven-Whalley model explains why differences in after-tax rates of return can persist in equilibrium. This omission has troublesome implications, as the following example illustrates. The models may show that a policy that induces purchase of foreign assets yielding a higher return than domestic assets raises welfare. If there were some offsetting disadvantage to holding foreign assets, however, then this induced portfolio shift would not necessarily represent a welfare improvement. A superior modeling approach would explicitly introduce the source of the imperfect capital mobility, so that investors would be making optimal marginal portfolio decisions subject to the constraints that they face.

Uncertainty

The models presented so far omit two important influences on investments: investments are risky, and investors try to avoid risk.[28]

28. Uncertainty can take many different forms in an economic model, including uncertainty about preferences or endowments. Because the focus of this paper is capital

Recognizing that the return to capital is uncertain and that individuals are risk averse reduces the tendency for the model to predict specialization in the international pattern of asset ownership when equations 1a and 1b do not both hold. If the return to capital income is uncertain, both domestic and foreign investors are likely to diversify their portfolios and to own both domestic and foreign assets.[29] As long as the real returns of owning foreign and domestic assets are not perfectly correlated, diversification permits investors to reduce risk without sacrificing expected return. Returns may be imperfectly correlated because of country-specific business cycles or exogenous shocks. Moreover, uncertainty and risk aversion justify the inelastic response to interest rate differentials assumed in the models of imperfect capital mobility. When risk-averse individuals are choosing optimal portfolios, an increase in the expected after-tax return of one asset typically induces a shift, but not a plunge, toward holding that asset. Thus there are no explicit barriers to mobility; rather, individuals choose not to react to interest rate differentials in an extreme way. In other words, capital is *mobile* across countries, but capital goods located in different countries are not perfectly *substitutable* in portfolios.

A simple way to think about this problem is to posit that representative domestic and foreign wealth owners are concerned both with the expected after-tax return on their portfolios and with the variance of the after-tax yield on their portfolios. Assume that there are two risky assets, the returns to which are positively correlated because of the common effect of international shocks but imperfectly correlated because of the presence of country-specific uncertainty. Domestic and foreign wealth owners would hold identical diversified portfolios if there were no taxes, if they had the same attitudes toward risk, and if there were no risks tied to the residence of the owner, such as exchange rate uncertainty or the threat of expropriation of foreign-held assets. Taxes, differential risk

income taxation, this section focuses on technological randomness, which renders the return to real investment uncertain. Pomery provides an excellent guide to the implications of uncertainty for a broader range of international trade issues. John Pomery, "Uncertainty in Trade Models," in Ronald W. Jones and Peter B. Kenen, eds., *Handbook of International Economics*, vol. 1 (Amsterdam: North-Holland, 1984), pp. 419–65.

29. Introducing risk aversion and capital income uncertainty does not preclude the possibility that unconstrained optimal portfolios will contain negative holdings of some assets.

aversion,[30] or resident-specific risks may cause the optimal portfolios of the domestic and foreign wealth owners to differ.

One logical question to ask of a portfolio model is whether it can generate the empirical fact that wealth owners tend to specialize in assets denominated in the domestic currency. Exchange rate risk, in the absence of purchasing power parity, will cause optimal portfolios to differ across residents of countries with different currencies.[31] It can be shown, however, that each resident should hold the security that is the best hedge against his own country's inflation—probably a short-term nominal instrument, such as treasury bills—and also hold a diversified portfolio of the other assets that is common to all residents.[32] This proposition implies that if there were no transaction costs and everyone had the same information, exchange rate risk might not be sufficient to induce as much specialization in domestic assets as is actually observed.

The political risk of expropriation or default varies according to the residence of the wealth owner and could cause wealth owners to favor investments in their own country's assets. A well-specified model of political risk should recognize that if behavioral responses to the threat of expropriation are ignored, the losses from expropriation exactly offset the gains. In essence, the threat of expropriation or default on externally held debt is that such risk is a random tax assessed only on nonresidents.

Because uncertainty makes it likely that all countries will export and import capital simultaneously, the effect of tax policies need not be analyzed separately for different cases. Consider, for example, an

30. If a riskless asset existed, then differential risk aversion by itself would not cause the portfolio of risky assets to differ, although the fraction of wealth held in the riskless asset would differ.

31. Note that if purchasing power parity held at all times (that is, if countries' relative price indexes were exactly in line with exchange rates), exchange rate risk would not be a reason for the portfolios held by different countries' residents to be different, because all countries' investors would view the real return of a given security identically. For example, an American holding a yen-denominated bond would suffer a loss if the yen depreciated against the dollar and if the two countries' relative price level remained unchanged. With purchasing power parity, this depreciation would be accompanied by an increase in the Japanese price level (in which case a Japanese holder of the bond would suffer an identical real loss), by a decrease in the U.S. price level (in which case neither owner would suffer a real loss), or by some combination of the two price effects. In all cases both investors would be affected identically.

32. See Michael Adler and Bernard Dumas, "International Portfolio Choice and Corporation Finance: A Synthesis," *Journal of Finance*, vol. 38 (June 1983), pp. 925–84.

increase in t_{DD}. Under certainty this policy in a capital-importing country would simply reduce the net return to domestic wealth holders on domestic investment but would leave the domestic capital stock unchanged. In a capital-exporting country, however, it would reduce the domestic capital stock and leave the return to saving unchanged.

If capital income is uncertain, the domestic wealth owners are likely to move some of their wealth abroad when t_{DD} rises. As a result, g_D will increase, causing foreign wealth owners to shift some of their wealth to the domestic country. The likely net effect is a lower domestic capital stock (but not as much lower as in the capital-exporting case under certainty) and increased cross-ownership of capital.

The effect of uncertainty on the results for incidence is similar to the effect of "imperfect capital mobility." The tax on domestically owned, domestically located capital cannot be completely avoided by capital owners because the alternative of foreign capital ownership is not a perfect substitute for domestic capital ownership. Capital flight can reduce tax liability, but only at the cost of holding a portfolio that would be inferior in the absence of tax considerations.

With uncertainty it is also no longer necessarily true that a tax levied on domestic wealth regardless of location ($t_{DD} = t_{DF}$) will be borne fully by domestic wealth owners with no allocational effect. Under uncertainty such a tax may cause an adjustment of portfolios and a shift in the location of capital, thus imposing some burden on owners of domestic wealth factors that are complementary to capital.

The welfare analysis of portfolio allocations must encompass risk as well as return. A tax may lower welfare, even if it does not reduce expected national income, by increasing the risk borne by residents. Furthermore, if the pattern of return offered by a country's equity cannot be reproduced by other available securities, a tax that reduces capital flow can increase the welfare of the taxing country. Roger Gordon and Hal Varian argue that any country in this situation has the incentive to restrict international flows of equity ownership by imposing a corporate tax and a set of taxes on residents' capital income to induce them to hold domestic equity.[33] This incentive applies to any country for which the distribution of its equity returns cannot be duplicated elsewhere and the

---

33. Roger H. Gordon and Hal R. Varian, "Taxation of Asset Income in the Presence of a World Securities Market," National Bureau of Economic Research Working Paper 1994 (Cambridge, Mass.: NBER, August 1986).

country therefore has some market power over the world price of its equity.

The analysis of capital income taxation in an open economy with uncertainty is in its infancy. It is a promising avenue of research, both because uncertainty is a reality and because models with uncertainty generate more plausible responses to tax changes than do models that ignore uncertainty. Simple models of uncertainty seem, however, to be incapable of explaining the degree of home-country asset specialization that is observed.

Dynamic Models of an Open Economy: A Heuristic Model

What are the implications of allowing saving and wealth to vary with the after-tax rate of return to saving? In this case, opening an economy to international capital flows may change not only the worldwide allocation of capital but also the quantity of saving at home and abroad. Such changes in saving have important ramifications for the incidence of capital income taxation and its effects on efficiency. Only if one considers changes in saving can one address the question of the appropriate mix of taxes on labor and capital income.[34]

Two straightforward changes must be made to the diagrams presented earlier. First, the supply-of-capital schedule, WW, is upward sloping in figures 1 through 5, reflecting the standard assumption of a positive interest rate elasticity of saving. Second, in the large-economy case, the slope of the capital import-export schedule, as depicted in figure 5, becomes more elastic (flatter), reflecting the interest rate responsiveness of foreign saving. A given increase in the rate of return offered by a capital-importing country will attract more foreign-owned capital because it not only decreases the amount of profitable foreign-located investment but also increases the amount of foreign saving. A given capital export of a large country that drives down the world marginal product of capital, by reducing the interest rate, also reduces foreign saving.

A residence-based capital income tax imposed in a small country is still borne by domestic capital owners, although now the tax reduces

---

34. If factor supplies are fixed, a general tax on any factor has no distortionary effect. Thus, such a tax does not reduce efficiency. One tax can be preferred over another only on the basis of distributional considerations.

domestic saving. If one assumes that the supply-of-saving schedule represents the true social opportunity cost of postponed consumption, this assumption causes a welfare loss because saving is reduced below its optimal level. The size of the welfare loss depends only on the size of the tax and on the interest elasticity of saving. Contrast this result with the closed-economy case, in which the welfare loss from a capital income tax also depends (positively) on the elasticity of demand for capital.[35]

A source-based tax will have no effect on domestic saving because the domestic interest rate will rise by just enough to offset the increased taxation, leaving the after-tax return to saving unchanged. The reduction in the domestic capital stock remains as the source of a welfare loss.

A tax imposed by a capital-importing country on the capital income earned by foreigners raises the rate of return domestically. Such a tax has two potentially offsetting welfare effects: a welfare loss, because domestic investment with a marginal product that exceeds the world interest rate is forgone; a welfare gain (if saving is already being taxed), because the higher domestic interest rate induces increased domestic saving.

This heuristic approach helps to develop intuition about the role of an elastic saving response in an analysis of the incidence and allocational effects of capital income taxation. But it is no substitute for a careful analysis of the welfare effects of such taxation. Saving is desirable not in itself, but for the future consumption that it enables. For that reason welfare analysis of taxation should focus on how taxes affect present and future consumption, not on saving itself. Because the welfare analysis presented above assumes that any divergence of saving from its zero-tax level will reduce welfare, it is not helpful in analyzing cases in which the optimal tax system does tax (or subsidize) saving. It is not helpful, moreover, in understanding the welfare cost of a suboptimal capital stock. The Appendix deals with models in which saving and the capital stock are derived from explicit lifetime utility maximization problems.

35. In a closed economy, a decline in saving necessarily translates into a decline in the domestic capital stock, which increases the before-tax return and thus to some degree offsets the effect of taxation on the after-tax rate of return. In a small open economy, the domestic capital stock may be unaffected by a tax on the return to domestic wealth owners. Domestic capital holdings of foreign wealth owners adjust to offset changes in domestic saving.

Concluding Remarks

Analysis based on the simplest model of a small open economy leads to the rejection or modification of many of the standard propositions about capital income taxation. Certainly the analyst must carefully specify the kind of capital—its location and ownership—to which a tax policy applies. Alas, the world is not simple. Tax analysis must recognize the multiplicity of tax systems, the importance of market power in capital and goods markets, and the substitutability of foreign and domestic capital in portfolios as well as production.

The greatest challenge for future research in this field is to develop models of an integrated world economy that are theoretically rigorous and that can generate results consistent with such empirical evidence as the Feldstein-Horioka finding and the observation that wealth owners tend to hold the majority of their wealth in domestic assets. Model builders must direct their attention to real-world behavior and institutions. No one can maintain any longer that the U.S. economy, or virtually any other, is closed. Whether an economy responds to taxation more like a closed or an open economy is another question, and answering it requires a marriage of theoretical and empirical investigation.

Appendix: Dynamic Considerations in Open-Economy Tax Analysis

This appendix reports on how the recognition of international capital flows modifies two types of models found in the economic literature: two-period models and overlapping-generation models.

A Two-Period Model

Martin Feldstein analyzed the optimal taxation of capital versus labor income in a closed economy by using a two-period model in which the representative individual cares about consumption in each of two periods and about leisure in the first period.[36] The optimal tax formula is merely

---

36. Martin Feldstein, "The Welfare Cost of Capital Income Taxation," *Journal of Political Economy*, vol. 86 (April 1978, pt. 2), pp. S29–S51.

a reinterpretation of the standard formula for optimal commodity taxation in a static framework, where the relative tax rates depend on the own- and cross-elasticities of demand. Zero taxation of capital income (equivalent to uniform taxation of first-period and second-period consumption) is optimal only in certain special cases, and the optimal tax on capital income could be negative (a subsidy) as well as positive.[37]

A parallel model of a small open economy in essence expands the transformation possibilities so that first-period and second-period consumption can be traded at a rate of $1 + r_F$ through foreign lending or borrowing. One conclusion that follows immediately from work by Peter Diamond and James Mirrlees is that, when taxes on consumption goods can be set optimally, it is always desirable to have production efficiency.[38] Production efficiency implies that the marginal product of capital should equal the world rate of interest, r_F. This result is achieved in a capital-importing country by setting t_{FD} equal to zero, and in a capital-exporting country by setting t_{DD} equal to t_{DF}. Furthermore, any system of capital income taxation that interferes with production efficiency cannot be optimal.[39] This conclusion implies that a residence-based capital income tax $(t_{DD} = t_{DF})$ may be part of an optimal tax system, but neither a source-based capital income tax $(t_{DD} = t_{FD} \neq 0, t_{DF} = 0)$ nor a tax on international capital flows $[(t_{FD} = - t_{DF}/(1 + t_{DF}) \neq 0, t_{DD} = 0]$ may be. As Roger Gordon argues, a corporation tax will never be part of an optimal tax system because its incidence is identical to that of a wage tax (borne by labor, not capital), so that although its effect on labor supply is identical, it also causes an inefficient capital stock, as a wage tax does not.[40] In general, once production efficiency is assured, the optimal taxation of capital versus labor income in this model does not differ from the closed-economy case.

37. Although this analysis assumes fixed producer prices, similar conclusions apply when production occurs under constant returns to scale.

38. See Peter A. Diamond and James A. Mirrlees, "Optimal Taxation and Public Production: I—Production Efficiency," *American Economic Review*, vol. 61 (March 1971), pp. 8–27; and "Optimal Taxation and Public Production: II—Tax Rules," *American Economic Review*, vol. 61 (June 1971), pp. 261–78. This statement reflects the fact that the required amount of revenue can always be raised in a second-best way with other taxes (that is, a labor income tax and a residence-based capital income tax) that cause no production inefficiency.

39. This conclusion follows only in the absence of foreign tax credits and applies only to a small open economy.

40. See Gordon, "Taxation of Investment and Savings in a World Economy."

A Two-Period, Overlapping-Generation Model

Peter Diamond was the first to examine the welfare economics of a model in which individuals live two periods and generations overlap.[41] Such a model differs in significant ways from the two-period model discussed above. A planner interested in maximizing steady-state consumption would choose the capital-labor ratio so that the marginal product of capital was equal to the rate of population growth, n,[42] and would choose first- and second-period consumption levels such that the representative consumer's marginal rate of intertemporal substitution equaled $1 + n$. Although both of these conditions would hold in a competitive economy in which the rate of interest equaled n, Diamond showed that a competitive economy would not necessarily attain an equilibrium in which these conditions were met.

When a competitive equilibrium yields a suboptimal capital stock and the government cannot alleviate the problem by directly transferring resources among generations,[43] in general some tax or subsidy on capital income is desirable, even if lump-sum taxes are available, because the tax can be used to increase the capital-labor ratio toward the level at which the marginal product of capital equals n, sometimes called "the golden rule" level. It is not optimal to use this instrument to establish the capital-labor ratio exactly at the golden rule, because in the absence of intergenerational transfers such a tax would excessively distort lifetime consumption patterns, with too little first-period consumption and too much second-period consumption. A. B. Atkinson and Agnar Sandmo have shown that, when the government must raise revenue and lump-sum taxes are not available, the formula for the optimal taxation of wage and capital income must be modified in consideration of the divergence among the marginal product of capital, the private cost of second-period consumption, and the social cost of increased capital (n).[44]

The planner of a small open economy who can choose the steady-

41. Peter A. Diamond, "National Debt in a Neoclassical Growth Model," *American Economic Review*, vol. 55 (December 1965), pp. 1126–50.

42. In general, the marginal product of capital should be set equal to the rate of population growth plus the rate of Harrod-neutral technical progress.

43. The bar on intergenerational transfers applies to the use of debt policy.

44. A. B. Atkinson and Agnar Sandmo, "Welfare Implications of the Taxation of Savings," *Economic Journal*, vol. 90 (September 1980), pp. 529–49.

state values of K, C_1, and C_2 will want to set the marginal product of capital equal to the world interest rate. This point is moot, however, because no interior steady-state optimum exists for steady-state saving.[45] As long as r_F exceeds n, steady-state welfare can be increased without limit by lending on the international market. Because the return to lending, r_F, exceeds the social cost of postponing consumption, n, national welfare is always increased thereby.

A government constrained to use only taxes on capital income (which may be differentiated by residence of owner) may, as in the closed-economy example, find it optimal to impose a tax or subsidy even when lump-sum taxation (but not debt policy) is possible. A tax on foreign capital owners imposed by a capital-importing country implies that the country will forgo some domestic investment for which the marginal product exceeds r_F. The result is a welfare loss. But note that, in the presence of a fixed tax on domestic wealth owners, the tax on foreign wealth owners also increases the after-tax rate of return toward the world level, improving the intertemporal allocation of consumption. John Dutton and David Hartman show that, although the optimal tax on foreign wealth owners in this case ordinarily lies between zero and the tax on domestic wealth owners, dynamic efficiency considerations may alter this result.[46]

Hartman also argues that, when a capital-importing country can adjust taxes on both domestic and foreign wealth owners, the tax rates should be equal and, in general, not zero. The optimal rate, it turns out, is equal to the rate of tax that a closed economy would choose. This result is best understood in two steps. The value of t_{FD} is set so that the equilibrium domestic capital stock is optimal. Setting the tax rate on domestic wealth owners equal to the tax rate on foreign investors implies that the after-tax return received by domestic wealth owners is equal to the world rate of return, thus ensuring that the amount of saving is optimal. This result differs from the finding in the two-period model, where a capital-importing country should always set t_{FD} to equal zero. The key difference

45. This point was noted by Koichi Hamada in "Economic Growth and Long-Term International Capital Movements," *Yale Economic Essays*, vol. 6 (Spring 1966), pp. 49–96.

46. See John Dutton, "The Optimal Taxation of International Investment Income: A Comment," *Quarterly Journal of Economics*, vol. 97 (May 1982), pp. 373–80; and David G. Hartman, "On the Optimal Taxation of Capital Income in an Open Economy," National Bureau of Economic Research Working Paper 1550 (Cambridge, Mass.: NBER, January 1985).

here is that, even before the imposition of any capital income taxes, the government is confronted with a suboptimal capital stock.

All of these results apply to a model with no labor-leisure choice and where lump-sum taxes are allowed. The extension to an open economy of the optimal tax question posed by Atkinson and Sandmo—where labor supply is endogenous and lump-sum taxes are not allowed—has not, as far as I know, been made.

Other Considerations

As in the world of fixed capital stocks, the conclusions drawn from dynamic models may be different for an open economy that is sufficiently large for optimal tariff motives for taxation to arise. David Hartman shows in an overlapping-generation model that largeness does not affect the optimal tax rate on domestic capital income (when lump-sum taxes are available) but does imply that the optimal tax rate on capital movements increases toward unity as its elasticity falls to zero.[47]

The presence of foreign taxes and of foreign tax credit systems can also dramatically alter some of the conclusions drawn above. As shown earlier, foreign countries' use of a foreign tax credit provides an argument for a positive value of t_{FD} in a capital-importing country. Furthermore, in a capital-exporting country where the domestic investor is indifferent between domestic and foreign assets, the return (including taxes paid to the home government) to a domestic investment is g_D, but the domestic return to a foreign investment is $g_F (1 - t^*_{DF})$. But, as shown earlier, $g_F [1 - \max(t_{DF}, t^*_{DF})] = g_D(1 - t_{DD})$ when the domestic wealth owner is indifferent to the choice between domestic and foreign assets. Using that equation to substitute for g_F, the domestic return to a foreign investment is also equal to $[g_D(1 - t_{DD}) (1 - t^*_{DF})]/[1 - \max(t_{DF}, t^*_{DF})]$. As long as t^*_{DF} is positive, production efficiency (that is, where the domestic return to domestic investment, g_D, equals the domestic return to foreign investment) is no longer ensured by setting t_{DD} equal to t_{DF}; it can be obtained only if t_{DF} is greater than t_{DD}.

Note that if t_{DD}, t^*_{DF}, and t_{DF} are approximately equal, as they are for residents of the United States, the domestic return to foreign investment is significantly less at the margin than the return on domestic invest-

---

47. Hartman, "On the Optimal Taxation of Capital Income in an Open Economy."

ment.[48] In this situation it makes a considerable difference whether additional saving is invested domestically, yielding g_D, or abroad, yielding the lower value of $[g_D(1 - t_{DD})(1 - t^*_{DF})]/[1 - \max(t_{DF}, t^*_{DF})]$ to the country. A tax incentive to domestic investment (lowering t_{DD}) will yield the former; an incentive to saving (lowering t_{DD} and t_{DF} in proportion) in a small economy will yield close to the latter. It is certainly plausible in these circumstances that an increase in domestic investment would be desirable, whereas an increase in domestically owned foreign investment would not be desirable.

Of course the tendency for the foreign tax credit to misallocate domestic portfolios could be offset by setting t_{DD} sufficiently less than t_{DF}. Such a difference would violate the spirit of the foreign tax credit. If t_{DD} must be close to t_{DF}, then the benefits of a tax policy intended to increase saving diminish substantially for a small country.

Goulder, Shoven, and Whalley reached this conclusion in their computable general equilibrium analysis of a consumption tax.[49] They found that replacing the U.S. income tax with a consumption tax caused large welfare gains if one disregarded international capital flows, but caused a "substantial" welfare loss when capital mobility was considered. The turnaround reflected the finding that introducing the consumption tax in the United States caused capital to move abroad, where it earned a lower return net of taxes paid to foreign governments. This result led the authors to suggest that the United States might gain from having additional taxes on capital income received from abroad by revoking the foreign tax credit.

Comments by Lawrence H. Summers

Joel Slemrod's paper analyzes the optimal tax literature as it applies to capital taxation in open economies. Slemrod succeeds quite well in his objective, but it is in his commentary on both the optimal tax analysis

48. In the United States t_{DD} is somewhat less than t_{DF}. For example, accelerated depreciation and the (now repealed) investment tax credit cannot be used for direct investment abroad. But the benefit of deferral of any positive difference between U.S. and foreign tax on earnings retained abroad offsets this disadvantage to some degree.

49. Goulder, Shoven, and Whalley, "Domestic Tax Policy and the Foreign Sector," p. 362.

and his own paper that the discussion seems rather removed from actual tax policy debate, where incentives of various sorts are regularly urged on policymakers in the name of competitiveness.

This paper shares a common weakness with several other papers in this volume: the only numbers are applied to the pages and footnotes. Actual tax policy surely should not be based only on a priori theory, especially given the natural experiments that Ronald Reagan has provided in recent years, and it is hard to see where useful factual input will come from, if not from Brookings books and the economists who contribute to them.

The paper enunciates five primary propositions about international taxation. Let me summarize these points and then turn to the question of competitiveness, which I think is more important.

First, Slemrod notes that when an economy is open a distinction must be drawn between taxes based on the location of capital, which might be called investment taxes, and those based on the location of the owner of capital, which might be labeled as taxes on saving.

In the simplest closed economy, taxes on saving and investment have very similar effects. Yet in the open economy the effects are very different. Suppose Rhode Island levies a tax on the capital income of its citizens—a savings tax. In the short run, before there is a change in the accumulation of wealth in Rhode Island, there is no effect at all on capital intensity or factor returns. Rhode Island residents would allocate their capital in the same way, to maximize their return, regardless of whether or not that return was taxed. A tax on saving does not change the interregional or international allocation of capital.

An investment tax, on the other hand, would lead capital to flow out of Rhode Island until the point where after-tax returns were equalized in Rhode Island and elsewhere. This means that the incidence of the investment tax cannot be on Rhode Island capital because the return to capital will be equalized around the world, both before and after the tax. Instead, the loser from the capital tax in Rhode Island will be immobile factors such as land and labor. This just illustrates that there is a fundamental difference between the effects of taxes on saving and those on investment.

Slemrod's second point stresses the complexity of complex situations. He considers cases where the interaction of domestic and foreign tax provisions lead to cases where taxes are not pure taxes on saving or on investment, but are instead some kind of hybrid. To illustrate his point, suppose that a country does what the United States more or less does and tries to have it both ways, by taxing foreigners on their capital investments in the United States and also taxing Americans on their worldwide income. How will capital respond to such a set of tax rules?

U.S. domestic investors who are taxed equally, regardless of whether they invest in the United States or invest abroad, will invest so as to equate the after-tax returns to both kinds of investment, but of course if the taxes are equal, they will be investing so as to equalize the before-tax rates of return.

What about foreigners? Foreigners are, by assumption, taxed on their U.S. income but not on their foreign income. It is clear then that if U.S. investors are indifferent at the margin between investing here and abroad, foreigners cannot also be indifferent. Foreigners will earn a higher return by investing abroad where they do not pay tax than they will by investing in the United States where they do pay tax. They will be driven to a corner where they hold no capital. That is just one possibility.

The other possibility is that the United States is small relative to the world capital market. In this case, it would be reasonable to assume that foreigners would end up holding some capital in the rest of the world and some in the United States. With foreigners holding capital in both places, the before-tax return to capital abroad would have to equal the after-tax return to capital in the United States. U.S. residents would then hold capital only in the United States.

Slemrod's point is that proper analysis will, in general, require a determination of which of these cases is true, or equivalently, an answer to the traditional question: who is the marginal taxpayer? This point is not unique to international settings. Similar issues arise all the time in a progressive income tax system in identifying, for example, who the marginal taxpayer is in considering the effect of dividend taxes or proposed taxes on municipal bond interest.

Slemrod's third observation is essentially that foreign governments are the best candidates for taxation. There is a very general principle that it is good to tax things that are in inelastic supply. The government of France is presumably in inelastic supply, though perhaps no current government is likely to remain in office forever.

Where it is possible to levy a tax that will be creditable by another country's treasury, it is surely desirable. Such a tax will have no distortionary effect at all and is therefore an ideal tax from the point of view of the home country. It is, however, a bad tax from the world's point of view. This principle has been used by many developing countries with the aid of tax attorneys employed by American multinationals. Such nations optimally configure their tax credits to take advantage of the largess provided by U.S. foreign tax credits. Of course, the difficulty with this plan is that taxing foreign governments is likely to invite reprisals.

Fourth, Slemrod considers the possibility that the United States has some monopoly power in the world capital market. This power could arise because the United States bulks large in the world economy, because assets in different currencies are not perfect substitutes, or because uncertainty about future exchange rates creates risk. A country in such a situation should exploit its monopoly power. If the United States is an exporter of capital, it will pay to limit its exports so as to raise the return; if it is an importer of capital, it will pay to impose an optimal tariff on capital to obtain capital more cheaply. Capital, which can be thought of as a claim on future consumption, is no different from any other product. If a country has power in world markets, it should exploit it.

Finally, Slemrod considers issues relating to capital accumulation. Here it is difficult to reach any strong conclusion. Increased capital accumulation will benefit future generations at the expense of current ones. Whether this is desirable as an ethical choice cannot be resolved on an a priori ground. My own feeling is that, given the payoffs to increased investment, raising the level of capital intensity in the United States should be a high priority. But there is an ethical as well as an economic component to this judgment.

Let me turn to the questions that I would have preferred the paper to have discussed. I think the crucial policy question at the present time is how taxes affect American firms' ability to compete in world markets. A principal argument made against the tax changes enacted recently, which raised tax burdens on business investment, is that they will somehow reduce American international competitiveness. I will consider the validity of this proposition.

It is good to start with an assertion that no one can argue with: a basic identity of national income accounting holds that a nation's current account is equal to its national saving less its national investment. Simple identities have simple implications, and this one is no exception. Increased investment without increased saving must necessarily be associated with a reduction in the trade balance. How does this happen?

Capital flows to finance the increased investment cause an increase in the demand for dollars. The increase in the demand for dollars leads to an appreciation in the real exchange rate. This appreciation makes the price of American tradable goods more expensive relative to the price of foreign tradable goods, and that leads to a deterioration in the country's trade balance.

The apparent implication of this argument is that a revenue-neutral program that increases investment incentives and does not promote national savings will reduce competitiveness and impair the performance of the traded-goods sector of the economy. These effects are potentially important. Assume that the before-tax return to capital is 10 percent. If there is a policy that changes the effective tax rate on business capital by 15 percent, in order to restore the after-tax rate of return that exists in the rest of the world a change of about 20 percent in the capital stock will be required. Such a 20 percent change in the capital stock corresponds to about 30 percent of GNP. Some of that is going to come from investments in owner-occupied housing, and some of it is going to come from increased savings. It is clear that relatively modest investment incentives could have huge effects on foreign capital inflows. Recall that the much-maligned U.S. current account deficit has run at only about 3.5 percent of GNP in recent years.

If one takes the view that capital is freely mobile and that marginal funds for investment will come from abroad, the implication is that tax policy changes of the kind enacted in 1981 and again in 1986 should lead to enormous changes in the current account. Measures that promote investment should lead to capital inflows and therefore to very large and protracted trade deficits.

If this analysis is correct, one wonders why those concerned about the size of the traded-goods sector—firms and labor that produce traded goods—are so enthusiastic about investment incentives.

I can think of five hypotheses. First, people either do not know better or pretend not to know better and sense that arguments about beating the Japanese will elicit a better political response than arguments about achieving optimal second-best tax structures. Therefore they couch their arguments in terms of international competitiveness. The fallacy is an appealing one. It is true that any industry, if subsidized, will perform better on international markets. But if investment in all industries is subsidized, our current account does deteriorate. It is much like standing up at a football game. Any individual who stands up sees better. But if everyone stands up, no one's view is improved.

A second possibility is what might be called the Keynesian argument that demand creates saving. If resources are not fully employed in the economy because wages are relatively rigid and do not fall in response to unemployment, an increase in investment that raises demand will increase GNP and lead to an automatic increase in saving. There will be crowding in of saving and so there will be no need for the trade balance to fall when investment is increased. In the current policy environment, where monetary policy tries to set a certain target for output with a view to inflationary pressures and where, in the long run, there is a tendency to return to some natural level of output, I am skeptical that this Keynesian explanation could be very important in supporting the conclusion that investment incentives will increase competitiveness.

A third possible argument positively relating competitiveness and investment incentives is what might be referred to as the "bash-the-farmers" argument. The argument is that tax policies that encourage investment do make the trade balance worse, but that investment is being encouraged in only some parts of the traded-goods sector and so, while the trade balance as a whole will deteriorate, those parts of the traded-goods sector that receive tax benefits will improve. The difficulty here is that there is not much of the traded-goods sector that is not affected by tax incentives like the investment tax credit. The principal exception is the farm sector, and it is hard to believe that the farmers could bear so much of the loss that the rest of the traded-goods sector would sell more if investment incentives were enacted.

The fourth possible hypothesis is that it is inappropriate to interpret the term "competitiveness" as referring to short-run trade performance. A different sense of competitiveness would emphasize the long-run growth rate of real wages that is consistent with maintaining a balance of trade. On this definition, improved investment incentives, by increasing capital intensity, do spur competitiveness. There is the additional point that if the country goes deep into debt, ultimately that debt will have to be paid back by exporting more than is imported. This will mean improved performance of the traded-goods sector. Such a scenario is likely to apply to U.S. manufacturing in coming years. But I doubt that going into debt so that large repayments would have to be made is what advocates of tax incentives for international competitiveness have in mind.

The fifth, and I believe most important, consideration that helps to resolve this riddle of political economy is that the premise of the discussion—that capital is perfectly mobile—is not a useful approximation for thinking about the competitiveness problem. I do not mean that capital does not "slosh" freely around the world and that there are not billions of dollars poised to move between countries in response to small changes in the rate of return. These factors are clearly present. Instead, I would suggest that governments systematically pursue policies that inhibit incipient capital mobility. Sometimes these policies take the form of direct capital controls; other times they take the form of response to pressures arising from high interest rates or a poor trade balance. For example, countries with severe trade balance problems tend to reduce government budget deficits and thereby increase their national saving.

The empirical fact, first highlighted by Martin Feldstein and not discredited despite a large number of attempts, is that across countries one finds an extremely high correlation between national saving and investment rates. Essentially, all high-saving countries are high-investment countries, and all high-investment countries are high-saving countries. No one has succeeded in linking high saving and high investment to common third factors in any persuasive way.

There is the possibility, originally stressed by Feldstein, that capital does not flow very freely across international borders. But this is challenged by the observation that the relatively small net flows of capital that do occur represent the offsetting effects of very large gross flows of investment in all directions.

I think the most plausible explanation for the correlation between national saving and investment rates is that countries find it difficult to live with large capital inflows or outflows for reasons relating to political pressures of the kind that are building up in the United States at the moment. They therefore systematically manipulate the levers of economic policy to alter national saving and investment and bring them into balance.

If this view is correct, the assessment of investment incentives becomes a delicate matter requiring both political and economic insight. One can analyze the effect of an investment incentive by assuming that no other policies take place and that there are large capital inflows from abroad, but history and experience teach us that this outcome almost certainly will not obtain. Some other policy will come along that will drive investment and saving back into balance. If that policy does not involve undoing the investment incentive, but instead involves changing national saving, then the policy mix of investment incentives followed by high interest rates and pressures to increase national saving will be in the interest of the traded-goods sector of the economy.

Other than that explanation, I think that one has to conclude that arguments for investment incentives on grounds of international competitiveness are largely specious. That does not mean that policy has taken the right tack in recent months by reducing investment incentives. An alternative policy, which follows equally well from the saving-investment identity and is much more conducive to economic growth, would be to increase national saving by reducing budget deficits. This is a policy that I suspect most economists can support. It means that there will be more tax reforms in the future for us to study.

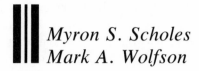

Myron S. Scholes
Mark A. Wolfson

The Cost of Capital
and Changes in Tax Regimes

IN HIS 1976 presidential address to the American Finance Association, Merton H. Miller presented an equilibrium analysis of how taxes affect the optimal amount of debt in a firm's capital structure. Miller presented a clear and simple model demonstrating that when the tax positions of both the suppliers and demanders of debt are considered, the amount of debt in the capital structure of a firm may be a matter of indifference.[1]

Throughout the years following the publication of papers by Modigliani and Miller on taxes and the cost of capital,[2] researchers had been looking for the nontax costs associated with debt that balanced the benefits of the tax deductibility of interest.[3] Thus Miller's 1976 conclusion

We are grateful to Mark Mazur for assistance in collecting and structuring data. The suggestions of George Constantinides, John McConnell, James Patell, Joseph Stiglitz, and Sheridan Titman are gratefully acknowledged. A version of this paper geared more to an audience of financial economists appears as "Issues in the Theory of Optimal Capital Structure," in Sudipto Bhattacharya and George Constantinides, eds., *Frontiers of Modern Financial Theory* (New York: Rowman and Littlefield, 1987).

1. Merton H. Miller, "Debt and Taxes," *Journal of Finance,* vol. 32 (May 1977), pp. 261–75.

2. Franco Modigliani and Merton H. Miller, "The Cost of Capital, Corporation Finance and the Theory of Investment," *American Economic Review,* vol. 48 (June 1958), pp. 267–97; and Modigliani and Miller, "Corporate Income Taxes and the Cost of Capital: A Correction," *American Economic Review,* vol. 53 (June 1963), pp. 433–43.

3. These costs included deadweight bankruptcy costs; loss of tax shields such as net operating loss carryforwards in bankruptcy; and various deadweight costs associated with operating inefficiencies that result when "agents" act on behalf of "principals" in settings where the actions of agents are imperfectly monitored. For examples of writings on these types of costs, see Alan Kraus and Robert Litzenberger, "A State-Preference Model of Optimal Financial Leverage," *Journal of Finance,* vol. 28 (September 1973), pp. 911–22; James H. Scott, Jr., "A Theory of Optimal Capital Structure," *Bell Journal of Economics,* vol. 7 (Spring 1976), pp. 33–54; E. Han Kim, "A Mean-Variance Theory

was all the more striking. He pointed out that an important cost of issuing debt that had been ignored was the premium required by bondholders in equilibrium to cover the tax penalty on interest income they earned from holding corporate bonds. To induce these individuals to hold bonds rather than tax-favored stock, issuers must pay a higher before-tax rate of interest. Miller showed that the resulting corporate after-tax cost of debt finance could be exactly the same as the risk-adjusted after-tax cost of equity finance. Although there would be an optimal aggregate amount of debt in the economy, there would be no tax advantage for any particular firm to issue either debt or equity.

To illustrate, assume that the corporate tax rate is 50 percent, the marginal personal tax rate on interest income is 50 percent, and the marginal tax rate on dividend and capital gains income is zero. Assume that the after-tax rate of return on bonds is 6 percent. To realize 6 percent after taxes, the marginal investor in bonds must earn 12 percent (or 6 percent/(1 − 0.5)) before taxes. Since the marginal investor pays no tax on dividend or capital gains income, the equilibrium price of shares must be such that after controlling for risk the before- and after-tax rate of return on shares is also 6 percent. In this equilibrium, the firm's risk-adjusted cost of issuing shares is 6 percent; the firm's risk-adjusted cost of issuing debt is also 6 percent (or 12 percent (1 − 0.5)) after the corporate interest deduction. Since the after-tax cost of issuing shares is exactly the same as the after-tax cost of issuing debt, there is no apparent advantage to issuing either stock or debt to finance economic activity. Before the Tax Reform Act of 1986, the marginal corporate income tax rate was 46 percent, the marginal tax rate of individual investors on income from holding corporate bonds could have been 50 percent,[4] and the marginal tax rate on individual investors from holding shares could have been approximately 8 percent (due to the 60 percent exclusion for capital gains, the ability to convert dividends into unreal-

of Optimal Capital Structure and Corporate Debt Capacity," *Journal of Finance*, vol. 33 (March 1978), pp. 45–63; M. J. Brennan and E. S. Schwartz, "Corporate Income Taxes, Valuation, and the Problem of Optimal Capital Structure," *Journal of Business*, vol. 51 (January 1978), pp. 103–14; Michael C. Jensen and William H. Meckling, "Theory of the Firm: Managerial Behavior, Agency Costs and Ownership Structure," *Journal of Financial Economics*, vol. 3 (October 1976), pp. 305–60; and Stewart C. Myers, "Determinants of Corporate Borrowing," *Journal of Financial Economics*, vol. 5 (November 1977), pp. 147–75.

4. See Jeffrey L. Skelton, "Banks, Firms, and the Relative Pricing of Tax-Exempt and Taxable Bonds," *Journal of Financial Economics*, vol. 12 (November 1983), pp. 343–55.

ized capital gains by using margin to buy stock, and the ability to avoid or defer payment of the capital gains tax through installment sale arrangements, charitable contributions, gifts, or bequests). With this configuration of tax rates, the marginal investor would be indifferent between holding stocks and bonds, and corporations would also be indifferent between issuing bonds and stocks. Other configurations of marginal tax rates on shares result in different conclusions as to the relative advantage of issuing debt, as will be discussed later.

In summarizing the debate that followed the publication of the Miller equilibrium theory, Kim points out that if there is no tax advantage to issuing debt rather than equity, firms would not issue risky debt, given information costs such as those of negotiating risky loan terms, monitoring the performance of corporations with such loans, coping with inefficiencies that may result when managers are more concerned with the welfare of stockholders than with the welfare of creditors, and reorganizing such corporations in the event of loan defaults.[5] However, there are also many circumstances in which the information costs of issuing equity exceed those of issuing debt, either because of "adverse selection" problems or because of "moral hazard" problems associated with issuing outside equity.[6]

5. E. Han Kim, "Optimal Capital Structure in Miller's Equilibrium," in Bhattacharya and Constantinides, eds., *Frontiers of Modern Financial Theory*.

6. Hayne E. Leland and David H. Pyle, "Information Asymmetries, Financial Structure, and Financial Intermediation," *Journal of Finance*, vol. 32 (May 1977), pp. 371–87; Stephen A. Ross, "The Determination of Financial Structure: The Incentive-Signalling Approach," *Bell Journal of Economics*, vol. 8 (Spring 1977), pp. 23–40; and Jensen and Meckling, "Theory of the Firm." By an adverse selection problem, we mean that a party to a transaction possesses information not available to the other party. Arrow terms this the "hidden information" problem. See Kenneth J. Arrow, "The Economics of Agency," in John W. Pratt and Richard J. Zeckhauser, eds., *Principals and Agents: The Structure of Business* (Harvard Business School Press, 1985), pp. 37–51. In the context of issuing equity, hidden information costs include underwriters' fees, accountants' fees, costs associated with legal conflicts relating to allegations of misrepresentations by sellers, and operating inefficiencies (such as the cost of passing up profitable projects) that result when equity must be sold to uninformed buyers at a price different from what the informed sellers know it to be worth. Moral hazard problems arise when a principal hires an agent to take actions that are imperfectly observable. For example, the agent may not be working hard, but the principal cannot monitor the agent's efforts without cost. Arrow terms this the "hidden action" problem. In the context of issuing equity, hidden action costs include those related to establishing internal control systems within the firm and those relating to distortions both in the sharing of risks (agents are often exposed to more risk than is otherwise desirable to align incentives properly) and in making decisions (in choosing actions, managers will be more concerned with their own welfare than with the welfare of passive shareholders).

On the other hand, if the corporate tax can be viewed as progressive (for example, at low levels of taxable income, interest deductions cannot be fully utilized at the statutory corporate tax rate) or if the information-related costs of issuing debt beyond those of issuing equity are increasing at an increasing rate as more debt is issued (even if the difference is negative), then there can be an optimum amount of debt to be included in the capital structure of a particular corporation. That is, capital structure can matter. Indeed, as we will discuss later, the empirical evidence on how stock prices respond to exchange offers (such as debt-for-equity swaps), equity issuances and repurchases, and convertible debt issuances can be interpreted as evidence of a progressive corporate income tax in a setting in which managers are better informed about the prospects of their firms than are passive owners.

Even if we were to accept the premise that issuing equity entails no deadweight costs and that the deadweight costs associated with the issuance of risky debt increase at an increasing rate as more debt is issued, we would still have difficulty resolving one of the key puzzles that inspired Miller to produce a model in which there is a small maximum possible tax advantage to issuing debt. That puzzle is, how can we explain the modest amount of debt issued by the IBMs of the world, firms that not only have plenty of taxable income to shield but also could issue essentially default-free debt at negligible deadweight costs?

We argue below that such puzzles may be resolved if a richer menu of capital structure components than simply debt and equity is considered. There are many classes of claimants to the assets of the firm, including the firm's suppliers, employees, customers, bankers, limited partners, coventurers, lessors, various classes of bondholders, preferred and common stockholders, competitors, the public at large (to the extent they participate in litigation claims and redistributive claims brought about by legislation), and various government agencies, especially the taxing authority. The capital structure problem is but a small piece of a larger tax planning problem, which itself is a problem of the optimal design of organizations. The optimal tax planning strategy depends heavily on the tax rates of the firm and of all of its claimants, both now and in the future. The optimal strategy also depends heavily on the costs, especially the idiosyncratic information costs of issuing and retiring various types of securities. Adding to the problem are the costs of structuring and restructuring the asset side of the balance sheet to affect both the marginal tax rate and the information costs associated with issuing various classes of securities.

Optimal tax planning must also consider the taxation of the economic activities of the firm in all the tax jurisdictions in which it faces liability, including those of states and localities, federal taxation in the United States, and a host of foreign country taxes. In addition, if differences in capital structures among firms are to be understood, models must include the effects of the dynamic elements of the tax system (for example, the Tax Reform Act of 1986) as well as differences in the ways various industries and economic activities are taxed. If one were to ignore the dynamic and uncertain elements of tax planning, as well as the costliness of reorganizing economic activity, the resulting theory of the effects of taxes on the investment and financing decisions of firms inevitably would become sterile and hopelessly weak in predictive power.[7]

For example, the "IBM debt puzzle" might be explained, in part, by considering multinational tax planning problems. U.S. tax rules for the effective deductibility of interest (for income tax and foreign tax credit purposes) require that firms apportion interest deductions between U.S. and foreign tax jurisdictions based on the book or market value of assets (unless the interest is on debt collateralized by assets concentrated in a specific tax jurisdiction). Even for corporations with plenty of taxable income, the marginal tax rate effectively applied to interest deductions may be insufficient to compensate for the risk-adjusted yield premium on debt (relative to equity) required by the marketplace. Alternatively, a firm that generates most of its income in a state without an income tax has less tax incentive to issue debt than one operating primarily in a state with high income taxes. Before the Tax Reform Act of 1986, similar considerations applied to a firm that generated enough tax preferences (such as accelerated depreciation) to be subject to the corporate add-on minimum tax, in which case its maximum marginal federal tax rate dropped from 46 percent to only 39.1 percent, due to the interaction between the add-on minimum tax and the regular corporate tax.[8] Such a firm might rationally choose to issue no debt, even though it was generating considerable amounts of taxable income and was able to issue default-free debt without incurring any issuance costs.

The above discussion suggests that to build a rich model of capital

7. As suggested by Stewart C. Myers, "The Capital Structure Puzzle," *Journal of Finance*, vol. 39 (July 1984), pp. 575–92.

8. Although the add-on tax was applied at a 15 percent rate on tax preferences, the amount of tax preference subject to the tax was reduced by any regular tax paid. Hence, when the add-on tax was binding, the marginal tax rate dropped from 46 percent to 39.1 percent (or $0.46 [1 - 0.15] = 0.391$).

structure planning one must abandon a neoclassical perspective where transactions can be effected costlessly and information is freely and equally available to all participants in the market.[9] It also requires consideration of the interactions between corporate investment decisions (which assets to acquire) and corporate financing decisions (how operations are financed).

Taxation and Corporate Finance

We certainly are not the first to point out the lack of independence between investment decisions and financing decisions. For example, DeAngelo and Masulis extended the Miller model by incorporating uncertainty and introducing substitutes for interest deductions (notably depreciation) to serve as tax shields in tax planning.[10] An important limitation of their work, however, is that production decisions are taken to be specified exogenously and optimal debt-to-equity ratios are determined for a given level of depreciation shields and for a given distribution of corporate income. One could just as well fix debt-to-equity ratios and determine the optimal level of investment in depreciable equipment along with the optimal form of contracting for control of such assets (for example, buying or leasing). A more general approach, however, is to determine the most cost-effective means of organizing the productive activities of the firm. This includes not only the information and transaction costs of contracting but also their interaction with the costs of producing tax shields. Taxes can be shielded not only by issuing debt and purchasing depreciable equipment but also by engaging in research and development activity, accelerating compensation to employees, entering into long-term construction contracts, and selling products on an installment basis, among a broad list of other alternatives. In short, the tax planning problem is considerably broader than simply choosing the correct mix of debt and equity.

9. See Myron S. Scholes and Mark A. Wolfson, "Taxes and Organization Theory," Working Paper (Stanford University, April 1987), for an elaboration of this theme.
10. Harry DeAngelo and Ronald W. Masulis, "Optimal Capital Structure under Corporate and Personal Taxation," *Journal of Financial Economics*, vol. 8 (March 1980), pp. 3–29.

Efficient Tax Planning versus Tax Minimization

There are myriad institutional arrangements that are driven by a desire to mitigate the costs of taxation. In the presence of costly contracting, however, efficient tax planning often requires abandoning the goal of tax minimization. The goal of minimizing taxes often conflicts with other goals, such as minimizing transaction costs. This has important implications for organizational design in general and corporate financial policy in particular, as we intend to show.

To illustrate, consider the incentive of stockholders to encourage corporate managers to make investments in projects that increase the variability of the cash flows of the firm. This would make stockholders wealthier at the expense of bondholders.[11] Without taxes and other constraints, stockholders gain at the expense of bondholders by increasing the value of their right to default on the bonds. Bondholders, in effect, sell to stockholders a put option, an option to sell the firm to the bondholders for the face amount of the debt.[12] The value of this option increases by investing in projects that increase cash-flow risks or by replacing equities with additional liabilities of equal or greater priority than those already outstanding. The presence of taxes, however, alters the incentive problem. In those states of nature where the option would be exercised but for the tax considerations, the firm is most likely to have incurred net operating losses. If, because of transaction costs, the firm cannot eliminate its net operating losses within its tax year (for example, by issuing equity and using the proceeds to buy fully taxable bonds), it faces a progressive tax schedule. In the extreme, the stockholders could lose the value of their net operating losses in the course of selling the firm to the bondholders. Because these losses represent a potential claim against the government, they reduce the value of the option and influence the initial investment and financing decisions of the firm. A progressive schedule of corporate tax rates induces a degree of risk aversion, insofar as the selection of investments is concerned, which mitigates the preference for risk induced by the option.[13]

11. Dan Galai and Ronald W. Masulis, "The Option Pricing Model and the Risk Factor of Stock," *Journal of Financial Economics*, vol. 3 (January–March 1976), pp. 53–81; Jensen and Meckling, "Theory of the Firm"; and Myers, "Determinants of Corporate Borrowing."

12. Fischer Black and Myron Scholes, "The Pricing of Options and Corporate Liabilities," *Journal of Political Economy*, vol. 81 (May–June 1973), pp. 637–54.

13. The tax rules may reduce significantly the demand for explicit and costly debt

Market Frictions and Tax Rule Restrictions

In a world of no transaction or information costs, the corporate tax planning problem would be trivial. As long as there were two assets whose returns were taxed differently, opportunities for tax arbitrage would be available if there were any differences in tax rates across taxpayers. Highly taxed taxpayers would be inclined to increase their investment in tax-favored assets and finance their investment by borrowing tax-disfavored assets. Low-bracket taxpayers would be inclined to take the reverse investment and financing positions. It would be efficient for taxpayers to recontract until all personal and corporate marginal tax rates were the same (possibly zero). Hamada and Scholes argue that one of the crucial assumptions of the Miller model is that entities in different tax brackets cannot engage in tax arbitrage: they cannot sell assets with returns that are taxed at one rate to profit from buying securities that are taxed at a different rate. Stiglitz presents similar arguments.[14] Without costs, it is possible for tax planners to eliminate the differences between corporate and individual tax rates; and, depending on the particular configuration of rules and restrictions, the system could yield no tax revenue at all. Many models in the finance literature finesse this difficulty by imposing (implicitly or explicitly) exogenous restrictions such as fixed supplies of securities, arbitrary restrictions on the ability of investors to sell stock that they do not own (short sale), or infinite costs

---

covenants, since taxes can alter the very nature of the incentive problem. For an analysis of how bond covenants are used to mitigate conflicts of interest between bondholders and stockholders, see Clifford W. Smith, Jr., and Jerold B. Warner, "On Financial Contracting: An Analysis of Bond Covenants," *Journal of Financial Economics*, vol. 7 (June 1979), pp. 117–61. Although a firm does not lose its net operating losses in bankruptcy, there are explicit restrictions in the tax code against "selling" these losses to other firms. Under the 1986 act, it will be even more difficult to sell such losses: following most changes in control of a company with net operating losses, the net operating losses will be restricted from offsetting other taxable income at a rate greater than the long-term after-tax rate on riskless bonds times the purchase price of the firm. This rate of utilization is reduced even further if at least one-third of the loss company's assets are nonbusiness assets (such as cash and marketable securities). Other changes that impair the ability to sell losses relate to new "continuity of business" requirements.

14. Robert S. Hamada and Myron S. Scholes, "Taxes and Corporate Financial Management," in Edward I. Altman and Marti G. Subrahmanyam, eds., *Recent Advances in Corporate Finance* (Richard D. Irwin, 1985), pp. 187–226; and Joseph E. Stiglitz, "The General Theory of Tax Avoidance," *National Tax Journal*, vol. 38 (September 1985), pp. 325–37.

to implement certain tax-planning strategies. But such restrictions are questionable in the frictionless, perfectly competitive settings that are otherwise assumed.

Five important characteristics of tax codes encourage economic agents to expend resources in the tax planning process. One, to which we have alluded already, is statutory differences in tax rates as a function of income. The second is differences in tax rates over time. The third characteristic is that alternative legal organizational forms used to produce the same goods and services or to hold the same assets are taxed differently. The fourth is that the returns from investing in different economic activities for a given taxpayer are taxed differently. And the fifth is that various states and nations may tax income differently.

It is the tax rules themselves, however—complemented by the reality that contracting is costly—that constrain the elimination of all differences in marginal tax rates. This combination of market frictions and tax rule restrictions precludes tax arbitrage. Indeed, new tax rules often become necessary to prevent arbitrage as a change in technology (for example, the creation of an active market in a new financial instrument) reduces the force of a friction.

Tax Clienteles and Implicit Taxes

To appreciate the role of taxes and transaction costs in the optimal capital structure decision, it is necessary to introduce the concepts of tax clienteles and implicit taxes. Tax clienteles arise because the ways in which taxpayers organize productive activities have different tax implications for the parties to a contract. Consider, for example, a buy-versus-lease decision in which the user of an asset compares two alternative ways to allocate the property rights to a particular asset. Company A plans to manufacture a product requiring machinery currently owned by Company B. Although Company A can use the investment tax credits and rapid depreciation deductions if it buys the machine, suppose that Company B places a higher value on these tax benefits. For example, suppose that Company B is flush with taxable income, but Company A is uncertain whether its taxable income will be sufficient to use all of the tax benefits of ownership (that is, the anticipated costs of restructuring to generate taxable income are high). Company B has a tax incentive to lease the machinery to Company A. Company A will capture indirectly some of the tax benefits of using the machine through the terms of the rental contract (such as a reduced rental rate). Companies (such as B) that buy depreciable assets to use or to lease out and companies (such as A) that capture tax benefits indirectly by leasing are examples of tax clienteles.[15]

Related to the concept of clienteles is the concept of implicit taxes. Implicit taxes represent the before-tax differences in cash flows from investments that are taxed differently.[16] The yield differential between municipal bonds and corporate bonds is an example. The lower before-tax rate of return on an exempt bond (or on an investment that gives rise to generous investment tax credits and accelerated depreciation allowances) when compared with that on a taxable bond is an implicit tax. As pointed out earlier, the risk-adjusted required rate of return on shares in the Miller equilibrium could also be well below the rate on fully taxable bonds. Naturally, a taxpayer whose marginal explicit tax rate on taxable interest income is below the implicit tax rate on municipal bond income would prefer to hold taxable bonds; that is, taxpayers who face relatively low explicit tax rates are the natural clientele to hold tax-disfavored

15. In the absence of investment tax credits, whether low-rate taxpayers form a natural clientele as lessees depends upon the depreciation schedule permitted for tax purposes relative to economic depreciation. A generous depreciation allowance results in taxation of investment returns to the lessor that is more favorable than the taxation of returns to holding a taxable bond, and a competitive market would force the lessor to reduce the lease rate to below the taxable bond rate. In the special case of immediate expensing of the cost of the investment (and with no investment tax credits), the after-tax return to the investment is equal to the before-tax return. In a competitive market, this return, on a risk-adjusted basis, must be equal to the municipal bond rate. On the other hand, certain intangible assets (such as a trademark) that have finite economic lives but are nonamortizable for tax purposes are most efficiently owned by low-taxed entities. The equilibrium before-tax return to such assets should exceed the taxable bond rate.

16. See Harvey Galper and Eric Toder, "Measuring the Incidence of Taxation of Income from Capital," Brookings Technical Series Reprint T-026, 1983; Galper and Toder, "Transfer Elements in the Taxation of Income from Capital," in Marilyn Moon, ed., *Economic Transfers in the United States* (University of Chicago Press for National Bureau of Economic Research, 1984), pp. 87–138; Myron S. Scholes and Mark A. Wolfson, "Employee Compensation and Taxes: Links with Incentives and with Investment and Financing Decisions," Working Paper (Stanford University, Graduate School of Business, October 1984); and Mark J. Mazur, Myron S. Scholes, and Mark A. Wolfson, "Implicit Taxes and Effective Tax Burdens," Working Paper (Stanford University, August 1986). As an aside, empirical estimates of personal tax rates in the United States as a function of gross income do not factor in implicit taxes (and implicit subsidies). We are convinced that marginal tax rates have been far more progressive than, say, the estimates of Pechman. See Joseph A. Pechman, *Who Paid the Taxes, 1966–85?* (Brookings, 1985).

assets, such as fully taxable bonds. It is in this sense that tax clienteles and implicit taxes are interrelated.

One could factor contracting (and recontracting) costs into the analysis by defining implicit taxes to include such costs. Clienteles then arise not only because of differences in tax treatment across organizational forms but also because of cross-sectional differences in transaction costs. Such costs are an additional source of cross-sectional differences in total (explicit plus implicit) marginal tax rates. Moreover, the presence of recontracting costs introduces a degree of intertemporal dependence in tax planning: history plays a role in the sense that the tax costs of landing in the "wrong" clientele (following a change in market conditions or tax status) interact with the transaction costs of reorganizing corporate activities (mobility costs) in order to move the taxpayer into the "right" clientele.

Uncertain Future Tax Status and Changing Tax Clienteles

When the tax status of a firm changes, it generally will consider whether to alter its capital structure and its asset allocations. Low-taxed firms would want to buy assets that bear high explicit taxes and sell assets that bear high implicit taxes. For example, a firm that purchases equipment that is eligible for rapid depreciation for tax purposes when its tax rate is high may find it efficient to sell the equipment and perhaps lease it back when its tax rate falls. When managers are better informed about the prospects for the firm than are outsiders (hidden information), such restructuring might lead other market participants to infer that there is a change in the current or expected future tax-paying status of the firm. Since tax-paying status and real productivity are positively correlated, tax-induced changes in asset structure or capital structure could be accompanied by changes in the prices of publicly traded securities. Firms are "forced" to make the change in capital structure or asset makeup because of the implicit tax associated with being in the wrong tax clientele.

Empirical evidence to date is consistent with the valuation implications of this hypothesis. For example, it has been documented that leverage-increasing exchange offers (such as debt exchanged for common stock) are associated with increases in stock price. The opposite is true of leverage-decreasing exchange offers. Moreover, equity issues and convertible debt issues are associated with reductions in stock prices, whereas equity repurchases are associated with increases in stock prices.[17] This evidence increases confidence in using capital structure data to make inferences about a firm's tax-paying status.[18]

There are many alternative ways to restructure organizations that serve as substitutes for changes in debt or equity to respond to a change in tax status. For example, those firms expecting to move from low to high tax brackets might consider all of the following tax-motivated changes in strategy. (The opposite would be true for firms expecting a fall in marginal tax rates.)

DIRECT CHANGES IN CAPITAL STRUCTURE. The firm could issue more straight debt rather than common stock, warrants, preferred stock, or convertible debt. Although the interest rate on straight debt will be higher, interest payments are tax deductible. The calculus required here is one of trading off the implicit subsidy received from issuing capital structure components that give investors a tax advantage against the explicit subsidy from the tax deduction for interest on debt.

More specifically, the tax system encourages those firms with the highest expected marginal tax rates to issue "straight" debt with coupon interest fully deductible from taxable income. Among firms that issue straight debt, one would expect those with the highest expected marginal tax rates to issue the least secured debt, since risk premiums are deductible as paid even though they represent payments that compensate for expected future defaults.

The costs associated with reorganizing the capital structure in the face of a change in tax status have implications for the optimal duration of debt. For example, when refinancing is costly, the issuance of noncallable long-term debt will be less expensive than rolling over short-term debt to the same term provided that the issuer remains inframarginal with respect to borrowing long term for the duration of the loan. Not all firms can afford the luxury of relatively cheap after-tax long-term debt.

17. See Larry Y. Dann and Wayne H. Mikkelson, "Convertible Debt Issuance, Capital Structure Change and Financing-Related Information: Some New Evidence," *Journal of Financial Economics,* vol. 13 (June 1984), pp. 157–86, especially table 9; Ronald W. Masulis, "The Impact of Capital Structure Change on Firm Value: Some Estimates," *Journal of Finance,* vol. 38 (March 1983), pp. 107–26; and Clifford W. Smith, Jr., "Investment Banking and the Capital Acquisition Process," *Journal of Financial Economics,* vol. 15 (January–February 1986), pp. 3–29.

18. More evidence remains to be collected, however, especially with respect to changes in asset structure and compensation policy. Moreover, it will be important to show a direct association of tax-paying status with both financing policy and investment policy as well as with a change in share prices.

If the marginal tax rate becomes insufficient to use the tax shields of the long-term debt cost effectively, then the recapitalization costs associated with long-term debt may make short-term debt the more efficient financing strategy. Hence, issuers of long-term debt signal either that they expect to remain in high marginal tax brackets or that they expect reorganization costs to be low.[19]

Firms with expected marginal tax rates below those of the marginal holder of straight debt are induced by the tax rules to finance operations in ways that give the borrower smaller explicit tax subsidies (the value of which is increasing in marginal explicit tax rates)—for example, convertible debt, leases, warrants, preferred stock, common stock, limited partnerships, and joint ventures. The motivation for issuing each of these classes of debt or equity is the implicit subsidy paid to the firm by the suppliers of capital.

Firms with the lowest marginal explicit tax rates are encouraged to issue those instruments that offer the largest *implicit* tax subsidy. This means that the tax rules lead to financing with preferred stock and common stock for firms that expect marginal tax rates below those of firms making extensive use of convertible bonds, since convertible bonds provide both explicit and implicit tax subsidies to the issuer. On the other hand, when management is better informed about the prospects of the firm than are outside investors, equity issues might entail giving away too much of a bargain to outsiders.

The popularity of convertible bonds is interesting, because they would appear to have some undesirable tax characteristics. Although low current deductions for interest (relative to straight debt) are consistent with a lower marginal tax rate for issuing firms (relative to firms issuing straight debt), conversion into common stock takes place when the firm's stock increases in price. Such a conversion would alter the capital structure in a way that is less sensible for the firm than before its good fortune. A more efficient tax policy would be for the bonds to be convertible into straight debt, using the stock price as a conversion metric. Hence it is unlikely that the issuance of convertible bonds is motivated primarily by tax considerations.

Another important class of firms that forms a natural clientele for

19. Note that it is costly for a firm that does not expect to generate enough taxable income to use the interest deductions cost effectively to imitate the behavior of a firm that does expect to generate enough taxable income, because such behavior puts the firm in the wrong tax clientele.

particular financial instruments is those with significant uncertainty about their future tax status. Owing to the cost of changing the composition of capital structures, these firms must use relatively inefficient financing and investment policies to enable them to respond quickly to changes in their marginal tax rates. For example, as we discussed above, they would tend to use short-term debt when their tax rate is high. Alternatively, if marginal tax rates for these firms are highly correlated with reported income, income bonds would be a particularly tax-efficient form of financing. Such bonds require a payment that may depend on the level of corporate income. Tax-deductible payments are made to bondholders when income and tax rates are high. Although Miller lamented that few corporations issue such claims, many corporations do issue them indirectly.[20] Common examples of indirect income bonds include (1) risky bonds with promised fixed coupon payments payable only if the issuer is solvent; (2) operating leases with payments tied to revenue; (3) patent royalty agreements; (4) employee bonus plans tied to profitability; (5) pension plans where funding is timed to coincide with high tax rates; and (6) nonqualified employee stock option plans if there is a positive correlation between the stock price and the profitability of the firm.[21] As with income bonds, many of these contracts involve payments that are contingent upon the realization of a random variable (such as revenue or profit) that may be subject to manipulation by management. In addition, the contracts differ in their degree of correlation between interest payments and tax rates. Nontax costs of using direct income bonds might be greater than for these indirect instruments.[22]

20. Miller, "Debt and Taxes."
21. An employee stock option offers the employee the right to buy common stock at a fixed price (the "exercise price") for a fixed period of time. Such options are typically granted with an exercise price equal to the stock price on the date of grant. Despite being valuable, such options do not give rise to taxable income at the date the options are granted. Nonqualified options give rise to ordinary income to the employee (and compensation expense to the employer) equal to the difference between the stock price on the date the option is exercised and the exercise price. A qualified stock option (which requires a number of restrictions in the option contract) allows the employee to receive capital gains treatment if the stock is held for a period of at least two years. The capital gain is the difference between the sale price of the stock and the exercise price of the option. The corporation receives no deduction on exercise of the qualified stock option or on a subsequent sale of the stock if the employee receives capital gains treatment. See Gailen L. Hite and Michael S. Long, "Taxes and Executive Stock Options," *Journal of Accounting and Economics,* vol. 4 (July 1982), pp. 3–14, for further discussion.
22. Another possibility is that the taxing authority would reclassify direct income

CHANGES LINKED TO EMPLOYEE COMPENSATION CONTRACTS. Deferred compensation contracts (both those conditioned on the passage of time as well as those tied to future performance) become more attractive when the employer's tax rate is expected to be higher in the future (whether due to a reduced probability of not being able to use tax losses or for other reasons).[23] Similarly, nonqualified stock options become more attractive relative to incentive stock options. With more highly taxed income it becomes desirable to increase pension funding. Moreover, because of more generous funding opportunities, defined benefit pension plans become relatively more attractive than defined contribution plans. Overfunded pension accounts earn, tax free, at the before-tax rate of interest.[24] The desirability of overfunding pension plans depends on the extent of costs related to resolving any ambiguity of the property rights to such assets.

CHANGES LINKED TO CUSTOMER OR SUPPLIER CONTRACTING. Firms that expect their future tax rates to increase will find contracts that defer income to be relatively undesirable. Hence installment sales (where taxable income from the sale of goods is realized in proportion to

---

bonds as equity. See also John J. McConnell and Gary G. Schlarbaum, "Return, Risks and Pricing of Income Bonds, 1956–76 (Does Money Have an Odor?)" *Journal of Business*, vol. 54 (January 1981), pp. 33–63; McConnell and Schlarbaum, "Evidence on the Impact of Exchange Offers on Security Prices: The Case of Income Bonds," *Journal of Business*, vol. 54 (January 1981), pp. 65–85; and Sang Yong Park and Joseph Williams, "Taxes, Capital Structure, and Bondholder Clienteles," *Journal of Business*, vol. 58 (April 1985), pp. 203–24.

23. There may also be a rather severe identification problem in sorting out whether compensation packages are driven by tax considerations, incentive considerations, or both. See Merton H. Miller and Myron S. Scholes, "Executive Compensation, Taxes, and Incentives," in William F. Sharpe and Cathryn M. Cootner, eds., *Financial Economics: Essays in Honor of Paul Cootner* (Prentice-Hall, 1982), pp. 179–215; Clifford W. Smith, Jr., and Ross L. Watts, "Incentive and Tax Effects of Executive Compensation Plans," *Australian Journal of Management*, vol. 7 (December 1982), pp. 139–57; Smith and Watts, "The Structure of Executive Compensation Contracts and the Control of Management," Working Paper 81-7 (University of Rochester, Center for Research in Government Policy and Business, March 1984); and Scholes and Wolfson, "Employee Compensation and Taxes."

24. A defined benefit pension plan defines the employee benefit (for example, 50 percent of final salary each year after retirement at age 65 until the death of the employee). A defined contribution pension plan defines the contributions into the plan (for example, 10 percent of current salary is contributed to a pension account for the employee). Determination of the level of funding of a defined benefit plan requires projections of such things as the growth rate of fund assets and salaries as well as the rate of turnover of employees. Estimates can be conservative (leading to overfunding of the pension plan) or liberal (leading to underfunding of the pension plan). See Scholes and Wolfson, "Employee Compensation and Taxes," for further discussion of these tax planning issues.

principal payments received on a note issued by the seller to the buyer) become less attractive from a tax standpoint. Installment sales become more attractive, however, once the tax rate of the firm has increased and is expected to remain high.

Another way to shift income across periods is to sell or buy on credit, using credit terms that differ from market terms. The bargain or punishment element of the credit terms translates into a higher or lower "price" charged for the goods or services that are being financed. For example, if the seller of a good offers the buyer cheap financing, this results in a higher sale price, which in turn leads to higher current taxable income to the seller (lower taxable income to the buyer as the asset is expensed for tax purposes) and lower interest income to the seller in the future (and correspondingly higher income to the buyer due to reduced interest expense in the future).[25]

Note how careful one must be here in linking changes in capital structure to changes in tax status. A firm that generates net operating losses may actually issue debt (at below-market rates to finance the sale of assets) rather than equity to *reduce* its tax burden. A powerful empirical test of how taxes affect financing and investment decisions requires factoring much more structure into experimental designs rather than simply using first differences in debt-to-equity ratios.

CHANGES LINKED TO INVESTMENT POLICY. Lease obligations represent an important capital structure component. When the tax rate of a firm increases, it may be efficient to engage more heavily in buying rather than leasing long-lived assets. As we discussed above, it is tax efficient for low-tax firms to make extensive use of leasing (rather than buying) of durable assets.[26] As with the issuance of equity, the before-tax

25. The Deficit Reduction Act of 1984 introduced new original issue discount rules to reduce the use of below-market rate loans to increase the reported sales price of an asset. Under the new rules a loan is viewed as being below the market rate when the rate on the loan is below the "applicable federal rate" (a riskless government bond rate matched to the term of the loan). Although firms that issue risky loans at this riskless rate clearly issue a loan with a below-market interest rate, it is not treated as such under the tax code. As discussed in Scholes and Wolfson, even with the new rules, many tax planning opportunities still exist to use below-market-rate demand loans effectively in the compensation programs for employees. See Myron S. Scholes and Mark A. Wolfson, "Compensatory Loans to Executives Before and After the Tax Act of 1984," Working Paper (Stanford University, Graduate School of Business, September 1985).

26. Shaw documents striking evidence of a propensity to engage in leasing as a means of exploiting firms' low marginal tax rates. In particular, 85 percent of the firms in his sample that sold tax benefits under "safe harbor lease" contracts during 1981

financing cost is reduced relative to that associated with the issuance of straight debt. The nature of the information problems, however, may be quite different with lease financing than with equity financing. It is not difficult to construct examples in which leasing gives rise to no information-related costs of issuance at all (hidden information costs), whereas such costs are quite high when equity is issued. On the other hand, owned property tends to be better maintained and hence more valuable than leased property, a hidden action problem.[27] Hence the optimal capital structure will depend not only on the firm's tax status but also on the nature of its information problems (that is, the contracting cost component of the implicit taxes associated with various elements of the capital structure). Moreover, the firm need not stop at buying its own equipment. It could lease equipment to other companies that are inframarginal with respect to the tax benefits of ownership. General Electric Credit Corporation and many commercial banks provide dramatic examples of this phenomenon.[28]

CHANGES IN INVESTMENT POLICY. The above discussion suggests that there are investment policy changes that represent substitutes for capital structure changes as a potential response to changes in tax status. Four examples of such changes are the purchase of other companies, research and development, other tax-favored investments, and multinational investments.

The expectation of an increase in taxes could trigger a firm's purchase of other companies (in the same or other industries) that have net operating losses. This strategy does not drive the firm's effective tax rate to zero, for it must pay an implicit tax on acquiring the tax shelter; that is, it must share the tax advantage with the shareholders of the

disclosed tax loss or credit carryforwards and at least $50 million in capital expenditures in their 1980 annual reports. See Wayne H. Shaw, "Measuring the Impact of the Safe Harbor Lease Law on Security Prices," Working Paper (Cornell University, Johnson Graduate School of Management, August 1987).

27. See Jensen and Meckling, "Theory of the Firm"; Mark A. Wolfson, "Tax, Incentive, and Risk-Sharing Issues in the Allocation of Property Rights: The Generalized Lease-or-Buy Problem," Journal of Business, vol. 58 (April 1985), pp. 159–71; and Clifford W. Smith, Jr., and L. MacDonald Wakeman, "Determinants of Corporate Leasing Policy," Journal of Finance, vol. 40 (July 1985), pp. 895–908.

28. Stickney, Weil, and Wolfson estimate that General Electric Credit Corporation paid roughly seventy cents on the dollar for over $1.5 billion in tax benefits related to safe harbor leasing contracts in 1981. See Clyde P. Stickney, Roman L. Weil, and Mark A. Wolfson, "Income Taxes and Tax-Transfer Leases: General Electric's Accounting for a Molotov Cocktail," Accounting Review, vol. 58 (April 1983), pp. 439–59, especially p. 443.

acquired company. For example, if a purchase premium (including all costs of effecting the purchase) of thirty cents is paid for each dollar of tax loss carryforward of a target company, the acquiring company's implicit tax rate would be 30 percent. (We mentioned companies in the same industry because of a firm's expertise in this field.) An imperfectly competitive market for corporate combinations could leave a buyer with a larger share of the tax benefits and therefore a lower implicit rate of tax. Gilson, Scholes, and Wolfson describe various other ways in which taxes and information problems interact to determine the efficacy of a merger or other asset restructuring.[29]

The firm that faces an increase in tax rates could increase the scale of its own internal research and development (R&D) programs. Some firms contract out R&D programs (either directly or through limited partnerships) for the same tax reasons that they lease rather than buy durable goods. Internal R&D programs create their own tax credits and the immediate deductibility of the expenditures incurred in running them. As with ownership of durable assets, internal R&D also mitigates costly incentive problems that would otherwise naturally arise when the research is conducted by outsiders or is conducted by insiders but financed with outsiders' funds through a partnership or joint venture.[30]

The advertising policies and charitable contributions of firms should be affected by their tax rate. Firms facing lower tax rates because of reduced profitability might find it desirable to increase the budget for these items. This would reduce current taxable income (at a high marginal tax rate) in exchange for increased future income from, for example, sales generated by advertising campaigns that are designed to have a long-term effect on demand. Similar incentives exist to increase market research and personnel costs to lay the foundation for expansion of product offerings. In addition, the firm could replace nontaxable municipal bonds with taxable high-yielding interest-bearing securities. More

29. Ronald J. Gilson, Myron S. Scholes, and Mark A. Wolfson, "Taxation and the Dynamics of Corporate Control: The Uncertain Case for Tax Motivated Acquisitions," in John C. Coffee, Jr., Louis Lowenstein, and Susan Rose-Ackerman, eds., *Knights, Raiders, and Targets: The Impact of the Hostile Takeover* (Oxford University Press, 1988). As described above, the 1986 Tax Reform Act made it more difficult to use net operating losses where there is a significant change in the ownership of the loss firm.

30. Shevlin presents empirical evidence that is consistent with these arguments. See Terrence J. Shevlin, "Research and Development Limited Partnerships: An Empirical Analysis of Taxes and Incentives" (Ph.D. dissertation, Stanford University, 1986), chap. 5.

generally, firms in low tax brackets avoid tax shelters such as real estate, advertising, and R&D (unless they sell the tax benefits to highly taxed entities), and firms in high brackets naturally hold municipal bonds, high-dividend-paying common and preferred stock, and a variety of other tax-sheltered investments.

The explicit marginal tax rate is lower, in present value, on foreign-source income generated in certain countries (for example, Ireland or Hong Kong) than it is on domestic income, because the U.S. tax on this income (other than so-called subpart F income, which is passive income) is deferred until it is repatriated to the United States. In addition, certain countries (for example, Japan, Germany, and a number of other European countries) impose higher tax rates than does the United States (even more so under the 1986 act). Limitations on the use of foreign tax credits depend, in part, on the distribution of worldwide income and tax rates. When a firm's profitability increases, its demand for shelter may increase or decrease, depending on whether the increase comes primarily from low-tax jurisdictions or high-tax jurisdictions. A change in the firm's tax status can have dramatic implications for its multinational investment and financing decisions, especially with respect to its repatriation policies.

Implications for the Efficient Design of Experiments

We have explored some of the ways in which the economic balance sheet of a firm might be reorganized in response to a change in the firm's tax status. These reorganization opportunities are only suggestive of a broad menu of possible strategies available to firms with changing prospects for profitability. One point should be kept clear: firms have strong incentives to engage in costly tax planning that exploits cross-sectional and intertemporal differences in marginal tax rates. However, as argued above, although there are ample opportunities for them to do so, costs might preclude them from exploiting many of these opportunities. The marginal tax rate could be quite different from the rate that a naive analysis would suggest, namely, either zero or the maximum statutory rate. To determine the correct rate requires consideration of many tax planning options, how tax benefits are shared among the various tax clienteles (implicit taxes), the cost of switching from one clientele to another, and the fundamental underlying uncertainty not only of prospects for future profitability but also of the tax rules themselves.

Myers points out that the empirical evidence collected to date of the relation between the form of financing and investment and the firm's tax status is weak.[31] He claims there is no study that clearly demonstrates that a firm's tax status affects its debt policy (or asset allocation). He also claims that the prospects are bleak for documenting such relations in the future. Although we agree that the evidence to date has been weak, so have the experimental designs underlying the evidence. The studies do not exploit the rich set of substitutes in tax planning, the role that history and transaction costs play in locking in certain aspects of asset and capital structure (the tests are cross-sectional rather than longitudinal), or the importance of industry-specific or multinational tax rules. Cross-sectional tests using seasoned firms in a variety of industries are unlikely to yield powerful results.

To illustrate some of the possibilities, we have conducted a pilot study, summarized below, on the relation between financing, asset allocation, and compensation policies of sixty firms that went public during 1979 and whose financial statements were available in the library of the Stanford Business School. These firms are interesting because a majority of them start with tax loss carryforwards and tax credits, without any previous history of taxable income. This contrasts with companies that were once profitable, experienced financial distress, and changed components of their asset and capital structures without a complete reversal of policy because of the costs of restructuring operations or the costs of reorganizing specific elements of the capital structure.[32] By conducting cross-sectional tests on seasoned firms, one may well miss changes in policies that are related to changes in tax status. It is important to recognize that with costly restructuring, the most efficient response for some firms to a change in tax status will be to change leasing policy first; for others, to change debt policy; for still

31. Myers, "The Capital Structure Puzzle."
32. Leasing is a good example of the restructuring problem. Although changing from leasing to owning could reduce agency costs and other costs, it might not be possible for a firm to switch in the short run. Owing to the depreciation and investment tax credit recapture provisions of the tax laws, contracts might preclude a firm from terminating its lease. Similarly, a firm with a large portfolio of appreciated municipal bonds might find it too costly to sell such assets (due to the acceleration of the capital gains tax) despite a drop in its marginal tax rate that would render a *new* purchase of municipal bonds suboptimal.

others, to change asset allocations. Tests devised to account for changes among a set of policies could be more efficient than univariate or multivariate cross-sectional tests. There is a drawback here as well. Since we argue that the dimensionality of the tax planning problem is so large relative to that reflected in the traditional experiments, improved specification of the problem might impose a loss of too many degrees of freedom in estimating the many parameters of the system.

After the fact, it is obvious that from a tax planning standpoint a firm with net operating losses would prefer to have no debt in its capital structure. If there were no reorganization costs, it would prefer to use such strategies as exchanging its outstanding debt issues for equity. Such reorganization plans, however, really cannot be implemented without costs. For example, some risky debt may be redeemable only at par; or costs to exchange public debt as reflected in the premium paid to effect the exchange could easily be large enough to wipe out the tax advantage. The reason for the required premium is that an exchange of equity for some fraction of outstanding risky debt would increase the value of the remaining risky debt, since it becomes less risky. This increase in the value of the risky debt is at the expense of shareholders; again, the tax planning benefits may be vitiated. It is for reasons such as these that casual empirical observers might conclude that firms were not following optimal tax planning policies or that taxes appeared not to matter to the capital structure decision. They might observe debt in the capital structure of firms with net operating losses. Such observations are by no means anomalous, however, when reorganization costs are sufficiently high that apparent tax benefits rationally are left on the table.

It is for the reasons discussed above that we were motivated to consider the case of newly public companies. A high fraction of these firms begin public life with net operating loss carryforwards. History should pollute their decisions much less than those of seasoned companies. And our evidence suggests that tax status *does* affect their decisions. For example, these firms use relatively little debt and rarely have pension plans. On the other hand, deferred compensation that is tied to future profitability (and hence tax status) is pervasive. Moreover, only four of the sixty firms in our pilot study used the last-in, first-out (LIFO) method to value inventories: when prices are rising and tax rates are not, LIFO minimizes taxable income. None of these four firms had net operating loss, investment tax credit, research and development tax credit, or foreign tax credit carryforwards during the three years after going public, although thirty-four other sample firms had such carryforwards, something that could occur by chance only 3.5 percent of the time.[33]

The upshot of the analysis is not only to exhort the researcher to look more broadly in search for evidence of the relation among tax status, capital structure, and asset structure, but also to argue that the marginal cost of capital will be idiosyncratic. This occurs for two sets of reasons: (1) entity-specific tax characteristics (for example, accumulated capital gains and recapture taxes on long-lived assets that are a function of the date of purchase and purchase price of assets; industry-specific tax rules, including those that pertain both to tax rates as well as to special income and recognition rules; and multiple tax jurisdiction considerations); and (2) entity-specific transaction costs that affect the desirability of various tax plans and reorganizations.

When changes in tax regimes occur, these idiosyncrasies in tax status become even more pervasive, because many taxpayers find themselves situated in the wrong clientele under the new rules. We turn next to a consideration of the 1986 Tax Reform Act to illustrate how a change in tax rules can affect both the desirability of alternative organizational forms for new investment activities and the desirability of reorganizing ongoing economic activities.

Organizational Form: The Implications of the 1986 Act

The 1986 act changed the tax rules dramatically for both individuals and corporations. The top marginal tax rate is scheduled to be reduced from 50 percent to 28 percent in 1988 for the highest-earning individuals (although there is a broad income range over which individuals face a 33 percent marginal tax rate before the rate once again becomes 28 percent). The top corporate rate is scheduled to be reduced from 46 percent to 34 percent, and the corporate add-on minimum tax, which resulted in a 39.1

33. For example, the 1983 balance sheet and income statement of Genetic Systems Corporation reveal that since its inception in 1980 it has suffered losses. It has established investment partnerships with profitable firms, committed to noncancelable operating leases, financed research and development through limited partnerships, issued incentive stock options for tax purposes to a far greater degree than nonqualified options, issued warrants and common stock, held interest-bearing marketable securities on corporate account, and issued little long-term debt. It has no pension plan. These are good examples of the expected associations of capital structure, asset structure, and compensation policy with the tax-paying status of the firm.

percent marginal tax rate when binding, was replaced by an alternative minimum tax, which results in a 20 percent tax rate when binding.[34] The rates are phased in over a two-year period. In 1987 the top marginal rate for individuals is 38.5 percent; the top marginal rate for (calendar year-end) corporations is 40 percent.[35]

When changes in tax rates occur over several tax years, it is desirable to time deductions to coincide with high tax rates and to time income to coincide with low tax rates. Tax planning becomes a bit more delicate when planning involves entering into contracts in which the tax rates of all of the contracting parties are changing in the same direction at the same time. In such a case it may not be possible to effect a tax arbitrage even without transaction costs. Moreover, it may become rational for a firm to accelerate the recognition of taxable income despite a falling tax rate, if this results in a tax deduction being symmetrically accelerated for another contracting party whose tax rate is falling even faster.[36]

Transition years such as 1986–88 or 1981–84 serve as a valuable laboratory to observe transactions among individuals and corporations with different fiscal years and different marginal tax rates. Owing to the importance of transaction costs, many reorganization strategies that would be efficient in a frictionless setting will be too expensive to

34. The alternative minimum tax is equal to 20 percent of the corporation's regular taxable income increased by tax preferences. For most corporations, the main preferences include accelerated depreciation and, for a three-year period, one-half of the excess of before-tax book income reported to stockholders over alternative minimum taxable income. This latter adjustment will affect those corporations that generate income that is exempt from the regular income tax, such as municipal bond interest and dividend income otherwise subject to 80 percent exclusion (down from 85 percent), both of which are included in book income. The adjustment also applies to the large number of accounting items that give rise to book income or book expenses at different times than do taxable income or tax deductions.

Note that reduced federal tax rates effectively increase state and local income and property tax rates, and such taxes become a more important ingredient in planning for capital structures. In addition, U.S. tax rates are much lower now than rates in many foreign countries. Unless these countries respond by reducing their rates, many corporations will restructure foreign operations and will repatriate profits earlier than woud have been the case under pre-1986 rules. The new alternative minimum tax credit, however, may soften the blow of the alternative minimum tax on such timing differences.

35. Companies with noncalendar fiscal years face higher marginal tax rates early in 1987 and lower marginal rates later in 1987. For example, a corporation whose fiscal year runs from June to June faces a 46 percent marginal rate throughout its fiscal year ending in June 1987, when its marginal rate drops to 34 percent.

36. For further discussion, see Myron S. Scholes and Mark A. Wolfson, "Taxes and Employee Compensation Planning," Taxes—The Tax Magazine, vol. 64 (December 1986), pp. 824–34.

implement in the more realistic settings from which empirical observations will be drawn. For this reason, transition periods provide the researcher with a golden opportunity to gather indirect measures of the costs of recontracting among entities and the effects of changes in tax rules on economic activity.

The Miller Equilibrium under the 1986 Act

If it were not for information and transaction costs, the 1986 act would cause massive restructuring of productive activities. Corporations would be replaced as an organizational form by partnerships for new equity-financed ventures; many existing firms would convert to partnership form; and without this conversion many corporations would add debt to their capital structures.

To see this, we begin with a comparison of the after-tax returns available to investment in corporate and partnership form. Let us denote the required rate of return on debt by r_b. For illustrative purposes assume that the rate is 9 percent and the tax rate of the marginal investor setting prices in the market, t_{pb}, is 28 percent. The municipal bond rate, r_o, would then be 6.48 percent, as required by the following relation:

$$(1) \qquad r_o = r_b (1 - t_{pb}) = 0.09 (1 - 0.28) = 0.0648.$$

The marginal investor is indifferent between holding municipal bonds yielding 6.48 percent and taxable bonds yielding 9 percent. Moreover, in equilibrium, the after-tax risk-adjusted rate of return to stockholders must also be equal to 6.48 percent. Similarly, those activities conducted in partnership (or sole proprietorship) form would also return 6.48 percent after all price adjustments in the market (including implicit taxes resulting from market frictions).

For the corporate organizational form to be competitive, the corporation must earn at a before-tax rate high enough that it can pay corporate taxes, its stockholders can pay personal taxes, and stockholders will still be left with 6.48 percent after tax. Assume for the moment that the tax on income from holding shares, t_{ps}, is equal to zero and that the corporate tax rate, t_c, is equal to 34 percent. In equilibrium, the corporation, before paying corporate taxes, would have to earn at the following rate, r_c, per unit of capital investment:

$$(2) \quad r_b (1 - t_{pb})/(1 - t_c) = 0.09 (1 - 0.28)/(1 - 0.34) = 0.09818.$$

That is, if corporations return 9.818 percent on a risk-adjusted basis before corporate tax, shareholders will be left with 6.48 percent after corporate tax, or 0.09818 (1 − 0.34). Note that if the marginal tax bracket of investors in partnerships is 28 percent, then partnerships dominate corporations even if the tax on shares were equal to zero. The partnership would have to earn only 9 percent before tax to be competitive with passive investments. If, on the other hand, the marginal investor setting prices in the market were in a 33 percent bracket, and before-tax bond returns remained at 9 percent, the required before-tax returns for the alternative organizational forms would be much closer (r_c = 9.136 percent for the corporation versus r_p = 9 percent for the partnership).[37]

Now relax the assumption that the tax on holding capital assets such as bonds and stock is equal to zero. After all, the 1986 act eliminated the exclusion for long-term capital gains at both the personal level and the corporate level. After 1987 capital gains (losses) will be taxed as ordinary income (loss); and losses will still be limited to $3,000 per year. These changes influence dramatically the explicit shareholder-level tax, t_{ps}. It is still possible to bequeath appreciated assets upon death to escape capital gains tax, or to donate appreciated stock to tax-exempt organizations (although the untaxed gain potentially is subject to the alternative minimum tax for individuals, at a rate of up to 21 percent), or to make a gift of appreciated securities to low-income relatives, other than children under 14 years of age (to have the gain taxed at their lower rates). Those investors selling shares, however, will be subject to a marginal tax rate on the related gain that increases from a maximum of 20 percent (28 percent for corporate investors) under the rules in 1986 to 28 percent or 33 percent (34 percent for corporate investors) in 1988 and beyond. The 1986 act also eliminates the opportunity to use installment sales to defer the gain on the sale of publicly traded shares. Moreover, corporate investors will be able to exclude only 80 percent of dividends received from these investments, and may be subject to the 20 percent alternative minimum tax on 60 percent of the dividend.[38] The rate of tax on shares

37. Before the 1986 act, corporations could be competitive with partnerships from a tax standpoint even with a moderate tax on shares at the stockholder level. For example, a 46 percent corporate-level tax and a 7.4 percent shareholder-level tax imply a before-tax required rate of return to corporate investments that is equal to that on partnership investments if the partners are taxed at a 50 percent rate.

38. Hence the marginal explicit tax rate on dividends to corporate holders is 6.8 percent when the alternative minimum tax is not binding and up to 12 percent when it

is likely to be far greater after the Tax Reform Act takes effect than before.

There are those who might argue with the claim that the tax on shares was low enough before 1986 so that the risk-adjusted before-tax rate of return on shares was close to the municipal bond rate.[39] In fact, Gordon and Malkiel address these issues directly.[40] They argue that even if one could defer the tax on capital gains, corporations pay out over 55 percent of their earnings as dividends. They conclude that the resulting tax on shares could be as high as 50 percent of the tax on interest. Others argue that even if a tax is paid on dividend and capital gains income by a substantial number of highly taxed investors, the marginal investor setting prices in the market might be a taxpayer for whom the tax on dividends and capital gains is very low (for example, below 10 percent) on the margin. For example, Miller and Scholes argue that the marginal investors in shares can convert dividends into untaxed (or tax-deferred) capital gains by leveraging their stock holdings so that the interest deductions erase the taxable dividend income.[41] Kalay, Miller and Scholes, and Stiglitz argue that short-term traders such as brokers can profit if the returns on dividends differ from the returns on capital gains.[42] Such traders ensure that the prices of high dividend-paying securities are not very different from the prices of low dividend-paying securities. It is not appropriate to use the average tax paid on dividend and capital

is (although it is only 4 percent when the alternative minimum tax is binding and dividends are not tax preference items).

Although one might be tempted to argue that pension funds are the marginal investor in shares and, for this reason, t_{ps} can be assumed to be zero, this would further imply that the return on shares would be equal to the return on bonds, a relation that is inconsistent with the Miller equilibrium.

39. The extensive literature on the cost of capital is reviewed in Alan J. Auerbach, "Taxation, Corporate Financial Policy and the Cost of Capital," *Journal of Economic Literature,* vol. 21 (September 1983), pp. 905–40.

40. Roger H. Gordon and Burton G. Malkiel, "Corporation Finance," in Henry J. Aaron and Joseph A. Pechman, eds., *How Taxes Affect Economic Behavior* (Brookings, 1981), pp. 131–98. See also James M. Poterba and Lawrence H. Summers, "New Evidence That Taxes Affect the Valuation of Dividends," *Journal of Finance,* vol. 39 (December 1984), pp. 1397–1415.

41. Merton H. Miller and Myron S. Scholes, "Dividends and Taxes," *Journal of Financial Economics,* vol. 6 (December 1978), pp. 333–64.

42. Avner Kalay, "The Ex-Dividend Day Behavior of Stock Prices: A Reexamination of the Clientele Effect," *Journal of Finance,* vol. 37 (September 1982), pp. 1059–70; Merton H. Miller and Myron S. Scholes, "Dividends and Taxes: Some Empirical Evidence," *Journal of Political Economy,* vol. 90 (December 1982), pp. 1118–41; and Stiglitz, "The General Theory of Tax Avoidance."

COST OF CAPITAL AND CHANGES IN TAX REGIMES

gains income to infer the tax paid on shares by the marginal investor. The tax on dividends and capital gains is likely to be far lower than is implied by these methods. Although the empirical evidence is mixed,[43] estimates tend to suggest that the returns on dividend-paying securities are not very different from the returns on nondividend-paying securities of similar risk. In any case, if the tax on shares was significantly greater than zero before 1986, one must still rely on nontax costs to explain why corporations financed so many new projects by equity rather than by partnerships or debt financing.

Even after 1986, deferral of the tax on shares until sale helps to lower the present value of the explicit tax on shares to a rate that is below the maximum statutory rate. Holding nondividend-paying shares now gives rise to explicit tax treatment similar to that from holding a single premium-deferred annuity: taxation of the interim share appreciation is deferred until realized by sale or liquidation. To illustrate this effect, assume that the marginal investor setting prices in the stock market holds shares for n years. To find the equivalent annual rate of return on shares, r_s, that will make investors indifferent between paying the tax currently or at the end of n years, we must solve the relation:

$$(3) \qquad [(1 + r_s)^n (1 - t_{pb}) + t_{pb}]^{1/n} - 1 = r_b (1 - t_{pb}).$$

If we assume that n, the average holding period on shares (including the liquidation represented by dividends), is six years, and we continue to assume that $r_b = 9$ percent and $t_{pb} = 28$ percent, then $r_s = 8.54$ percent per year. That is, even though the tax on holding shares is deferred for six years, the required annual rate of return on shares before stockholder taxes is 8.54 percent; thus, after stockholders pay personal taxes at that time, they earn an annualized return of 6.48 percent, which is equivalent to what they would have earned from holding taxable bonds on which they would pay the tax each year. This translates into an equivalent annual explicit tax on shares, t_e, of 22.897 percent (24.15 percent tax on the reduced before-tax yield of 8.54 percent, or $[0.0854 - 0.0648] / 0.09$) and an implicit tax on shares of only 5.11 percent (or $[0.09 - 0.0854] / 0.09$). The total tax rate is 28 percent (22.89 percent explicit plus 5.11 percent implicit), and this makes shares and bonds perfect substitutes

43. See, for example, Miller and Scholes, "Dividends and Taxes" (1978); and Robert H. Litzenberger and Krishna Ramaswamy, "The Effects of Dividends on Common Stock Prices: Tax Effects or Information Effects?" *Journal of Finance*, vol. 37 (May 1982), pp. 429–43.

for the 28 percent explicitly taxed taxpayer who would hold stock for six years.[44]

With an explicit tax on shares of 24.15 percent of the before-tax return, the required rate of return on equity-financed investments in corporate form must now increase from $r_c = 0.0982$ before tax to $0.0982/(1 - t_e) = 9.82/(1 - 0.24) = 0.1295$ before tax.[45] If the required before-tax risk-adjusted rate of return on new investments in corporate form is 12.95 percent, and in partnership form is only 9 percent, corporations cannot compete with partnerships to attract equity capital to be used in the production of goods and services. Growth of the corporate form of organization requires enormous nontax advantages of corporations over partnerships.

It is obvious from this exercise that under the new tax regime it will be difficult to achieve a Miller equilibrium in which the corporate tax advantage to issuing debt is small. Although the tax shield on debt has been reduced because marginal statutory corporate tax rates have fallen from 46 percent to 34 percent, this does not imply that corporations will issue additional equity, as has been naively claimed in the popular press. In our example, the required rate of return on equity-financed corporate investments is 12.95 percent before tax and 8.55 percent after a 34 percent corporate tax; the cost to issue bonds is 9 percent before tax and 5.94 percent after a 34 percent corporate tax reduction. If a corporation

44. Assuming that before the 1986 act the municipal bond rate was 6.48 percent, the marginal holder of bonds was in a 50 percent tax bracket, and the marginal holder of shares deferred gain recognition for only six years and paid tax at a 20 percent rate at that time (40 percent of the gain taxed at a rate of 50 percent), the required annual rate of return on shares would have been 7.829 percent and the required before-tax bond rate (and return to partnership investments) would have been 12.96 percent. In this example, the equivalent annual explicit tax on shares would have been only 10.4 percent per year (the implicit tax on shares would have been 39.6 percent). By using an installment sale to defer the payment of the capital gains tax on the sale of the asset, the annual explicit tax on shares could have been reduced to substantially less than 10.4 percent (and as indicated in footnote 37, a 7.4 percent rate of tax on shares would equate the required before-tax rates of return for investments in corporations and partnerships).

Since empirical evidence suggests that before the 1986 act the equilibrium value of dividend income was little, if at all, different from the equilibrium value of capital gains, it is unimportant to distinguish between dividend-paying stocks and nondividend-paying stocks in these examples. See ibid.

45. Alternatively, the required rate, r_c, must satisfy: $\{[1 + r_c(1 - t_c)]^n(1 - pt_{pb}) + t_{pb}\}^{1/n} = (1 + r_b)(1 - t_{pb})$. For $t_c = 0.34$, $t_{pb} = 0.28$, $r_b = 0.09$, and $n = 6$, $r_c = 0.1295$. For $n = 20$, $r_c = 0.1181$; and for $n = 100$, $r_c = 0.1035$. For infinite holding periods, $r_c = 0.09818$, the same as if the explicit tax on shares were 0 percent.

taxed at 34 percent could issue debt at an after-tax cost of 5.94 percent and invest the proceeds at an after-tax return of 8.53 percent, it would be quite eager to increase leverage.[46]

If reorganization costs are ignored, corporations facing this set of required rates of return under the new tax regime would prefer to reorganize as partnerships. With tax and other reorganization costs, however, an alternative is to substitute debt for equity to finance marginal investments.[47] The reason that substituting debt for equity is an alternative to reorganizing as a partnership is that both types of restructuring result in profits being taxed only once. As discussed earlier, the corporation will also have an increased demand for tax shelters (such as holding municipal bonds or engaging in leasing transactions). By converting its income from being explicitly taxed at the corporate level to being implicitly taxed at a rate that is determined by the price of tax shelters in the marketplace, the corporation may achieve a tax outcome that is closer to that of a partnership than its legal form might suggest. The new corporate alternative minimum tax, however, represents a major constraint on this endeavor. If corporations invest sufficient

46. We still can think of situations in which the advantages of issuing debt would be small under the 1986 act, but such situations would seem to be perverse. For example, if the marginal holder of shares were an individual who avoided capital gains taxes by contributing shares to a charitable organization or by holding the shares until death, the tax on shares would be zero for a nondividend-paying stock. If, in addition, the marginal investors setting prices in the bond market were taxed at a rate of 33 percent, rather than 28 percent, then the advantages of issuing debt would be significantly smaller. The after-tax required rate of return on shares in this special case becomes 6.03 percent (or $0.09[1 - 0.33]$), and the required before-tax rate of return on new corporate investment becomes 9.14 percent (or $0.0603/[1 - 0.34]$). In this situation the after-tax advantage of issuing debt is 6.03 percent minus 5.94 percent for the 34 percent marginal tax rate corporation.

47. The tax costs of converting to a partnership include the realization of a capital gain at the stockholder level. After 1986 the corporation will also be subject to a capital gains tax on the sale of assets that have a market value above tax basis; that is, it can no longer use the liquidation rules that allow stockholders to escape the capital gains tax at the corporate level (the effect of eliminating the so-called General Utilities doctrine). Conversion to a partnership also triggers recapture of depreciation as well as a loss of tax attributes such as net operating losses and investment tax credit carryovers. (See Gilson, Scholes, and Wolfson, "Taxation and the Dynamics of Corporate Control," for further discussion of these issues.) Moreover, if the conversion takes place after 1986, the partnership may inherit a less attractive depreciation schedule for its durable assets than the corporation would have enjoyed before the conversion. Finally, conversion effectively forces some tax-exempt investors to sell their shares (or to hold them indirectly in other organizational forms) since such investors must pay tax on "unrelated business income" earned through partnership interests.

amounts in tax-sheltered investments, the alternative minimum tax will exceed the regular tax. When this occurs, the marginal explicit tax rate becomes as low as 20 percent. At this low rate, the corporation becomes inframarginal with respect to holding taxable bonds and other tax-disfavored investments. In addition, it would no longer be optimal to issue debt as long as t_{pb} is set by investors with marginal tax rates above 20 percent. Instead, the corporation would want to increase taxable income by buying tax-disadvantaged assets such as bonds until its next dollar of income was taxed at a rate above the alternative minimum tax rate.[48] With uncertain taxable income, year-end tax planning becomes much more important for the corporation than in the prereform era, and optimal strategies become much more heavily dependent on the transaction costs associated with year-end reorganization of economic balance sheets.

Dividend Policy under the 1986 Act

Without an ability to reorganize at the corporate level to achieve tax treatment equivalent to that imposed on partnerships, a logical question arises as to whether the corporation should shrink its size by paying (liquidating) dividends. An important consideration here is that the required rate of return on retained earnings is less than that on new investment. To see this more clearly, consider the firm with $1 of retained earnings. Assume that the marginal tax bracket of its stockholders is t_{po} today and t_{pn} at time period n. Assume that on personal account stockholders can earn $r_{at,\,pn}$ per period after personal taxes and that the

48. Note that it would be suboptimal for a firm to finance additional capital investments with debt and to forgo accelerated depreciation allowances to avoid generating tax preferences. Although such a strategy enables avoidance of not only the alternative minimum tax but also all regular income tax, the before-tax return available on such investments bears an implicit tax because highly taxed investors compete for the right to take accelerated depreciation.

Many leasing companies will cease to play the role of lessor once their level of leasing activities gives rise to tax preferences of sufficient magnitude to subject them to the alternative minimum tax. Assuming such lessors have developed expertise in arranging leasing contracts, however, they will likely syndicate leasing deals with those corporations still paying tax at the marginal explicit rate of 34 percent. Such syndication deals will impose implicit taxes on their lessors through extra costs associated with such multiparty transactions. The propensity to syndicate leasing deals is also affected by the availability of an alternative minimum tax *credit* in years following the imposition of the alternative minimum tax.

firm can earn $r_{at, cn}$ per period after corporate taxes. Shareholders would wish the firm to retain the $1 of earnings if and only if:

(4) $$(1 - t_{po}) (1 + r_{at, pn})^n < (1 + r_{at, cn})^n (1 - t_{pn}).$$

If the corporation can invest its retained earnings at the same after-tax rate as its shareholders (that is, $r_{at, pn} = r_{at, cn}$), the advantage of the retention of earnings depends on whether the marginal tax rate of the shareholder is greater currently or in the future (that is, whether $[1 - t_{po}]$ is greater than or less than $[t - t_{pn}]$). If the tax rate of any shareholder is expected to decline, retention at the corporate level is tax advantageous. Even if tax rates are expected to remain the same on average, but vary through time, retention provides all shareholders with a valuable timing option to realize a capital gain and pay a tax when their tax rate at some period s is such that $t_{ps} < t_{po}$. This occurs, for example, when a shareholder is subject to the personal alternative minimum tax rate of 21 percent, when statutory tax rates change, when a shareholder desires to make a charitable contribution (in which case $t_{ps} = 0$), when a shareholder holds until death (in which case $t_{ps} = 0$), or when a shareholder makes a gift of stock to a lower-income relative (in which case $t_{ps} =$ the tax rate of the relative at time s). Each alternative requires a consideration of implicit taxes. If there are nontax advantages to being in corporate form, such that $r_{at, cn} > r_{at, pn}$, there are further incentives to invest retained earnings in corporate form rather than pay dividends. Moreover, if the firm retains earnings, shareholders are less likely to realize capital losses on their shareholdings at the time of sale, which could otherwise prove costly due to the $3,000 capital loss limitation.

Still, dividends impose a smaller tax cost on investors under the 1986 act than under the old tax rules, where capital gains were subject to a maximum tax rate of 20 percent, compared with a tax on dividends of up to 50 percent. This may have the very significant effect of reducing the tax costs of using dividends as a means of conveying favorable information ("signaling") regarding cash flows.[49] Whether dividends will be increased in the aggregate is an interesting empirical question that we would expect some research entrepreneurs to address.[50] Sorting out

49. See Sudipto Bhattacharya, "Nondissipative Signaling Structures and Dividend Policy," *Quarterly Journal of Economics*, vol. 95 (August 1980), pp. 1–24.

50. For corporate holders of dividend-paying stocks, the 85 percent exclusion of dividends from corporate taxation before reform resulted in a 6.9 percent tax rate (0.46×0.15), which might appear to compare favorably with an explicit corporate capital

whether aggregate dividends increased due to the 1986 act will require a model of dividend-paying behavior that incorporates the effect of the substantial advance in stock prices that preceded passage of the legislation.

This still leaves the question of whether share repurchases dominate the payment of dividends to shareholders under the 1986 act. Taxable investors with a positive basis on their holdings of stock would prefer that the corporation repurchase part of their stock each period instead of paying them dividends of equal amount. This would further defer personal tax on that part of the payment that is considered to be a return of capital. Moreover, it enables shareholders to retain the timing option as to when they sell their shares to the corporation; shareholders will step forward as sellers when it is in their interest to do so. On the other hand, share repurchases may not have the same signaling properties as do dividends. A precommitment to a policy of systematic share repurchases might duplicate the signaling and monitoring properties of a systematic dividend-payment policy, but it would also result in share repurchases being treated as dividends for tax purposes.

Corporate Restructuring under the 1986 Act

As discussed above, the 1986 act contains many changes that collectively increase the costs of selling assets to restructure the balance sheet of the firm. Asset sales followed by liquidations no longer escape the corporate capital gains tax, shareholders can no longer use the installment sales method to defer their realizations of capital gains, and for many assets the depreciation deductions are much less generous than under pre-1986 rules. Although the corporation can still use the install-

---

gains tax of 28 percent. In a frictionless setting, however, the corporation could reduce the capital gains tax to its shareholders to zero by liquidating the firm to escape any corporate-level capital gains taxes (the General Utilities doctrine), and its individual and corporate shareholders, in turn, could use installment sales to reduce (or eliminate) the present value of the capital gains tax. As we noted above, however, under the new law, the tax rate on dividends for corporate holders will be approximately 6.8 percent, and the capital gains tax on realized gains at the corporate level will be 34 percent. With the repeal of the alternative corporate tax on long-term capital gains and the General Utilities doctrine, and with the elimination of the opportunity to use installment sales for marketable securities, corporations are stuck with paying a high tax rate on capital gains. Hence the corporate investor may have a strong preference for dividends under the 1986 act, which, in turn, provides an incentive for corporations to increase dividend payments.

ment sales method to defer taxation on assets that are not publicly traded, the 1986 rules impose more restrictive provisions than existed previously. A clear prediction is that there will be fewer mergers and acquisitions that are motivated by tax considerations; indeed, there will be less tax incentive to turn over assets in general.

There are also important implications of the increased cost of asset restructuring for capital structure changes. As we emphasized earlier, asset restructurings are in many ways substitutes for capital restructuring as a response to changes in tax status. The new bill increases the cost of employing such strategies as selling tax-favored depreciable assets and leasing them back. Since reducing debt and increasing equity (or equity substitutes such as preferred stock) are a substitute (albeit an imperfect one) for the sale-leaseback transaction insofar as tax planning is concerned, the new tax bill could make such equity-for-debt restructurings relatively more cost effective. On the other hand, the gross tax benefit of restructuring by repurchasing or issuing common shares or bonds is less in the postreform era. Stocks offer their corporate issuers a smaller implicit tax subsidy (relative to bonds) under the 1986 act, both because explicit tax rates on ordinary income have been reduced and because the capital gains tax rate has been increased. Moreover, if the before-tax transaction cost of capital restructuring is as great after the new tax bill as before (as seems reasonable), the reduced tax rates will cause after-tax transaction costs to overwhelm the gross tax benefits in a larger number of cases.

Conclusion

We have argued that capital structure issues subsume a broad variety of financing and investment considerations. The optimal instruments (debt versus equity versus a rich menu of other asset and capital structure alternatives) cannot be chosen independently of information and tax considerations. An understanding of the dynamics of capital structure planning requires an understanding of the related problem of the dynamics of asset structure planning. These in turn require an analysis of the transaction costs associated with a reorganization of economic balance sheets in the face of changes in tax rates, as well as analysis of the tax costs associated with *not* undertaking such reorganizations (that is, the costs associated with being stuck in the ''wrong'' tax clientele).

If a reasonable predictive theory is to emerge, one that is designed to explain differences in observed capital structures across different taxpayers and across time, such a theory must recognize that the dimensionality of cross-sectional differences in tax status is vastly larger than whether a taxpayer has net operating losses. In a world of costly contracting, the marginal tax rates of firms (including all implicit taxes) can vary dramatically, even if each firm faces the same statutory tax rate schedule. Moreover, each firm does not face the same statutory tax schedule. For example, thrift institutions, life insurance companies, and a host of tax-exempt corporations have faced significantly lower statutory marginal tax rates than have other corporations for many years. Firms operating in many tax jurisdictions may face very different explicit tax rates from those that operate in a single jurisdiction. Finally, as Miller has emphasized, efficient corporate tax planning is inextricably linked to the idiosyncracies of noncorporate taxes (such as the personal income tax).

Comments by Joseph E. Stiglitz

The paper by Scholes and Wolfson revolves around nine major points concerning the effects of taxation on business and personal behavior. I shall describe these nine points and then make some additional observations.

The first point is that to understand the impact of taxes one must treat the corporation and personal income taxes jointly. Too often papers that purport to describe the behavioral effects of the corporation income tax ignore this fundamental truth. This paper stresses the interaction throughout.

The second point, like the first, has been made before, but the authors give it proper weight. To understand the effects of taxes, one must take explicitly into account the fact that people and businesses are in different tax brackets and that these differences condition their responses. The way I like to think about the first and second points is that the private sector of the economy behaves as if it were engaged in a game with the federal government in which the federal government sets down the rules and the private sector—households and corporations together—is trying to figure out how to minimize its total tax bill. The result is that it is very hard to figure out empirically how taxes affect after-tax incomes. Scholes and Wolfson make clear that one can deduce almost nothing about these effects from the amount of taxes that people or businesses actually pay. For example, the fact that General Electric did not pay any taxes because of safe harbor leasing and other provisions does not mean that their after-tax income has been unaffected by taxes.

The third point that they emphasize is the importance of progressivity. This point may surprise those who think of corporation taxes as proportional. The limitations on loss carryforwards and loss carrybacks mean that the corporation tax is not strictly proportional.

The fourth point—which the authors develop with distinctive flair—is the wide range of instruments available to individuals and businesses to minimize taxes. These instruments include leasing agreements, various kinds of debt instruments, pension plans, stock option plans, and a host of other devices by which taxpayers try to take deductions when rates are high and realize income when rates are low.

Among these instruments, and this is the fifth point, is the form of business organization; the choice of the form of business organization is one of the most important decisions affecting tax liabilities. By raising this point, they call attention to a serious shortcoming in much tax analysis—the failure to study explicitly the nontax advantages of alternative forms of business organization. Some of the early literature begins with assumptions under which the form of business organization is a matter of indifference apart from its tax consequences. Recent work on the economics of information has stressed that this result is not generally correct. Debt and equity, for example, are very different financial instruments, each with its own special problems of moral hazard and adverse selection. Even apart from tax considerations, one can derive an optimal debt-equity ratio. This fact means that changes in taxes that cause companies to alter their financial structure have real effects. On the other hand, so many ways to avoid taxes exist that the consequences of changing any one provision may be relatively modest.

The sixth point is that the little previous discussion of the effect of taxes on organizational form paid insufficient attention to the costs of reorganization. The recent tax bill has increased some of those costs. A change in tax rules might cause a company that is beginning operations to choose a different ratio of debt to equity from the one it would have chosen under prior rules. An existing company, in contrast, might conclude that the costs of moving to such a ratio of debt to equity through changed borrowing or changed dividend payments exceed the gain in reduced taxes. Some of these costs arise from the fact that the act of changing dividends or borrowing conveys information to financial markets. Much recent literature, for example, has stressed the fact that when firms try to buy back outstanding equity, this action may generate costs or benefits, as financial markets respond to the information conveyed by these actions by increasing or decreasing the price of shares.

The result of many of these points—and this brings me to my seventh point—is that the analysis of how taxes affect behavior requires the solution of a dynamic programming problem of extraordinary complexity. One cannot characterize what actions to take to avoid taxes by looking only at current conditions. The act of changing borrowing, of issuing stock, of changing dividends, or of engaging in any of a large number of other actions changes the environment in which future decisions will be made, for instance, by conveying information that changes the expectation of financial markets concerning the status of the firm.

This brings me to the eighth point, that it is wrong to separate real and financial decisions, as is done frequently in neoclassical analysis. I shall return to this point presently.

The final point is that real advantages to tax planning arise from the fact that different companies are in different tax situations. Traditional analysis has suggested that prices of various assets would adjust so that in equilibrium investors could enjoy similar after-tax rates of return on all assets. The general story was that it mattered little whether a company chose one ratio of debt to equity rather than another. Once one recognizes that companies are distinguished by a host of idiosyncratic characteristics, the significance of tax planning is restored. Despite the fact that tax lawyers probably have as much work as they can handle, hearing this piece of news from an economist will no doubt make all of them breathe easier.

This paper is a major step forward in another respect. The dirty little secret of tax economists is that our models do not work very well, in the sense that they lead to conclusions that are transparently false. A few years ago, partly at the urging of Harvey Galper, I demonstrated that if people behaved as the models used by public finance economists say they should behave, they would pay no taxes at all. I am not an empirical economist, but introspection sufficed to reject that conclusion. Something was clearly wrong with the model. The model that I used was based on pure arbitrage activities, for instance, in which people earned income that was taxed at low rates and generated deductions that could be claimed at high rates without thereby exposing themselves to serious risk. Clearly people do pay taxes. And they do so partly because tax avoidance activities involve costs of one kind or another that exceed the gains they might realize in reduced taxes, partly because they are imperfectly informed, and partly because capital markets look far different from those envisaged by the traditional models. In any case, it is very difficult to figure out just what the effect of a given tax rate or of a change in that tax rate is if we do not have a model that explains convincingly why individuals and firms pay more taxes than our simple theory predicts; and we cannot have much confidence in analyses based on the ad hoc modifications of the standard model that are required because without such modifications the models would yield clearly counterfactual predictions.

A concrete example illustrates the problem. Scholes and Wolfson mention the role of dividends as a signaling device and suggest that this function helps to explain why companies pay dividends. In general, however, taxes would be reduced if companies bought back shares of their own or other companies rather than pay dividends. To be sure, some dividend recipients may not have to pay taxes on them because the receipt of dividends allows them to increase their interest deductions. But people in this position constitute a minuscule fraction of all dividend recipients. Unless decisions on dividends are dictated by this small minority of shareholders, one must come to terms with the stubborn insistence companies display in paying dividends when the standard model says that they should not.

The equally stubborn and, by the lights of the traditional model, equally irrational insistence of many firms on using FIFO rather than LIFO inventory accounting also must be recognized. Scholes and Wolfson find that only four of sixty new companies behave in the way the traditional model says they should behave. As John Shoven has shown, LIFO dominates FIFO as long as there are loss carryforwards—with or without interest. To be sure, profitable companies are more likely than unprofitable companies to use LIFO rather than FIFO accounting. But this superficially gratifying correspondence of theory with practice may simply reflect the fact that smart managers are more likely than foolish managers both to make profits and to use the most advantageous form of inventory accounting.

Scholes and Wolfson also point to the tendency of new companies to offer unqualified stock options rather than qualified pensions. The supposed difficulty of disentangling tax from incentive motives is really bogus as companies could easily tie compensation to stock prices without using stock options. But why one should want to base incentives on stock prices, which are moved by variables that have nothing to do with either the absolute or relative performance of the company, is hard to understand.

My final comment concerns the observations by Scholes and Wolfson regarding the opportunities presented by events such as the Tax Reform Act of 1986 to learn more about how people respond to taxes. They observe that "transition periods provide the researcher with a golden opportunity to gather indirect measures of the costs of recontracting among entities." In some sense, it is surely true that the new tax law will offer a good opportunity to measure the effects of tax changes on financial structure or on the organization of companies, especially of corporations. It is clear that if the cost of debt, relative to equity, has gone down, one should see increased debt financing. On the other hand, it was hard, even before, to see any advantage to (new) equity financing. I interpret the quoted passage by Scholes and Wolfson, in good Chicago-school tradition, to mean: "Whatever we see is consistent with our theory, because we can posit that transaction costs explain whatever we see." It is surely comforting to know, in advance, that whatever surprises the world may serve, the result of this experiment will be consistent with theory.

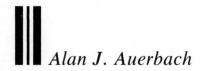 *Alan J. Auerbach*

Should Interest Deductions Be Limited?

THE TAX LAW treats interest deductibility as entirely appropriate—even as a desirable vehicle for achieving important social objectives—and at the same time as an abusive and unwarranted device for reducing taxes. Moreover, these conflicting tax treatments may apply to borrowing by a single individual, who is allowed to deduct business and investment interest in accordance with the dictates of income tax principles and home mortgage interest because of an avowed social policy of encouraging homeownership, but (if the investment results in a loss) not interest on debt used to finance an apartment building he owns, because that is a tax shelter.

Much of the discussion of borrowing limitations appearing in the tax policy literature has concentrated on the cosmetic benefits of making the tax system appear fairer. This appears to be a symptom of a general uncertainty about the real problems associated with borrowing. Vague discussions about "perceptions of fairness" indicate that there has been a failure to delineate the goals of tax policy and too little effort has been devoted to understanding the effects of borrowing limitations and the cases in which they might really be justified.

Certain interest deductions have been seen by some tax policy analysts as abusive. In response to this view, the Tax Reform Act of 1986 limited the extent to which tax losses on "passive" and real estate investments, often associated with interest deductions, could be claimed by individual

I am grateful to the Brookings Institution and the University of Pennsylvania's Institute for Law and Economics for financial support, and to Calvin Johnson, George Mundstock, David Shakow, and especially Al Warren for helpful comments on earlier versions.

195

taxpayers.[1] For businesses, even those investing in tax-favored property, interest deductions appear to remain acceptable as expenses that appropriately reduce measured income before taxes.[2] Still other types of interest deductions remain where no proper measurement of income is pretended, as in the case of mortgage interest deductions, because the associated activity has been deemed worthy of encouragement.

This selective approach to determining whether interest deductions are acceptable introduces two problems, one practical and one conceptual. The practical problem is the difficulty of tracing borrowing to specific activities, as is attempted under the new law (and even under previous law, to a lesser extent). The conceptual problem is whether such tracing has any meaning or justification. Put another way, are there any cogent equity or efficiency arguments for having limits on borrowing based on the proximate use of the borrowed funds? More generally, what justification exists even for overall limits on borrowing?

In this paper, I argue that the use of borrowing limits may be justified only on the ground that better, more direct methods of controlling undesirable activities are unavailable. In some cases, the imposition of borrowing limits appears to derive from a failure to understand the real source of the problem that the limits are intended to control. Moreover, the limits themselves may worsen the inequities and inefficiencies supposedly caused by the unrestricted opportunity to borrow. In some cases, measures that appear to reduce tax avoidance activity exacerbate its distortions and inequities.

Few of the conclusions or analytical points made below are entirely original; many of the most important ones have been presented forcefully and convincingly by other authors. However, points of conflict remain, which I argue are largely a result of differences in assumptions (often implicit) about the operation of the economy and the firms and households that populate it. Under a realistic view of the world, where assets are imperfect substitutes and information (particularly that of the Internal

1. In 1984, for example, real estate partnerships had an aggregate net tax loss of $21.2 billion, with $10.4 billion of interest payments. See Alan Zempel, "Partnership Returns," U.S. Department of the Treasury, *Statistics of Income Bulletin*, vol. 6 (Summer 1986), p. 54. It is worth noting that a substantial aggregate loss would have occurred even without *any* interest deductions.

2. There have been changes in business accounting rules that tighten the rules requiring the capitalization of construction period expenses, including interest. Although these provisions are important in terms of the revenue they are expected to generate, they do not seem aimed specifically at transactions that involve borrowing.

Revenue Service) is also imperfect, there are few easily analyzed polar cases and more reason to understand, if not justify, the case for limits on borrowing activity. It is important that realistic cases be considered so that the flaws of borrowing limitations are understood and that cosmetic solutions are not confused with real ones.

Interest Deductions under a Pure Income Tax

Defenders of unlimited interest deductibility often argue that, as a negative component of capital income, interest is rightfully deductible regardless of the purpose to which borrowed funds are put. Such a case could be made under a pure "Haig-Simons" income tax.[3] A pure income tax would include in an individual's tax base all capital income, net of losses, regardless of its source or liquidity. This would include such items as unrealized capital gains, imputed rent on owner-occupied housing, and interest on municipal debt. In this context the important property of this tax system is that an investor borrowing to invest in an asset with risk characteristics identical to those of the debt itself would experience no change in tax liability by doing so. The outcome would be the same as if the lender had invested directly in the asset. Hence paper transactions involving borrowed money could not have real effects on tax liabilities.

If all assets were riskless (or, more generally, had the same risk characteristics), the very existence of debt would be of no consequence. Households would be indifferent about which assets their wealth was invested in. As long as such wealth were positive, borrowing would have no real effects and it would never be necessary to borrow. Even in an economy with risky assets, the importance of debt would be as an asset with particular risk characteristics. The standard approach to the problem of an investor's portfolio choice between safe and risky assets

3. The Haig-Simons concept of income as consumption plus all accretions to wealth was developed by Robert Murray Haig, "The Concept of Income—Economic and Legal Aspects," in Robert Murray Haig, ed., *The Federal Income Tax* (Columbia University Press, 1921), pp. 1–28; and Henry C. Simons, *Personal Income Taxation: The Definition of Income as a Problem of Fiscal Policy* (University of Chicago Press, 1938). For a discussion of the Haig-Simons approach, see Richard A. Musgrave, *The Theory of Public Finance: A Study of Public Economy* (McGraw-Hill, 1959), pp. 160–73; or Joseph A. Pechman, *Federal Tax Policy*, 5th ed. (Brookings, 1987), pp. 94–98.

usually envisions the former as some form of debt.[4] Restricting individuals to positive positions in bonds would have real effects on the behavior of those who wished to borrow, but only because it would induce a shift in their portfolios and distort the market mechanism for allocating risks among individual investors.

Thus the portfolio choice problem in the presence of risk would be a substantive one, since the amount of debt held would influence the riskiness of an investor's portfolio. Nevertheless, the decision to invest less in the safe asset and more in the risky asset would, at least under a proportional pure income tax, have no effect on aggregate tax revenue, adjusted for risk and under competitive conditions.[5] However, there are few who would argue that the U.S. tax system even remotely resembles a pure income tax. In addition to the intentional deviations for incentive purposes, there are differences attributable to the clear and insurmountable problems involved in taxing all returns at all dates and in all states of nature at a uniform rate. Given how far removed the tax system is from the pure income tax under which unrestricted interest deductions would be appropriate on the basis of first principles, it is a non sequitur to justify full deductibility of interest under the current tax system on the basis that such treatment is appropriate under a pure income tax base.

Why Is Debt a Problem?

There are four properties of the current tax system that may be identified as sources of the problems associated with borrowing.

1. The tax system is progressive, so that different individuals receive different after-tax rates of return from the same fully taxed assets.

2. Different assets have different rates of exclusion or deferral of the income they generate from the tax base. Debt normally qualifies for neither exclusion nor deferral.

3. Debt may not only be held in negative as well as positive amounts, but it also receives symmetric tax treatment. Interest payments are generally deductible at the rate at which interest receipts are taxable.

4. Real income on debt is more than fully included in the tax base

4. James Tobin, "Liquidity Preference as Behavior towards Risk," *Review of Economic Studies,* vol. 25 (February 1958), pp. 65–86.
5. This is shown in the Appendix.

(and real interest expenses are more than fully deductible) when there is inflation, because there is no indexing of capital income in the tax base.

It is the interaction of these characteristics that leads to difficulties. The first and third properties would not, themselves, represent a violation of the principles of pure income taxation; they were assumed to hold in the previous analysis as well. However, in conjunction with the other conditions, they facilitate the borrowing activities that are perceived as problematic. For example, if the tax system were not progressive, then the violations of pure income tax principles contained in the second and fourth characteristics would be of little significance.

Properties 1 and 2 together imply that different investors will receive different relative after-tax returns from the same pair of assets. Higher-bracket taxpayers will gain relatively more from the exclusion of favored assets than will low-bracket taxpayers.[6] This will necessarily occur if the base exclusion is independent of the investor's tax bracket, as is the case with such preferences as capital gains exclusions and the tax exemption for municipal debt. If a favored asset has a fraction, x, of its returns included in the tax base, then an investor with tax rate θ on fully taxed income will receive a return from the tax-favored asset relative to that of a fully taxed asset of $(1 - x\theta)/(1 - \theta)$ times the ratio of the before-tax returns on the two assets. This ratio strictly increases with respect to θ.[7] Likewise, for two assets with different fractions of the base included, the relative return of the more favored asset will also increase with the investor's marginal tax rate.

6. Early discussions of this point, and its implications, may be found in Martin J. Bailey, "Progressivity and Investment Yields under U.S. Income Taxation," *Journal of Political Economy*, vol. 82 (November–December 1974), pp. 1157–75; David F. Bradford, "Issues in the Design of Savings and Investment Incentives," in Charles R. Hulten, ed., *Depreciation, Inflation, and the Taxation of Income from Capital* (Washington, D.C.: Urban Institute, 1981), pp. 13–47; and Harvey Galper and Dennis Zimmerman, "Preferential Taxation and Portfolio Choice: Some Empirical Evidence," *National Tax Journal*, vol. 30 (December 1977), pp. 387–97.
7. Suppose, for example, that the tax-favored asset had 60 percent of its return excluded from the tax base, as was the case for long-term capital gains under previous law (ignoring the additional benefits of deferral). If one investor were in the 40 percent bracket, the after-tax return on the tax-favored asset relative to the fully taxed asset would be 1.4 ($= [1 - (1 - 0.6) \times 0.4]/[1 - 0.4]$) times the ratio of the two assets' before-tax returns. If the tax-favored and fully taxed assets had returns of 8 and 10 percent respectively, for example, the after-tax return of 6.72 percent on the tax-favored asset, divided by the after-tax return of 6 percent on the fully taxed asset, would equal 1.4 multiplied by 0.8, the ratio of the before-tax returns. For the 20 percent bracket investor, the ratio would be 1.15 instead of 1.4.

The fact that the ranking of the after-tax rates of return may differ from one investor to another means that tax-favored assets should be concentrated in the portfolios of higher-bracket investors, thereby increasing the aggregate tax savings from the base exclusions. In a world of perfect certainty, one would expect complete sorting, since the prices of tax-favored assets would be bid up until only groups with sufficiently high marginal tax rates would find them profitable to hold. If one ranks assets by the fraction of income included in the tax base, x, those assets with the lowest value of x would be held by individuals in the highest tax bracket until their wealth was exhausted, with the remaining assets being allocated to the remaining investors according to the base inclusion fraction, x, and the marginal tax rate, θ.

Table 1 presents an illustration of this result. In the example used there, there are two primary assets, each with a total supply of 150. Asset 1 is fully taxed, while 50 percent of the income from asset 2 is excluded from the tax base. There are three investors in the example, each with wealth of 100 (summing to the total stock of assets) and with marginal tax rates of 40 percent (investor 1), 20 percent (investor 2), and zero (investor 3). I assume that zero-bracket investors can receive a fixed real before-tax return of 5 percent, perhaps on the world market. (Some assumption of this sort is necessary to determine the overall level of returns.) The first case shows the outcome without any sorting by tax bracket, where investors hold identical portfolios. Because the tax-exempt investor holds both assets, each must yield the return that is available to him elsewhere, which is 5 percent.

In the second case, portfolio sorting without borrowing, there is only one configuration of portfolios consistent with an equilibrium in which each investor prefers his portfolio to the alternatives available. The tax-exempt investor holds only the fully taxed asset, which therefore continues to yield his alternative return of 5 percent before taxes. The high-bracket investor holds only the tax-favored asset, and the middle-bracket investor continues to hold both assets. Because this investor holds both assets, capital market equilibrium requires that he be indifferent between their after-tax returns, and since the fully taxed asset must yield 5 percent before tax, this determines the before-tax yield of 4.44 percent on the tax-favored asset.[8] This lower yield would encourage

---

8. The equality between the after-tax returns on the two assets is calculated as follows: $[1 - 0.2 \times (1 - 0.5)] \times 0.0444 = (1 - 0.2) \times 0.05 = 0.04$.

Table 1. *The Effects of Borrowing, Inflation, and Taxation on Portfolio Choice*[a]

Portfolio	Asset type			Income and taxes			
	Asset 1[b]	Asset 2[c]	Asset 3[d]	Income	Taxable income	Taxes	Net income
Equal portfolios							
Investor 1[e]	50	50	. . .	5.00	3.75	1.50	3.50
Investor 2[f]	50	50	. . .	5.00	3.75	0.75	4.25
Investor 3[g]	50	50	. . .	5.00	0	0	5.00
Rate of return or total	0.050	0.050	. . .	15.00	7.50	2.25	12.75
No borrowing							
Investor 1[e]	0	100	. . .	4.44	2.22	0.89	3.56
Investor 2[f]	50	50	. . .	4.72	3.61	0.72	4.00
Investor 3[g]	100	0	. . .	5.00	0	0	5.00
Rate of return or total	0.050	0.044	. . .	14.17	5.83	1.61	12.56
Unrestricted borrowing with no inflation							
Investor 1[e]	0	150	−50	3.13	0.31	0.12	3.00
Investor 2[f]	75	0	25	5.00	5.00	1.00	4.00
Investor 3[g]	75	0	25	5.00	0	0	5.00
Rate of return or total	0.050	0.038	0.050	13.13	5.31	1.13	12.00
Unrestricted borrowing with 2.5 percent inflation							
Investor 1[e]	150	150	−200	−1.25	−8.13	−3.25	2.00
Investor 2[f]	0	0	100	5.00	7.50	1.50	3.50
Investor 3[g]	0	0	100	5.00	0	0	5.00
Rate of return or total	0.033	0.025	0.050	8.75	−0.62	−1.75	10.50
Restricted borrowing with 2.5 percent inflation							
Investor 1[e]	0	135	−35	3.50	0	0	3.50
Investor 2[f]	150	15	−65	3.90	1.98	0.40	3.50
Investor 3[g]	0	0	100	5.00	0	0	5.00
Rate of return or total	0.044	0.039	0.050	12.40	1.98	0.40	12.00

a. Assuming a real interest rate of 5 percent.
b. Fully taxed.
c. Half of the income from this asset is included in taxable income.
d. Represents debt; fully taxed under no inflation and taxed on 1.5 times real return under inflation.
e. Taxed at marginal rate of 40 percent.
f. Taxed at marginal rate of 20 percent.
g. Taxed at zero rate.

greater supply of this asset over time.[9] Both taxable investors pay taxes that total $1.61, or 11.4 percent of before-tax income, compared with 15 percent in the previous example. Tax avoidance activity thus reduces each taxable investor's taxes, but also reduces the returns required on the tax-favored asset. The combination of greater holding of tax-favored

9. Note that this change in the yield on the existing supply of assets does not require a change in the assets' underlying returns, only in the price of the assets. Over time,

assets by taxable investors and lower yields on these assets leads to a greater percentage decline in taxable income than in economic income.

Property 3 enhances this sorting procedure by relaxing the limit of personal wealth that would otherwise constrain the holding of tax-favored assets by high-bracket individuals. The introduction of debt (asset 3) leads to even greater tax savings from the holding of tax-favored assets. This is illustrated in the third case in table 1, which shows what happens when there is no inflation, so real interest is fully taxed. With the ability to borrow, the high-bracket investor now holds the entire supply of the tax-favored asset. The remaining assets have identical tax characteristics and so are arbitrarily divided evenly between the two remaining investors. Taxes are now only 8.6 percent of before-tax income, and the yield on the tax-favored assets has been lowered still further. This shift in asset holdings causes a *reduction* in the after-tax income of the high-bracket investor, because he is now the marginal investor in the tax-favored asset and will bid the after-tax return on that asset down to his after-tax return on debt.[10] Thus, through more complete portfolio sorting, the ability to borrow leads to a reduction in taxes, a reduction in before-tax yields on tax-favored assets, and a reduction in the after-tax income of high-bracket investors. Since assets 1 and 3 have the same tax characteristics, it is the ability to hold negative amounts of the debt that makes this case special. Permitting short sales of asset 1 (with symmetric tax treatment) would have led to the identical outcome.

Property 4 is the other key attribute of debt. Under inflation, the full taxation of nominal interest means that taxable income from debt exceeds economic income, making asset 3 tax disfavored.

For the example used in the table, with a real return of 5 percent and an inflation rate of 2.5 percent the nominal interest rate is therefore 7.5

---

the difference between the yield on existing assets and the higher productivity of new ones would spur increased supply. This is, essentially, Tobin's "q" theory of investment. See James Tobin, "A General Equilibrium Approach to Monetary Theory," *Journal of Money, Credit and Banking*, vol. 1 (February 1969), pp. 15–29. Since it may take time for before-tax returns on the underlying assets to fall to the levels consistent with the before-tax yield required by investors, the values of the assets themselves may vary substantially in the short run with changes in the required yield resulting from tax policy changes. These windfalls are received by those holding the assets at the time of the change, and not at all by those who purchase the assets immediately after it, even before the underlying asset returns have yet to adjust.

10. The equality between the after-tax cost of debt and the return on the tax-favored asset is calculated as follows: $[1 - 0.4 \times (1 - 0.5)] \times 0.0375 = (1 - 0.4) \times 0.05 = 0.03$.

percent, all of which is taxable. Thus the tax base of 7.5 percent is 150 percent of the asset's real return before taxes. By the same process, however, financial liabilities are tax favored, since their nominal interest costs are fully deductible. This introduces the opportunity for investors to create additional tax-favored instruments, that is, financial liabilities. Although these instruments are in the aggregate netted against an equal increase in tax-disfavored instruments (financial assets), the financial assets and liabilities are held by investors in different tax brackets and therefore have a real effect on aggregate tax payments, portfolio decisions, and asset yields.

This point is demonstrated by the fourth case in table 1, for which it is still assumed that all investors have free access to debt, but the inflation rate is 2.5 percent and the nominal returns to debt (positive or negative) are taxable. The only outcome consistent with portfolio equilibrium is for the high-bracket investor to hold all of the economy's real wealth, borrowing from the middle-bracket investor and the tax-exempt investor. The relative before-tax returns on these assets are such that the high-bracket investor breaks even on purchases financed by borrowing,[11] and the other two investors prefer not to hold any of either asset, because each receives a higher after-tax return on debt. Inflation drives down the before-tax yields on both of the economy's real assets. The bigger tax advantage to borrowing reduces the after-tax incomes of both taxable investors. The behavior of investor 1 drives this process by pushing down yields on both real assets until these assets have the same after-tax yield as debt to that investor. He is now the marginal investor in each asset. While before-tax yields have gone down, so have tax payments. In this example, they have become negative in the aggregate, as has total taxable income. As with the advent of borrowing in the prior example, however, the reduction in taxes is less than the reduction in before-tax income, so that after-tax income declines.

Thus borrowing does increase the aggregate tax benefits associated with tax incentives in two respects. First, it allows tax-favored assets to migrate more completely to the portfolios of high-bracket investors. Second, it allows the creation of additional tax-favored instruments—

11. For the fully taxable asset, a return of 3.33 percent makes the high-bracket investor indifferent between borrowing and holding the fully taxed asset, since $(1 - 0.4) \times 0.0333 = (1 - 0.4) \times 0.075 - 0.025 = 0.02$. For the tax-favored asset, the return of 2.5 percent also yields 2.0 percent after tax as follows: $[1 - 0.4 \times (1 - 0.5)] \times 0.025 = 0.02$.

financial liabilities. Although in the aggregate these are netted against an equal increase in tax-disfavored financial assets, they are held by investors in different tax brackets and therefore have a negative effect on aggregate tax payments.

This use of borrowing to purchase tax-favored assets has been referred to as "normal tax arbitrage."[12] The crucial property of such normal arbitrage is that it is anchored by the before-tax returns of the underlying real tax-favored assets and limited by their amount. If social wealth equals the stock of real assets, then net financial liabilities of high-bracket investors cannot sum to more than the stock of the real assets. This not only limits the aggregate amount of income that can be excluded from the tax base and the value of tax savings that can be obtained from investing in tax-favored assets, but also relates the tax savings directly to the purchase of those assets.

A second type of arbitrage has been termed "pure tax arbitrage." In general, such arbitrage occurs whenever it is possible to alter the amount of income excluded from the aggregate tax base without altering the underlying supply of real assets. A frequently cited example of pure arbitrage is borrowing money to invest in an individual retirement account (IRA). The investor can, essentially, borrow money from himself and hold it in a tax-favored but otherwise similar form, thus reducing his tax liability without creating a new asset or affecting anyone's portfolio allocation. But pure arbitrage opportunities are not limited to cases in which one has the ability to lend to oneself and receive different tax treatment on the two sides of the transaction.

In general, what permits pure arbitrage to occur is the existence of a second asset besides debt, with different tax attributes, that can also be held in negative quantities. The presence of such an asset allows two investors, typically in different tax brackets, to gain from trade. A clear example of this would be if the tax-favored asset in the example in table 1 could be sold short. Then the tax-exempt investor would wish to sell the asset short at any before-tax return below 5 percent, and the high-bracket investor would wish to borrow to invest in the additional assets so created at any before-tax return greater than 2.5 percent (in the case of positive inflation). The difference of 2.5 percentage points represents the tax saving such a two-way transaction would generate, divided between the two investors. In the unrestricted borrowing case described

12. See Bradford, "Issues in the Design of Savings and Investment Incentives"; and C. Eugene Steuerle, *Taxes, Loans, and Inflation* (Brookings, 1985).

in table 1, the before-tax rate of return on the tax-favored asset has been bid down to 2.5 percent because there is only one marginal investor, the high-bracket individual. If the nontaxable investor could sell the tax-favored asset short, however, there would no longer be a financial equilibrium, because this investor would stand to gain the full 2.5 percent per dollar of lending financed by short sales.

All that is required for this pure tax arbitrage is a difference in the two investors' relative returns on the two assets. The only natural limit to such activity under a progressive income tax without specific restrictions on interest deductions would be the equalization of marginal tax rates among individuals. This might occur, for example, if the high-bracket investor shifted his taxable income to the middle-bracket investor by borrowing from him to purchase tax-favored assets issued by him. Even this implausible equilibration process would have its limitations, however, since some zero-bracket investors, such as foundations, universities, and state and local governments, have tax brackets that are not based on their income. Indeed, a good example of a second asset that could be held in negative quantities is municipal bonds, which are tax favored and may be issued by tax-exempt municipal governments. Without existing restrictions there would be no natural limit on the tax arbitrage gains achievable through the process of a government borrowing from taxable investors and issuing them tax-exempt debt.

The case of the IRA may appear different because it is customary to view an IRA not as an asset but as a way of holding assets; however, this difference is more apparent than real. One may conceive of a separate asset, an IRA, the return on which is deductible to the borrower (a bank or another investor, for example, who pays interest on the funds contributed to the IRA) but not taxable to the lender (the individual establishing the IRA).[13] There are then two assets that can be held in positive or negative quantities: debt and IRAs. Because of the asymmetric treatment of the two sides of the IRA transaction, it is no longer even necessary for the two investors to be in different tax brackets to gain from trading: two investors in the same tax bracket will have different relative after-tax returns on the two assets (debt and the IRA) because the investor with a long position in the IRA receives a tax exemption on the income from it while the investor with the short

13. The actual treatment of IRAs is now and was before the recent tax changes more complicated than a simple exemption from tax, but for the purposes of the present argument this distinction is unimportant.

position in the IRA receives a deduction for interest paid to it. Since investors in the same tax bracket can in this way generate tax reductions, it follows that a single individual can play the role of the two investors. Rather than having another investor obtain funds through the IRA and lend to the IRA contributor, the latter may simply obtain the funds directly from the IRA.[14]

It is useful to summarize the results of the foregoing discussion. The view that borrowing enhances investment incentives may be correct, but its validity depends on a number of institutional factors. First, debt as an asset is relatively tax disfavored. Second, debt may be held in negative as well as positive amounts. Finally, debt occupies a unique position in this respect. The existence of a second asset that can be held in negative amounts detaches the borrowing decision from the investment decision and creates the opportunity for pure tax arbitrage. When the tax treatment of different assets is symmetric with respect to long and short positions, individuals in different tax brackets can gain from trade. When the tax treatment of long positions is at a lower rate than that of short positions (as in the IRA example just given), even investors in the same tax bracket and, indeed, a single individual, can generate reductions in tax liabilities.[15]

Pure arbitrage may become a more serious problem because of the continuing innovations occurring in financial markets and the reduced costs of creating new types of assets and liabilities,[16] but this does not

14. A conclusion of this line of argument is that what Steuerle has distinguished as "financial" or "reverse" arbitrage, in which two investors trade, is fundamentally identical to pure arbitrage, in which a single individual reduces taxes independently.

15. On the other hand, if short positions were taxed (that is, if their costs were deductible) at a lower rate than long positions, the ability to hold negative amounts of an asset might not result in any potential for tax arbitrage. If, for example, municipalities were taxed at the high-bracket individual's marginal tax rate on positive financial investments, then the scope for pure tax arbitrage would disappear. The differential tax treatment of positive and negative holdings of the taxable debt by the municipality would make it unprofitable for the taxable and tax-exempt investors to trade in either direction (the other being where taxable investors issue tax-exempt debt to municipalities).

16. For example, there is no reason in principle why an investor couldn't "issue" an apartment building, offering to match the before-tax returns from some other building already in existence. This would make the number of apartment buildings held as assets independent of the number actually in existence. As this example illustrates, however, symmetry of tax treatment (see footnote 15) is by no means assured even when the asset itself can be issued. In this example, the creator of the "building" would also

indicate a role for borrowing restrictions. Borrowing restrictions have effects similar to the complete elimination of borrowing, as the last case in table 1 demonstrates. This example illustrates the effect of restricting interest deductions to taxable investment income, as provided for in the Tax Reform Act of 1986. The effect is to push some of the tax-favored asset into the middle-bracket investor's portfolio, forcing up the before-tax returns to that asset as well as the high-bracket investor's after-tax income. The provision does reduce aggregate borrowing and increase tax revenue, although borrowing by the middle-bracket investor actually increases as he becomes the marginal investor in both real assets, holding some of the tax-favored asset and all of the other, fully taxed asset.[17]

The above discussion shows how, under perfect certainty, the ability to borrow increases the tax benefits associated with tax base exclusions by increasing the sorting of portfolios. In the presence of inflation, the borrowing itself creates additional tax benefits, but these benefits are limited by the supply of assets in the economy. This limitation disappears when there are other assets that, like debt, may be held in negative amounts, creating the opportunity for pure tax arbitrage.

Borrowing restrictions reduce the sorting process associated with the ability to borrow by increasing the after-tax returns to high-bracket investors and the before-tax returns on the tax-favored assets in which they invest. The equity consequences of such restrictions are therefore undesirable, but the efficiency consequences depend on the benefits of encouraging the tax-favored activity in the first place: for a given before-tax yield on the investment, it is inefficient to provide higher after-tax returns to some investors (since these must ultimately be financed by other distortionary taxes), but restricting the activity itself could produce an efficiency gain (if it had been excessively encouraged) or an efficiency loss (if it had not). Even if it were desirable to discourage the activity, borrowing restrictions could be justified only to the extent that direct limitations on the activity were unavailable.

---

have to issue "depreciation allowances," a right not given to private taxpayers. As discussed below, one of the activities of "abusive" tax shelters is the construction of transactions aimed at getting around such restrictions.

17. Equilibrium for the fully taxed asset would occur when that asset had a yield of 4.375 percent; there would be no marginal benefit from borrowing to invest in this asset. In other words, $(1 - 0.2) \times 0.04375 = (1 - 0.2) \times 0.075 - 0.025 = 0.035$. For the tax-favored asset, the equilibrium is as follows: $[(1 - 0.2) \times (1 - 0.5)] \times 0.0389 = (1 - 0.2) \times 0.075 - 0.025 = 0.035$.

Can Borrowing Restrictions Be Justified?

To many observers of the tax shelter process, the preceding analysis must appear lacking in verisimilitude. Where are the "pigs feeding at the trough," the tax shelters of questionable legality promising enormous first-year tax deductions? In the real world, the tax policy process is a complex one. Assets are not perfect substitutes, policy goals are not well defined, information and auditing are imperfect, and the tax treatment of similar transactions may differ markedly. This section discusses the complications that must be considered and how they influence the conclusions above regarding the effects of borrowing and the desirability of restricting it.

Risk and Imperfect Asset Substitutability

If borrowing to invest in an individual retirement account really constitutes pure tax arbitrage, then there is a lot of public stupidity to be explained. Most taxpayers did not establish IRAs during 1981–86, when their tax advantages were greatest.[18] Some of this may be attributable to ignorance, but there were also individuals whose need for liquidity was so great that they would not have been able to repay the loans used to establish the IRAs without digging into the IRAs themselves soon after. Such early withdrawals would have been subject to a 10 percent excise tax, thus eliminating the tax advantages of the IRAs.[19]

An IRA then really is different from the debt used to fund it. This has two implications regarding the conclusions of the previous section. First,

18. According to Galper and Byce, only 14.1 percent of all taxpayers filing returns in 1983 made IRA contributions. Harvey Galper and Charles Byce, "Individual Retirement Accounts: Facts and Issues," *Tax Notes,* vol. 31 (June 2, 1986), p. 918.

19. This is consistent with the fact that IRA participation increased with income. According to Galper and Byce, in 1983 this rate rose from 0.8 percent of taxpayers with adjusted gross incomes below $5,000 to 68.0 percent for taxpayers with adjusted gross incomes between $100,000 and $200,000. Ibid. There is evidence that the lack of full participation is attributable to other factors, too, such as lack of information about the tax benefits available. Until the Tax Reform Act of 1986, the supplemental retirement annuity (section 403b) plans to which employees of nonprofit institutions were permitted to contribute had the tax characteristics of IRAs without the excise tax penalty on early withdrawals. At most educational institutions such plans typically were participated in by only a minority of employed faculty members, many of whom were presumably moderately well educated.

the introduction of the universal IRA by the Economic Recovery Tax Act of 1981 was not simply an invitation to engage in pure tax arbitrage. It may be interpreted as having provided a very strong tax incentive for individuals to reduce the liquidity of their portfolios. For those without substantial preexisting assets, this incentive may have encouraged additional saving to replace the funds locked away in the IRAs. One could support the introduction of such portfolio distortions for paternalistic reasons (people would not save enough otherwise) or on more traditional grounds involving "second-best" welfare economics—that the new distortion would work against other, preexisting ones (such as the disincentives for retirement savings due to the general taxation of capital income or the provision of social security benefits). Whether this was a desirable policy goal, and if so whether the IRA was an appropriate tool for achieving it, remains open to very serious question, but it is somewhat misleading to describe the IRA as a pure tax arbitrage opportunity.

Indeed, few truly "pure" arbitrage opportunities are likely to exist, since there will almost always be real differences in behavior induced by the tax variations. Where the differences in asset characteristics are small relative to the tax variations, however, the tax benefits will be large and one must question whether any sensible policy goal could be involved. Consider, for example, the pre-1981 commodity straddles based on futures contracts for the same or related commodities in nearby months.[20] One might argue that the associated tax benefits encouraged financial investors to bear the risks of intermonth price changes. But the bearing of such risks makes little sense given that the risks borne by different straddle investors were largely offsetting and hence diversifiable. For example, two investors trading opposite sides of the same two contracts with each other would bear risks with a perfectly negative

20. Although such transactions did not involve borrowing, they had the general characteristic of pure tax arbitrage indicated above. The straddles operated by having taxable private investors realize losses and defer gains. These tax benefits could be realized because there were other investors (such as traders) for whom the reverse transaction did not generate a tax disadvantage of comparable magnitude. Another difference between this example of pure tax arbitrage and those considered above is that in this case the tax-favored asset was identifiable only after the initial investment had been made, when it was known which contract went up in value and which one went down. A general discussion of different types of pure arbitrage transactions involving capital gains deferral may be found in Joseph E. Stiglitz, "Some Aspects of the Taxation of Capital Gains," *Journal of Public Economics,* vol. 21 (July 1983), pp. 257–94.

correlation. Such allocation of risks might be justified if each investor had other risks with offsetting characteristics. The standard example in this context is the farmer and the crop purchaser, each of whom wishes to hedge against the risk of future crop price uncertainty. However, since the number of long and short contracts greatly exceeded the number of individuals with any direct connection to the underlying commodity markets themselves, the primary "goal" encouraged by the tax incentives in this example seems to have been the production of deadweight loss, caused by individual investors' bearing of risks that could have been reduced through pooling.

Hence there is an additional dimension necessary in the classification of tax arbitrage schemes. Pure arbitrage requires not only that some other asset can be held in negative quantities, but also that it be very substitutable for debt. If it is not, then real effects will result from the arbitrage activity, involving the altering of individual portfolios. If this portfolio shift is, in itself, deemed an appropriate social goal, then the activity may be justified along lines similar to those for the "normal" arbitrage already discussed: tax incentives leading to an increase in a socially desirable activity. On the other hand, the portfolio shift may simply represent a coincident distortion that, while preventing pure arbitrage from occurring, misallocates risky assets and achieves no recognizable policy goals. If the portfolio distortion is not very large and the policy goals are not clear, as in the commodity straddle example, then the substantial transactions one would expect from pure arbitrage opportunities will undoubtedly occur and give rise to policy measures to restrict them.

The riskiness of assets also affects the analysis of normal tax arbitrage. Assets have different characteristics regarding liquidity and financial risk. Investors respond to the assets' relative returns, but only the hypothetical risk-neutral investor would attempt to eliminate completely differences in expected returns on different assets. As long as no asset exists whose after-tax returns will always exceed those of another,[21] an investor will normally choose to hold finite quantities of all assets (although if negative holdings are not feasible, the quantity for some will be zero). This reduces not only the likelihood of pure arbitrage, but also

---

21. This would be the case for pure tax arbitrage under perfect certainty. This property is referred to in the economics literature as "stochastic dominance." See, for example, Michael Rothschild and Joseph E. Stiglitz, "Increasing Risk: A Definition," *Journal of Economic Theory*, vol. 2 (September 1970), pp. 225–43.

the possibility that investors will sort their portfolios completely according to relative tax advantages. Even if permitted to borrow, investors will be unlikely to dissipate fully the tax advantages of tax-favored assets through lower expected returns.

Standard models of portfolio choice in the absence of taxes call for investors to diversify their portfolios to reduce risk.[22] This objective clearly works in opposition to the sorting of portfolios in response to relative tax advantages. Indeed, when both risk and relative tax advantages are present, it is still generally optimal for investors to diversify, but their portfolios will be shifted in the direction indicated by the tax advantages, with the relative importance of the two motivations depending on the magnitude of risk and risk aversion on the one hand and the tax advantages on the other.[23] What these models suggest is that investors will not dissipate all the tax advantages from arbitrage, even otherwise "pure" arbitrage, stopping at the point where the additional tax advantages from tax arbitrage are balanced by additional distortions to portfolio balance.

The implications of this model of investor behavior are most easily illustrated by considering a standard example, that of borrowing to invest in tax-exempt municipal debt. There has been much discussion in the literature about whether such borrowing increases the benefits of the municipal debt tax exemption. As indicated in the previous section, if all assets were perfect substitutes, and indeed even if just taxable and tax-exempt debt were perfect substitutes, then borrowing would facilitate a complete sorting of tax-exempt debt into the portfolios of the highest-bracket investors, with complete capitalization of the tax advantage of tax-exempt debt in its before-tax yield. In this case, borrowing would facilitate the sorting and capitalization and therefore benefit the issuers of the debt by providing them with a lower cost of capital. Its desirability would therefore depend primarily on whether the government wished to encourage tax-exempt borrowing and, if not, whether it had the ability to regulate the encouraged activity independently.

22. Indeed, under some circumstances, it would be optimal in the absence of taxation for different investors to hold the same mix of risky assets. See, for example, David Cass and Joseph E. Stiglitz, "The Structure of Investor Preferences and Asset Returns, and Separability in Portfolio Allocation: A Contribution to the Pure Theory of Mutual Funds," *Journal of Economic Theory*, vol. 2 (June 1970), pp. 122–60.

23. See Alan J. Auerbach and Mervyn A. King, "Taxation, Portfolio Choice and Debt-Equity Ratios: A General Equilibrium Model," *Quarterly Journal of Economics*, vol. 98 (November 1983), pp. 587–609.

If the two types of debt are not perfect substitutes, however, the effect of borrowing will be less sharply defined. Without borrowing, there will be incomplete sorting and capitalization. However, the ability to borrow need not lead to full capitalization, for this would require the high-bracket investors to dispose of substantial quantities of taxable assets and perhaps borrow in addition in order to absorb the entire stock of tax-exempt debt. What is more likely is that the sorting will increase but stop short of complete capitalization, since the additional sorting involves additional reductions in the efficiency of portfolio balance. Though it has been argued that this distorted portfolio allocation is a potential cost of tax arbitrage even with complete capitalization of the tax advantage of tax-favored investments,[24] it is likely that the two problems will coexist. The portfolio choice problem is substantive in precisely those (realistic) cases where complete capitalization is unlikely to occur. The capitalization fails to occur because investors have nontax reasons for caring which assets they hold. At the margin, high-bracket investors will not wish to hold more of the tax-favored assets, but the existence of the tax differential will still provide them with benefits on their existing holdings.

Another result of this incomplete capitalization will be a smaller decline in the issuing authorities' cost of capital. This outcome may be good or bad, depending on how much the federal government wishes to encourage tax-exempt borrowing. The differential after-tax rate of return between tax-exempt and taxable bonds for high-bracket investors would decline with the removal of borrowing restrictions, but the total "windfall" to such investors need not,[25] since their absolute holdings of tax-exempt bonds might increase substantially.[26] Furthermore, the lack of complete sorting is attributable to a worsening allocation of assets among investors from the perspective of diversification of risk.

Moreover, not all high-bracket individuals would gain equally. Inves-

24. See, for example, Alvin C. Warren, Jr., "Accelerated Capital Recovery, Debt, and Tax Arbitrage," *Tax Lawyer*, vol. 38 (Spring 1985), pp. 549–74.

25. I will follow previous authors in the use of this terminology, although it is somewhat at odds with the more usual definition in the economics literature as an unanticipated shock to wealth induced by a policy shift.

26. This situation is analogous to what happens to profits when output increases to a level that is still below that which would deliver only normal economic returns, in a market where output was previously restricted even further. Profits per unit of output will fall, but output will rise. Unless output expands all the way to its competitive level, one cannot be sure in general about the direction of change in profits unless the output was originally determined by a profit-maximizing monopolist.

tors who are not especially risk averse would engage in substantial borrowing to increase municipal bond holdings, while those who are very risk averse would borrow relatively little, if at all. Such an outcome suggests a potential justification for restricting borrowing on equity grounds, because extensive borrowing by an investor would indicate that he is able to take greater advantage of the differential after-tax return on tax-exempt assets than more risk-averse investors. One could also justify borrowing restrictions because investors who borrow to invest in tax-exempt debt also could have financed the purchase by reducing holdings of taxable assets.[27] Such actions are not necessarily equivalent, however, once risk is considered. The fact that high-bracket investors hold any such fully taxable assets in the first place (which of course they do)[28] is direct evidence of this. While the imposition of restrictions on borrowing might lessen the problem of horizontal equity, it would still restrict the capitalization of the tax advantage to debt, produce windfalls, and raise the cost of capital for the tax-favored activity. These factors would have to be weighed to determine whether this represents a desirable policy.

Since the potential trade-off between horizontal equity and windfalls relates to the imperfect substitutability (that is, differences in risk characteristics) of assets, the trade-off might be improved by making assets more substitutable. This could be accomplished by government policy, as in the case of the safe harbor leasing provisions introduced in 1981. These provisions facilitated the leveraged purchases of tax-advantaged assets by taxable corporations by permitting transacting parties to tie the debt obligations to the returns on the leased assets and allowing a separation of the assets from some of their legal characteristics.[29] Some of the opposition to the safe harbor provisions was due to another of the effects of increased capitalization; many saw the reduced cost of capital as encouraging even more investment in assets that were already

27. See, for example, William A. Klein, "Borrowing to Finance Tax-Favored Investments," *Wisconsin Law Review*, vol. 1962 (July 1962), pp. 608–36.

28. For example, King and Leape estimated that the average marginal tax rate for taxable bonds, weighted by holdings of the assets, was actually higher than that of corporate equity for a sample of households surveyed in 1978. Mervyn A. King and Jonathan Leape, "Wealth and Portfolio Composition: Theory and Evidence," National Bureau of Economic Research Working Paper 1468 (Cambridge, Mass.: NBER, September 1984), table 5.

29. See Alvin C. Warren, Jr., and Alan J. Auerbach, "Transferability of Tax Incentives and the Fiction of Safe Harbor Leasing," *Harvard Law Review*, vol. 95 (June 1982), pp. 1752–86.

excessively encouraged because of the accelerated cost recovery system.

Another example of packaging debt and assets to reduce overall risk is the use of nonrecourse debt in the design of tax shelters (although there are additional complications in some cases, discussed below). Indeed, any packaging of debt and tax-favored investments that reduces, or appears to reduce, the underlying portfolio shift required to obtain the tax advantages of the tax-favored assets would have the same effect. However, there may be other attributes that distinguish the tax shelter operation from the introduction of safe harbor leasing and make it more objectionable.

The Special Problem of Tax Shelters

Although tax shelters have no exact definition, their key purpose seems to be to reduce taxes for a limited number of well-connected investors. Such tax shelters might be attributable to a number of factors, including limitations on investor information or on the ability to package the shelters, and differences in investor risk aversion.

Permitting borrowing encourages the process of normal tax arbitrage, and provisions aimed at making tax-favored assets more substitutable for debt carry the process still further. Such provisions are less desirable if only some investors are capable of taking advantage of them, because their transactions alone will be too insignificant to drive down the yield on the tax-favored asset. This is one interpretation of what tax shelters are, or are intended to be.

A common argument is that tax shelters are innocuous because they can usually be decomposed into activities that individually are entirely acceptable.[30] This argument presumes that combining the assets in the tax shelter package is costless or at least equally possible for all investors. Indeed, the tax shelter entrepreneurs may only appear to have better access to the technology. However, they may possess the knowledge of how to structure investments to reduce the risk that investors incur when engaging in normal arbitrage, such as the combination of a risky real investment with nonrecourse debt. Finally, though, they may reduce risks through the use of techniques that distort the intention of the tax

30. See, for example, the discussion in George Mundstock, "Accelerated Depreciation and the Interest Deduction: Can Two Rights Really Make a Wrong?" *Tax Notes*, vol. 29 (December 23, 1985), pp. 1253–58.

preference and may be of questionable legality. A good example of this type of activity was the "movie" shelter that existed before the introduction of the at-risk rules limiting the advantages of nonrecourse debt. It is instructive to consider the operation of this shelter in light of the previous discussion.

Through the use of existing tax provisions, promoters were able to convert normal arbitrage involving movies into pure arbitrage. A normal leveraged movie investment might involve one investor borrowing from another to buy a movie, perhaps from the lender. The next logical step is to suppose that the lender could engage in pure arbitrage by selling movies short, providing the borrower with a nonexistent "movie" for a fair purchase price, with the borrower receiving taxable movie royalty income and depreciation deductions from the lender and making interest payments on the loan, reversing the lender's tax position. In fact, the law did not allow such symmetric treatment of real assets sold short (see footnote 16), but a similar outcome was achieved by overstating the value of a real movie, letting the borrower receive depreciation deductions from the government rather than the lender (with the lender taking the substantial excess of sale price over basis into income), and, through the use of nonrecourse debt, replacing the borrower's interest payments and the lender's royalty payments with a cancellation of indebtedness in the distant future, resulting in taxable income for the borrower and a tax deduction for the lender. Just as if the asset had been sold short, the borrower's tax payments were deferred and the lender's tax payments accelerated, making pure tax arbitrage possible.

If the government knows that such undesired behavior is occurring but cannot uncover it without incurring great expense, it may be preferable simply to restrict the entire class of activity of which it is a part. This could justify borrowing restrictions, though one might view overall restrictions on the deductibility of tax losses as more appropriate if the questionable activities do not all involve borrowing, or one might prefer the at-risk rules actually adopted if the activities depend on the use of nonrecourse debt.

Alternatively, participation in tax shelters may indicate that some individuals are not very risk averse and hence, as discussed above, they benefit more from the incomplete capitalization of tax advantages than do other investors. Although restrictions on the borrowing of such individuals might increase the before-tax yield on tax-favored investments (which could be desirable or undesirable, depending on the circumstances) and possibly worsen the overall extent of windfalls on these assets, they could conceivably be justified on equity grounds.

If the technology of the tax shelter involved the introduction of a unique type of debt, as would be the case if the debt were tied to the tax-favored asset to reduce the risk of normal tax arbitrage, then it might be acceptable to institute a tracing rule basing the limitation on the interest earned by whatever the borrowed funds were used for. Only in such a case would it make sense to ask where the funds came from to purchase a tax-favored investment. Otherwise, borrowed funds are borrowed funds, and no unique allocation rule exists. Indeed, one of the difficulties involved in imposing such rules is the financial flexibility investors do have in structuring their transactions.[31]

Borrowing Restrictions as a Substitute for Direct Subsidy Reductions

As already indicated, borrowing restrictions can be used to curtail the degree of normal tax arbitrage. Although they may also increase the windfalls associated with incomplete capitalization of the tax advantages of tax-favored assets, borrowing restrictions may also be supported on equity grounds when investors in a given tax bracket have differing abilities to take advantage of such windfalls. However, it is important to recognize that there are alternative approaches to the limitation of tax incentives and the equitable distribution of investor tax benefits that do not involve the inefficiencies and residual inequities caused by incomplete capitalization.

Consider the case of tax-exempt municipal bonds. Suppose it is anticipated that relaxing the section 265 restriction on borrowing to invest in such bonds would not result in complete capitalization at the highest marginal tax rate, and that some investors in the highest tax bracket would take much greater advantage of the ability to borrow than others. Rather than maintaining the restriction on their borrowing to prevent such an outcome, the government might instead institute other changes, similar to the safe harbor leasing rules, that would reduce the riskiness of leveraged purchases of municipal bonds. For example, investors could be permitted to tie the interest payments on the borrowed

31. See, for example, Calvin H. Johnson, "Is an Interest Deduction Inevitable?" *Virginia Tax Review*, vol. 6 (Summer 1986), pp. 123–82; and David J. Shakow, "Confronting the Problem of Tax Arbitrage," *Tax Law Review*, vol. 43 (Fall 1987).

funds to the payment of interest on the municipal bonds. Such a change would lead to nearly complete capitalization and very possibly to a reduction in the aggregate level of windfalls. It would also encourage borrowing by municipal authorities, something that the federal government might not wish to do. Borrowing restrictions could be justified only if it were infeasible for the government to reduce the direct value of the tax incentive.

In this example, the government might wish to make interest on municipal debt partially taxable to counteract the reduction in before-tax interest rates caused by the increased level of arbitrage activity. However, for legal or political reasons such a policy might not be possible.[32] Indeed, the preference itself might be seen as undesirable but difficult to limit directly.[33] This justification for borrowing restrictions suggests a much more complicated view of the legislative process than is normally considered in tax policy analysis. It appears to incorporate a certain amount of inconsistency or irrationality on the part of legislators, lobbyists, or both. Similar arguments have been made with respect to other tax provisions, such as the minimum tax.[34] The growing importance of the minimum tax suggests that, although the political economy of the tax legislative process is not well understood, it plays an important role in the determination of how particular fiscal objectives can be achieved.

Thus, when normal tax arbitrage is at issue, borrowing limitations may be the best alternative given that others are politically unattainable.

Borrowing Restrictions Equivalent to Other Policies

The previous section suggested that there may be cases in which a desirable policy is not feasible, and that restricting borrowing is a better

32. This policy combination would have quite similar effects to making municipal debt fully taxable and instituting a direct interest subsidy to bond issuers equal to the yield differential that previously existed, a policy that has been advocated to reduce windfalls. See, for example, George F. Break and Joseph A. Pechman, *Federal Tax Reform: The Impossible Dream?* (Brookings, 1975), pp. 52–57.

33. This argument has been made by various commentators. See, for example, Klein, "Borrowing to Finance Tax-Favored Investments"; and Warren, "Accelerated Capital Recovery."

34. See Michael J. Graetz, "The 1982 Minimum Tax Amendments as a First Step in the Transition to a 'Flat Rate' Tax," *Southern California Law Review*, vol. 56 (January 1983), pp. 527–71; and the paper by Graetz and Sunley in this volume.

policy than none at all. There has also been some discussion of the use of borrowing restrictions to replicate a desired policy that does not involve borrowing restrictions.[35] For example, consider a policy that allocates the benefit of tax base exclusion on a tax-favored asset according to the source of funds rather than the ownership of the asset. An asset financed fully by borrowing would then have all its basis exclusion given to the lender rather than the borrower; in general, an investor's own basis exclusion could not be increased by borrowing.[36] Therefore, this policy would be equivalent to one in which interest incurred on borrowing to purchase such assets was only partially deductible, to the extent that the income of the tax-favored asset was taxable.

But recognition of such equivalences makes borrowing restrictions neither more nor less attractive as a policy option and begs the question of why one should be interested in enacting either version of this type of limitation on tax preferences. Except in the circumstances outlined above, restrictions on borrowing may be difficult to justify. The fact that such policies may be shown to be equivalent to others that do not involve borrowing merely suggests that both are equally suspect. The real benefit of this type of analysis is not to justify borrowing restrictions but to clarify the implications of their adoption.

Conclusions

My objective has been to analyze the effects of maintaining interest deductibility under a tax system where some assets receive favorable tax treatment. The analysis suggests that the ability to borrow does indeed further the process of normal tax arbitrage by increasing the migration of tax-favored assets to the investors who value them most highly, but that borrowing may be undesirable for a number of reasons, including incomplete capitalization of tax advantages, differential access to arbitrage opportunities, differences in investor attitudes toward risk, and the desire not to provide further encouragement for the underlying tax-favored activity itself.

35. For example, J. Gregory Ballentine's comments below.
36. In the presence of inflation, this result would also require that only real interest were taxed. Otherwise, as discussed above in relation to table 1, borrowing itself would also affect the allocation of real income between borrower and lender.

I have also attempted to clarify the distinction between the activities that have been termed "pure" and "normal" arbitrage. The fundamental difference between the two is that normal arbitrage requires a "real" transaction (that is, purchasing a tangible tax-favored asset) while pure arbitage involves transacting only with another taxpayer (or the same taxpayer in a different taxpaying status). Put very simply, pure arbitrage involves assets that would be netted out in aggregate national income accounts (incorporating the different government sectors).

However, there is a second important dimension to the characterization of arbitrage opportunities relating to the degree to which debt is a substitute for the other asset involved in the transaction. In all cases of arbitrage, activity is limited by risk considerations, as investors balance tax benefits against distortions in their desired portfolios. In cases of pure arbitage, such considerations may be the only limit (barring explicit restrictions) on infinite use of the arbitrage, but they may also relate fundamentally to the reason for the existence of arbitrage opportunities in the first place. For example, the *objective* of the IRA system may be to encourage savings earmarked for retirement by forcing taxpayers to reduce the liquidity of their portfolios more than they themselves would consider optimal. In this case, the portfolio distortion associated with the arbitrage activity is the government's objective. While the introduction of such distortions normally violates the rules of welfare economics, one may argue (although perhaps not very convincingly in this example) that the new distortion helps to counteract a preexisting one. In cases of normal arbitrage, where the objective is to encourage the supply of the tax-favored asset, imperfect asset substitutability will again lead to distorted portfolios, as well as imperfect capitalization of the asset's tax advantage and an uneven distribution of the benefits of this incomplete capitalization.

The very idea of a tax shelter suggests that there is more to it than the straightforward combination of its apparent parts. This may simply be an illusion, but if not, there may be cases in which limitations on borrowing, and, in particular, on borrowing to invest in tax shelters, may be justified. Whether these circumstances exist in all the cases in which such provisions have been enacted is certainly doubtful. Even where they do exist, it is not clear that borrowing limitations are the most direct remedies available. To identify superior alternatives, it is important to focus discussion not on the tools of tax policy but on the ultimate, perhaps uncertain, goals of tax policy.

Appendix: Tax Revenue and Risk Taking under a Pure Income Tax

Under a pure Haig-Simons income tax, risky assets would be taxed on their returns at a constant tax rate regardless of the outcome or "state of nature" that occurred. Hence, the government's share of a risky asset's return would always be the investor's tax rate, say θ, the same as its share of the riskless return. Since these returns, adjusted for risk, would have equal value to investors, the same would be true for the government's share, as long as private risks were being efficiently pooled.

For example, suppose there were two states of nature, with debt yielding a return of r_f in both states and the risky asset yielding r_1 in state 1 and r_2 in state 2. An investor who shifts one dollar from the safe asset to the risky asset receives $(r_2 - r_f)(1 - \theta)$ in state 2 and $(r_1 - r_f)(1 - \theta)$ in state 1, while the government receives $\theta/(1 - \theta)$ times these amounts. Hence the government's portion of social returns and the value of these returns, evaluated using private risk premiums, are unaffected by the investor's decision. If the risk-free rate were 4 percent, and the risky asset returned 12 percent half of the time (say state 1) and zero the other half of the time (state 2), then an investor in the 25 percent bracket would have an expected after-tax return of 3 percent on the safe asset and 4.5 percent on the risky asset. The government's expected revenue would be 1 percent of the investment in the safe asset and 1.5 percent of the investment in the risky asset. However, investors value the 4.5 percent after-tax return on the risky investment as equal to the 3 percent after-tax safe return. Hence the government's shares of each, having the same risk characteristics and relative magnitudes, are also of equal value when evaluated using the same criteria.[37]

Under a progressive tax system, however, the tax bracket of an investor with a sufficiently risky portfolio would depend on the state of nature that occurred. This would lead to the same type of portfolio distortions discussed above, with different investors encouraged to invest in different assets. For example, an investor expecting to be in

37. See generally Agnar Sandmo, "The Effects of Taxation on Savings and Risk-Taking," in Alan J. Auerbach and Martin S. Feldstein, eds., *Handbook of Public Economics,* vol. 1 (Amsterdam: North-Holland, 1985), pp. 265–311; and Roger H. Gordon, "Taxation of Corporate Capital Income: Tax Revenues versus Tax Distortions," *Quarterly Journal of Economics,* vol. 100 (February 1985), pp. 1–27.

the same tax bracket regardless of the outcome would receive a higher after-tax return (relative to that on the safe asset) than an investor who faced a higher tax rate when the risky asset did well than when it did poorly. This suggests that consistent application of the Haig-Simons principles would restrict tax progressivity to cases in which an individual's decisions would not affect his marginal tax rate. The simplest progressive tax system satisfying this criterion would be a linear income tax with a single rate. More generally, one could allow marginal rates to vary according to individual characteristics such as age. The new tax system's broad tax brackets and flat marginal rate schedule appear to reduce the importance of the aspect of the tax arbitrage problem associated with variations in marginal tax rates for a single individual.

Comments by J. Gregory Ballentine

While presented as a comment on Auerbach's article, this paper was actually written before Auerbach wrote his paper. Auerbach demonstrates that borrowing limits as interest deduction limits may be justified "only on the grounds that better, more direct methods of controlling undesirable activities are unavailable." This paper deals with the case in which debt-financed assets receive tax preferences that are assumed to be *desirable* because the underlying activity—for example, investing in depreciable assets—is assumed to be desirable and worthy of a tax preference.

In the current debate over tax reform, some have argued that borrowing to purchase assets with an income tax preference (for example, assets that are depreciated using ACRS) causes tax distortions that should be remedied.[38] One remedy that has been discussed is a limitation on the deductibility of interest on debt used to finance certain investments. For example, this rationale has been used to defend limitations on the deductibility of partnership interest in real estate limited partnerships. Others who tend to oppose such limitations have concluded that borrowing, and interest deductions, cause no separate problem.[39]

38. See, for example, Calvin H. Johnson, "Tax Shelter Gain: The Mismatch of Debt and Supply Side Depreciation," *Texas Law Review*, vol. 61 (March 1983), pp. 1013–55. A general review of this issue is given by Warren, "Accelerated Capital Recovery."

39. See, for example, Frederic W. Hickman, "Interest, Depreciation, and Indexing," *Virginia Tax Review*, vol. 5 (Spring 1986), pp. 773–823; and Mundstock, "Accelerated Depreciation and the Interest Deduction."

Limitations on interest deductibility can be examined in two different contexts, one being the advantages of limiting interest deductibility when the underlying debt-financed asset has a tax preference that is felt to be undesirable. An alternative context, and the one I deal with here, is whether interest deductibility should be limited when the tax preference on the underlying asset is deemed desirable. A case can be made for limiting interest deductibility even when the underlying tax preference is desirable, depending on the way the tax preference is allocated across investors. When such a case for interest limitations applies, however, interest exclusions for the recipients of interest income are also justified.[40]

While demonstrating that such a case for interest limitations can be made is my central purpose, I really hope to clarify the issues in the debate over interest limitations. The debate begins with the stipulation that some tax benefit—accelerated depreciation, for example—is desirable. The issue then is whether there should be limitations on interest on debt used to purchase assets with accelerated depreciation. Proponents of limitations say they are needed to prevent interest deductions from combining with accelerated depreciation to produce a total tax benefit greater than the (desirable) accelerated depreciation alone. Opponents contend that interest deductions do not enhance the benefits of accelerated depreciation and that allowing interest deductions is the correct rule to allocate income among all the investors in a project even when the project has a tax preference.

The debate will be much clearer if, instead of focusing on interest deductions directly, it focuses on the way in which the tax benefit is allocated among investors. Allocating all of the tax benefits of accelerated depreciation to the equity investors—as is done under current law—has far different results from allocating the benefits pro-rata to debt and equity investors. (The pro-rata allocation rule is equivalent to the allocation of the benefits of expensing in a consumption tax of the type considered in the U.S. Treasury Department's 1977 *Blueprints for Basic Tax Reform*.)[41] If the all-equity allocation is preferred, there is no reason to limit interest deductions. If, however, the pro-rata allocation rule is

40. Throughout this paper, I assume no inflation, thus avoiding the special issue of indexing interest for inflation.

41. The particular element of the consumption tax described in *Blueprints* that is important here is the deduction for loans made and the inclusion in taxable income of loans received.

preferred, but is not administratively practical, then a limitation of interest deductions and an exclusion of some interest income are clearly justified.

The debate over limitations on interest deductions would be clarified greatly if the participants would state and defend their preferred rule for allocating the desired tax benefit. Once that is done, the correct rule for interest deductions follows in a straightforward manner.

The Allocation of Investment Incentives

The issue of the allocation of investment incentives can be most easily described by beginning with the polar cases of a true income tax and a true consumption tax. In a true income tax there is no investment incentive. The economic burden of true depreciation is borne by the equity holder, and therefore the true depreciation deductions are all allocated to the equity holder, independent of the extent of debt finance.[42] In such a tax system, all interest costs should be deductible by the borrower and all interest expense included in the income of the lender.

In a true consumption tax there are no depreciation deductions; instead, assets are expensed. However, equity investors do not take the full expensing deduction; instead, in effect, it is prorated between debt and equity investors. This may not be apparent from the usual description of the consumption tax, but it can be demonstrated easily. Suppose that an individual buys an asset for $100, using $50 of equity funds and borrowing $50. The usual description of the tax effects of this investment has the equity investor expense the full $100, but also include in income the $50 loan, while the lender deducts the loan. Exactly the same tax effect can be described as a pro-rata allocation of the expensed $100 between debt and equity investors. That is, the equity investor expenses his share ($50) of the investment and the lender his share (also $50). The result is the same as the loan inclusion and deduction structure of a consumption tax. In either case, all interest is deductible by the equity holder and includable by the lender.

42. This assumes a clear distinction between debt and equity. In cases of non-recourse debt and high leverage relative to the market value of the asset, circumstances can arise in which the debt holder bears the burden of the decline in value of the asset. Normally, such circumstances would imply bankruptcy and the debt holder would become the equity holder. When that does not happen, but the true value of the asset falls below the outstanding debt on the asset, the rationale for letting the equity holder deduct true depreciation is less clear even in a pure income tax.

Now consider a hybrid tax system that is between a pure consumption tax and a pure income tax. Specifically, suppose that 50 percent of the cost of an asset can be expensed and the remainder depreciated over the true life of the asset. Before considering the deductibility of interest in this setting, consider how the tax benefit of expensing should be allocated when debt and equity finance is used. The general approach of current law would allocate the true depreciation and *all* of the expensing benefits to the equity holder. An approach analogous to the pure consumption tax would still allocate the true depreciation to the equity holder, but would prorate the expensing benefit between debt and equity investors. The effects of the differences between these two rules can be dramatic. Further, each of the two different allocation rules has its attractions. Most important, if the pro-rata allocation is deemed desirable but is not feasible as a practical matter (as is likely to be the case), then there is a sound case for limiting interest deductibility to offset the effects of allocating all of the expensing benefit to the equity holder.

The Effects of the Different Investment Incentive Allocation Rules

Again, it will be useful to begin by examining a pure income tax. The analysis will deal with the purchase of a $100 asset that lasts for one year and then immediately becomes valueless. At the end of one year it produces $110 of sales, thus earning a 10 percent before-tax return. The equity investor has a 50 percent tax rate and the lender has a 10 percent tax rate. The interest rate is 10 percent. The relevant outcomes for three different financing arrangements are shown below.

Financing	Total private investment (dollars)	Total after-tax receipts (dollars)	After-tax equity return on investment (percent)	After-tax debt return on investment (percent)	After-tax total return on investment (percent)
100 percent equity	100.00	105.00	5	. . .	5.0
50 percent debt	100.00	107.00	5	9	7.0
70 percent debt	100.00	107.80	5	9	7.8

Now consider the same investment with 50 percent of the investment expensed, all of which is allocated to the equity holder, while the rest receives true depreciation. All interest is deducted in this example. (The arithmetic of this example and the pro-rata example discussed below is described in the Appendix.)

Financing	Total private investment (dollars)	Total after-tax receipts (dollars)	After-tax equity return on investment (percent)	After-tax debt return on investment (percent)	After-tax total return on investment (percent)
100 percent equity	75.00	80.00	6.67	. . .	6.67
50 percent debt	75.00	82.00	10.00	9	9.33
70 percent debt	75.00	82.80	30.00	9	10.40

While the asset still costs $100, the total private investment is only $75 due to the $25 tax savings arising from expensing $50 by the equity investor.

A comparison of these two cases shows why many argue that borrowing does not enhance the value of the underlying tax incentives and thus why, if that tax incentive is desirable, no restrictions on interest deduction are justified. In both a true income tax and the tax incentive case, borrowing more adds to after-tax receipts and the total after-tax rate of return. *The effect of borrowing is the same in both cases, however.* In both 50 percent debt examples, debt finance adds $2 in after-tax receipts and raises the total after-tax return by 40 percent relative to all equity finance (for example, 7 percent is 40 percent larger than 5 percent and 9.33 percent is 40 percent larger than 6.67 percent).[43] The same is true with 70 percent debt finance: it adds $2.80 and raises the all-equity return by 56 percent in both cases. Put differently, allowing 50 percent expensing, all allocated to the equity holder, increases the total after-tax return by 33 percent for comparable financing. (That is, for all-equity financing, 6.67 percent is 33 percent larger than 5 percent; for 50 percent debt financing, 9.33 percent is 33 percent larger than 7 percent; and for 70 percent debt, 10.4 percent is 33 percent larger than 7.8 percent.)

Thus, if the goal of the 50 percent expensing tax incentive is to raise the total after-tax return by 33 percent at given interest rates, then allocating all of the benefits to the equity investor is the correct rule.[44]

43. The fact that leverage adds the same total dollars of after-tax return is made by George Mundstock in his argument that interest deductibility does not enhance a tax incentive. "Accelerated Depreciation and the Interest Deduction," p. 1254.

44. The goal is stated for given interest rates, 10 percent in the example, because if interest rates rise when the tax incentive is introduced (as is likely), two cases with the same borrowing will not be fully comparable. That is, if the income tax case has a 10 percent interest rate and the investment incentive case a 13 percent interest rate, 50 percent debt finance corresponds to a different sharing of debt and equity income in the two cases. Since debt and equity income are taxed at different rates, this interest rate differential would make the two 50 percent debt examples noncomparable.

Further, borrowing does not add to that incentive, and any interest deduction limitations will thwart the goal of the 33 percent increase in after-tax returns.

While the above examples show why many have argued that borrowing does not enhance a tax incentive, they also show why many argue exactly the opposite. Notice that in the investment incentive case with 70 percent borrowing, the after-tax return exceeds the before-tax return (10.4 percent versus 10 percent). Thus, with that financing, the 50 percent expensing tax incentive results in an overall negative tax rate. This is *not* an inevitable result of allowing half expensing; it results from the way the half-expensing benefit is allocated. It is quite reasonable to advocate half expensing in order to lower each investor's tax rate, but it is also reasonable to advocate the pro-rata allocation rule in order to achieve that result while avoiding negative tax rates for any one investor or for the total investment.

The examples below show the results of the same investment with the 50 percent expensing allocated pro-rata to the debt and equity investors. Before turning to those results, the operation of that pro-rata allocation needs to be explained. The result of 50 percent expensing is $50 deducted when the asset is purchased and $50 a year later, as opposed to true depreciation deductions of $100 in the year after purchase. The tax benefit is the timing benefit of accelerating the $50 deduction; it is only the timing benefit that is allocated pro-rata. For a 50 percent debt finance case, the way this is done is to allow the lender to deduct $25 (half of the $50) in the first year, then to recapture that $25 (include it in taxable income) in the second year. The equity investor deducts $25 in the first year and $75 in the second.[45]

---

45. Notice that this is exactly the same result that occurs if two $50 assets are bought, each financed half by debt, and one asset is treated under income tax principles and the other under consumption tax principles. The asset taxed under income tax principles has a $50 depreciation deduction a year after purchase. The asset taxed under consumption tax principles has $50 expensed when purchased by the equity holder, but, since he also includes the $25 loan on that asset, there is only a net deduction of $25. The lender for this asset deducts the $25 loan and includes the $25 repayment the next year. In the second year, the equity holder deducts the $25 loan repayment on the asset loan. Overall, the equity holder expenses $25 when the asset is purchased and deducts $75 the next year. The lender deducts $25 when the loan is made and includes $25 when it is repaid at the end of the year.

Financing	Total private investment (dollars)	Total after-tax receipts (dollars)	After-tax equity return on investment (percent)	After-tax debt return on investment (percent)	After-tax total return on investment (percent)
100 percent equity	75.00	80.00	6.67	. . .	6.67
50 percent debt	85.00	92.00	6.67	9.47	8.24
70 percent debt	89.00	96.80	6.67	9.47	8.76
100 percent debt	95.00	104.00	. . .	9.47	9.47

The key points about this example are that the equity investor's after-tax rate of return is increased by the same amount independent of the extent of debt finance and, even with 100 percent debt finance, the investment as a whole still pays a positive tax rate. Half expensing with this allocation rule ensures that all investors receive a cut in their effective tax rate (a 33 percent cut for the 50 percent tax-bracket investor and a 47 percent cut for the 10 percent tax-bracket investor). For investors in a given statutory rate bracket, the reduction in their effective tax rate is the same, whether they are equity investors or debt investors. (The 100 percent debt case has the same result as the 100 percent equity case.) Further, the effective rate reduction for equity investors is independent of the degree of leverage they use.

Implications for the Debate over Interest Deductibility

The issue here is not whether the pro-rata allocation rule is inherently superior to the all-equity allocation rule or vice versa. Each has what some will see as advantages. The point is to explore the differences between the two rules and the implications of that difference for the debate over limitations of interest deductibility. In particular, suppose that half expensing with pro-rata allocation is the desired rule, but administrative or other reasons require that the all-equity allocation rule be used. The question is, can an interest limitation rule be combined with the all-equity rule to achieve the same result as the pro-rata allocation? The answer is yes.

Suppose that the all-equity allocation rule is used, but that one-third of all the equity holders' interest payments are not allowed as a deduction *and* 47 percent of all of the interest income of the lender is not taxed.[46]

46. The fraction of interest deductions or expense that is disallowed is given by X

ALAN J. AUERBACH

Financing	Total private investment (dollars)	Total after-tax receipts (dollars)	After-tax equity return on investment (percent)	After-tax debt return on investment (percent)	After-tax total return on investment (percent)
100 percent equity	75.00	80.00	6.67	. . .	6.67
50 percent debt	75.00	81.40	6.67	9.47	8.54
70 percent debt	75.00	81.96	6.67	9.47	9.28
100 percent debt	100.00	109.47	. . .	9.47	9.47

The results are shown above.[47] Clearly, the results are essentially the same as for the pro-rata allocation case.[48] It is important to note that the interest disallowances and interest exclusion rates are the same no matter what the financing ratio is: 33 percent of all interest deductions are disallowed and 47 percent of all interest income is exempt. The 33 percent disallowance rate arises from the fact that the equity holders' tax rate is to be reduced 33 percent, from the 50 percent statutory rate to the 33 percent effective rate. Similarly, the 47 percent exemption arises because the lender's tax rate is to be reduced 47 percent, from the 10 percent statutory rate to the 5.3 percent effective rate. Thus the reduction in effective tax rates that would occur under pro-rata allocation of the tax benefit gives the deduction limitation rate and the exemption rate to be used under all-equity allocation.

Conclusion

The debate over interest limitations in the presence of desirable investment incentives has been largely miscast. The debate should focus on which allocation rule for the tax benefit is desirable—the all-equity rule that raises the total after-tax rate of return by a fixed percentage, or

---

$(1 - t)/[X(1 - t) + X]$, where t is the borrower's or lender's tax rate and X is the share of the asset that is expensed.

47. The 100 percent debt example has $100 of private investment because the lender provides $100 and the government provides $25, so the total *private* investment is $100. The example assumes that the equity investor invests the government funds at 6.67 percent (his highest return available). This allows the equity investor to pay his tax bill in the second year of $26.67, leaving the total after-tax return of $109.47 all to be received by the debt holder. The key point, of course, is that the total private rate of return is only 9.47 percent, indicating a positive tax rate.

48. The overall after-tax rates of return differ slightly. Those overall rates of return are essentially a weighted average of the two individual rates of return where the weights are the shares in income. The interest disallowance alters these shares slightly, causing the overall rates of return to differ.

the pro-rata rule that raises each investor's rate of return by a fixed percentage. The debate will be furthered by drawing out the advantages and disadvantages of each allocation rule. Interest limitations in the presence of desirable tax preferences should be viewed as only a means of achieving a pro-rata allocation of the tax benefit when that cannot be done directly. The fundamental issue is the desirability of pro-rata allocation in the first place.

Appendix

This appendix presents the arithmetic behind the examples given in the text. The first case involves half expensing with all the expensing benefits allocated to the equity owner. For 100 percent equity finance, the equity owner's out-of-pocket cost for a $100 asset is $75: the government puts up $25 from the tax saving of expensing $50. In the next year, the asset produces revenues of $110, against which there is only $50 of true depreciation deductions. That means taxable income is $60 in year 2, and the tax is $30. This in turn implies that after-tax receipts are $80 ($110 − $30 in taxes) for a 6.67 percent return on $75.

If 50 percent debt finance is used, the equity owner has out-of-pocket costs of $25, the debt owner has out-of-pocket costs of $50, and, as before, the government contributes $25 due to the equity owner's expensing $50. The total private cost is still $75. The next year's taxable income for the equity owner is $55 ($110 receipts − $50 true depreciation − $5 interest). After-tax net receipts for the equity owner are $27.50 ($110 receipts − $55 principal and interest payments and $27.50 in taxes on $55 taxable income). Receipts of $27.50 imply $2.50 net income, or a 10 percent return on $25 out-of-pocket costs for the equity owner. The debt owner receives $5 in before-tax income and $4.50 after taxes for a 9 percent return. The total after-tax receipts are $27.50 plus $54.50, or $82, for a total return of 9.33 percent on total private costs of $75.

In the second case the expensing benefits are allocated pro-rata across the debt and equity investors. In this case the total private costs are no longer $75. Suppose 50 percent debt is used. The equity owner expenses $25, his share of the total $50 to be expensed. Expensing $25 saves him $12.50 in taxes, making his total out-of-pocket costs $37.50. The debt owner loans $50, but also expenses $25, making his out-of-pocket costs $47.50 (the tax saving for the debt owner is 10 percent of $25, or $2.50). Thus total out-of-pocket costs are $85. Taxable income for the equity owner after a year is $30 ($110 − $5 in interest and $75 in true depreciation). Notice that the equity owner still depreciates $100 in total; $25 is accelerated and $75 is not. The equity owner owes $15 in taxes and pays $55 in interest and principal, leaving him with $40 after taxes from the $110 in revenues. This is a return of 6.67 percent on a $37.50 investment.

The lender has taxable income after a year of $30, which arises from $5 of interest and $25 of recapture of expensing benefits. (Notice that the recapture ensures that, in total, $50 is expensed in the first year and $50 is deducted in the second.) The lender pays $3 in taxes, leaving $52 in after-tax returns on an investment of $47.50, for a 9.47 percent return. The total after-tax return is $92 on an $85 investment, for a return of 8.24 percent.

The reader can easily demonstrate that the rates of return to the equity holder and debt holder are invariant to the debt share as the leveraging ratio is increased. Further, the reader can also recast this example along the lines of a pure consumption tax. That is, the equity owner can take all the expensing benefits, but include the borrowed funds in income while the lender deducts them, and later the equity owner can deduct repayments of the loan and the lenders include those repayments in taxable income. The result of that approach is identical to the example of pro-rata expensing.

Finally, consider the 50 percent debt case with all the expensing benefits allocated to the equity holder, but 33 percent of interest deductions disallowed and 47 percent of interest income exempted. The equity owner must put up $25 and the debt owner $50, while the government contributes $25. The taxable income of the equity owner after a year is $56.67 from $110 of revenues, $50 of depreciation deductions, and $3.33 of interest deductions (two-thirds of the $5 interest cost). After-tax net receipts are $26.67 ($110 − $55 interest and principal and $28.33 in taxes). This gives a 6.67 percent return on $25.

The lender receives $5 in interest income and pays $0.26 in tax on 53 percent of the interest income, leaving after-tax income of $4.74 for a 9.47 percent return. Clearly this result is identical to the pro-rata case.

Comments by Stanley A. Koppelman

Under our federal income tax system, the income from many types of assets is partially or fully excluded from the tax base. Interest on debt deemed to finance these tax-preferred assets is subject to limitations on deductibility in some cases but not in others. Where the interest deduction is not limited, so that tax-preferred income may be combined with currently deductible interest, "tax arbitrage" is said to arise.

Alan Auerbach addresses the conceptual question of whether limits on the deductibility of the interest component of tax arbitrage may be justified. He also observes without much discussion that such limitations raise the practical problem of determining to what extent interest expenditures relate to the tax-favored assets (or income) subject to limitation. I will comment on his analysis of the conceptual problem of whether interest limitations can be justified and offer some thoughts on the practical problem of determining what portion of a taxpayer's interest expenditures should be subject to limitation if limits on deductibility are imposed.

Can Interest Limitations Be Justified?

Auerbach first presents a clear and insightful analysis of the components of tax arbitrage in an idealized world of perfect certainty (no risk) and information. He first describes how yield adjustments will occur where the tax system has progressive rates and the income from some assets is taxed more favorably than others, but no borrowing is permitted. Under these conditions, the tax-favored assets tend to gravitate toward the high-bracket taxpayers for whom the tax benefits are the most valuable, while the fully taxable assets tend to be held by tax-exempt persons. The increased demand for the tax-favored assets by the high-bracket taxpayers reduces the yield (increases the price) from the tax-favored assets.

He next analyzes how this sorting procedure (and the price of tax-favored assets) increases when debt financing is permitted. Under these circumstances, although the increased holding of tax-preferred assets by high-bracket taxpayers increases their tax savings, the reduced yield exceeds these savings, thus reducing their after-tax return. The sorting of assets thus has the effect of driving out inequities by eliminating any windfall to high-bracket taxpayers. This return is further reduced if inflation exists and the tax system does not index capital income. Auerbach also distinguishes "normal tax arbitrage," resulting from borrowing to purchase tax-preferred assets, from "pure tax arbitrage," where two assets have different tax attributes and may be held in negative amounts.

Auerbach goes on to indicate how the presence of risk and the resulting imperfect asset substitutability would likely prevent the full capitalization of tax benefits even if no interest limitations existed. Windfalls thus will not be entirely eliminated even if interest is fully deductible. If limitations are imposed upon the interest deduction, capitalization will be further limited.

Auerbach believes that interest limitations should be evaluated in conjunction with basic tax policy goals. If the provisions reducing or eliminating the tax burden on some types of property income represent bad policy, they should be dealt with directly. Interest limitations are justified only if "more direct methods of controlling undesirable activities are unavailable." Even here, caution is required because the limitations may "worsen the inequities and inefficiencies" that would otherwise exist. If the activities are desirable, then efforts might be made to achieve full capitalization. For example, assets might be made more substitutable by enacting provisions such as safe harbor leasing. The role of interest limitations is thus quite limited. Auerbach is particularly disdainful of imposing interest limitations in order to improve the perception of fairness, which he views as symptomatic of the failure to delineate tax policy goals.

Although I agree with Auerbach's analysis of how tax arbitrage works, I differ with him in several respects regarding the implications of this analysis for limiting the deductibility of interest.

I agree that if we know that a tax benefit represents bad policy, the best approach is to deal with that provision directly. Yet in reality political considerations often render this approach difficult, if not impossible. While Auerbach recognizes this possibility, I believe it is more pervasive than he suggests. The history of attempts at tax reform reflects that many provisions widely believed to represent bad policy have proven to be quite resilient. For example, some of the existing interest limitations were enacted precisely because of the reluctance by politicians to take a more direct approach. The original version of section 163(d), enacted in 1969, is one such example. On the one hand, Congress was reluctant to eliminate provisions that reduced taxes on capital income. Yet Congress was greatly disturbed by Treasury reports indicating that some millionaires paid no federal income tax as a result of these incentives. One of the responses was to limit the deductibility of investment interest. There is a significant political constraint upon direct approaches. Interest limitations represent a "second best" alternative that should merit serious consideration.

I also believe there are good reasons for imposing interest limitations even if a tax preference represents good policy. The lessons of tax expenditure analysis provide numerous reasons why a direct appropriations provision is almost always a better vehicle for achieving good policy than a tax provision. A careful delineation of policy goals would thus remove from the tax laws good policy tax expenditures as well as the bad. Comprehensive interest limitations might help convert tax expenditures into more efficient direct appropriations by reducing the attractiveness of tax expenditures.

Even if, as a practical matter, many good policies may be achieved only through tax provisions, interest limitations serve the useful function of helping satisfy political constraints on the nature of the tax system. The example of investment interest limitations suggests there is a constraint on the extent to which wealthy taxpayers may reduce their nominal tax payments. Interest limitations help control the extent to which nominal taxes may be reduced.

Thus, if a tax preference represents good policy, it is likely that a better approach would be to promote that policy outside the tax system. Interest limitations may help promote a shift to this more direct approach. Even if this shift does not occur, interest limitations may be justified as a way of satisfying the political constraint that the tax system appear equitable.

Where a tax preference represents good policy, methods like safe harbor leasing should not be employed even if they might increase the extent to which the tax benefit is capitalized. A separate political constraint is that rules in the federal tax code generally must be consistent with income measurement rules. The safe harbor leasing provisions provide an example of a provision that violated this constraint and was repealed as a consequence. Although safe harbor leasing did help further the investment incentives of the accelerated cost recovery system (some people thought ACRS represented good policy), the appearance of large companies selling tax losses proved politically unacceptable. Safe harbor leasing also violated the first constraint in allowing profitable corporations to reduce or eliminate their nominal taxes. Just as the fact that millionaires paid no nominal or explicit taxes led to interest limitations and the introduction of the alternative minimum tax, the existence of profitable corporations paying little or no nominal taxes contributed to the repeal of safe harbor leasing. Price adjustments or other implicit taxes, although borne by both the millionaires and the profitable corporations, do not ease these constraints.

I have one comment regarding Auerbach's analysis of the equity implications of interest limitations. Where full capitalization is not achieved, I do not think we know what the distributional effects will be. I am not sure if Auerbach is saying something different when he indicates that interest limitations may worsen inequities. He does observe that although interest limitations reduce the price adjustments, thus increasing the windfall to high-bracket taxpayers for each unit of investment, the total number of units purchased is reduced by the limitations. Thus it is not clear whether the aggregate windfall is increased or decreased.

Further uncertainty arises with regard to the price adjustments to taxable assets. Auerbach's example assumes that the taxable return, including the interest rate, is unaffected by the tax preferences and the increased borrowing that they stimulate. In fact, the taxable rate of return, including the interest rate, is likely to increase. The distributional effects of these price adjustments are uncertain. Although interest limitations are likely to reduce these effects, we do not know the effects of these adjustments upon vertical equity.

Allocating Interest

If interest limitations are imposed, tax arbitrage interest must be distinguished from other interest. I would like to offer some thoughts regarding the advantages and disadvantages of possible allocation methods. Current law takes a variety of approaches. Each of the four methods I will discuss is currently employed to allocate interest in some situations.

One approach is tracing. Section 265(a)(2), disallowing interest on loans used to purchase or carry tax-exempt bonds, relies in part on a tracing rule. This approach has been roundly criticized as unworkable. Physical tracing is often impossible, as where borrowed money is commingled with other money before being spent. A tracing rule based on the taxpayer's purpose is difficult to prove and easily avoidable in most cases. Notwithstanding these criticisms, tracing probably best comports with the way most people think of allocating interest.

A second approach is to allocate debt in proportion to the assets held by the taxpayer. This approach is used to distinguish foreign from domestic interest, to apply the new limitations on the use of the installment sales method, and to some extent in administering section 265(a)(2). In theory, allocations under this method should be made in proportion to the fair market value of the assets held. In practice, however, the adjusted basis of assets is used to avoid valuation difficulties, notwithstanding a sacrifice in accuracy. Proportionate allocation has been justified on the basis that money is fungible. It is a rule that thus addresses the average, not the marginal, transaction. There are some situations under this approach where the interest deduction on the marginal transaction will not be limited enough to make tax arbitrage unprofitable.

A third approach is "permissive" stacking. This approach presumes that the debt is first associated with taxable investments. Under this approach, only interest on debt exceeding taxable investments is subject to restriction. A practical variation is to allow a deduction for interest to the extent of property income. This variation, which I believe was first suggested by Richard Goode, is adopted in section 163(d) with regard to investment interest. This approach has the advantage of being the easiest to administer. It has been justified on the basis that it recognizes that taxpayers may liquidate assets to finance new purchases. A contrary argument is that asset liquidations usually cannot be achieved without some tax cost.

The fourth approach is "strict" stacking. This approach makes the opposite presumption from permissive stacking: debt is first associated with tax-favored assets. Thus interest is disallowed or limited to the extent a taxpayer holds tax-favored assets. The "avoided-cost" method of allocating interest under the new capitalization rules is a variation of this approach. If interest limitations are designed to preclude tax arbitrage, then this type of stacking may be the best approach. Unlike pro-rata allocations and permissive stacking, strict stacking addresses the marginal transaction. And, unlike tracing, it is not dependent upon taxpayer intent. Where a tax preference represents bad policy but cannot be removed for political reasons, strict stacking may present the best approach.

Even where the tax preference does not represent bad policy, there may be at least some theoretical support for strict stacking. Assume that there are only two types of investments, one taxable and yielding 10 percent, the other tax-exempt and yielding 8 percent. A taxpayer with no salary but substantial capital should invest in the taxable investment until the 20 percent marginal tax bracket is reached. At this point, he should shift to the tax-exempt investment. At marginal rates over 20 percent, the benefits from the tax exemption exceed the implicit tax. Thus, if the marginal tax rate is 15 percent on income up to $20,000 and

30 percent on income exceeding $20,000, the first $200,000 of assets should be invested in the taxable asset. If a taxpayer holds $200,000 of taxable assets, $100,000 of tax-exempt assets, and $100,000 of debt, to which assets should the debt be allocated? If one asks which assets the debt enabled the taxpayer to purchase, I think it is the tax-exempt assets. If the taxpayer did not borrow, or now had to repay the loan, and thus may hold only $200,000 of assets, he likely would hold only the taxable assets because these would produce the greatest after-tax return. It thus may be appropriate to view the tax-exempt assets in this example as the marginal assets. These are both the assets that would not have been purchased if the borrowing had not occurred and the assets that would be liquidated if the debt had to be repaid.

There are, of course, problems with this approach. Taxpayers do not always exhibit the type of behavior suggested in the example. If they do not behave this way because of variations in the riskiness of assets, as Auerbach suggests, the rationale for stacking becomes less clear.

As this discussion indicates, it is not clear which approach offers the best combination of sound and administrable rules. But this question must be answered if meaningful interest limitations are to be implemented.

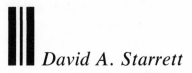 *David A. Starrett*

Effects of Taxes on Saving

THE DETERMINANTS of savings behavior have proved elusive in both the theoretical and empirical economics literature. Indeed, one might argue that the failure to explain macroeconomic trends in the recent past can be traced largely to the lack of a satisfactory model for savings behavior.

This paper explores some alternative theoretical models of savings behavior and explains how taxes affect saving within these models. I shall also evaluate the distortions introduced through the taxation of saving and the associated effects on welfare.[1] I shall examine both the possible motivations for saving and the question of appropriate functional forms.

I shall focus on only general taxes on saving. My major concern will be the sensitivity of saving to the tax rate on income from capital. However, I shall also explore the effect of offsetting changes in taxes on capital income and labor income.

I shall start with a simple life-cycle model in which people receive no inheritances and grant no bequests. Later I consider the effect of a bequest motive. In general, I treat consumption as an aggregate, but I do allow for "big-ticket" consumer durables. I ignore changes in labor supply that might be induced by taxes on capital income.

My most important conclusion is that it is not possible on the basis of theory to predict how taxes will affect saving. The reason is that saving is quite sensitive to the motivation behind it as well as to the mathematical representation of preferences. While I cannot resolve any of the outstand-

1. See A. B. Atkinson and A. Sandmo, "Welfare Implications of the Taxation of Savings," *Economic Journal,* vol. 90 (September 1980), pp. 529–49; or David F. Bradford, "The Economics of Tax Policy toward Savings," in George M. von Furstenberg, ed., *The Government and Capital Formation* (Ballinger, 1980), pp. 11–71, for a more detailed discussion of the welfare implications of the savings tax.

ing controversies about how taxes affect saving, I outline an agenda for the research needed to achieve a resolution.[2]

Computing Savings Elasticities

Almost all practical questions concerning the responsiveness of saving to the net rate of return are complicated by issues of uncertainty and expectations. People will behave differently if they think a change in the net rate of return is permanent than they will if they think it is temporary. Indeed, the short-run elasticity of saving with respect to the net rate of return cannot be defined without reference to some explicit assumption about future rates of return.

If the net rate of return changes and then remains at its new level, one can determine by what amount saving eventually will change after all agents have fully adjusted their behavior to the new level. I shall refer to such responses as *long-run responses* and label corresponding elasticities *long-run elasticities*. Short-run elasticities may differ from long-run elasticities for several reasons. One of the more important reasons is that at any given time a tax change will find only a few people just beginning their economic lives. These people will not be influenced by previous tax rules. Older people, however, will have spent part of their lives under the old rules and accumulated some assets or liabilities in the expectation that these old rules would endure. Typically, these asset holdings will cause the responses of such older people to be different from the long-run or "steady-state" effects.

I focus primarily on long-run responses, partly because more can be said about them than about short-run responses and partly because of the recent interest in how tax reform might affect the long-run capital stock. However, one should recognize that it may take many years for

2. For earlier discussion of these issues, see Lawrence H. Summers, "Capital Taxation and Accumulation in a Life Cycle Growth Model," *American Economic Review*, vol. 71 (September 1981), pp. 533–44; Alan J. Auerbach and Laurence J. Kotlikoff, "National Savings, Economic Welfare, and the Structure of Taxation," in Martin Feldstein, ed., *Behavioral Simulation Methods in Tax Policy Analysis* (University of Chicago Press for National Bureau of Economic Research, 1983), pp. 459–93; Alan Auerbach and Laurence J. Kotlikoff, "An Examination of Empirical Tests of Social Security and Savings," in Elhanan Helpman, Assaf Razin, and Efraim Sadka, eds., *Social Policy Evaluation: An Economic Perspective* (Academic Press, 1983); and Laurence J. Kotlikoff, "Testing the Theory of Social Security and Life Cycle Accumulation," *American Economic Review*, vol. 69 (June 1979), pp. 396–410.

long-run changes to materialize. The long-run response to change will not be realized fully until all persons partially affected by the "old" net rates of return have died. Furthermore, the concept will not be meaningful unless the new agents are similar in tastes and endowment to the old ones.

Savings responses can be computed in principle from aggregate data. Letting B_t stand for aggregate net wealth at date t, the aggregate budget constraint may be written as

$$(1) \qquad S_t = \partial B_t/\partial t = rB_t + W_t - C_t,$$

where S_t is net saving, r is the rate of return on wealth net of taxes, W_t is the value of earnings at date t, and C_t is the value of aggregate consumption. The rate of return, r, may include cash payments or capital gains. Assuming that these variables can be measured correctly (already a tall order), short-run responses to *unanticipated* policy changes can be computed by treating B as fixed and inferring the saving response from the corresponding consumption response. This type of analysis has been performed econometrically by a variety of authors;[3] however, to infer anything useful by this route, the practitioner must know a great deal about future expectations. One plausible hypothesis would be that agents believe that all policy changes are temporary, in which case useful information about short-run responses can be inferred from a representation of the consumption function in which future parameters are held fixed.

The long-run considerations are quite different, since B must be treated as determined through the adjustment process. Indeed, in a long-run steady state, B must grow at the natural rate of growth of the economy, m, so $S = mB$. Consequently, in the long run

$$(2) \qquad B = (C - W)/(r - m).$$

Assuming that resource supplies are fixed, aggregate savings responses can be computed from knowledge of an aggregate long-run consumption function. For example, sensitivity to interest rate changes

---

3. See, for example, Michael J. Boskin, "Taxation, Saving, and the Rate of Interest," *Journal of Political Economy,* vol. 86 (April 1978, pt. 2), pp. S3–S27, and the references therein.

can be computed by differentiating equation 2 with respect to this rate.[4] Converting to elasticity form yields

(3) $\eta^s = [C/(C - W)]\eta^c - r/(r - m)$,

where η^s stands for the long-run interest elasticity of saving (percentage increase in saving per percentage increase in the interest rate) and η^c stands for the corresponding elasticity of consumption.

Two points are worth emphasizing at this level of generality. First (assuming an efficient regime in which $r > m$), η^s is sure to be negative unless η^c is positive. This fact seems a bit odd, since if η^c were interpreted as a price elasticity one would expect it to be negative. However, η^c is *not* a pure price elasticity; it also exhibits properties of a wealth elasticity. It incorporates *both* the fact that the young will consume less *and* the fact that the old will consume more as the interest rate they all anticipate rises. This wealth effect is going to be positive as long as $r > m$ so that the return on saving to old cohorts outweighs the extra saving of young cohorts.

Second, any errors in specifying the consumption function (or elasticity) will be magnified in the corresponding savings elasticity, because consumption is so much larger than saving. This effect will be particularly acute when the interest rate is relatively close to the growth rate. Indeed, small percentage changes in η^c may imply relatively large differences in η^s. For example, if $C/(C - W) = 15$, $r = 0.04$, and $m = 0.035$, then $\eta^c = 0.6$ leads to $\eta^s = 1$, while $\eta^c = 0.5$ leads to $\eta^s = -0.5$.

These observations suggest that it is very hard to estimate long-run savings elasticities from aggregate consumption data. For one thing, consumption in the long run is positively related to r, but most empirical studies show negative consumption elasticities.[5] None of them is able to capture the fact that the old will consume more in their old age when faced with a higher interest rate throughout their lifetime. Furthermore, even if the correct function can be estimated, any specification error is going to be magnified, as I have just shown.

---

4. Differentiating yields $\partial B/\partial r = (\partial C/\partial r)/(r - m) - (C - W)/(r - m)^2$. Therefore, substituting from equation 2 we find $(r/B)(\partial B/\partial r) = C/(C - W)(r/C) \cdot \partial C/\partial r - [r/(r - m)]$. Equation 3 now follows from the conventional elasticity definitions $\eta^s = (r/B)(dB/dr)$ and $\eta^c = (r/C)(dC/dr)$.

5. See, for example, Boskin, "Taxation, Saving, and the Rate of Interest," p. S14.

The Theoretical Argument for High Interest Elasticities

There are some theoretical reasons for believing that the long-run interest elasticity of saving ought to be large even if there is a relatively low degree of substitutability from one period to the next.[6] These reasons derive from properties of models in which the agents have indefinitely long lives. For a broad class of utility functions (involving wide variation in the degree of period-to-period substitution), these models have the property that only one interest rate is consistent with long-run equilibrium. Any attempt to maintain some other rate will lead to an infinite accumulation or reduction of savings balances (relative to the capital stock). In other words, the long-run savings elasticity is infinite in these models. Now, if the effective lifetime horizon is finite but long, an appeal to continuity suggests that the corresponding interest elasticity still will be high.

This observation is important because until recently most discussion of saving in the overlapping-generations model was conducted in the context of two-period lives, where interest elasticities turn out to be quite low. Summers sought to deal properly with the time horizon issue.[7] To avoid discrete-period effects, he examined a continuous-time model in which the effective lifetime could be thought of as a continuous parameter (T). He proceeded to compute long-run elasticities for an overlapping-generations model using the following preference function:

$$(4) \qquad U = \int_{t=0}^{T} \frac{(c_t)^\gamma}{\gamma} e^{-\delta t} dt.$$

In this equation δ is the subjective rate of discount and γ is a variable that indicates the household's willingness to give up consumption in one period for added consumption in another. The variable γ can take on any value less than or equal to one. A value of one indicates indifference about the timing of consumption. As the value of γ declines, consumers are progressively less willing to trade consumption in one period for that in another.

6. Robert E. Hall was perhaps the first to make this conjecture in "Stochastic Implications of the Life Cycle–Permanent Income Hypothesis: Theory and Evidence," *Journal of Political Economy*, vol. 86 (December 1978), pp. 971–87. See also Summers, "Capital Taxation and Accumulation," pp. 536–37.

7. Summers, "Capital Taxation and Accumulation," pp. 534–35.

Summers showed that for a wide range of variation in the degree of intertemporal substitutability of consumption, the elasticities of savings with respect to the rate of return were greater than 1.5 when $T = 50$, representing a working life of forty years and retirement of ten years.[8] These elasticities were large compared with empirical estimates. They implied that taxes caused much larger distortions of savings than had been typically assumed.

Summers and later authors used this type of model to simulate the effect of various types of tax changes on long-run savings and capital formation in the U.S. economy.[9] These studies took baseline values for γ from empirical studies,[10] but showed that their results were insensitive to what they regarded as plausible variations in γ. They did not, however, test the sensitivity of their results to the form of the assumed consumption function. Two features of the welfare function in equation 4 are particularly questionable. First, that function incorporates the assumption that changes in consumption during one year have no effect on the value of consumption in other years. Second, it incorporates the assumption that a decline in consumption of, say, 10 percent has the same proportionate effect on welfare regardless of the initial level of consumption. The authors do not explore whether consumption functions that incorporate different assumptions would yield similar results.

There are strong informal reasons to doubt the simultaneous validity of these two assumptions. As the interest rate changes, the relative price of consumption changes far more in distant periods than in early ones. Unless consumers are extremely unwilling to trade future for present consumption (γ much below zero), current consumption will be very sensitive to the rate of interest. Indeed, this is the reason why savings elasticities are large. However, if this story is correct, then small changes in interest rates should generate large swings in early consumption. For example, in Summers's model with $\gamma = 0$ (a number he uses for baseline

8. Ibid., p. 536.

9. See Auerbach and Kotlikoff, "National Savings, Economic Welfare, and the Structure of Taxation"; Auerbach and Kotlikoff, "An Examination of Empirical Tests of Social Security and Savings"; and Alan J. Auerbach, Laurence J. Kotlikoff, and Jonathan Skinner, "The Efficiency Gains from Dynamic Tax Reform," *International Economic Review*, vol. 24 (February 1983), pp. 81–100.

10. Some of the relevant studies are cited in Auerbach, Kotlikoff, and Skinner, "Efficiency Gains." See also Robert E. Hall, "Intertemporal Substitution in Consumption," National Bureau of Economic Research Working Paper 720 (Cambridge, Mass.: NBER, July 1981); and Michael Hurd, "Mortality Risk and Bequests" (State University of New York at Stony Brook, Department of Economics, 1986).

simulations), as the real interest rate moves between 4 percent and 8 percent, consumers switch from borrowing 6 percent of their income to saving 42 percent. Such swings seem implausible. One can mitigate these swings by choosing smaller values of γ, but even if the best fit is chosen, there remains the possibility that the corresponding elasticities would be altered by changes in the functional form.

I shall suggest two reasons for modifying the functional form above and explore their implications for long-run savings elasticities. First, some fraction of consumption involves necessities that people virtually cannot do without. These will be purchased in each period regardless of the interest rate. Consequently, the representation in equation 4 is inappropriate because the degree of inelasticity should increase as the necessity level is approached from above. Rather, one ought to employ a Stone-Geary generalization with consumption base built in. That is, the objective equation 4 ought to be replaced with

$$(5) \qquad U = \int_{t=0}^{T} \frac{(c_t - \bar{c}_t)^\gamma}{\gamma} e^{-\delta t} \, dt,$$

where $\bar{c}_t$ represents the level of necessities at date t. Since the presence of a consumption floor may mitigate swings in early consumption, such a formulation is likely to exhibit reduced sensitivity of savings to interest rate changes.

Second, a significant fraction of consumption spending involves big-ticket items such as houses and children's education. Although the timing and size of these purchases are not completely rigid, there is much less discretion in their choice than in the other elements of flow consumption. Again, this limited discretion is likely to introduce inelasticity into savings response functions.

Purchase of big-ticket durables involves a certain type of complementarity in preferences across time. Of course, there are many other types of complementarity also worthy of consideration. For example, there is a wide variety of goods and services (such as barber services, lawn care, or opera performances) that people want to consume in more than one period, if at all. Such complementarities imply that consumption in one period influences the utility of consumption in later periods. Although such interrelationships are consequently difficult to analyze formally, I shall make some informal comments below concerning their effect on saving.

Long-Run Savings Elasticities in the Model without Bequests

To test the sensitivity of savings elasticities to variations in these and other parameters, I carried out a variety of simulations similar in general form to Summers's.[11] Since problems of estimating a suitable cohort preference function are quite formidable,[12] I resorted to simulations over a range of parameter values for functional forms that incorporate these features. In this section, I treat big-ticket items as fixed both in timing and in size. Later I explore the importance of the timing choice and show that it has a relatively small effect on overall saving behavior. The variables I use in the simulation are listed below. In general, I find that estimated savings elasticities are sensitive to what one assumes about the proportion of consumption devoted to necessities and many of the other variables. In fact, one cannot be sure whether steady-state savings elasticities are positive or negative. The short-run elasticities are even more uncertain, for reasons set forth later.

Parameter	Definition	Range of values
T	Consumer lifetime	50 years
$\hat{T}$	Time of retirement	40 years
h	Wage growth within lifetime	2–3.5 percent
r	Consumer interest rate	4–8 percent
Γ	Size of big-ticket purchase relative to initial yearly income	0–10
v^*	Time of big-ticket purchase	15–20 years
n	Population growth rate	2 percent
g	Rate of productivity growth	1.5–3 percent
α	Percentage of standard of living required for necessities	0–50 percent
δ	Subjective rate of discount	3–5 percent
γ	Substitution parameter	0 to -5
M	Borrowing constraint (times wage of initial year)	0–8
W	Present value of wage income (times wage of initial year)	30.08–40

11. For similar simulations, see Owen J. Evans, "Tax Policy, the Interest Elasticity of Saving, and Capital Accumulation: Numerical Analysis of Theoretical Models," *American Economic Review,* vol. 73 (June 1983), pp. 398–410; and David A. Starrett, "Long Run Savings Elasticities in the Life Cycle Model," Research Paper 24 (Stanford University, Department of Economics, 1982).

12. See Mervyn King, "The Economics of Saving: A Survey of Recent Contributions," in Kenneth J. Arrow and Seppo Honkapohja, eds., *Frontiers of Economics* (Basil Blackwell, 1985), pp. 227–94, for a discussion of the difficulties encountered.

Members of a cohort live T periods after they form a separate household and work during the first $\hat{T}$ of these. During their working life wages grow at the rate h. There are no bequests. Everyone can borrow or lend freely at the rate r. Consequently, the present value of wages equals the present value of all consumption. (I address the effects of liquidity constraints and other imperfections later.) In addition to ordinary consumption, cohorts purchase a big-ticket item of size Γ at date v^*. Cohort populations are assumed to grow at the rate of n, while cohort productivity grows at the rate g. Thus the rate of growth of the economy in a steady state (m) will be $n + g$. Further, I assume that both the initial consumption base and the size of big-ticket purchase grow at rate g; that is, the perception of necessities is seen as relative, so that each generation perceives such spending as a constant percentage, α, of the general standard of living.[13]

The results from simulating this model appear in tables 1–3. The savings rate reported there is saving relative to noninterest income, so the rates will be somewhat higher than if I had used saving relative to GNP. The model generates average savings rates on the order of 6–8 percent. Although these rates may seem low, the underlying baseline parameter choices correspond relatively closely to those used in the aforementioned simulation studies.

Among the many parameters of the model, savings elasticities were most sensitive to γ, α, and T. Interestingly, the size and timing of big-ticket outlays—Γ and v^*, respectively—were relatively unimportant. I explore the reasons for this result later and show that big-ticket outlays may still have important implications for savings elasticities when there are effective borrowing constraints.

There is no big-ticket spending in the first table. Elasticities are quite sensitive to α. When α moves from zero to one-half, elasticities decline considerably; indeed, for $\gamma = -2$, the interest elasticities become negative. For example, when $r = 0.04$, and $\gamma = -2$, the interest elasticity is 2.72 at $\alpha = 0$; 0.38 at $\alpha = 0.25$, and -0.13 at $\alpha = 0.5$. What explains this decline? If everything depended on intertemporal substitutability, it would be explained as follows: the degree of intertemporal substitut-

---

13. Although these latter assumptions are required if one is to have steady states (otherwise the relative importance of necessities and big tickets will fall over time), I think they are reasonable in their own right due to the so-called ratchet effect. Note also that this modeling choice is broadly consistent with the view (held by some) that preferences are homothetic in income for cross sections of "similar" individuals.

Table 1. Sensitivity of Savings Elasticities to Changes in Various Parameters in the Utility Function[a]

Interest rate (percent)	Substitution and necessity parameters											
	$\gamma = 0$			$\gamma = -1$			$\gamma = -2$			$\gamma = -5$		
	$\alpha = 0$	$\alpha = 0.25$	$\alpha = 0.5$	$\alpha = 0$	$\alpha = 0.25$	$\alpha = 0.5$	$\alpha = 0$	$\alpha = 0.25$	$\alpha = 0.5$	$\alpha = 0$	$\alpha = 0.25$	$\alpha = 0.5$
Initial consumption												
4	1.06	1.01	0.95	1.17	1.08	1.00	1.20	1.11	1.01	1.24	1.13	1.03
5	0.90	0.90	0.90	1.07	1.02	0.98	1.14	1.07	1.01	1.20	1.12	1.03
6	0.77	0.81	0.85	1.00	0.98	0.96	1.09	1.04	1.00	1.17	1.10	1.04
7	0.67	0.74	0.81	0.91	0.94	0.94	1.04	1.01	0.99	1.14	1.09	1.04
Savings rate												
4	0.06	0.08	0.10	0.03	0.06	0.09	0.02	0.05	0.08	0.01	0.04	0.08
5	0.12	0.12	0.12	0.05	0.07	0.09	0.03	0.06	0.08	0.01	0.04	0.07
6	0.19	0.17	0.14	0.08	0.08	0.10	0.04	0.06	0.08	0.01	0.04	0.07
7	0.26	0.22	0.18	0.10	0.10	0.10	0.06	0.07	0.08	0.02	0.04	0.06

Interest elasticity

4	3.70	1.82	0.68	3.20	0.86	0.09	2.72	0.38	−0.13	1.08	−0.24	−0.38
5	2.55	1.73	0.90	2.26	0.96	0.21	2.06	0.51	−0.09	1.30	−0.22	−0.43
6	2.23	1.74	1.13	1.93	1.05	0.35	1.79	0.62	−0.01	1.43	−0.15	−0.46
7	2.16	1.84	1.36	1.78	1.14	0.49	1.64	0.72	0.07	1.49	−0.06	−0.47

Income elasticity

4	1.04	0.79	0.63	1.09	0.54	0.34	1.14	0.41	0.25	1.34	0.24	0.13
5	1.09	1.09	1.09	1.20	0.87	0.69	1.32	0.73	0.50	1.98	0.50	0.28
6	1.10	1.23	1.40	1.22	1.09	0.98	1.38	0.97	0.75	2.24	0.73	0.44
7	1.10	1.31	1.63	1.23	1.23	1.23	1.39	1.15	0.98	2.30	0.96	0.61

Equal-yield elasticity

4	3.71	1.79	0.62	3.20	0.83	0.06	2.72	0.36	−0.16	1.07	−0.26	−0.39
5	2.51	1.64	0.77	2.23	0.90	0.13	2.04	0.46	−0.15	1.28	−0.25	−0.46
6	2.12	1.58	0.90	1.86	0.94	0.20	1.74	0.53	−0.11	1.40	−0.21	−0.52
7	1.92	1.58	1.02	1.66	0.97	0.28	1.56	0.60	−0.08	1.45	−0.13	−0.55

a. Baseline parameter values are: $n = 0.015$, $\delta = 0.03$, $\Gamma = 0$, $W = 30.08$, $T = 50$, $g = 0.02$, $h = 0.02$, and $\hat{T} = 40$. The necessity parameters, α, are the percentage of the standard of living required for necessities. The elasticities show the percentage change in the indicated quantity (initial consumption, the savings rate, and so on) with respect to a 1 percent change in the net rate of return. "Initial consumption" refers to the amount of consumption relative to initial income. "Savings rate" refers to the ratio of savings to noninterest income. "Interest elasticity" refers to the percentage change of long-run saving with respect to a 1 percent change in the net rate of return. "Income elasticity" refers to the percentage change in long-run saving with respect to a 1 percent change in wealth, where wealth is altered by changing income equally in all periods. "Equal-yield elasticity" refers to the percentage change in saving with respect to a 1 percent change in the net rate of return attributable to a change in taxes where the tax increase (decrease) is returned to (taken from) the taxpayer in lump-sum fashion.

ability depends on the the elasticity of marginal utility represented by $\gamma - 1$ in equation 4. When α is increased, ceteris paribus, this elasticity falls (taking lower negative values), so the savings elasticity will fall as well.

To see how much variation this argument can explain, look at the elasticity of marginal utility $(\eta^{u\prime})$ as a function of α and γ: $\eta^{u\prime}_t = [U''_t/U'_t](c_t)$ $= (\gamma - 1)[c_t/(c_t - \bar{c}_t)]$. On average (as a rough approximation), $c_t/(c_t - \bar{c}_t) = 1/(1 - \alpha)$, so

$$(6) \qquad \eta^{u\prime}_t = (\gamma - 1)/(1 - \alpha) \equiv (\gamma - \alpha)/(1 - \alpha) - 1.$$

Thus a positive α does alter (and generally will lower) this elasticity for any given γ. What value of γ in the isoelastic formulation will best correspond to a combination (α, γ) in the Stone-Geary formulation? From equation 6 this value should be $\hat{\gamma}(\alpha,\gamma) = (\gamma - \alpha)/(1 - \alpha)$. Suppose $\alpha = 1/2$; then if $\gamma = 0$, $\hat{\gamma} = -1$; $\gamma = -1$ corresponds to $\hat{\gamma} = -3$; and $\gamma = -2$ generates $\hat{\gamma} = -5$. Thus raising α from zero to one-half would be roughly equivalent to changing the substitution parameter, γ, from 0 to -1 (or from -2 to -5) and keeping α equal to 0. Looking at table 1, the reader will see that the effect on interest elasticities is much greater than this. Something more must be going on. The change in functional form does more than simply change the effective intertemporal elasticity of substitution. It inhibits the big swings in early consumption more than would be implied by this factor alone.

This observation highlights the fact that savings elasticities may be quite sensitive to the mathematical form of the function that relates utility to consumption. In particular, if the Stone-Geary form is correct, then simulations of tax policy that ignore necessities will overstate the sensitivity of saving to net rates of return, especially if γ is assumed to lie between -1 and -5, the range used in most recent simulations.

Changing the value of α has another interesting effect: the higher α is, the more sensitive the interest elasticity is to values of γ. Compare $\gamma = 0$ with $\gamma = -2$. When $\alpha = 0$, the interest elasticity falls only from 3.70 to 2.72 at $r = 0.04$.[14] However, with $\alpha = 0.25$, the corresponding elasticity falls from 1.82 to 0.38, and when $\alpha = 0.5$, it falls from 0.68 to -0.13. This discrepancy again illustrates the importance of justifying the choice of functional form before engaging in simulation studies.

14. It was partly on the basis of this insensitivity that Summers argued that long-run savings elasticities would not depend much on the intertemporal elasticity of substitution. See Summers, "Capital Taxation and Accumulation," pp. 536–37.

Table 2. *Sensitivity of Savings Elasticities to Changes in Various Parameters in the Utility Function, with Purchase of Big-Ticket Item*[a]

Interest rate (percent)	Substitution and necessity parameters							
	$\gamma = 0$		$\gamma = -1$		$\gamma = -2$		$\gamma = -5$	
	$\alpha = 0$	$\alpha = 0.5$	$\alpha = 0$	$\alpha = 0.5$	$\alpha = 0$	$\alpha = 0.5$	$\alpha = 0$	$\alpha = 0.5$
	Initial consumption							
4	0.98	0.87	1.07	0.90	1.10	0.91	1.14	0.93
5	0.83	0.82	0.98	0.89	1.05	0.92	1.11	0.94
6	0.71	0.79	0.93	0.88	1.00	0.91	1.08	0.95
7	0.62	0.77	0.87	0.87	0.97	0.91	1.06	0.95
	Savings rate							
4	0.06	0.10	0.03	0.09	0.02	0.09	0.01	0.08
5	0.12	0.12	0.06	0.09	0.04	0.09	0.02	0.08
6	0.18	0.14	0.08	0.10	0.05	0.09	0.02	0.08
7	0.25	0.17	0.11	0.11	0.06	0.09	0.03	0.07
	Interest elasticity							
4	3.43	0.56	2.78	0.09	2.26	−0.09	1.08	−0.27
5	2.46	0.79	2.09	0.20	1.83	−0.04	1.16	−0.30
6	2.18	1.03	1.82	0.33	1.63	0.03	1.19	−0.31
7	2.13	1.28	1.70	0.47	1.52	0.11	1.21	−0.30
	Income elasticity							
4	1.02	0.62	0.95	0.34	0.89	0.24	0.75	0.12
5	1.10	1.10	1.10	0.66	1.11	0.47	1.13	0.25
6	1.12	1.44	1.16	0.94	1.19	0.69	1.34	0.39
7	1.13	1.70	1.18	1.18	1.23	0.90	1.42	0.52
	Equal-yield elasticity							
4	3.43	0.50	2.77	0.05	2.25	−0.11	1.07	−0.28
5	2.41	0.65	2.05	0.11	1.80	−0.10	1.84	−0.33
6	2.06	0.79	1.75	0.18	1.58	−0.10	1.16	−0.33
7	1.92	0.93	1.58	0.25	1.43	−0.04	1.16	−0.38

a. Baseline parameter values are: $n = 0.015$, $\delta = 0.03$, $\Gamma = 5$, $W = 30.08$, $T = 50$, $g = 0.02$, $h = 0.02$, $v^* = 20$, and $\hat{T} = 40$. See table 1 for definition of elasticities.

The impact of big-ticket spending can be gauged by comparing tables 1 and 2. In table 2, I assume that the big-ticket outlay costs five times the starting wage rate ($\Gamma = 5$) and choose a purchase date halfway through the working life ($v^* = 20$). I assume here that households can borrow to finance the large outlay if current income plus accumulated saving is insufficient to pay for it.

The introduction of big-ticket spending usually lowers savings elasticities, but not much. At $\gamma = -2$ and r = 0.04, the interest elasticity falls from 2.72 without such spending to 2.26 with the spending when α = 0 and actually rises from −0.13 to −0.09 when $\alpha = 0.5$. Table 3

Table 3. *Sensitivity of Savings Elasticities to Changes in Various Substitution Parameters, with Doubled Purchase of Big-Ticket Item*[a]

Interest rate (percent)	Substitution parameters[b]			
	$\gamma = 0$	$\gamma = -1$	$\gamma = -2$	$\gamma = -5$
	Initial consumption			
4	0.89	0.97	1.01	1.04
5	0.76	0.91	0.96	1.01
6	0.65	0.85	0.92	1.00
	Savings rate			
4	0.07	0.04	0.03	0.02
5	0.12	0.06	0.04	0.03
6	0.18	0.08	0.06	0.03
	Interest elasticity			
4	3.18	2.46	1.97	1.08
5	2.36	1.94	1.66	1.10
6	2.13	1.73	1.51	1.10
	Equal-yield elasticity			
4	3.17	2.45	1.96	1.07
5	2.31	1.90	1.63	1.08
6	2.00	1.65	1.45	1.06

a. Baseline parameter values are: $n = 0.015$, $\delta = 0.03$, $\Gamma = 10$, $W = 30.08$, $T = 50$, $g = 0.02$, $h = 0.02$, $v^* = 20$, and $\hat{T} = 40$. See table 1 for definition of elasticities.
b. $\alpha = 0$ in all instances.

reveals that even if the size of big-ticket outlays is doubled ($\Gamma = 10$), the effects are still moderate.

Thus, when the timing of big-ticket purchases is fixed, they have little effect on savings elasticities. Although the assumption of fixed timing is reasonable for such items as children's educational expenses, it is less reasonable for housing. Because positive net savers benefit from rising interest rates, they may respond by purchasing their housing earlier, especially if there are liquidity constraints. Such timing responses might, in principle, have substantial effects on savings elasticities.

However, in the absence of liquidity constraints, the timing choice has little effect on the savings elasticity as long as the growth rate is close to the net rate of return. Intuitively, the reason is as follows: if high rates of return cause people to purchase housing earlier in life, then each person will save less in total, but the saving occurs earlier in life, so that there is more of it relative to the size of the economy. These two effects tend to cancel. The same type of argument suggests that pure target saving will have less of a negative effect on savings elasticities in the life-cycle model than it does for a given individual. Of course, if people are induced to purchase later in life, these considerations work in reverse and any positive effect on saving is correspondingly muted.

To explore the magnitude of these effects, I performed the following experiment. Suppose that a fixed collection of resources is devoted to purchase of a big ticket; the item (which is fixed in size) is purchased at the earliest date when it can be afforded using these resources. I made the big-ticket item large enough relative to the resources so that positive saving was needed to acquire it. Consequently, when the interest rate increases, households will be better off and will use this increased wealth to purchase the item earlier.

In the absence of growth, such a process generates an interest elasticity of minus one—a standard result in target saving models. However, with positive growth, there is a positive contribution deriving from the fact that aggregate saving *per person* tends to increase as saving occurs earlier in life. The following table (based on an aggregate growth rate of $m = 0.035$, a wage growth rate within lifetime of $h = 0.02$, a working life of $\hat{T} = 40$, and a status quo purchase date of $v* = 19$) illustrates the importance of this effect.

	$r = 0.04$	$r = 0.05$	$r = 0.06$	$r = 0.07$
Savings rate	0.05	0.07	0.09	0.12
Interest elasticity	0.76	0.19	-0.09	-0.25

Here, the elasticity is positive until the interest rate approaches 6 percent. The alleged negative effect of target saving on elasticities appears to be largely unjustified.

If consumers face borrowing constraints, however, the purchase of a big-ticket item may involve an independent motive for saving, and the effect on savings functions turns out to be more significant. In the cases of housing and children's education, as well as other big-ticket outlays, advance saving is required because purchasers face borrowing limits or borrowing costs that rise as borrowing increases.

Of course, households may have voluntarily accumulated sufficient retirement saving to cover these expenses when they come up. However, since one typically cannot borrow against money contributed to a formal retirement plan, it seems likely that such constraints are binding for many people at some time in their lives. This view is also consistent with the observation that people generally do not fully "undo" social security–type transfer programs (a process that would require added borrowing by those who are constrained).

DAVID A. STARRETT

Table 4. *Sensitivity of Savings Elasticities to Changes in Various Substitution Parameters, with Borrowing Constraint*[a]

Interest rate (percent)	Substitution and necessity parameters							
	$\gamma = 0$		$\gamma = -1$		$\gamma = -2$		$\gamma = -5$	
	$\alpha = 0$	$\alpha = 0.25$	$\alpha = 0$	$\alpha = 0.25$	$\alpha = 0$	$\alpha = 0.25$	$\alpha = 0$	$\alpha = 0.25$
	Initial consumption							
4	1.01	1.00	1.05	1.02	1.06	1.03	1.07	1.04
5	0.96	0.96	1.02	1.01	1.05	1.02	1.07	1.04
6	0.90	0.93	1.00	0.99	1.03	1.00	1.07	1.04
	Savings rate							
4	0.05	0.05	0.04	0.05	0.04	0.05	0.04	0.05
5	0.07	0.07	0.05	0.05	0.04	0.05	0.03	0.04
6	0.09	0.09	0.06	0.06	0.04	0.05	0.03	0.04
	Interest elasticity							
4	1.32	0.85	0.58	0.28	0.25	0.04	−0.15	−0.16
5	1.31	0.95	0.66	0.35	0.31	0.08	−0.18	−0.22
6	1.34	1.05	0.73	0.43	0.37	0.12	−0.19	−0.26

a. Baseline parameter values are: $n = 0.015$, $\delta = 0.03$, $\Gamma = 5$, $W = 40$, $T = 50$, $g = 0.02$, $h = 0.035$, $v^* = 15$, $\hat{T} = 40$, and $M = 4$. See table 1 for definition of elasticities.

Borrowing constraints ought to reduce savings elasticities because they prevent substitution across long periods of time. As long as households have borrowed as much as they can at the date of purchase, effective substitution across time can occur separately only within two periods, one before and one after purchase.[15]

Tables 4 and 5 illustrate the quantitative effect of borrowing constraints at the date of the big-ticket purchase. If such constraints are imposed without changing any of the other parameters, the model explains too much saving. Therefore, in order to calibrate so that all my examples explain the same amount of saving on average, I made compensating changes in other parameters to discourage saving. For table 4, I raised the growth of wages within lifetime (h) from 2 percent to 3.5 percent and moved the big-ticket purchase (v^*) from the twentieth to the fifteenth year. Both changes would tend to lower savings. I set the required savings balance at that date (M) at four times initial wages. This constraint turned out to be binding for all but one entry in the table. Comparing table 4 with table 2 where $\alpha = 0$ and $r = 4$–6 percent, one

15. This assertion is justified rigorously in David A. Starrett, "Properties of Saving Functions in the Life-Cycle Model" (Stanford University, Department of Economics, 1986).

Table 5. *Sensitivity of Savings Elasticities to Changes in Various Substitution Parameters, with Doubled Borrowing Constraint*[a]

Interest rate (percent)	Substitution parameters[b]			
	$\gamma = 0$	$\gamma = -1$	$\gamma = -2$	$\gamma = -5$
	Initial consumption			
4	1.02	0.98	0.96	0.95
5	0.96	0.96	0.96	0.96
6	0.90	0.94	0.95	0.96
	Savings rate			
4	0.05	0.06	0.06	0.06
5	0.06	0.06	0.06	0.06
6	0.07	0.06	0.06	0.06
	Interest elasticity			
4	0.77	0.18	0.01	−0.14
5	0.85	0.24	0.03	−0.18
6	0.93	0.29	0.05	−0.21

a. Baseline parameter values are: $n = 0.015$, $\delta = 0.05$, $\Gamma = 10$, $W = 30.08$, $T = 50$, $g = 0.02$, $h = 0.02$, $v^* = 20$, $\hat{T} = 40$, and $M = 8$. See table 1 for definition of elasticities.
b. $\alpha = 0$ in all instances.

can see that the borrowing constraint dramatically lowers elasticities across the board. For example, when $\gamma = -2$, elasticities drop from numbers at least as large as 1.6 to numbers smaller than 0.4. And looking at table 4, one can see that as the proportion of consumption absorbed by necessities (α) increases, interest elasticities fall, much as they did in table 1.

As a second method of discouraging saving, the discount rate (δ) was raised while retaining $v^* = 20$ and $h = 0.02$. With $\delta = 0.05$, it was still necessary to require a savings balance of eight times initial wages in order to make borrowing constraints binding. Table 5 reports one set of simulations for purposes of comparison. The elasticities in table 5 are even lower than those in table 4 (when $\alpha = 0$). This observation suggests (and other computations support) the view that the importance of borrowing constraints has to do with the time horizon effects they generate. Table 4 entails a maximum time horizon for substitution of thirty-five years, as compared with thirty years in table 5.

I conjecture that any other factors that tend to break up substitution into distinct subperiods of life would have similar effects. For example, the consumption of many household capital items (such as washing machines, yard services, or outdoor equipment) is generally restricted to the period of homeownership. Other types of complementarity across time ought to have similar effects. It seems that it will be necessary to identify such factors before reliable statements about the responsiveness of saving will be possible.

My analysis of big-ticket items up to this point has assumed that participation is universal. The effects on saving may be quite different if the rate of return influences the likelihood of making big-ticket purchases. To the extent that saving is forced through borrowing constraints, the tax law can dramatically affect saving through its effect on participation rates, quite apart from its effects on net rates of return or incomes. For example, if special treatment of capital gains induces more home-ownership, and if the decision to buy a house forces saving, then lowering the tax on capital gains will increase saving. The elasticity of this effect will depend on the rate at which participation is generated as a function of tax and the amount of forced saving involved per transaction. One can imagine very high elasticities in a situation where many similar people are right at the margin of purchase.

Transition Paths and Short-Run Effects

I turn now to the question of how saving behaves during the transition from one equilibrium to another. Unfortunately, little can be said without some strong assumptions concerning expectations. In a world of perfect foresight, if the interest rate changes at date t from the constant level r^0 to a new constant level r^1, all agents fully anticipate this change. What is savings behavior during the transition between a steady state associated with one interest rate (r^0) and that associated with another (r^1)?

I shall not solve the transition problem here, but rather identify plausible transition patterns based on reasonable beliefs about prefer-ences. I focus on what is likely to happen at the beginning and end of the transition. Given perfect foresight, the transition begins long before the actual date when the interest rate changes; indeed, it starts when members of the newest generation will face r^1 at the end of their life.

Suppose $r^1 > r^0$ and the long-run interest elasticity is positive. One might expect that saving will increase smoothly from the level associated with r^0 to that associated with r^1 during the transition. However, this may not be the case. For example, generations facing r^0 now and r^1 later may well save less now (and more later when the interest rate is favorable) than they would if facing r^0 throughout their lives. Of course, this conclusion does not have to hold, but it will hold for reasonable preferences. Only the saving of this group matters in the initial phase of the transition, since all older generations face r^0 throughout in this phase; so transition saving falls initially even though it rises eventually.

Furthermore, transition saving may well rise higher than the eventual equilibrium. At the end of the transition, the only people not in the new steady-state behavior are members of the oldest generations who faced r^0 at the beginning of life. If this group saved less early in life, they may now be saving more late in life than they would in the new steady state.

None of these results need hold in the absence of perfect foresight. For example, when people expect current policy to remain in effect, any change is a surprise and there will be no transition before the date of the change. Under some circumstances, it can then be shown that saving will move smoothly to its new equilibrium. Clearly, one must understand how savers form expectations before one can predict the shape of transition paths.

Equal-Yield Elasticities and the Income Effect on Saving

Much of the recent literature on tax reform has focused on changes in the tax system that do not change revenues. This focus seems appropriate because it is the best way to isolate allocative effects of the tax system from those of government expenditures and intergenerational transfers that would result from the use of debt. This observation suggests that one should examine the effect on saving of balanced tax changes, for example, a reduction in the tax on savings offset by an increase in other taxes. For each such combination, the elasticity of savings is different. Since other taxes involve only an income effect in the model under study, I shall analyze the long-run income elasticity of saving in the process of evaluating equal-yield elasticities.

There are many different income elasticities in the present model, each associated with a different timing of the income increment. On the assumption that consumption depends on lifetime resources, income given to an individual early in life will induce more net saving than income given later. The appropriate elasticity is one that corresponds to income increments that would result from lowering existing taxes in some specified way.

It turns out that the income elasticity will be positive for most reasonable distribution rules governing tax relief when the interest rate exceeds the discount rate. For example, this elasticity has the same sign as $r - \delta$, when the increments are uniform over time.[16] Although the subjective rate of discount is unobservable, there is some indirect evidence that r must be generally bigger than δ. Consumption profiles tend to rise over time for a given cohort. This behavior will be chosen in the present model only if the reward to postponing consumption (r) exceeds the rate of impatience (δ).[17] Largely for this reason, I used relatively small values for δ in most of the simulations. Referring again to tables 1 and 2, one can see that income elasticities (computed as above, using a constant increase in income over the lifetime) are positive and generally quite close to one.

The finding of a positive income elasticity may seem surprising, since the income effect of a higher interest rate is negative in the two-period model as long as first-period consumption is a normal good. The discrepancy can be explained as follows: in the two-period model, all the extra income from an interest increase accrues in the second period. And when people receive money in the last period, they will tend to consume more in both periods (saving less in the first period). However, if people receive additional income when they work (for example, because of a reduction in a labor income tax) or if the increase in income is spread uniformly over life, then saving will generally rise. The crucial factor is whether the change in income stream tends to come earlier or later than the desired consumption stream.

To compute an equal-yield elasticity, I introduce a savings tax and assume that before-tax returns are unchanged, so that the incidence of such a tax falls entirely on households. That is, I suppose that the before-tax rate of return (ρ) is fixed exogenously so that the after-tax rate (r) drops as much as the tax rate (τ) increases. Revenue neutrality requires that any change in revenue from this source must be made up from an equal and opposite change in other taxes. I offset a change in taxes on capital income with a change in a lump-sum tax by an equal amount.[18] In the computation reported, this change was imposed uniformly over household lifetimes.

---

16. See ibid. for a demonstration.

17. Of course, in nonseparable preference models, observing a rising consumption path need not have any implications for the relationship between r and δ.

18. Letting Π stand for revenue from the interest tax and assuming that interest payments on debt are tax deductible, $\Pi = \tau B$, so $\partial\Pi/\partial\tau = B - \tau(\partial B/\partial r)$. The appropriate "equal-yield" adjustment lowers other taxes by the amount $\partial\Pi/\partial r$.

Given a positive income elasticity, the elasticity of savings to change in capital income taxes together with an offsetting lump-sum tax will be smaller than the corresponding elasticity of the capital income tax alone.[19] The importance of this effect depends on the size of the savings tax (τ), since the marginal increase in revenue tends to be a decreasing function of that rate. I assumed $\tau = 0.15$ in the computations reported; larger values for τ will lead to smaller differences between adjusted and unadjusted elasticities, and vice versa.

The difference between the interest elasticity and the equal-yield elasticity is fairly small when $\alpha = 0$ (see table 1). The loss in saving from an increase in lump-sum taxes usually is dominated by the increase from lowering the tax on capital income. Of course, the required increase in lump-sum taxes is small when $\alpha = 0$ because, with high interest elasticities, lowering the interest tax increases the corresponding tax base. On the other hand, when α is large (and interest elasticities correspondingly smaller), the relative importance of these influences shifts. For example, when $\alpha = 0.5$ and $\gamma = -1$ in table 2, the equal-yield elasticities tend to be about half the size of the unadjusted ones.

Bequests

Up to this point, I have assumed that people save only for their own later consumption. However, many have argued that a substantial fraction of saving is accounted for by bequests.[20] Once bequests are included, one can think of a variety of reasons why savings functions might be altered. On the one hand, bequests serve to extend the effective planning horizon, so given the discussion above concerning infinite elasticities in the infinite horizon case, one might expect bequests to

19. This conclusion holds as long as lowering the tax on saving lowers revenue from the saving tax, requiring an increase in other tax rates.

20. An extensive literature tests the life-cycle model of saving against a number of alternatives, most of which involve bequests. See Albert Ando and Franco Modigliani, "The 'Life Cycle' Hypothesis of Saving: Aggregate Implications and Tests," *American Economic Review*, vol. 53 (March 1963), pp. 55–84; P. A. Diamond and J. A. Hausman, "Individual Retirement and Savings Behavior," *Journal of Public Economics*, vol. 23 (February–March 1984), pp. 81–114; and Michael Hurd, "Savings of the Elderly and Desired Bequests," and "Mortality Risk and Bequests" (State University of New York at Stony Brook, Department of Economics,1986). Laurence J. Kotlikoff and Lawrence H. Summers, "The Role of Intergenerational Transfers in Aggregate Capital Accumulation," *Journal of Political Economy*, vol. 89 (August 1981), pp. 706–32, provide some direct evidence for the importance of bequests in aggregate saving.

increase derived elasticities. On the other hand, if the donor treats his bequest as his own consumption, it will play a role more like that of a big-ticket item. And, as shown above, the presence of such items tends to lower interest elasticities somewhat.

Given this intuition, it is not surprising to find that savings elasticities are quite sensitive to the form of the bequest function, and that the size and indeed the sign of the long-run elasticity depend crucially on how families perceive bequests. The resulting sensitivity can be elucidated as follows. Consider the class of bequest valuation defined by the function

(7) $V(B) = \sigma(B - \bar{B})^{\gamma}/\gamma,$

where B stands for the level of bequests and σ and $\bar{B}$ are new parameters that reflect potential ranges of variation in the bequest motive; in fact, for some versions of this motive it is reasonable to think of these parameters as being sensitive to interest rates.

When bequests are valued because they augment consumption of heirs, the "base" $\bar{B}$ might be negative since bequests should be thought of as merely adding on to the substantial discretionary resources that will be commanded anyway by future generations. Furthermore, the value of σ might be quite sensitive to the interest rate in this case, reflecting the fact that the higher that rate, the more valuable bequests will be in generating consumption in the distant future. Negative values for the base will raise interest elasticities just as positive ones lowered them in earlier sections. And the sensitivity of σ has similar implications. These two factors combine to generate very high interest elasticities in such an intergenerational bequest model.

However, suppose that the bequest is viewed as consumption (at the date of death) by the giver. Then its size is not sensitive to future interest rates, and the appropriate value of "bequests base" would be zero. When simulations were conducted on the basis of these assumptions, interest elasticities dropped dramatically. Indeed, the presence of a "consumption" bequest motive had a negative effect on such elasticities similar to that observed in table 1 when the consumption base was raised.[21] Thus savings elasticities are indeed quite sensitive to the underlying bequest motive, a particularly unfortunate result since little is known about such motives.

21. For a full exposition of these issues, see Starrett, "Long Run Savings Elasticities in the Life Cycle Model."

Concluding Remarks

What does all this mean for tax policy? Unfortunately the main message is that economists know little about long-run savings responses or short-run adjustments to many potential policy changes. The lack of data makes it difficult, if not impossible, to select the single mathematical form that best characterizes consumption preferences. And saving behavior is extremely sensitive to this choice. I have tried to highlight key missing pieces in the overall puzzle. But until they are found I recommend extreme caution in the use of simulation models to predict the effects of tax policy changes.

Comments by Lawrence H. Summers

David Starrett's paper addresses a crucial issue in the design of tax policies: the relationship between tax policy and saving. If, as many economists and others believe, U.S. private saving should be increased, it is important to know what role tax policy can play in achieving this objective. In my view, Starrett's paper fails to shed new light on this important issue. He calls for "an agenda for the research needed to achieve a resolution" of outstanding controversies but does not present one. Moreover, I am persuaded that his analysis of past research is misleading.

The Theoretical Relationship between Saving and Rates of Return

Starrett argues that the conclusion reached in my earlier research that "[life cycle models] establish[es] a prima facie theoretical case for a high interest elasticity of savings"[22] is theoretically fragile. To begin with, I was careful to acknowledge that "a question of central importance is the realism of the life cycle hypothesis" and that "there are certainly internally consistent theoretical models which lead to a different conclusion, but their premises do not seem compelling."[23] I think that it is

22. Summers, "Capital Taxation and Accumulation," p. 537.
23. Ibid., p. 543; and Lawrence H. Summers, "The After-Tax Rate of Return Affects Private Savings," *American Economic Review*, vol. 74 (May 1984, *Papers and Proceedings, 1983*), p. 251.

260 DAVID A. STARRETT

incumbent on critics not just to suggest theoretical possibilities but also to document their importance. I shall argue that Starrett has raised no credible challenge to my earlier conclusion that realistic intertemporal models predict a significant response of savings to changes in the rate of return.

First, despite Starrett's criticisms, I hold that a homothetic utility function lends itself to reasonable representations of how consumers smooth consumption over time and that a Stone-Geary formulation does not. If utility from consumption is a function of actual consumption less some constant that represents necessities, the savings rate should rise steadily through time as per capita income grows. The absence of such a trend has been recognized since Kuznets's pioneering work. Indeed, the secular stability of the savings rate provided much of the motivation for initial development of the life-cycle and permanent-income hypotheses. Starrett avoids this difficulty by postulating that the amount of consumption of necessities rises proportionally with income. Looking at the range of consumption enjoyed by Americans today, I find it difficult to believe that anything like half the average level of consumption is in any sense a necessity.

Second, Starrett demonstrates that allowing for the possibility that consumers save in part to make "big-ticket" purchases does not greatly influence the interest elasticity of savings as long as the assumption of perfect capital markets is maintained. This result, which supports the view that savings are interest elastic, would be strengthened had he recognized that investment in consumer durable goods, like other investment, responds negatively to increases in rental costs. The simulation evidence of Modigliani suggests that increases in interest rates significantly reduce consumer durable expenditures and so increase the savings rate.[24]

Third, Starrett argues that taking account of bequests would reduce the estimated interest elasticity of savings. This conclusion depends on his assumption that bequests are made without taking account of the welfare of the recipient. My 1982 paper demonstrated that as long as the utility of even one family is based on expected consumption, not only by itself but also by its heirs, the long-run interest elasticity of savings

24. Franco Modigliani, "Monetary Policy and Consumption," in Federal Reserve Bank of Boston, *Consumer Spending and Monetary Policy: The Linkages,* Monetary Conference No. 5 (Boston: FRBB, 1971), pp. 9–84.

will be infinite.[25] Alternatively, if most bequests are left accidentally because of premature death, and if recipients are reasonably far along in the life cycle, taking account of bequests will actually increase the estimated interest elasticity of savings. Seidman's analysis supports the conclusion that capital taxes depress savings.[26]

Finally, Starrett treats the possibility that consumers are liquidity constrained. Interestingly, he finds it rather difficult to generate plausible savings rates with his life-cycle model when he allows for liquidity constraints. He also ignores a crucial aspect of the problem that has been treated in other studies of the interest elasticity of savings. Replacing capital income taxes with other taxes tends to increase savings because it redistributes income away from liquidity-constrained consumers who have a high marginal propensity to consume toward others who have a low marginal propensity to consume. Even ignoring this effect, it is noteworthy that in every case where the intertemporal elasticity of substitution algebraically exceeds -2, Starrett finds a positive relationship between savings and rates of return in his simulations focusing on liquidity constraints.

Starrett claims that his simulations establish the fragility of the theoretical conclusion that savings should respond positively to rates of return. Even so, more than three-quarters of his simulations yield positive interest elasticities of savings. If he had allowed for the effects of rates of return on consumer durable investment, altruistic bequests, and tax-induced redistributions among consumers, the count would have been even higher. The effect of interest rates on saving is larger still if one recognizes that consumers receive social security and pensions when retired and that age consumption profiles peak before retirement.

Observed Relationships between Saving and Rates of Return

The theoretical considerations that I have discussed imply that a dramatic increase in real interest rates, like that experienced by the United States in recent years, should have markedly raised the private savings rate. In fact, the private savings rate as measured in the national

25. Lawrence H. Summers, "Tax Policy, the Rate of Return, and Savings," National Bureau of Economic Research Working Paper 995 (Cambridge, Mass.: NBER, September 1982).

26. Laurence S. Seidman, "Taxes in a Life Cycle Growth Model with Bequests and Inheritances," *American Economic Review*, vol. 73 (June 1983), pp. 437–41.

262   DAVID A. STARRETT

Table 6. *Savings Rates in the United States, 1961–85*
Percent

Period	Private saving	Inflation-adjusted private saving	Change in net worth
1961–64	7.80	7.27	15.82
1965–69	8.72	7.52	12.39
1970–74	8.39	6.24	0.10
1975–79	8.11	5.10	21.08
1980	6.39	1.66	22.81
1981	6.64	3.05	0.19
1982	5.49	2.99	-4.36
1983	5.60	4.20	27.91
1984	6.88	5.03	9.71
1985	6.28	4.67	17.42

Source: Chris Carroll and Lawrence H. Summers, "Why Have Private Savings Rates in the United States and Canada Diverged?" *Journal of Monetary Economics*, vol. 20 (September 1987), pp. 249–79; and James M. Poterba and Lawrence H. Summers, "Finite Lifetimes and the Effects of Budget Deficits on National Saving," *Journal of Monetary Economics*, vol. 20 (September 1987), pp. 369–91.

income and product accounts has declined slightly in recent years (see table 6). This shift appears to be evidence against a positive elasticity of saving with respect to the real rate of return, and I would be the first to acknowledge the relevance of such evidence.

Nevertheless, two basic difficulties in interpreting recent movements in private savings—issues of measurement and identification—make it premature to conclude that after-tax rates of return do not influence private savings. First, the private savings rate should be adjusted for the effects of inflation on measured disposable income. Treating all nominal interest payments received by the private sector as income is clearly wrong in an inflationary environment. Making this correction raises disposable income in recent years relative to that during the high inflation years of the late 1970s; inflation-adjusted private savings have actually increased somewhat in the 1980s (see table 6).

Second, the private savings rate as calculated from national accounts data does not treat increases in wealth caused by revaluations of capital assets as a form of savings. The dramatic post-1982 stock market rally, which has created over a trillion dollars of private wealth, is not represented at all in the measured savings rate. James Poterba and I have examined the behavior of a broad measure of wealth savings.[27] Because this component of savings is highly volatile, determining whether it has increased in recent years is impossible. The data do

27. James M. Poterba and Lawrence H. Summers, "Finite Lifetimes and the Effects of Budget Deficits on National Saving," *Journal of Monetary Economics*, vol. 20 (September 1987), pp. 369–91.

suggest that consumption in recent years has been weaker than movements in real disposable income and stock prices would lead one to expect. This fact provides further evidence that increased rates of return may have increased saving beyond the levels that would otherwise have been reached.

The empirical record contains other important ambiguities as well. The fact that hotel prices are higher in Washington during the week than on the weekend and that occupancy rates are also higher during the week is not generally interpreted as evidence that higher hotel prices do not discourage occupancy. In the same way, simultaneous increases in real interest rates and the share of income that is consumed do not necessarily invalidate the proposition that increases in rates of return tend to increase savings. The crucial question is the source of the increase in the rate of return.

A number of arguments can be constructed to explain strength in consumption and high rates of return as a joint consequence of other events. If the disinflation of the last few years has increased the growth of income expected in the future or has reduced uncertainty about future incomes, one would expect both consumption demand and interest rates to rise. The fact that the stock market has risen so dramatically in the face of increased real rates makes this scenario plausible. Bernheim reports that the index of consumer sentiment has been very strong in recent years, providing further support for this view.[28] On the other hand, as Poterba and I note, consensus forecasts of long-term future income growth have declined over time.[29]

Alternatively, it is widely recognized that the availability of consumer credit has increased through time. As Starrett's simulations suggest, even a small relaxation of liquidity constraints could have a large effect on the savings rate. For example, home equity credit lines, which were essentially unknown five years ago, now provide consumers with several hundred billion dollars of extra liquidity. If only a small fraction of these funds are spent, the savings rate would change substantially. An increase in the ability of consumers to borrow, like an increase in their optimism about the future, would push real interest rates up and the savings rate down.

The problem of simultaneity that I have stressed here receives too

28. B. Douglas Bernheim, "Ricardian Equivalence: An Evaluation of Theory and Evidence," in Stanley Fischer, ed., *NBER Macroeconomics Annual* (MIT Press, 1987).
29. Poterba and Summers, "Finite Lifetimes and the Effects of Budget Deficits on National Saving."

little attention in analyses of tax policy effects. Economists believe that increases in interest rates reduce investment and increase savings. Given that at least until recently private savings and investment rates have moved in parallel, it is no surprise that these relationships do not both show up in simple correlations. Nor is it clear what variables are appropriate to use as instruments in order to identify structural savings and investment relations.

Considerations other than recent experience provide more support for the view that savings are responsive to rates of return. In my 1982 paper, I used a number of different empirical approaches in examining the responsiveness of saving to rates of return.[30] These include structural consumption function estimates, direct estimation of consumers' utility functions, and estimates of relationships describing wealth accumulation. Each of these methodologies supports the conclusion that savings respond to rates of return. In a more informal vein, Chris Carroll and I have examined the divergent trends in private savings between the United States and Canada.[31] We find that a significant part of the relative increase in Canadian savings can be explained by increases in the relative rate of return enjoyed by Canadians and tax incentives for personal savings that were put into place in the mid-1970s. Giuseppe Tullio and Francesco Contesso report similar findings in a comprehensive study of the relationship between savings and the rate of return.[32] This evidence is striking because, as emphasized above, simultaneity considerations work toward a positive association between consumption and real rates of return. Given the simultaneity problem, as well as the other econometric difficulties discussed in my 1982 paper, I do not find it surprising that some investigators have not found evidence that saving responds to rates of return.

Conclusion

Unfortunately, the available empirical evidence is not fully satisfactory for evaluating the responsiveness of savings to rates of return. While

30. Summers, "Tax Policy, the Rate of Return, and Savings."

31. Chris Carroll and Lawrence H. Summers, "Why Have Private Savings Rates in the United States and Canada Diverged?" *Journal of Monetary Economics,* vol. 20 (September 1987), pp. 249–79.

32. Giuseppe Tullio and Francesco Contesso, "Do After Tax Interest Rates Affect Private Consumption and Savings? Empirical Evidence for 8 Industrial Countries: 1970–1983," Economic Paper 51 (Commission of the European Communities, December 1986).

statistical evidence of an association between savings and rates of return can be uncovered, I find the empirical relationship more tenuous than the theoretical arguments suggest. It is unclear whether the statistics invalidate the theoretical arguments or simply illustrate how hard it is to interpret the data. I remain persuaded that permanent tax measures that raise the rate of return to savings are likely to increase private saving. But at this point, the magnitude of the effect is difficult to gauge.

The data do speak clearly on one point, however. Changes in public saving that occur as the government runs budget deficits have a direct and large impact on national saving. The most potent and reliable way to increase national saving is to reduce government deficits. Any adverse effect that tax increases have on private saving is almost surely dwarfed by their favorable effect on national saving.

Comments by Barry Bosworth

David Starrett's paper examines whether pure theory can predict the response of private saving to changes in taxes and other determinants of the return to capital. He extends the type of analysis made popular by Lawrence Summers. He concludes, as have several others, that Summers's arguments in favor of a large positive interest elasticity depend sensitively on the assumed form of the underlying utility function and on the presence or lack of constraints on borrowing by consumers.

Starrett's basic model is a relatively standard life-cycle formulation in which individuals maximize utility subject to a known stream of future lifetime income. That is essentially the same model employed by Summers, but Starrett goes on to consider four variants. First, he incorporates a Stone-Geary type of utility function in which consumers must have some minimal level of consumption necessities in every period. Second, he considers the effect of big-ticket purchases such as the purchase of a home, consumer durables, or college tuition. He then extends that model to include borrowing constraints. Finally, he examines the effects of bequests.

In all these cases, Starrett emphasizes a long-run elasticity of saving with respect to the rate of return. This aspect of his analysis is important in inferring any correspondence with observed changes in the aggregate saving rate, because such a correspondence would emerge only after a very long period of adjustment.

Any actual change in the rate of return will affect people of various ages differently. For the young, who have no accumulated wealth, the saving decision simply involves the allocation of a future stream of labor income. For older people, however, an unanticipated change in the rate of return alters the consumption value of previously accumulated wealth. If their wealth was invested in short-term assets, a rise in the interest rate increases their income, encourages current consumption, and reduces saving. Starrett's analysis largely ignores this short-run wealth effect by focusing on age cohorts who live continuously under one rate-of-return regime. Even if saving were eventually increased for such groups, the aggregate saving rate might fall after an increase in the rate of return because of increased consumption by older cohorts.

In actual practice, changes in the return to capital cause a wide range of capital gains and losses. They also alter interest receipts among creditors and debtors, which greatly complicate the determination of short-term effects.

Starrett's initial results, reported in table 1, are similar to those reported by Summers. The interest elasticity of saving is large and relatively stable over a wide range of alternative rates of interest and rates of intertemporal substitution, which is a transformation of his γ. However, the elasticity declines rapidly as he increases the share of necessities in total consumption. At high levels of consumption on necessities the interest elasticity also becomes very sensitive to changes in the value of γ. These results are not surprising because consumption has been divided into two parts, one with zero elasticity and one with an elasticity similar to that obtained by Summers. The average is bound to be lower. In fact, any assumption that reduces the degree of freedom in the consumption decision reduces the ability of the individual to respond to changes in interest rates.

The assumption about necessities, because the amount is proportionate to income, might be more realistically thought of as comparable to the relative income hypothesis of James Duesenberry, in that a substantial proportion of consumption is dictated by the consumption standards of one's social group, leaving very little discretionary consumption.

The inclusion of liquidity constraints in financing the purchase of large-ticket items sharply reduces the interest elasticity of saving. This result is similar to those obtained with the Stone-Geary formulation. The intrinsic explanation, once again, is that such restrictions reduce the degree of freedom in the consumption-saving decision.

I think that the type of dynamic modeling employed by Starrett is very useful in clarifying some of the relationships between assumptions and results. I also think that he is correct in concluding that such simulations cannot resolve the debate over the magnitude of the interest elasticity of saving. Whether saving rises or falls when interest rates increase, and by how much, can be resolved only by analysis of actual behavior. In particular, he clearly demonstrates the sensitivity of any results to the functional form of the utility function.

I would also like to discuss a different set of concerns with this type of steady-state analysis. That concern is provoked especially by the beginning of Starrett's paper, where he finds that the long-run interest elasticity of saving will be negative unless the interest elasticity of consumption is positive. That is not the normal context in which the issue is discussed since saving and consumption are expected to be negatively related. The result reflects the long-run nature of the analysis: if people increase saving and investment at any rate of return, their lifetime income and consumption possibilities are increased. These conclusions emerge from a growth model, in which an initial increase in capital raises the long-run level of income. It is only loosely related to the debate over the interest elasticity of saving. Furthermore, such a long-run analysis should incorporate a production function to capture the reduction in the rate of return from increased saving in a closed economy. In effect, Starrett's paper is an open-economy analysis in which an increase in saving can be invested abroad with no effect on the rate of return.

Finally, I believe that much of the current discussion of taxes and saving behavior confuses two different issues: the distorting effect of taxes on individual saving decisions and the effect of tax policy on the overall private saving rate. To date, the empirical evidence has been quite conclusive in discounting any substantial effect on overall private saving rates of changes in the return to capital. Tax incentives for saving, in short, have a very small bang for the buck.

Such a negative finding for tax policy, however, does not rebut the case for a less distorting tax system, and it does not deny the desirability of a higher national saving rate. If the country truly believed that increased national saving was desirable, a reduction in public dissaving—the budget deficit—could achieve it. I do not understand the current focus on incentives for increased private saving at a time when two-thirds of net private saving is required to finance the budget deficit. Nor do I understand the desirability of tax incentives for additional domestic investment at a time when less than half of current net investment can be financed with domestic saving. At the present time, tax policy should be a minor element in the debate over how to increase the national saving rate.

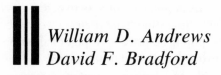 **William D. Andrews**
David F. Bradford

Savings Incentives
in a Hybrid Income Tax

RECENT policy analysis of the income tax has recognized two models or
ideals for evaluating income tax policy. One is the Haig-Simons accretion
ideal in which taxable income is defined to reflect a taxpayer's total
accretion in a period. Accretion is the sum of consumption plus accumulation. Henry C. Simons thus expressed the classic formulation of
this model: "Personal income may be defined as the algebraic sum of (1)
the market value of rights exercised in consumption and (2) the change
in the value of the store of property rights between the beginning and
end of the period in question."[1]

The second ideal is a personal consumption expenditure tax in which
accumulation is systematically excluded from the tax base. The simplest
version is one in which the tax base is set equal to net cash flow from
business and investment activities. The consumption model admits some
flexibility in implementation by reason of the general equivalence between deferring tax on an item and exempting its yield. In the case of

1. Henry C. Simons, *Personal Income Taxation: The Definition of Income as a
Problem of Fiscal Policy* (University of Chicago Press, 1938), p. 50. As to property
rights, the Simons formulation clearly requires periodic valuation of material wealth to
get taxable income to reflect accretion accurately. But few practical proposals to
implement the Haig-Simons ideal carry out such a program of accrual accounting with
full consistency. See, however, David J. Shakow, "Taxation without Realization: A
Proposal for Accrual Taxation," *University of Pennsylvania Law Review*, vol. 134 (June
1986), pp. 1111–1205. In their treatment of capital gains, even such ambitious designs
as the *Blueprints* comprehensive income tax and the November 1984 Treasury reform
plan abandon the attempt at accrual accounting. See David F. Bradford and the U.S.
Treasury Tax Policy Staff, *Blueprints for Basic Tax Reform*, 2d ed. (Arlington, Va.:
Tax Analysts, 1984); and U.S. Department of the Treasury, *Tax Reform for Fairness,
Simplicity, and Economic Growth: The Treasury Department Report to the President*,
3 vols. (Department of the Treasury, 1984).

consumer durables, for example, it is most convenient not to allow any deduction for a taxpayer's investment but then not worry about imputing any return; taxing the purchase price of a personal automobile is the virtual equivalent of taxing its use and much easier. Indeed, paying tax on the purchase price of the car is a prepayment of tax from a consumption standpoint, and so the yield-exemption method can properly be called the tax-prepayment approach to implementing a consumption-type tax.[2]

The current income tax is in some respects a cross between these two ideals.[3] Like an accretion tax, it taxes ordinary investment income, such as interest and dividends, and does not have any general deduction for saving. Like a consumption tax, it fails to tax unrealized appreciation in value of assets, provides a number of particular deductions for items that realistically represent capital expenditures, and omits from taxable income returns on owner-occupied housing and consumer durables.

It is not only the current tax that is a hybrid;[4] the inclination of tax policymakers is also mixed. They show little determination to go all the way in either direction toward a pure accretion or a pure consumption tax. Many of the recent proposals for comprehensive tax reform appear to be modeled on the accretion ideal but preserve important consumption tax traits.

The notion of a savings incentive is more difficult to explain than a hybrid income tax. In a broad sense it is a catchall for most of the general consumption or cash-flow aspects of the current tax.[5] But the term itself, *savings incentive,* seems to refer to a departure from the norm for the purpose of inducing an increase in saving. In this sense the term is not neutral concerning the accretion and consumption ideals since the provisions in question are only departures from the accretion ideal. The

2. We think the use of the term *tax prepayment* first appeared in *Blueprints* and was invented by a committee inspired by Harvey Galper. Some proposals for implementing a consumption tax have extended the tax-prepayment method to a wide variety of assets, often on an elective basis. See U.S. Department of the Treasury, *Blueprints for Basic Tax Reform* (Government Printing Office, 1977), p. 128.

3. For an exposition of both ideals and extensive references to the literature, see David F. Bradford, *Untangling the Income Tax* (Harvard University Press, 1986).

4. Some rules in the actual income tax have nothing to do with either *accretion* or *consumption* as the terms are used in theoretical discussions. The term *hybrid* in this context concerns rules relating to the treatment of saving and investing. Andrews appears to have coined the term *hybrid income tax.* See William D. Andrews, "A Consumption-Type or Cash Flow Personal Income Tax," *Harvard Law Review,* vol. 87 (April 1974), pp. 1113–88.

5. We are not distinguishing here between savings incentives and investment incentives.

term therefore implies that the current tax is not essentially a balanced hybrid but rather a Haig-Simons accretion tax with departures from that norm. As the term *incentive* suggests, the principal ground on which the departures are to be accounted for is that they induce people to behave differently, by saving more, than they otherwise would. The idea suggested by this term is of a tax expenditure, a departure from the accretion norm for a purpose essentially unrelated to those of the tax system as such.[6]

The current tax is not just a defective accretion tax, however; it is a rich hybrid combining positive aspects of both the accretion and consumption ideals. Accordingly, there is no more warrant for treating consumption-type traits as departures from a norm to be justified only by reference to nontax objectives than there is for so treating accretion traits because they are departures from a consumption or cash-flow norm. To explain the presence of one trait rather than another, one must turn to arguments concerning the choice between consumption and accretion models, arguments intrinsic to the business of taxation.

The title of this paper, "Savings Incentives in a Hybrid Income Tax," therefore suggests two quite different topics: (1) the problems that arise in trying to induce changes in savings behavior through provisions in the income tax, particularly the provisions of the kind that now exist; and (2) the variety of reasons why so much of real personal savings is left out of the income tax base. The first concerns, strictly speaking, savings incentives; the second has to do with consumption-type traits in the hybrid income tax, without any prejudgment about whether their main purpose is to induce an increase in saving.

Of course, inducing increased saving might be one of the reasons for leaving saving out of the tax base. (This possibility will be addressed separately.) But it is not necessarily the main reason or the best reason or even a very important reason. If the proposition is taken seriously that the current tax is a hybrid, not just a defective accretion tax, then other more convincing reasons for the provisions in question must be found. In fact, there are very great difficulties with the savings-inducement account of these provisions.

6. For extensive development of the idea that any income tax provision departing from the accretion ideal should be labeled and evaluated as a tax expenditure, see Stanley S. Surrey, *Pathways to Tax Reform: The Concept of Tax Expenditures* (Harvard University Press, 1973); and Stanley S. Surrey and Paul R. McDaniel, *Tax Expenditures* (Harvard University Press, 1985).

The major features of the U.S. income tax that make it a hybrid of accretion and consumption models are presented in the following section. Our paper then addresses the economics of savings incentives. In determining the effect of savings incentives, the degree of *capital market perfection* (loosely defined as a circumstance in which taxpayers can freely lend or borrow at the same market interest rate) is very important.[7] With perfect capital markets, these provisions typically do not provide an incentive to save more but instead are transformed into incentives to do what is necessary to relax constraints built into the rules. With imperfect capital markets (interpreted as the inability to borrow and lend at the same interest rate or, alternatively, as the requirement of certain kinds of collateral to support borrowing), savings-incentive effects are more likely. Imperfect capital markets also imply different incidence consequences of tax policies. Certain policies, such as statutory limits on deductible interest, have effects similar to those of capital market imperfections in the form of borrowing restraints.

Finally, the paper explores in more detail one of the most important so-called savings incentives in current law—the complex of rules by which certain forms of retirement savings are accorded preferential income tax treatment. The difficulties with such savings incentives force one to consider whether there may not be other, more general, reasons for the persistence of these provisions, reasons having to do with fairness and administration, which are quite germane to the business of taxation. The question is whether arguments in favor of consumption over accretion as a personal tax base have not been implicitly accepted, at least within the range covered by these provisions.

Major Features of a Hybrid Income Tax

In the accretion model of an income tax, income is set equal to total consumption plus net saving or accumulation. Put another way, in a true accretion-type income tax, saved income is taxed equally with consumed income.[8] In the consumption model, taxable income is set to reflect

7. Throughout this paper we use *perfect* and *imperfect* in a purely technical sense as applied to capital markets. We do not mean to suggest that it is obvious how existing capital market institutions could be improved upon, given information costs.

8. The terms *saved income* and *consumed income* have acquired currency even though they are conceptually inconsistent with Simons's specification, which defines income as the sum of saving and consumption.

consumption only, excluding accumulation. A hybrid income tax is one that combines features of the accretion and consumption models, with the effect that accumulation or saving is sometimes but not always reflected in taxable income. The term *savings incentives,* as noted earlier, refers to departures from the accretion model in the direction of effectively relieving saving from the burden of the tax.

Interest

Interest income is taxable in the accretion model. Principal is an existing property right whose repayment involves no income to the recipient, but interest, received or accrued, is an increase in the store of property rights to be included in taxable income as such. In some cases principal and interest may be misbranded, and then the tax system must make its own measurement of interest. If a corporation issues bonds at a discount, for example, then some part of the stated principal must be recognized and taxed as interest. And accrual is important; accretion income can be substantially mismeasured, either by waiting until receipt of interest to include it in income or by failing to accrue it on a compound basis. Moreover, inflation presents a problem; to the extent that interest only compensates for erosion in the real value of principal, it should not be included in income. But properly measured, interest (received or accrued) is in a sense the very paradigm of income in the accretion model.

In the consumption model, no distinction need be drawn between principal and interest. Under cash-flow treatment, money spent to acquire an interest-bearing obligation would be deducted, and then everything received, principal and interest alike, would be included in income. Under the tax-prepayment alternative, on the other hand, there would be no deduction for the cost of the obligation, but then nothing would be included in income for subsequent receipt of either principal or interest. Under either option there is no need to measure interest accurately or to distinguish between principal and interest.

Interest paid is the mirror image of interest received. In a true accretion income tax there should be an unlimited deduction for interest paid, while receipts and payments on account of principal should be excluded from the tax base. One needs to exercise the same care, therefore, in distinguishing interest from principal as in the case of interest income received. In a consumption-type tax, interest paid would not be deductible unless loan proceeds had been included, in which case both interest and principal repayments would be deductible; no distinction would be drawn in either event between principal and interest.

The current tax exhibits all of these modes of treatment. Ordinarily, interest received is taxable, and principal is neither deductible on acquisition nor taxable upon repayment. This is the essential accretion aspect of the income tax. It used to be that a cash-basis taxpayer could defer reporting of interest until receipt of payment, but in recent years extensive rules on original issue discount and the like have required accrual in many situations. At present, there is no provision for excluding the inflation component from interest income. An approximate method of doing this was proposed in Treasury I, but the method of approximation was criticized as excessively inaccurate in the case of taxpayers, such as financial institutions, that borrow at one rate and lend at another.[9]

Two particular exceptions to the general rule illustrate both forms of consumption tax treatment. Interest on state and municipal bonds is excluded from taxable income, as in the case of tax-prepaid treatment, and interest income in a qualified retirement savings account is treated on a cash-flow basis.

The purchase price of a municipal bond is not deductible. But then neither interest nor principal is subsequently included in income. (There is still a need, however, to distinguish interest from principal in some cases because capital gains and losses on municipal bonds are taxable or deductible, and computation of basis requires adjustment for receipts of capital and for accruals of interest.) The benefit of tax exemption is at least partly passed on from lenders to municipal borrowers in the form of interest rates lower than those on taxable bonds.

Investments in a qualified retirement savings account, like an individual retirement account (IRA), are deductible when made, and then whatever comes out of the account is included in taxable income at that time, be it interest or principal. This treatment applies without regard to what the account is invested in, and so its benefit will inure to the saver, not the payor of interest as in the case of the municipal bond exemption.

As to interest expense, our tax has exhibited considerable variety.

9. The method of approximation was to exclude a prescribed fractional share of interest income and expense, the fraction being computed periodically by the tax authorities on the basis of prevailing inflation and interest rates. Significantly, in the debate about this proposal, the relative balance of distortions—no indexing versus imperfect indexing—was little discussed.

Interest paid or accrued has generally been deductible, without regard to whether proceeds were used in a trade or business or income-producing activity, which is quite consistent with the accretion model. One longstanding exception relates to tax-exempt state or municipal bonds: specifically disallowed is a deduction for interest on indebtedness incurred or continued to purchase or carry such obligations. Recently, there has been a general limitation on so-called investment interest. The Tax Reform Act of 1986 tightened this limit and added others, so that when the law is fully phased in, there will be at least five different categories of interest expense: (1) trade or business interest is deductible without limit; (2) interest on investment indebtedness can be deducted only to the extent of investment income; (3) interest expense incurred in passive activities is deductible only to the extent that the total expenses incurred, including interest, do not exceed income from such activities; (4) qualified residential mortgage interest (that is, interest on no more than two homes) is fully deductible; and (5) consumer interest is not deductible at all. Because money is fungible, it is proving very difficult to distinguish sensibly among these several categories.

Since loan proceeds generally are not included in taxable income, interest would not be deductible under the consumption tax model, and limitations on deductibility under the income tax can be thought of as consumption model traits. Their purpose, apparently, is to limit taxpayer exploitation of the difference between full accretion model treatment of borrowing and less than full accretion model taxation of the return on investment of the borrowed funds. There is considerable controversy about whether the purpose and this mode of implementing it are sound.

Returns on Corporate Stock

Corporate dividends are taxable, and since the cost of a corporate stock investment is not deductible, this is essentially accretion treatment. Capital appreciation, on the other hand, is not taken into account currently (as would be required under a true accretion tax), nor is it exempted entirely (as it would be under the tax-prepaid version of consumption taxation if the cost had not been deducted).[10]

10. This description does not take any account of the corporate income tax. Under the *Blueprints* comprehensive income tax, inflation-adjusted income calculated at the corporate level is attributed to stockholders. Dividends result in a reduced basis for calculating capital gains, but they have no current tax consequences.

Capital Gains and Losses

Thoroughgoing accretion accounting for capital appreciation would require periodic valuation of all assets and taxation of any net appreciation (or deduction of any net decline) in value. Sales would not be substantively important under such a regime since gain or loss would be taken into account with or without a sale. Consumption tax treatment, however, would be based entirely on cash transactions, not changes in value. Under the cash-flow method, sales proceeds would be fully taxable, but purchases would be deductible. Under the tax-prepaid alternative, there would be no deduction, but then sales proceeds or any other investment returns would not be taxed.

In practice, realized capital gains are taxed without allowing any deduction for capital investments, which looks like accretion taxation. But changes in value usually are not taken into account until some event of realization. Before 1988, if the asset was a capital asset and had been held more than six months, even realized gain would be taxed at a significantly lower rate than ordinary income. On various kinds of exchanges the law permits further deferral, giving the new property a basis equal to that of the property exchanged, without any recognition of gain. And if property is held until death, there will never be any tax on the appreciation; death is not considered a realization of gain by the decedent, and the succeeding owner takes over with a basis equal to fair market value. A substantial portion of all capital gains thus escapes tax altogether, and much of the tax that is imposed is deferred in relation to actual accretion in value. As a consequence, the treatment of capital gains may be much nearer in effect to consumption tax than to accretion tax treatment.

Depreciation

Income taxes make some provision for capital recovery allowances, most typically in the form of a deduction of the cost of depreciable property spread over some period of its use. Financial accounting makes similar charges for depreciation of plant and equipment. These charges appear to be an essential element in any rational scheme of income determination.

In a true accretion tax system there would be no depreciation charges as such but rather a deduction for the actual decline in value of depreciable assets (and other assets) during each taxable period. Depreciation allowances in the tax system do not closely track changes in value, partly because that is so hard to do and partly because of a policy to encourage investment in such assets by allowing more accelerated deductions.

In a consumption tax, the cost of depreciable property would be written off on a cash-flow basis when paid.[11] Therefore, consumption tax treatment can be thought of as the ultimate extension of accelerated depreciation—depreciation deductions accelerated right down to the point of acquisition.

Of course, immediate deduction under a consumption tax would depend upon payment since the tax is computed on a cash-flow basis. If the cost of depreciable property is financed by borrowing, a cash-flow tax would allow deductions only as debt service payments were made. Under the tax-prepaid alternative treatment of debt, borrowing proceeds are not taxed, but no deduction is allowed for subsequent payments of interest. Neither would permit the negative effective tax rates on net equity return that result from full accretion treatment of borrowing and hybrid treatment of investment of the proceeds under current law.

To achieve true accretion treatment of depreciation in real terms would require inflation adjustments. Consumption tax treatment requires no such adjustments since costs are deducted in the period when they are paid. Explicit inflation adjustments, recommended under the current income tax, have not yet been adopted. Acceleration of depreciation is sometimes defended as a rough way to compensate for the erosion of depreciation deductions produced by inflation.

An investment credit, an allowance against tax liability of a percentage of the amount invested in specified real assets, has also been a frequent feature of the U.S. hybrid income tax. An investment credit does not raise any of the problems of tax arbitrage incentives that depend on marginal tax rates associated with accelerated depreciation, an advantage that has been little noted in recent discussion.[12]

11. Because it is usually difficult to sort out which of the receipts of a business are attributable to past investment and which to the provision of services by owners, the tax-prepayment alternative is not feasible for business investment by individuals. Thus, for example, the *Blueprints* cash-flow tax, which permits the taxpayer considerable flexibility between tax-prepayment and cash-flow treatment of assets, does not allow any choice for closely held business activities.

12. See Bradford, *Untangling the Income Tax*, p. 33.

Retirement Savings

Qualified retirement savings are excluded from the income tax base until they are withdrawn and available for consumption during retirement. This constitutes standard cash-flow, consumption tax treatment, except for the need to satisfy qualification requirements. These provisions are considered at greater length below.

Owner-Occupied Dwellings and Consumer Durables

The return on investments in owner-occupied housing and consumer durables is largely untaxed, which discriminates in favor of such investments as compared with investing in an income-producing security and using the yield to pay for consumer services. Under an accretion tax the only way to fix this defect would be to impute a value to services from consumer durables and include that value in income. This would raise valuation problems that are not involved in taxing cash flows.

Under a consumption tax one could also impute the value of services from consumer durables as taxable consumption. Then, however, a deduction should be allowed for investing in the consumer durable. This is the principal case in which it would be desirable to allow (or require) the tax-prepayment alternative, in which there is no deduction for purchase of the asset but then no need to include the return on it in income and therefore no need to face the valuation problem imputation would involve.

The current treatment of returns on consumer durables is thus very close to pure consumption tax treatment of the tax-prepaid variety. The main difference is that in a few circumstances a tax is imposed on realized capital gains.[13]

The Economics of Savings Incentives

The term *savings incentives* has been used to describe certain provisions of the tax law, provisions that induce, or ought to induce, persons

---

13. Tax on gain realized on the taxpayer's principal residence is deferred if the purchase price of a new principal residence exceeds the sales price of the old. Once in a lifetime, after reaching age 55, a taxpayer may exclude up to $125,000 of gain on sale of a principal residence, without reinvestment. Many other consumer durables, such as automobiles, are likely to depreciate in value with use and therefore not produce taxable gains.

to save more than they would under an alternative tax, presumably a pure accretion income tax. We now address the effect of savings incentives on saving.

Savings Incentives and the Incentive to Save

Just as the concept of wealth is elusive, so is the concept of change in wealth or saving.[14] It is generally preferable for purposes of analysis to avoid the question of defining and measuring wealth and to think instead about the effect of the tax system on the path of consumption chosen by the taxpayer over time. A rule that induces taxpayers with given endowments of skills and exogenously provided cash flows (gifts and transfers) to shift consumption toward the later part of life may reasonably be described as increasing the incentive to save.

Such a rule may or may not cause the person to accumulate more measured savings. Let us say, for example, that a person's lifetime is divided into two periods—youth and age. During youth the person obtains from working a sum of money and saves part of it to consume during retirement in the second life period. If the person seeks to divide his or her resources in a fixed proportion between spending on consumption in the first and second periods, the amount consumed in the first period will depend only on the amount of money earned in youth. It will be independent of the marginal return on saving.[15] First-period consumption will be a constant fraction of the amount of earnings, as will be measured private saving, which is the difference between earnings and first-period consumption. Reducing a tax on the receipt of earnings would increase both the amount of first-period consumption and the amount of private saving; increasing a tax on the return to saving would have no effect on either. If a tax on the return to saving is increased to finance a cut in tax on earnings, first-period consumption will increase,

14. Understanding exactly what is meant by wealth may be critical for defining Haig-Simons income, and therefore the tax liability of a particular taxpayer, but it may not have much bearing on the effect of the tax system on the trade-off between consumption today and tomorrow (see the Appendix).

15. This is the case of Cobb-Douglas preferences with respect to consumption in the two periods. For a slightly more elaborate analysis that takes into account labor-supply response, see David F. Bradford, "The Economics of Tax Policy Toward Savings," in George M. von Furstenberg, ed., *The Government and Capital Formation* (Ballinger, 1980), pp. 28–32.

second-period consumption will decrease, and measured private saving will increase, but public saving will decrease by more.[16]

The general subject of the incentive to save raises numerous analytical and empirical issues that we cannot resolve here. Partly for this reason we have taken more of an institutional approach to the concept of savings incentives, identifying them with features of the tax law that are believed to encourage saving in the sense of moving consumption from the present toward the future. In the language of economic analysis, we interpret the latter condition as a partial equilibrium increase in the marginal return to postponing consumption (which is to say, a rule that would make the after-tax interest rate higher if it did not itself change the interest rate). Even this apparent simplification presents difficulties, however. This is primarily because of the importance of arbitrage in the context of savings transactions. For example, suppose tax-exempt bonds did not exist. Analyzing the savings-incentive effect of introducing them would be senseless without taking into account the way in which the profit to be made by borrowing with tax-deductible borrowing and lending at tax-exempt interest might be limited.

Determining the effect of a provision on the marginal return to postponing consumption may be far from simple. Transactional complexity characterizes hybrid income taxes. In planning for retirement consumption, the taxpayer may have to solve a difficult dynamic programming problem. The marginal incentive to postpone consumption may be determined only from detailed knowledge of the taxpayer's situation. For example, a taxpayer will typically want to postpone realization of capital gains; depending on the degree of capital market perfection and the rules for deducting interest paid, the optimal savings plan may call for a last in, first out (LIFO) policy of asset acquisition and disposition. The marginal incentive to save now will depend upon the planned date of future dissaving.[17]

16. How the choice of a tax rule influences the equilibrium path of consumption is far more complex than this example. There is the classical problem of sorting out the relative force of income and substitution effects, whereby an increase in the rate of interest makes future consumption cheaper (which tends to encourage postponement of consumption); it also makes the person with some savings richer (which tends to encourage both present and future consumption). Expectations about future taxes and institutional aspects of capital markets also affect the path of consumption and the path of measured savings. Furthermore, income tax features such as the deduction for medical expenses, the inclusion of scholarships and social security benefits, and the graduated rate structure itself (which, for example, should influence the choice of time profiles and the riskiness of individual earnings paths) may play a role.

17. For good discussions of the technical problems confronting the hypothetical

In spite of the general usage, which we follow, it is not clear that one can draw an analytically useful line between savings and investment incentives. In a world of perfect capital markets, in which all interest received is taxed and all interest paid is deductible, it makes sense to think of the incentive to save as determined by the rate of interest. Provisions that influence the level of saving in the absence of any change in the rate of interest would be considered savings incentives, and investment incentives would be those provisions that influence the real asset composition in the absence of any change in the rate of interest. The assumptions required to make this distinction, however, are not very reasonable. In fact, introducing an investment incentive, such as accelerated depreciation, together with an offsetting measure to balance the budget, will typically influence both the composition of assets and the level of consumption. Indeed, in a closed economy a general investment incentive could not have any real effect if it did not influence the level of saving.

The Role of Capital Market Perfection

Hybrid taxes are characterized by income tax treatment of interest (effectively, accrual accounting, neglecting the problem of inflation correction) and consumption (realization) taxation of accruing gain on a wide class of assets. The resulting problems of inconsistency have increasingly been dealt with by special rules to limit arbitrage. To gain insight into the analysis, we look first at incentives to save in the absence of limits on interest deductibility and of capital market imperfections.

A PERFECT CAPITAL MARKET. Real life presents very complicated trade-offs between consumption today and consumption in the future at various times, and under various contingencies. It is common to model this complex choice as a simple one between consumption today and consumption tomorrow—where tomorrow is thought of as the end of some specified time (for example, a year or twenty years) or as a steady flow of consumption extending into the infinite future. Typically, the choice is embedded in a perfect capital market in which the individual can borrow or lend any amount at some specified rate of interest.

---

consumer seeking lifetime utility maximizing, see Yves Balcer and Kenneth L. Judd, "Effects of Capital Gains Taxation on Life-Cycle Investment and Portfolio Management," *Journal of Finance*, vol. 42 (July 1987), pp. 743–58; and R. Glenn Hubbard and Kenneth L. Judd, "Liquidity Constraints, Fiscal Policy, and Consumption," *Brookings Papers on Economic Activity 1:1986*, pp. 1–50.

In a rigorous Haig-Simons income tax the incentive to save is generally expressed as one minus the marginal tax rate times the real rate of interest prevailing in the economy. (We say "expressed as" because it is presumably the price of consumption in a whole series of future periods in terms of current consumption that corresponds to the margin of choice faced by the saving household. We usually think of that system of prices as derived from a single rate of interest, "the" going rate of interest, even though we should properly recognize a whole term structure of interest rates.) The incentive to save in a consistent consumption-type tax is expressed by the going real rate of interest itself. In short, in both of the polar forms of tax, the interest rate conveys all the information needed to calculate the marginal reward to saving.

The incentive to save in a hybrid income tax derives from the interaction of a whole set of taxes with different economic effects. But, to the extent that borrowing and lending at interest is always an alternative to other intertemporal transactions, the same principle applies as in the nonhybrid taxes. The incentive to save is expressed by the going rate of interest, less the taxes on interest that apply at the relevant margin, less the inflation rate. In other words, given the rate of interest, the incentive to save is unaffected by savings incentives. Only by influencing the applicable tax rates or the level of interest rates can savings incentives alter the intertemporal trade-off in a perfect capital market.

Take as an example the provisions whereby a person can deduct deposits to an IRA, up to a limit. Amounts set aside accumulate without tax until the time of withdrawal; all withdrawals are included in taxable income. The particular limit on deductions and the rules governing required withdrawals have no bearing on the marginal incentive to save in a perfect capital market. The person's strategy should be to maximize the discounted cash flow associated with the use of the IRA and any similar provisions, where the discount rate employed is the after-tax nominal interest rate. So long as the provisions do not lead to changes in the marginal tax rates, the separation of decisions about investment and consumption timing, mediated by borrowing and lending in a perfect capital market, continues to hold in the hybrid tax world with unlimited taxation of interest received and deductibility of interest paid.

What, in that world, are the effects of the IRA provisions? If the income tax rate of a person is fixed, the optimal strategy is to deposit as much as is allowable in the IRA and postpone withdrawal as long as possible. In this case any incentive effect is to be found in the determinants of those limits. If they can be relaxed by taxpayer action (for example, by earning more or retiring earlier), the provisions will affect those decisions. The graduated rate structure, however, might change the way IRA deposits and withdrawals are managed to maximize the (after-tax) discounted cash flow. For example, a requirement that the IRA balance be withdrawn at some point in the taxpayer's life may make it optimal to plan staged withdrawals late in life to avoid driving the marginal rate too high in any one period. In this case the savings incentive (the IRA provisions) will affect the path of marginal tax rates and therefore the applicable after-tax interest rate.[18]

Furthermore, the savings incentive will typically have income effects. In the simplest case the IRA provisions will be equivalent to a lump-sum reduction in the rate structure. It will be optimal for all taxpayers to make a deposit in the IRA up to the allowable limit, financed either by reducing other asset accumulations or by borrowing. Lump-sum tax reductions raise consumption at all ages, but this effect usually is not associated with savings incentives. Presumably, a general increase in the consumption levels of all taxpayers at all ages is not feasible. Changes must be made elsewhere to keep budgets in balance. If, for example, the IRA provision is financed by higher marginal tax rates, the incentive effect, as expressed by the net return to saving (or working) may be to increase consumption rather than saving. Taking into account the most obvious mode of budget balancing—increased tax rates—and neglecting the general equilibrium reaction of interest rates, leads to a presumption that the after-tax interest rate will be lower with than without the combined IRA and tax rate increase.

IMPERFECT CAPITAL MARKETS. The assumption of a perfect capital market implies no limits on borrowing and lending at the going rate of interest. The typical approach to modeling imperfect capital markets is to assume that the individual cannot be a net borrower or can be a net borrower only up to a specified limit.[19] Such an assumption significantly changes the operation of a savings incentive, such as the IRA. In a

18. For further discussion of the sometimes surprising implications of optimizing over time with graduated tax schedules, see Bradford, "The Economics of Tax Policy."
19. See, for example, Walter Dolde and James Tobin, "Wealth, Liquidity and Consumption," in Federal Reserve Bank of Boston, *Consumer Spending and Monetary Policy: The Linkages* (FRBB, June 1971), pp. 99–146; and Hubbard and Judd, "Liquidity Constraints."

perfect capital market, all taxpayers always confront the after-tax interest rate as the return on a marginal postponement of consumption. With borrowing constraints, the return on saving by the constrained and unconstrained taxpayers differs. The person who has a sufficiently positive accumulation along the pre-IRA path will simply shift funds from the taxable to the tax-exempt (IRA) form.[20] For such a taxpayer the marginal return on saving remains the after-tax interest rate. For the constrained taxpayer, however, extra funds sacrificed from consumption will be eligible to earn the before-tax interest rate in the IRA.

Borrowing constraints not only change lifetime consumption planning by the model taxpayer, but they also have somewhat surprising incidence effects. Consider, for example, what will happen if an IRA financed by higher marginal tax rates is introduced. For persons who choose not to take advantage of the IRA at all, this change must increase their tax burden. In general, the burden will shift from those most able or inclined to take advantage of the IRA to those least able or inclined (those without accumulated assets to put into sheltered form). The IRA thus tends to increase the incentive to save of those who are borrowing constrained and, through the tax rate increase, to decrease the incentive to save of those who are not constrained, that is, who have sufficient accumulation anyway. For two persons with the same lifetime earnings, the savings incentive shift, if any, is from the one relatively inclined to save to the one relatively disinclined. The burden shift is the other way, from the one predisposed to save to the one predisposed not to save. For unconstrained taxpayers, all of the incentive effect is in the marginal rates and in the provisions limiting the IRA deposit (for example, the level of earnings). For constrained taxpayers, the IRA deposit limit is unimportant, but the incentive to save is stronger than in the pre-IRA system.

Savings Incentives and Policy-Imposed Limits

As we have noted, limits on the ability of individuals to borrow influence significantly the effects of savings incentives. In some cases limits on the ability to borrow seem essential for there to be any equilibrium at all or at least one that generates positive revenue. For

20. See C. Eugene Steuerle, *Taxes, Loans, and Inflation: How the Nation's Wealth Becomes Misallocated* (Brookings, 1985), p. 129.

example, the realization rules by which capital gains are subject to tax (combined with the write-up in basis at death) can be used to eliminate income tax liability altogether in the case of perfect capital markets.[21] If, however, the posting of collateral is required to balance short and long transactions upon which the tax avoidance is premised, the equilibrium will be altered, and the relevant return on saving will be determined with reference to the marginal avoidance that can be financed by accumulating a marginal unit of collateral.

Consider the following hypothetical transaction. The purchase of an asset, the return on which is entirely in the form of capital gain or loss, is financed by selling the same asset short. In the absence of taxes and transaction costs, the net effect would be a wash. With taxes, however, the investor can realize the losing position (if one goes up, the other must go down), using the loss for tax purposes to offset other income and carrying forward the gain (until death, to avoid tax altogether). In fact, in the case of commodities, the tax laws require this pair of offsetting transactions to be aggregated. In the case of other securities, actual practices in capital markets apparently do not permit such a zero-net-worth transaction. The investor must put up some collateral (which is to say the investor must forgo consumption). The return on the collateral takes the form of extra tax avoidance.[22] (This particular form of tax arbitrage is actually restricted in another way, by the capital loss limitation.)

An even clearer example of the need for limits is provided again by the IRA. In this case the amount deposited, rather than the interest deducted, is limited. If there were no limit on deductions for IRA contributions, it would pay individuals to borrow from the IRA itself. Only the tendency for current deductions to lower the current marginal tax rate, and for larger future withdrawals to raise the future marginal tax rate, would prevent this procedure from generating infinite tax arbitrage profits.

It may be that tax policy in the past implicitly counted on imperfect

---

21. See Joseph E. Stiglitz, "Some Aspects of the Taxation of Capital Gains," *Journal of Public Economics,* vol. 21 (July 1983), pp. 257–94; and Stiglitz, "The General Theory of Tax Avoidance," *National Tax Journal,* vol. 38 (September 1985), pp. 325–37.

22. Were it not for transaction costs, the sorts of gaming of the system described by Stiglitz might lead all taxpayers to be in a constrained-borrowing situation. If this result prevailed, the introduction of an IRA would confront all taxpayers with the before-tax interest rate at the margin (up to applicable contribution limits).

capital markets to limit tax arbitrage. The ease with which taxpayers could borrow may not have been anticipated. But with the increasing perfection of capital markets and the increasing financial sophistication of taxpayers, the tendency to introduce statutory limits on the amount of interest that can be deducted seems to have grown.

The Qualified Retirement Savings Provisions

The law provides substantial income tax relief for those with retirement savings. The oldest and most important provisions govern qualified pension and profit-sharing plans. The central operative rules affecting such plans are as follows:

—Employees are not taxed on the accrual or vesting of pension rights before retirement, but only on the receipt of pension benefits whenever that may occur.

—Employers get a current deduction for payment of contributions into qualified pension or profit-sharing trusts, or for the payment of the premiums for qualified annuities.

—Qualified pension trusts are themselves exempt from tax on their investment income.

There are other beneficial provisions. Lump-sum settlements on account of death or separation from service are the subject of very generous rate provisions.[23] Moreover, the estate tax has often had favorable provisions for pension rights under qualified plans.

Beyond the foregoing, a variety of arrangements now exist for self-employed persons and employees whose employers do maintain qualified plans. The rhetorical technique for self-employed persons is to define them as employees.[24] The conditions for qualification for a plan including the employer as an employee are very similar to the conditions for qualification of a regular employer plan, though some standards are more stringent for plans in which owners of the business or stockholders have

23. These are commonly called special averaging provisions—a misnomer since the rate is that which applies if the recipient had received the lump-sum settlement over a period of several years without any other income. For taxpayers whose other income puts them in the top bracket anyway, true averaging would produce no benefit; these provisions, on the other hand, can be very generous.

24. The Internal Revenue Code, in sec. 401(c)(1), also allows "employees" to include participants in a plan of an unincorporated enterprise who are partners or sole proprietors.

a major interest.[25] For employees not covered by qualified plans, there are individual retirement accounts. These give individual employees an option to save on a deductible basis, without regard for what their fellow employees may do and without any kind of participation by their employers. IRAs are much more limited in magnitude, however, than are employer plans and Keogh plans. Like IRAs, 403(b) and 401(k) plans permit discretion on the part of individual employees about how much to contribute, but they are much more generous in the amount that can be contributed, and they do require an employer to maintain a plan or withhold amounts to be contributed. Moreover, a 401(k) plan limits what high-income employees can contribute, in the aggregate, by reference to what lower-paid employees elect to contribute.

Conditions: What Is a Qualified Plan?

The criteria for plan qualification are spelled out in detailed statutory rules, supplemented by innumerable regulations, rulings, and other administrative pronouncements involving various aspects of a plan's provisions and coverage and security. A common rationale for the qualified plan provisions is that they provide an inducement for employers to provide safe and sound pension coverage for a broad cross section of their employees. The qualification rules therefore serve to define the government's objectives as to broad pension coverage, and the tax benefits of qualified plan treatment are the currency with which the government seeks to achieve those objectives.

Originally, qualification criteria may have been conceived more in terms of income determination and definition than of tax benefit or incentive.[26] Deferring tax on an employee's accrual of pension rights was probably seen as a sensible, cash-receipts sort of construction of the term income in relation to pension benefits. Similarly, a deduction for the employer who contributed to a trust to fund pension benefits was considered a perfectly natural deduction in the accurate measurement of business income. Moreover, the pension trust was viewed as naturally nontaxable since it had no separate beneficial interest in anything, and all the real parties in interest were being properly taxed on their interests.

25. The relatively new term for this condition is *top heavy*.

26. Nancy J. Altman, "Rethinking Retirement Income Policies: Nondiscrimination, Integration, and the Quest for Worker Security," *Tax Law Review*, vol. 42 (Spring 1987), pp. 435–508.

Therefore, the trust need not be taxed as a proxy for beneficiaries. Indeed, only when the treatments of the several parties come into close juxtaposition does any remarkable tax benefit become apparent. In practice, this may occur when high-income employees conspire or contrive to have their salaries cast in the form of pension benefits in order to defer and reduce the burden of the tax that salaries are supposed to bear.

How, then, does one distinguish a true pension from a mere contrivance to cast salary in the form of a pension? The law's answer has been that a true pension is one paid pursuant to a general pension plan covering a broad range of employees, as contrasted with a private arrangement between an employer and a particular high-bracket or tax-conscious employee. The qualification requirements apparently have their origin in the effort to elaborate this distinction; only later did the idea appear that the purpose is to induce private employers to provide a particular sort of broad pension coverage that they might not otherwise have provided.

Besides corporate pension plans, there now exist various plans that are more a matter of individual employee discretion. Keogh plans take the form of pension plans but with individual entrepreneurs or partners defined as employees for this purpose. If a person who adopts a Keogh plan has any employees, the plan may have to cover them to meet qualification requirements. For those without real employees, Keogh plans cover only the entrepreneurs who adopt them, on terms that mainly are designed to meet their savings and tax-deferral objectives. In approving Keogh plans the Congress initially set rather modest dollar limits on what could be set aside for an owner-employee. Over time these limits have been raised, and analogous limits have been imposed on corporate plans. Today corporate employees and owner-employees are subject to the same limitations.

Extension of qualified retirement savings opportunities to the self-employed made such arrangements potentially available to most of the working population but not on the same terms; coverage of true employees depends upon their employer's adopting a plan. In fact, a substantial number of employees are not covered by any plan. They are denied the benefit of tax deferral for retirement savings just because their employers have left it up to them to carry out such saving on their own. To remedy this seeming injustice, Congress provided individual retirement accounts. Initially, they were available only for persons not covered by a qualified plan; then they were offered to everyone as a supplement to whatever plan coverage they might have. Now they have been restricted again.

Both IRAs and Keogh plans allow the prospective retiree substantial discretion in determining how much to set aside for qualified retirement saving. Such discretion may also be made a part of a qualified plan. Employee discretion does not by itself prevent a plan from qualifying for tax deferral, although the exercise of discretion must not be such as to make the plan operate disproportionately for the benefit of highly paid or supervisory employees.[27]

In sum, recent legislation governing retirement savings reflects an unresolved conflict between fostering individual savings at employees' own discretion and inducing employers to provide broad pension coverage by offering tax benefits for nondiscriminatory corporate plans that are not available for individual discretionary saving.

Retirement Savings Provisions as Savings Incentives

The primary effect of making contributions to a qualified retirement savings plan is to eliminate any income tax burden on the return on funds invested in this manner. Nothing is literally exempted from tax since everything that comes out of a pension trust into the hands of pensioners is taxed except to the extent it may have been taxed before, as in the case of optional, nondeductible employee contributions. As a result, the primary tax benefits associated with qualified plan status, from an employee's point of view, are benefits of deferral rather than exemption. But deferral of tax on earnings that are set aside for retirement is tantamount to exemption of the investment yield derived from those earnings. Beyond that, deferral offers some taxpayers a kind of automatic lifetime averaging by putting a portion of their earnings from active years into lower-income postretirement years for income tax purposes.

Moreover, deferral may drastically alter the impact of rate changes: persons who were able to divert pre-1987 earnings into retirement savings that will be taxed after 1987 may have enjoyed very substantial reductions in applicable tax rates; the reduction is even greater for high-bracket

---

27. So-called salary reduction agreements have long allowed employees of schools and hospitals to divert some of their salaries to purchase annuities on a tax-deferred basis. Such agreements are subject to a very complicated ceiling on permissible contributions.

earners who may have deferred earnings from before 1969 when the top rate applicable to earned income was even higher than 50 percent. In other time periods, of course, this effect may be detrimental since rates can go up between the time retirement benefits are earned and when they are paid.

PURPOSES. The origin of the qualified retirement savings provisions may well have been to provide a reasonable answer to the problem of income determination in the context of ordinary nontransferable pension rights or expectations, rather than to provide any particular tax benefit. But as the net tax benefit associated with these provisions has become more generally perceived, the provisions have taken on purposes that should now be the basis for their evaluation.

Supposedly, retirement savings are encouraged because they provide income security. It is considered to be in the public interest to prevent poverty, particularly for the aged who are no longer readily able to work or secure employment. Private pension plans are commonly viewed as valuable supplements to the old-age benefits provided by the social security system. Often discussions proceed on the apparent assumption that higher social security payments for all retired persons are desirable, but since the country cannot afford this, private pensions at least fill some of the gap for persons fortunate enough to work for employers with pension plans. It is generally considered a good idea to encourage employers to adopt plans that cover all or a substantial part of their work force.

Another reason given for continuing or expanding qualified retirement savings provisions is to increase aggregate private savings as a source of funds for capital investment.[28]

Still another purpose is to relieve an unfairness that would otherwise arise between persons who depend on their labor for a livelihood and those who live on inherited wealth. Persons living on income from property can generally afford to spend their whole income (or more) since their property already provides a source of income that will not come to an end as they grow older. Indeed, the measurement of income from property regularly provides some sort of allowance for depreciation of property of a sort that would wear out. Those who depend on personal earnings, on the other hand, cannot prudently spend their whole income since they are likely to outlive their period of productive earning capacity.

28. *The President's Tax Proposals to the Congress for Fairness, Growth, and Simplicity* (GPO, 1985), p. 340.

But if they save for retirement, and retirement savings were taxed on an undeferred, accretion basis, their lifetime disposable income would be reduced below its untaxed value by considerably more than the prescribed rate of the income tax.

Consider, for example, $1,000 of before-tax earnings set aside for retirement spending twenty-four years after being earned. At a 33 percent tax rate, this would represent forgone consumption of $670. At 9 percent compound interest, $1,000 would double every eight years and grow to about $8,000 in twenty-four. If the person were still taxed at a 33 percent rate, only $5,360 would be left for retirement spending. This is eight times the amount of consumption forgone, and just 67 percent of what would have been available in the absence of any income tax.

If this item had been taxed on a full accretion basis, only half as much would have been available on retirement. The original $1,000, reduced forthwith to $670, would have compounded at an after-tax rate of return of only 6 percent. At 6 percent the fund would double in about twelve years and in twenty-four would about quadruple, yielding a total of about $2,670. While this is four times the amount of consumption originally forgone, it is only about 34 percent of $8,000, the amount that would have been available in the absence of tax. One may feel that there is something drastically wrong if a 33 percent tax imposes a 66 percent reduction in retirement spending. Tax-deferred treatment of retirement savings can be defended as a direct and appropriate way of avoiding that result.

Whatever one may think about the taxation of other saved income, particularly that of wealthy people for whom savings may represent a surplus over personal needs, it seems only fair to eliminate the double tax effect on a reasonable level of retirement savings. This aspect of fairness in the treatment of earners as compared with independently wealthy property owners led John Stuart Mill to declare that no income tax would be just unless it contained a deduction for saving.[29]

This rationale helps to explain why the deferred taxation of retirement savings has been extended to taxpayers not adequately covered by qualified plans. It also may account for the prevalence of provisions of this sort in the income taxes of other countries.

DEFECTS AND ABUSES. Because the retirement income savings provisions operate only on a particular form of investment without regard to

29. John Stuart Mill, *Principles of Political Economy*, ed. by J. Laurence Laughlin (D. Appleton and Co., 1884), book 5, chap. 1, sec. 4.

the rest of a taxpayer's investment and spending activities, they fail to offer any encouragement or relief for savings that happen to fall outside the prescribed provisions for favorable treatment. Persons who save prudently and sensibly for their retirement but do not prevail upon their employers to fund their savings in a qualified retirement savings plan, and do not put their savings into an IRA or a Keogh plan, will not receive any benefit from these tax provisions. Except for the secondary effect on saving for other employees under a qualified corporate plan, it is hard to see any reason why savings should be encouraged only in an approved vehicle.

More important, there is no assurance that contributions to an approved vehicle represent any increase in net aggregate saving or indeed any net saving at all. Some amount of saving in qualified vehicles is apt to have occurred in any event in some other form. And some occurs that does not represent saving at all: persons who receive an inheritance, for example, may spend it while putting some of their earnings into a retirement savings arrangement.

Tax-favored treatment of corporate pension plans works in a particularly complicated way. The greatest benefits from favorable tax treatment of retirement savings inure directly to high-bracket employees; to achieve these benefits, high-bracket employees are supposed to prevail upon their employers to adopt qualified pension plans, and the qualified pension plans must meet various requirements designed to ensure pension coverage for some cross section of employees in the lower income brackets. Even without considering offsetting dissaving transactions, there are difficulties with this rationale. The qualified pension plan scheme represents an arbitrary and uneven way of inducing employers to provide pensions for low-income employees.

The nondiscrimination provisions have been criticized for not being strict enough for a tax-subsidized system of retirement income savings. There is, of course, a dilemma in the specification of nondiscrimination and other requirements. If standards are set too high—in the sense of requiring plan provisions or coverage that would not have been provided anyway—employers may be deterred from creating or continuing pension plans at all. This is an inherent dilemma in any attempt to induce action through an ultimately voluntary pension system.

Because of differences in ratios of high- to low-bracket employees in different industries, the extent of pension coverage provided to low-income employees in order to achieve the tax objectives of high-bracket employees will presumably vary among industries. Furthermore, differences in industrial organization may cause differences in the extent to which high- and low-bracket employees will turn up as employees of a single employer. Moreover, high-bracket employees may have different degrees of influence over pension policy in different companies. More important, the qualified pension scheme fails to provide any inducement to extend pension coverage to the self-employed. It is hard to justify a subsidy for increased pension coverage for employees that excludes those who make what they can in this world without the benefit of continuous employment.

Another disadvantage of current retirement savings schemes arises from the fact that they create zero-bracket players in investment markets. Moreover, these are artificial zero-bracket players since they act for the benefit of otherwise taxable principals; the profits they make, at a zero tax rate, inure to the benefit of those principals, whose profits would normally be subject to tax. This has led to what some writers have dubbed pure tax arbitrage, as contrasted with the tax arbitrage that arises out of investment incentives.

In form, an investment in an IRA is an investment in a particular type of asset. But the IRA is just an account through which one can invest in something else. Since earnings in the IRA are effectively exempt from tax, the most sensible investment of IRA funds is presumably in assets that are themselves fully taxable. IRAs, therefore, represent a way in which people can invest in fully taxable bonds on a tax-exempt basis. Because the bonds are fully taxable, they will sell in the market at a price that represents taxable bonds and will pay interest appropriate for that status. Ordinarily, the payment of interest on such bonds is fully deductible by the payor.

In an extreme case, A's IRA might invest in B's note, while B's IRA invested in A's note. No net saving would result since each person's IRA investment would be offset by liability on his or her note. And the arrangement would not produce or shift income on a before-tax basis since each party's interest payments on the note would be offset by interest receipts in the IRA. Before 1987, however, taxes would have made the arrangement quite profitable. Interest payments were deductible, while interest receipts in the IRA were effectively exempt from tax.[30]

30. In form, there would be a deduction for each party upon creating the IRA and

In practice, this would not be a good arrangement since reciprocal holding of notes would raise questions about bona fides that can easily be avoided. The essential effect is the same any time an IRA invests in taxable debt instruments while its contributor borrows on an interest-deductible basis. New restrictions have been imposed on the deductibility of interest on debt incurred or continued to purchase or carry tax-favored retirement investments, but the efficacy of such restrictions, as will be discussed later, is limited.

The interaction of savings incentives and investment incentives encourages complex investment arrangements to minimize overall tax burdens. Essentially, pension funds are substantial zero-tax-bracket investors; therefore, it is desirable to try to carve up the return on a real estate investment, for example, into taxable and nontaxable components and to place the former with a pension fund while the latter go to taxable investors. This technique is limited, to some extent, by provisions requiring in effect that certain partnerships with tax-exempt entities as partners allocate all items of income and deduction proportionately among their partners. (This is sometimes referred to as a requirement to have "straight-up allocations.") There are also restrictions applicable to leasing arrangements between taxable and tax-exempt entities. But one of the best ways of allocating taxable income is by interest payments, and so there is a very strong tax inducement for pension funds to be lenders to taxable equity holders, which produces taxable income to the tax-exempt participant with an equal and much more valuable deduction for the taxable participants. Frequently, the tax-exempt lender will seek conversion privileges or other features that will give its investment some of the favorable characteristics of an equity investment. How far this can be done without imperiling the desired tax treatment is not entirely clear.

Tax-favored savings vehicles, of course, are not the only zero-tax-bracket investors in the market. Net-loss corporations, for example, and tax-exempt charitable institutions have both been party to numerous schemes designed to divert taxable income disproportionately to the tax-exempt participant in a joint investment project. But tax-favored

---

deductions for payment of interest, and then a tax on the amount of the contribution plus interest when funds are withdrawn from the IRA. The net effect would be one of deferral. But if rates remain constant, the effect of deferring tax on the contribution itself is the same as exemption of the interest income but not the contribution. (See the paper by Alan J. Auerbach in this volume.)

savings vehicles sometimes act rather directly for the benefit of otherwise taxable beneficiaries.

Consider, for example, a tax-conscious professional woman who saves part of her earnings. She will quickly figure out that if she wishes to hold a certain portion of her assets in debt securities, she should do that first through her tax-favored savings accounts. That way she can get the benefit of taxable bond yields free of the burden of any tax. A taxable bond inside her IRA is the equivalent for her of a tax-exempt bond paying the same rate of interest, held outside (or inside) her IRA. One wonders whether this relationship partly explains the failure of long-term municipal bond interest rates to reflect anything like the full advantage of tax exemption.

The matter is less obvious in the case of employer pension plans since an employee does not have such control of investments by the plan, and investment through the plan is not so immediate an alternative to investment outside the plan. The fundamental tendency, however, is the same.

In the case of defined benefit pension plans, employees are not even directly affected by investment results in the pension plan. The party immediately interested in investment results is the employer since investment success will reduce the future contributions required to fund the benefits specified in the plan. If the employer is subject to tax, however, the same relations hold for it in terms of investing through the plan. An employer with funds to invest will enjoy the benefit of effective tax exemption if it makes the investment by contributing to its pension fund and letting the fund buy assets whose return is fully taxable. Investments of a large corporate pension fund are, at the margin, substitutes for investment by the employer but under the mantle of a tax exemption that would not be available if the employer were to make the same investment directly.

CURES? What cures, if any, are readily available for these misfunctions of the retirement income savings provisions? Some have been tried, and others should be considered.

To secure the benefits of the savings incentive provisions without doing any net saving at all, many taxpayers would need to borrow to fund contributions to a retirement savings plan or vehicle. A key to the tax benefit, therefore, is deductibility of interest, and one way to curb it is by disallowing interest deductions. As noted earlier, the 1986 rules disallow interest on debt incurred or continued to purchase or carry investments in tax-deferred savings accounts.

But disallowance of interest on debt incurred for a particular purpose is not always very effective because it is difficult and essentially rather arbitrary to allocate debt to one investment rather than to another. Under the new rules people probably will borrow more to finance their homes and less to finance their retirement plans since interest on the former kind of indebtedness is deductible while interest on the latter is not. But that discrimination is difficult to justify. Borrowed and owned funds are essentially fungible, and a taxpayer's capacity relates more rationally to his total debt than to some selected list of particular debts. Experience with the longstanding disallowance of deductions for interest on debt incurred or continued to purchase or carry tax-exempt bonds does not indicate that limitations of this sort are very effective or readily administrable.[31]

Even if interest deductions were effectively disallowed so that no net tax benefit would result from borrowing and investing an equal amount in a savings incentive account, wealthy persons could still secure the tax benefit attached to retirement saving without any net saving. They could disinvest from their existing wealth while diverting part of their earnings into a tax-favored retirement savings vehicle.

A more ambitious way of trying to cure the defects in the retirement savings provisions would be to make deduction conditional upon net saving measured in a comprehensive manner. A report of all dissaving and savings transactions—sales and purchases of investment assets and increases and decreases in indebtedness—would be required, and if these showed net dissaving, then any deduction for additions to a qualified retirement savings vehicle would be reduced accordingly. This would effectively limit tax benefits for contributions to a tax-favored account when they are financed either by net borrowing or by net disinvestment from other assets.

Such a scheme would require that net saving or dissaving be tracked over an extended period of time. It would hardly do to have deductible net saving in even years, while odd years showed net disinvestment. Moreover, to make the limitation fully effective, there should be a tax on any subsequent cumulative net dissaving to the extent of any deductions that may be allowed for retirement saving.

In addition to difficulties in effectuating the net savings part of the limitation, there may be others relating to the retirement savings part.

31. Philip D. Oliver, "Section 265(2): A Counterproductive Solution to a Nonexistent Problem," *Tax Law Review*, vol. 40 (Winter 1985), pp. 351–410.

Corporate pension plans do not involve deductions by employees that can be disallowed if they dissave from other sources. Employer deductions can be disallowed or deferred as a way of policing compliance with legal requirements and limitations, but it would not be easy to focus the impact of such disallowance on the employees whose dissavings were being investigated. Once one moves away from the world of IRAs and similar voluntary employee savings arrangements, measurement of individual accretion from the accrual of pension rights is not an easy matter.

Another form of hybrid income tax would have at least two partial taxes: a cash-flow tax on personal consumption and another tax on selected items of saved income. The tax on consumed income would pick up net dissaving from retirement savings or other assets and would automatically exclude all saved income. Then an additional tax could be levied on savings not intended to get the benefit of deferral. Net deductions for savings of all kinds could be limited to some specified function of income designed to represent reasonable retirement saving. But this would not by itself pick up excessive savings that take the form of employer contributions to a corporate pension plan unless, again, there were some allocation of contributions and earnings among employees. Alternatively, excessive corporate pension benefits might be limited by taxing pension trusts or denying or deferring employer deductions, but it would be hard to tailor this form of limitation to oversaving by individual employees.

With respect to pension plan savings as well as other forms of wealth, consumed income is easier to measure than is total income because the latter includes savings, which involve difficult questions of valuation and allocation beyond what are involved in measuring consumption. The difficulties of taxing saving on anything like a uniform basis persist, however, even if the tax is only on some saving.

Appendix: The Definition of Wealth and Saving and the Marginal Incentive to Postpone Consumption

Although the level of saving may be influenced by policy, it is preferable for analytical purposes to think about the timing of consumption, which is more easily defined in an unambiguous way. The national income accounting used as a framework for analyzing macroeconomic policy defines income in terms of factor payments and regards saving as a residual. Private saving is what is left after consumption and taxes are subtracted from income. The Haig-Simons model, however, defines income as the sum of consumption and the change in net worth during an accounting period. (There are many differences between the two concepts of income, a major one being the handling of capital gains, which are included in Haig-Simons income and ignored in national income accounting.)

In the Haig-Simons framework, saving is the change in net worth and thus depends upon what is considered part of the person's wealth. Wealth, in turn, is difficult to pin down. Does a person's wealth include the discounted value of anticipated inheritances, the value of anticipated retirement benefits or public transfers, or the change in value of assets held over a period? Whose valuation counts for assets without an active market? Wealth can be defined as the maximum amount of consumption a person could finance in a given period.[32] This definition includes what is usually called human capital to the extent that a person's future earnings can support current borrowing. Wealth in this definition is highly sensitive to expectations, information, and institutional features of capital markets.

Different definitions of wealth may imply differences in tax liabilities; but this does not necessarily mean differences in the incentive to postpone consumption. Consider this life-cycle savings problem. Imagine that life consists of h (for "horizon") periods and that the person is endowed with a certain flow of receipts in each period.[33] Let $z(t)$ stand for the exogenously given receipts of the person in period t, $c(t)$ for the person's consumption in period t, and i for the rate of interest (for simplicity, taken to be constant). If the person pays no taxes, and if it is possible to borrow or lend any amount at the going rate of interest subject to the requirement that debts must be paid, any consumption pattern is available that satisfies the lifetime budget constraint,

$$(1) \qquad \int_0^h c(s)e^{-i(s-t)}\,ds = \int_0^h z(s)e^{-i(s-t)}\,ds,$$

32. Bradford, *Untangling the Income Tax*, p. 22.

33. In economic theory such receipts are called income, to the disadvantage of clear thinking about income tax issues. The optimal income taxes of theory, for example, are almost invariably better described as optimal labor earnings taxes or even optimal first-period labor earnings taxes.

where consumption is understood to include amounts given away or bequeathed.

Saving is the change in wealth during a period. If the person owns the receipt flow of $z(t)$ in periods 1 through h (a fact assumed known to all), then he or she has an asset with market value at any time equal to the discounted value of all remaining cash inflows. In addition, in making up the difference between the amount consumed in a period and that period's cash inflow, there is always an accumulation from the past, which may be positive or negative. The person's wealth at any time will be the sum of this accumulation and the discounted value of the remaining portion of $z(t)$. The increase in this total during the year will be equal to the rate of interest times the amount of wealth, less the outlay on consumption. In other words, the person's Haig-Simons income will equal the rate of interest times his or her stock of wealth (there being no other source of spending power in this simple model).

The person's budget constraint in terms of consumption and wealth can be expressed as follows. By definition, $W(t)$, the person's wealth at time t, is

$$(2) \qquad \int_0^h z(s)e^{-i(s-t)}\,ds \; - \; \int_0^t c(s)e^{-i(s-t)}\,ds.$$

The person's saving at time t, $s(t)$, is defined to be $W'(t)$, which, differentiating equation 2, reduces to $iW(t) - c(t)$. Thus, Haig-Simons income, defined as the sum of consumption and saving, is $iW(t)$. Note that the budget constraint looking forward from any time t is

$$(3) \qquad \int_t^h c(s)e^{-i(s-t)}\,ds \; = \; W(t).$$

A slightly different picture emerges, one close to the national income concept, if we assume that future cash flows in the endowment are not counted as part of current wealth. This is the conventional treatment of future labor earnings. Then wealth consists simply of the person's accumulation (positive or negative) from the past. Haig-Simons income would be the sum of the rate of interest times the past accumulation and the current period's cash flow. The recorded income and savings levels would be different from those in the first concept discussed, even though, in the absence of income taxation, the person's choice would be the same. The person does not care how wealth or income is defined so long as his or her tax liability does not depend on it.

The distinction in wealth concepts can be formalized simply in the life-cycle savings model. If future endowment receipts are not regarded as a part of wealth, then $W(t)$, the individual's wealth at time t, is

$$(4) \qquad \int_0^t z(s)e^{-i(s-t)}\,ds - \int_0^t c(s)e^{-i(s-t)}\,ds.$$

The difference between expressions 2 and 4 is in the upper limit of the first integral, which extends to the horizon in 2 and only to the present in 4. As before, the person's saving at time t, $s(t)$, is defined to be $W'(t)$, which (differentiating) reduces to $iW(t) + z(t) - c(t)$. By virtue of the change in the definition of wealth, Haig-Simons income, defined as the sum of consumption and saving, shifts from $iW(t)$ to $iW(t) + z(t)$. Note that the budget constraint is now

$$(5) \qquad \int_t^h c(s)e^{-i(s-t)}\,ds = W(t) + \int_t^h z(s)e^{-i(s-t)}\,ds,$$

differing from equation 3 in the addition of the discounted value of future endowment flows to accumulated wealth on the right-hand side.

The usual arguments relating to the choice of Haig-Simons income as a tax base do not address the choice between these two concepts of wealth. As a measure of ability to pay, the version expressed by equation 2 might seem the more compelling since there is no obvious reason to distinguish between two taxpayers with the same discounted earnings but different time paths of earnings or other sources of cash inflow. But the equivalence between the positions of two persons with the same discounted value of earnings depends entirely upon their ability to borrow and lend without restriction at the going rate of interest. As a practical matter, it would seem rather difficult to implement expression 2 with respect to future labor earnings, and most discussions of income taxation implicitly accept the version expressed by expression 4 in this respect.

Comments by Louis Kaplow

These comments will address three issues: (1) the definitional concepts underlying Andrews and Bradford's analysis of the hybrid income tax and savings incentives, (2) the implications of their distinction between results under perfect and imperfect market assumptions, and (3) the current system of retirement savings provisions.[34]

Hybrid Income Tax and Savings Incentives

Andrews and Bradford begin by offering the familiar list of features of the U.S. hybrid income tax system. Because the purpose of this characterization is to place the system on a continuum ranging between an ideal Haig-Simons income tax and a pure consumption tax, I think it useful to categorize the primary features in the following manner.

First are *pure income tax attributes.* Among the most important are the lack of a general deduction for income that is not consumed, taxation of interest received and deduction of interest paid, and taxation of capital gains.

Second are *quasi-inherent departures* in the direction of a consumption tax. By this term, I have in mind the realization requirement, the failure to tax imputed income from housing and other consumer durables, and the expensing of items such as advertising that are, in principle, costs of intangible capital assets. Each of these features is a departure from the economic concept of income in the direction of a consumption tax. In addition, these features are most often understood and defended as necessary departures from the pure income tax on the ground that a more precise definition of income in these areas is infeasible, rather than as direct attempts to reject an income tax approach. Yet it may be possible to implement an income tax treatment more precisely in each instance. For example, one could imagine a mark-to-market approach for most traded securities and periodic valuation for many other assets.[35] Taxation of imputed rent from owner-occupied housing has been at-

---

34. Although not central to Andrews and Bradford's paper or these comments, readers with a theoretical interest are encouraged to examine the authors' Appendix, which begins to address some of the important aspects of how human capital could be considered from an income tax perspective.

35. I am not arguing that such alternatives are necessarily better, but only that they are more plausible than many often assume. For example, such valuations in the absence of objective market prices arising from simple sales are often necessary when assets are purchased as a group and for purposes of assessing property and estate taxes. If one desires an income tax, the question would be whether the second-best problems and administrative costs that would arise under such a modified system are worse than all those currently associated with the realization requirement.

tempted in other countries and would likely be far more accurate than the implicit zero valuation currently used. And depreciation schedules could be adopted to approximate the effects of advertising and related expenditures. To the extent these alternatives are rejected on grounds of practicality, these departures from income tax treatment are rather different from those in the next category.

A third set of departures are provisions motivated by the desire to provide favored treatment to certain activities, commonly known as tax expenditures. Those moving in the direction of a consumption tax are *savings and investment incentives*. The most prominent examples include the exemption of municipal bond interest;[36] accelerated depreciation; and retirement savings provisions, the focus of Andrews and Bradford's inquiry.[37]

Finally, there are *departures designed to limit certain transactions* that take advantage of interactions among the preceding hybrid provisions. Most notable, and most important for this discussion, are limitations on the deductibility of interest. Another well-known example is the limitation on the deductibility of capital losses, designed to curtail exploitation of the realization requirement.

This categorization is designed to isolate those features of the hybrid system that should be understood as savings incentives. As previously noted by the authors,[38] the combined effect of all the departures moves the system sufficiently in the direction of a consumption tax that calling it an income tax, even as a starting point for discussion, may be more misleading than helpful.[39]

It is useful to explore further the meaning of the term *savings*

36. One can recall the well-known relationship between consumption tax treatment and exemption of yield from tax.

37. As noted elsewhere in this volume, savings and investment incentives are largely identical in a closed economy, whereas important differences relating to the location of investment and effects on the trade balance arise when international capital flows are taken into account.

38. See, for example, Andrews, "A Consumption-Type or Cash Flow Personal Income Tax."

39. When one considers the portion of all savings that is in some sort of pension fund or retirement plan, is invested in municipal bonds, or constitutes equity in owner-occupied housing, it is clear that a very large portion of national savings receives something much closer to consumption tax treatment. To the extent social security represents, at least in part, a government-operated pension plan, another component of national savings could be viewed as receiving treatment that diverges from the income tax approach insofar as employer contributions are not subject to the income tax and earnings on social security contributions are implicitly tax exempt.

incentives. Andrews and Bradford adopt a particular, narrow definition that differs from customary usage. First, they explicitly have in mind the notion that more saving constitutes the shifting of a person's lifetime consumption profile to later years. This outlook is adopted to deal with life-cycle effects—particularly that more saving in early years is generally accompanied by more dissaving in later years, which potentially confuses the meaning of changes in saving if one examines a population of persons at different points in the age distribution. Second, they define savings incentives as provisions that increase the after-tax rate of return on savings. This definition bypasses the difficult issue, addressed in David Starrett's paper, concerning whether such increases in return increase saving. These definitions are a useful point of departure because discussion is clarified by separating the various links in the usual savings incentive arguments. In essence, Andrews and Bradford use these definitions to focus on the question of whether and when retirement savings provisions are effective on their own terms—assuming that interest rates have the posited effect on saving as they define it.

Finally, reasons why one might want savings incentives vary. First, from a consumption tax perspective, one might favor retirement savings provisions because they eliminate distortions in life-cycle consumption profiles or because they provide a more equitable distribution of the tax burden.[40] In principle, of course, this would lead one to adopt a consumption tax. Short of that, however, one might favor incremental moves in that direction. This rationale is not wholly dependent upon actual increases in savings because there are both efficiency and distributional consequences even if the level of savings in earlier periods is unaffected.[41]

Second, savings incentives are sometimes favored out of a desire to increase capital formation, to improve the productivity or competitiveness of the economy, or to further macroeconomic policies. Of course,

40. In their paper, Andrews and Bradford refer to a notion of fairness between workers and owners, that is, owners of capital can live off the whole income and still support their retirement, whereas workers must save. This leads to the question of the fairness of an income tax versus a consumption tax because, for example, if the owner of capital had obtained it through savings from prior wages, it is hard to see any inequity otherwise. Their quote of Mill on this issue underscores the point.

41. To the extent that the assumption of perfect markets, explored in the next section, holds for a large portion of taxpayers, retirement savings provisions are merely a lump-sum rebate for those groups and do not shift burdens in the manner contemplated by a consumption tax. The problem is the hybrid combination of consumption tax treatment of retirement savings and income tax treatment of interest paid.

in such contexts it is appropriate to consider alternative policies, particularly those affecting the overall size of the budget deficit.

Third, and of most direct relevance to this discussion, there is the desire to increase retirement savings for their own sake—a desire frequently expressed in legislative circles when retirement savings provisions are being addressed. This rationale falls most directly in the tax expenditure category, and it is often motivated by paternalistic considerations, which will be addressed further in the third section of these comments.

Economic Analysis of Savings Incentives

Andrews and Bradford provide a useful analysis of the effect of current retirement savings provisions by emphasizing the importance of the degree of market perfection. In particular, they focus on whether there exist effective borrowing constraints. If borrowing is freely available (and interest therefrom deductible), all taxpayers would engage in retirement savings up to the statutory ceiling, raising the funds, if necessary, through borrowing. No net savings would be induced. In that event, retirement savings provisions would provide only a lump-sum (although bracket-dependent) tax reduction. The sole incentive effect, as they note, would be to increase activities that relax the statutory ceiling.[42] Moreover, to the extent the revenue cost must be financed by higher marginal income tax rates, savings incentives—defined by the after-tax rate of return—would actually be reduced.

For those who must borrow to take full advantage of these provisions but cannot—either because of market constraints or rules limiting interest deductibility—there is a marginal incentive to reduce consumption to increase savings.[43] The effect is that current provisions produce three groups of taxpayers: (1) the unconstrained,[44] who receive a lump-

42. For example, if the statutory ceiling is a stated percentage of wages, there is an incentive to increase wage income; that is, the savings incentive in this instance is really a labor incentive.

43. As noted in the first section, this marginal incentive is meant only to refer to the substitution effect. Like the authors, I make no claims here concerning the aggregate effect on savings.

44. They could have sufficient savings that can be shifted into retirement accounts, or could be able to borrow funds and deduct interest. Over time, as taxpayers have become more sophisticated in adapting to the new tax rules, more probably fall into this category, unless direct borrowing constraints (rather than mere ignorance) prevent

sum tax reduction; (2) the constrained who still save enough to get some benefits from the provisions; and (3) the constrained who are unable to save under the provisions. Assuming an across-the-board tax increase to fund the revenue cost of the provisions, the result is a clear gain to the first group (typically upper income)[45] and a clear loss to the third (typically lower income), with no savings incentive for either. The middle group has some incentive, some gain from the provisions, and some loss due to the tax increase. Limits on interest deductibility move more people into the second and third groups, increasing the number who have an incentive but, under these assumptions, making the distribution of the resulting tax burden more regressive.[46]

Retirement Savings Provisions

This section focuses on the justification for the complex retirement savings provisions that currently exist—particularly those for employer-provided pension plans. Why does the United States have the current system instead of an alternative that allows tax-preferred retirement savings up to a given amount, or at a certain percentage of wages or income, or some combination? One simple instrument could be equally available to all, regardless of employment status or decisions of one's employer.

The only available rationalization appears to be a paternalism argument identified by Andrews and Bradford.[47] Consider the following argument that slightly expands on their characterization: (1) Low- or middle-income workers do not have the good judgment to save for their

---

them from engaging in the arbitrage transaction. Varying levels of home mortgages might be sufficient for many to circumvent any current limitations.

45. They gain because, under the stated assumptions, their portion of the savings benefit is greater than their portion of the tax increase.

46. Of course, the tax level adjustment could preserve the distribution of tax burdens across (although not within) income groups. The 1986 tax reform generally took this approach as to the aggregate effect of its changes, although the earlier reforms that created most of the retirement savings provisions generally did not adjust rates for the distributive effects of these or other provisions. In addition, since distortions generally rise with the square of the marginal tax rate, one would want to take such effects into account, and this consideration might deter one from making a distribution-neutral increase at higher income levels.

47. They note that this explanation may differ from the historical origin of current pension plan treatment. For present purposes, particularly since there have been so many alterations in the past fifteen years, it seems most useful to focus on the current rationale.

retirement.[48] (2) The tax incentive, although substantial, is still not enough to induce them to change their savings behavior. (3) Highly compensated employees (or employers) will be strongly attracted by the provisions and will be induced to force retirement savings on the rest. (4) Such arrangements of forced savings will survive in the market despite the reluctance of low- and middle-income employees to save.

This justification can be evaluated from a number of perspectives. First, if one adheres to the income tax perspective of efficiency and distributional equity, the result is much like that of any tax expenditure and thus may appear less desirable, despite the paternalistic benefits. Second, and more telling, one might ask why such a complex, indirect, partial, and clumsy system is used rather than obvious direct alternatives, such as regulations requiring employers to provide pensions at certain levels. Alternatively, one could supplement or expand social security in a number of ways.[49] Andrews and Bradford note the argument that such a system is one the United States cannot afford, but they do not endorse it, as it is obvious that the same dollars "induced" into retirement accounts by the current pension system could be placed in either alternative.

Third, the current system is incomplete, and in precisely those areas where it hurts the most, at least according to the posited rationale. There is no coverage for the self-employed. Some employers, especially those with mostly low-wage earners, may have an inadequate plan or none at all. Finally, to the extent participation is not required (a stated portion

48. The assumption is that these workers are not rational life-cycle maximizers, which has implications for many of the issues addressed elsewhere in this volume. An alternative assumption is that they are rational, but their preferences concerning discount rates are being rejected. Distinguishing shortsightedness from irrationality and from having a high discount rate is often difficult. If the only problem could be captured by the notion of a high discount rate, adjusting the level of savings incentive might be a sufficient response.

One could make a sort of moral hazard argument. Low- or middle-income workers may anticipate that they will be bailed out, most likely by the government, if they fail to provide for themselves. Thus, the same sort of justification might arise even with fully rational, calculating persons. Of course, the government could commit itself not to come to the rescue of those who do not save, but this may not be politically feasible (compare the awarding of disaster relief to those who do not purchase insurance), and it may be difficult to separate the free riders from others thought more deserving of government assistance.

49. If this was a problem due to the mixed nature of social security (retirement savings, intergenerational transfer, and intragenerational transfer among and within income groups), one could imagine a system in which the government withheld wages and had them transferred to special pension accounts and the taxpayer had control over the investment decisions and a vested right to the proceeds upon retirement.

of employees now suffices), some employees will fall through the cracks. Even if a significant majority were covered, those missed would be precisely those for whom the paternalism argument is strongest. If one really wished to allow employee choice, the entire complex system would be unnecessary, as noted at the outset.

The effectiveness of retirement provisions in terms of establishing plans for most workers is not the only issue. As Andrews and Bradford note, covered employees will be unaffected to the extent offsetting borrowing is freely available. Alicia Munnell's comments concerning the offset of retirement savings by reduced direct savings suggest that such plans may do little to affect the overall savings level even of those fully covered.

Andrews and Bradford place much of their emphasis on another line of criticism that I find less convincing. They point to the profit opportunities created because pension funds are essentially zero-bracket players in the investment game. This issue must be sharply distinguished from the pure arbitrage referred to by the authors, wherein taxpayers borrow to invest in retirement funds. Their example—where A's IRA lends to B, who places that money in an IRA, which lends to A—illustrates how the availability of borrowing can nullify any effect of retirement savings provisions.

In contrast, consider their objection that retirement savings provisions "create zero-bracket players . . . [which,] moreover . . . are artificial zero-bracket players." This objection, however, is not warranted because the zero bracket is precisely what is intended by the provisions. Recall Andrews and Bradford's definition of a savings incentive as one that increases the after-tax rate of return on savings. The zero effective tax rate on such savings is precisely the mechanism that accomplishes this result. They also note that IRAs allow persons to receive taxable-bond interest rates on an exempt basis. Yet if this were not the case, there would be no savings incentive. Finally, they note that complex investment arrangements (consuming resources in arranging the transactions) are produced by having such zero-bracket actors around. This argument is much like that which points to equipment leasing as an abuse of the accelerated cost recovery system (ACRS) and the investment tax credit. These arrangements, however, are indirect ways to accomplish what seems apppropriate to allow directly, to the extent one believes in the incentive provisions in the first place.[50] Of course, one must distin-

50. See Alvin C. Warren, Jr., and Alan J. Auerbach, "Transferability of Tax

guish the pure arbitrage transactions that directly undermine the savings incentive effect to begin with. Interest deduction limitations, and related alternatives the authors discuss, are directed to this rather different problem. Thus, when Andrews and Bradford refer to "cures" for the "misfunctions" of retirement savings provisions, this distinction must be kept in mind.

In summary, it is useful to review the beliefs one would have to hold to support the current system of retirement savings incentives for the currently offered reasons:

—One must endorse one of the rationales for increased saving.

—For many of the rationales, one must believe that "savings incentives," which increase the after-tax rate of return, actually increase saving.

—One must believe that markets are imperfect, or that rules such as those limiting interest deductibility can effectively prevent the sort of borrowing arbitrage that wipes out the incentive effects of retirement savings provisions.

—One must believe that the benefits outweigh the direct costs, taking into account the inevitable partiality of the preceding results and the administrative costs of the system, as well as the higher marginal tax rates necessary to finance the revenue loss.

And, in reference to the complex of provisions relating to qualified plans:

—One must accept some variant of the paternalism rationale.

—One must think that direct, more effective, and simpler alternatives are unavailable.

—One must assume that the complex buy-off of upper-income employees and employers works sufficiently often, and not mind that the current provisions let many, particularly those for whom the rationale most applies, slip through in a number of ways.

Thus, whatever the precise rationale or one's confidence in any particular step in the argument, it clearly takes quite a leap of faith to accept simultaneously the requisite combination of necessary conditions.[51]

Incentives and the Fiction of Safe Harbor Leasing," *Harvard Law Review,* vol. 95 (June 1982), pp. 1752–86.

51. Alternative rationales are less problematic. For example, if one favored the consumption tax approach, had reasonable confidence in the rationality of taxpayers or in the extent of coverage of pension plans, and thought the perfect market arbitrage

Comments by Alicia H. Munnell

Andrews and Bradford's paper considers issues surrounding savings incentives in the current U.S. tax system. In my view the interesting question is whether it is possible to introduce *effective* incentives for retirement saving in a hybrid tax system. Narrowing the topic in this fashion sidesteps two major questions: first, the issue of the optimal level of saving and therefore the need for any savings incentives on an aggregate basis; and second, the degree to which a movement away from a pure consumption tax reduces the incentive to save. Nevertheless, this smaller topic is not trivial: the theme of this volume is that the United States is unlikely to adopt either a pure consumption tax or a pure income tax, so the question of whether it is worth trying to encourage retirement saving in this hybrid-tax world merits serious consideration.

Because I agree with the authors' conclusion that existing savings incentives are ineffective, erode the tax base, and create inequities, I am somewhat surprised that our proposed solutions are so different. By process of elimination, Andrews and Bradford come out in favor of moving to a pure consumption tax, a politically improbable alternative that would allow many of the inequities in the current system to persist. My preference would be to eliminate the existing incentives as part of an effort to move the personal income tax toward the accretion ideal.

The costs of encouraging retirement saving are enormous. Excluding a major component of income, such as compensation received in the form of pension accruals, greatly reduces the size of the tax base. This forces Congress to increase marginal tax rates in order to raise a given amount of revenue. Although considerable controversy surrounds the precise magnitude of revenue loss, the amount of tax revenues forgone is unquestionably large.[52] The U.S. Treasury calculated that in fiscal

---

could be substantially limited, substantial retirement provisions might be justified even if some of the other conditions failed.

52. For example, see Employee Benefit Research Institute, "Retirement Program Tax Expenditures: A Case of Unsubstantiated, Undocumented, Arbitrary Numbers," *EBRI Issue Brief* (April 1983). The published figures jumped dramatically and apparently without explanation. For fiscal 1982 the estimates increased from $16.8 billion in the 1981 budget to $27.9 billion in the 1982 budget, and then to $45.3 billion in the 1984 budget. According to the Treasury, the first jump can be ascribed primarily to revised estimates of the earnings on pension fund reserves and an increase in the marginal

1986 the net exclusion of pension contributions and earnings from the tax base cost $53 billion for employer-sponsored plans, $14 billion for individual retirement accounts, and $2 billion for Keogh plans.[53] These revenue losses amount to roughly 20 percent of fiscal 1986 personal income tax receipts. If this retirement saving had been taxed in the same way as wage and salary income, personal income tax rates could have been roughly 18 percent lower, thereby reducing the distortions in labor supply and other savings decisions created by the rate structure.

Contributions to pension plans are excluded from the payroll tax base. These exclusions have never been considered "tax expenditures" because the Treasury and the Congressional Budget Office assume that the reduction in contributions will eventually be reflected in lower retirement and disability benefits. Future benefits are reduced less than proportionately, however. Thus the exclusion of pension contributions from the tax base not only causes the short-run loss of revenues, but also raises the long-run costs of the social security program.[54]

---

income tax rate from 25 to 29 percent; the second jump reflects the inclusion of the federal civil service retirement system and state and local retirement plans and another increase in the marginal income tax rate to 30 percent. The question remains, however, whether the figures as they are presently constituted accurately reflect the revenue loss associated with pensions.

The Treasury's tax expenditure estimates are computed on a cash-flow basis. Essentially, the calculation is designed to measure how much higher federal revenues would be in a given year if a particular subsidy had not been enacted. This approach is consistent with the expenditure aspect of the federal budget and is meaningful for permanent deductions and exclusions, but it does not properly account for tax concessions in those cases where tax payments are deferred. Its limitations for qualified pension plans are seen clearly by considering a situation in which (1) annual contributions to private plans and pension fund earnings exactly equal benefit payments during the year, and (2) workers face the same marginal tax rate in retirement as they do during their working years. Under these assumptions the revenue loss would equal zero, according to the Treasury calculations of tax expenditures. Yet persons covered by private plans would continue to enjoy the advantage of deferring taxes on employer contributions and investment income until after retirement. Clearly, such tax deferral is equivalent to an interest-free loan from the Treasury and reduces the present value of taxes to be collected from a person over his or her lifetime. A direct estimate of the annual revenue loss resulting from deferral would be the difference between (1) the discounted value of the revenue from current taxation of employer contributions and pension fund earnings as they accrue over the employee's working life, and (2) the present discounted value of the taxes collected when the employer's contributions and investment returns are taxable to the employee after retirement.

53. *Special Analyses: Budget of the United States Government, Fiscal Year 1987* (GPO, 1986), table G-2, p. G-45.

54. Although benefit payments are reduced somewhat by the decline in the payroll tax base that accompanies the expansion of nonwage compensation, they are reduced by less than the total amount of this decline because of the effect of the weighted benefit

In addition to requiring higher income and payroll tax rates, exclusion of pension contributions and earnings from the tax base creates problems of horizontal equity. Deferring taxes on a major component of compensation means that two persons who are equally well off in an economic sense pay different amounts of tax over their lifetimes. The favorable tax provisions also have an adverse effect on the distribution of income. Only half the work force is covered by a pension plan or an IRA, and pension coverage tends to be concentrated among the higher paid. Moreover, the value of exclusion and deferral increases with taxpayers' marginal tax rates. Hence the higher-income groups profit from the favorable treatment accorded retirement savings provisions, yet all taxpayers must pay higher rates to compensate.

This discrepancy perhaps could be overlooked if it could be shown that the incentives substantially improved the lot of those who would not have saved on their own or increased saving in the aggregate (should that be a desirable national goal). As I read the evidence, the favorable tax provisions achieve neither of these objectives.

Although the historical motivations for the favorable tax provisions may be debatable, the post-ERISA rationale is that the tax benefits can be justified only to the extent that they encourage the highly paid to have pension plans that benefit the rank and file. Contrary to the popular belief that social security fully replaces income of the low-paid worker, almost everyone needs supplementary benefits in order to avoid a decline in living standards after retirement. The misconception about social security arises from calculating replacement rates using the analytical construct of a hypothetical person retiring at age 65 with a history of low earnings and a nonemployed spouse; this exercise shows social security replacing nearly 100 percent of preretirement earnings. In contrast, data from the retirement history study, which are consistent with results from the recent survey of new beneficiaries, indicate that the actual replacement rate for couples in the lowest quintile was 56 percent.[55]

---

formula. This formula provides that a smaller percentage of wages are replaced at higher earnings levels than at lower ones. Since a substantial portion of the decline in the payroll tax base, caused by the growth in employee benefits, occurs at higher earnings levels, benefit payments are not reduced significantly. Thus the long-range costs of the program rise as the ratio of employee benefits to total compensation increases. See Yung-Ping Chen, "The Growth of Fringe Benefits: Implications for Social Security," *Monthly Labor Review*, vol. 104 (November 1981), pp. 3–10.

55. Alan Fox, "Earnings Replacement Rates and Total Income: Findings from the Retirement History Study," *Social Security Bulletin*, vol. 45 (October 1982), tables 7 and 10.

312 WILLIAM D. ANDREWS AND DAVID F. BRADFORD

Despite the near-universal need for supplementary pension income, the most recent data on pension coverage show that only 54 percent of the work force is covered by an employer-sponsored plan, and the incidence of coverage increases markedly as earnings levels rise.[56] For example, in 1983 only 30 percent of nonagricultural wage and salary workers earning under $10,000 were covered by a plan, compared with 85 percent of those with earnings over $50,000. Moreover, many of the low-paid participants are in plans with integration provisions that reduce the pension benefits they receive.

What about those people who are covered by private plans and who are not subject to integration provisions? Do they end up with substantially more savings than they would have in the absence of favorable tax provisions? The life-cycle model predicts that in an ideal world (characterized by perfect labor and capital markets, no taxes, and no uncertainty) people would simply substitute pension contributions for their own savings. Hence, the $1.7 trillion of assets held in private and public pension plans at the end of 1985 would represent a shift in the form of individual saving rather than an increase in the net amount.

On the other hand, the favorable tax provisions associated with pension plans would be expected to increase saving. This conclusion, however, depends crucially on the extent to which the tax preferences influence savings decisions at the margin. In the United States, pension contributions and benefits tend to be relatively small. According to a recent study by the Labor Department, the median annual retirement benefit for private pensioners was only $3,250 in 1984.[57] Hence, it is highly likely that desired saving exceeds pension saving for most middle-income and high-income people, and they experience no change in the rate of return to saving at the margin. Thus, the favorable tax provisions probably have had little effect on aggregate saving.

Some other nontax factors, however, might lead one to think that saving through pension plans might produce more capital accumulation than a procedure whereby each person saved directly. The illiquidity of the pension rights makes them less than perfect substitutes for private

56. Employee Benefit Research Institute, "New Survey Findings on Pension Coverage and Benefit Entitlement," *EBRI Issue Brief* (August 1984).
57. Richard A. Ippolito and Walter W. Kolodrubetz, eds., U.S. Department of Labor, Office of Pension and Welfare Benefit Programs, *Handbook of Pension Statistics 1985* (Commerce Clearing House, 1986), p. 121.

saving, with the result that people might reduce their other saving by less than one dollar for each dollar of pension accumulation. Similarly, retirement provisions accompanying private plans may stimulate saving by encouraging workers to retire early and therefore save more during their working years than they would have otherwise. Moreover, uncertainty about whether they will ultimately receive a pension benefit might cause people to be cautious about cutting back on their own saving. Conversely, because an inflationary environment hinders an accurate assessment of unindexed pension benefits, workers could just as easily overestimate future real benefits and reduce their own saving by more than their pension asset accumulation. Similarly, because pension benefits are paid as annuities that pool risk, total saving might be less than if workers saved individually for their own retirement and had to plan for extreme contingencies.

Since it is impossible to determine a priori whether the growth in private pension plans has fostered a net increase in saving or merely a shift in the form in which assets are held, a final assessment must rest on empirical evidence. Aside from early work by Phillip Cagan and George Katona, most of the studies indicate that persons covered by pension plans save less on their own than those without pension coverage.[58] A recent study by Robert Avery, Gregory Elliehausen, and Thomas Gustafson, based on the 1983 survey of consumer finances, showed very clearly that persons covered by pension plans reduce their other forms of saving and that the rate of trade-off was roughly sixty-eight cents for

58. See Phillip Cagan, *The Effect of Pension Plans on Aggregate Savings: Evidence from a Sample Survey* (Columbia University Press for National Bureau of Economic Research, 1965); George Katona, *Private Pensions and Individual Saving,* Monograph 40 (University of Michigan, Survey Research Center, Institute for Social Research, 1965); and Alicia H. Munnell, *The Effect of Social Security on Personal Saving* (Ballinger, 1974). Cagan and Katona concluded that workers covered by private pension plans actually saved more in other forms than workers not covered. Cagan's explanation of the surprising results is that pension coverage calls attention to retirement needs and prospects and thereby fosters a "recognition effect" that counteracts any disinclination to plan for the future. Katona added a second explanation for his results, hypothesizing a "goal feasibility" effect, wherein people intensify their saving efforts as they approach their retirement goal. Katona's results must be interpreted cautiously, however, since he focused on a narrow concept of saving—namely, changes in financial assets—which biases the results of his study. Similarly, subsequent detailed analysis of the Consumer Union survey, which was the basis of Cagan's study, found results that directly contradicted his earlier conclusions.

each dollar of pension wealth.[59] Most of the other studies also had results in the range of sixty to seventy cents per dollar.[60]

What does this number imply about aggregate saving? Between 1983 and 1985 total pension assets of private and public plans increased an average of $190 billion per year. (Assets rose from $1,358 billion at the end of 1983 to $1,738 billion at the end of 1985; the difference can be viewed as the sum of contributions and investment earnings if benefits are assumed to remain relatively constant.) If persons had reduced their other forms of saving by only seventy cents for each dollar increase in pension wealth, then savings would have increased by 30 percent of $190 billion, or $57 billion each year. It is impossible, however, to determine whether this net increase is due to the favorable tax provisions or to other features of pension plans such as uncertainty about future benefits, forced saving, and induced retirement. Nevertheless, if one were to assume that the entire increase was attributable to the tax treatment, would the net increment to saving justify the tax expenditure? In 1985 the tax expenditure for employer-sponsored plans was $45 billion, only slightly less than the estimated increase in saving from pensions. Given the large errors associated with both the saving and tax expenditure numbers, the increase in private saving may well have been offset almost completely by a comparable increase in the federal deficit.

If the wise people of the world decided that the United States as a nation was saving too little—a proposition I do not find very compelling— and that it could significantly improve the rate at which it accumulated capital by adopting a well-designed consumption tax, with a nice progressive rate structure and bequests included in the tax base, I would be willing to join the band of supporters. In the meantime, however, I think that almost nothing is gained from the current incentives for retirement saving. They cost a lot in forgone revenues, they create horizontal inequities, and they do not increase saving significantly. The hybrid system should be moved closer to an income tax by devising a mechanism for including in a person's tax base the change in the present discounted

59. Robert B. Avery, Gregory E. Elliehausen, and Thomas A. Gustafson, "Pensions and Social Security in Household Portfolios: Evidence from the 1983 Survey of Consumer Finances" (Board of Governors of the Federal Reserve System, October 1985).

60. See Alicia H. Munnell, "Private Pensions and Saving: New Evidence," *Journal of Political Economy*, vol. 84 (October 1976), pp. 1013–32; and Peter A. Diamond and Jerry A. Hausman, "Individual Retirement and Savings Behavior," *Journal of Public Economics*, vol. 23 (February–March 1984), pp. 81–114.

value of future retirement benefits.[61] An expedient approach for approximating this goal would be to levy an excise tax, say 15 percent, on employers' pension contributions and pension fund earnings. This would raise considerable revenue and create very little disruption; employers sponsor pension plans for numerous reasons that go far beyond tax considerations.

By significantly reducing the rates, the recent tax reform legislation has lessened the adverse impact of many of the remaining bad features in the tax code. The advantage of deferral has been reduced, and the incentive to receive deferred rather than current income has been lessened. In addition, the extent to which an income tax, relative to a consumption tax, is thought to have an adverse effect on saving has lessened. In the short run, however, saving as measured in the national income accounts may be adversely affected by the rate reduction. Many people have put money away on a deferred basis because they thought it would eventually be reclaimed at marginal rates of 30, 40, or even 50 percent. Suddenly, these people are going to be able to withdraw their funds at rates of 15 or 28 percent. The significant capital gains associated with the rate reduction may well have a negative impact on saving out of current income for some period of time.

61. Numerous approaches have been suggested for taxing pension contributions and earnings under a comprehensive income tax. For example, see Emil M. Sunley, Jr., "Employee Benefits and Transfer Payments," in Joseph A. Pechman, ed., *Comprehensive Income Taxation* (Brookings, 1977), pp. 77–84; and Department of the Treasury, *Blueprints for Basic Tax Reform*, pp. 56–58.

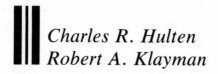

Charles R. Hulten
Robert A. Klayman

Investment Incentives in Theory and Practice

TWO MAJOR tax reforms have occurred during this decade, and investment incentives played a major role in both. The provision of generous investment incentives was at the heart of the supply-side philosophy of the Economic Recovery Tax Act of 1981. The Tax Reform Act of 1986, on the other hand, sought to establish a "level playing field" by minimizing the use of investment incentives in the tax system. The next major tax bill may well reestablish a role for investment incentives, particularly if tax "reform" occurs in response to a period of slow economic growth, as has happened so often in the past.

This history suggests profound disagreement over the role of investment incentives in the tax system. Indeed, several general views can be discerned: the Haig-Simons view that all income should be taxed and that the base of the income tax (consumption plus changes in net worth) should not be eroded by special incentives; the view that consumption should be taxed instead of income, which implies that a system of incentives that effectively eliminates the tax on capital income is desirable; the supply-side view that capital formation is essential for economic growth and that incentives help achieve this objective; and finally the Keynesian view that incentives should be used to stabilize the economy.

We review in this paper some of the major issues in the debate over investment incentives. After defining incentives in terms of marginal effective tax rates, we discuss the use of investment incentives in practice and note the major role they have played in the evolution of the U.S. business income tax system. Then the question of the optimal structure of investment incentives is addressed. We assess the "solution" pro-

We wish to thank Joseph Minarik, Robert Schwab, C. Eugene Steuerle, and Mancur Olson for their many helpful comments.

vided by the literature on optimal commodity taxation and examine the role of investment incentives when externalities and other market failures occur. A discussion of fairness issues follows.

Two basic conclusions emerge from this analysis. First, the optimal structure of taxation implies different effective tax rates on different types of capital income. These differential rates of taxation can be achieved by the appropriate use of investment incentives. Second, the analytical determination of the optimal structure of taxes and tax incentives involves information about the economy and social values that is virtually impossible to obtain. The optimal tax solution in its standard form is thus of limited practical significance for the formulation of tax policy.

This finding leads us to examine the evolution and implementation of tax policy, an extremely complex process that falls in the realm of political economy rather than traditional economic theory. We attempt to determine whether this process is likely to produce a system of investment incentives that approximates a theoretical optimal tax solution.

We conclude that it is not. Special interest groups seek the advantage of investment incentives for themselves, even though such incentives may not promote the general welfare.[1] Because the costs of the incentives are diffuse, public opposition may not form. Therefore, Congress is particularly subject to the influence of these special interests. Over time, a host of incentives enters the tax code. This erodes the tax base and leads to the need to raise revenues from other sources. It also promotes the formation of tax shelters and increasing disrespect for the system. Periodic reform is required to bring the system back into kilter. We conclude that it would be wiser for tax legislators to avoid the enactment of investment incentives and the eventual problems they produce.

Investment Incentives: A Definition

An investment incentive is a provision of the tax code that encourages capital formation. Examples include tax credits for investment in certain types of capital, the acceleration of depreciation allowances, and percentage depletion allowances for oil and gas and mineral deposits. Some

1. See Mancur Olson, *The Rise and Decline of Nations: Economic Growth, Stagflation, and Social Rigidities* (Yale University Press, 1982).

provisions serve as incentives even though their original rationale was not necessarily to encourage investment. The expensing of intangible investment and the exclusion of implicit income of owner-occupied housing are examples of this type of de facto incentive.

Investment incentives operate by reducing the effective rate of taxation on capital income.[2] The investment tax credit, for example, permitted taxpayers to reduce their tax liabilities by up to 10 percent of the purchase price of machinery and equipment. The effect was to reduce the effective rate of income taxation below the statutory rate. The effective tax rate can also be lowered by accelerating depreciation deductions. A dollar of tax deduction is generally worth more this year than next since a dollar of tax saved can earn interest over the year. Thus shortening the period over which an investment can be depreciated is generally advantageous, so long as there is sufficient taxable income to absorb the increased deductions. Similarly, acceleration in the method of depreciation—for example, from the straight-line form to the declining-balance method—is usually advantageous.

The lower effective tax rate associated with the provision of an investment incentive increases, at least initially, the after-tax rate of return to capital in the tax-favored use. Because capital in that use is now more profitable, the demand for that capital increases. This increased demand has two general effects: capital will tend to shift into the favored use from less favored uses, and the overall size of the capital stock will tend to change.

The first effect operates through the following mechanism. Investors are assumed to place their capital in the use with the highest after-tax rate of return, adjusted for risk. The provision of an investment incentive causes investment to flow to the tax-favored use until after-tax rates of return are equalized for assets of equal riskiness. This process, termed *arbitrage* to signify the exploitation of differential rates of return, results in a shift in the allocation of capital toward the tax-favored use. A tax incentive for one use of capital implies a relative disincentive for other uses. Investment incentives thus can alter the allocation of capital.

Incentives can also influence the absolute size of the capital stock. As noted earlier, the lower effective tax rate associated with incentives increases the overall demand for capital; unless the supply of capital is

2. The effective rate of income taxation is defined as the difference between the before- and after-tax rates of return, expressed as a percentage of the before-tax return. It measures the actual tax burden on investment income and, in general, differs from the statutory rate of taxation (see Appendix).

fixed independently of the rate of return, the higher after-tax return will influence how much is saved and how much is consumed. It is not possible on theoretical grounds to say whether saving will increase or decrease, but empirical estimates suggest that if saving is affected at all, it will tend to increase. The resulting increase in investment spending may have a Keynesian counterrecessionary effect, and the increased amount of productive capacity may lead to a supply-side surge in economic growth.[3]

Although investment incentives imply lower effective tax rates, lower effective tax rates do not necessarily imply an explicit intention to stimulate capital formation. There are many aspects of the tax code that lower effective tax rates on capital. For example, the exclusion of income from owner-occupied housing arose primarily from the administrative and political difficulty of imputing the implicit rental income of homeowners. More generally, the tax code is a maze of statutes, procedures, and rulings that frequently result in effective tax rates that differ markedly from the statutory rates.

Investment Incentives in Practice

Congress has enacted many investment incentives since World War II. Accelerated depreciation methods were adopted in 1954, and in 1962 write-off periods were substantially shortened and an investment tax credit for equipment was enacted. The adoption of the asset depreciation range (ADR) system in 1971 reduced write-off periods again, and the Economic Recovery Tax Act of 1981 provided for a further acceleration of write-offs.

As table 1 makes clear, the tax incentive programs adopted in 1954, 1962, 1971, and 1981 each significantly reduced the marginal effective corporate tax rate on new investment.[4] It is also evident that in the years

3. It is useful here to distinguish between tax provisions that increase the demand for investment (investment incentives like accelerated depreciation) and provisions that increase the supply of saving (like IRAs and tax-deferred pension plans). Both lower the effective tax rate on capital income but do so from different sides of the capital market. Furthermore, savings incentives tend to affect more strongly the size of the capital stock than its composition, while most investment incentives tend to affect the composition more strongly.

4. As noted in the Appendix, marginal effective tax rates embody changes in depreciation allowances and in the investment tax credit, as well as changes in the

Table 1. *Marginal Effective Corporate Tax Rates, 1952–83*[a]
Percent

Year	Total	Equipment	Structures
1952	61.2	63.4	57.4
1953	59.2	61.1	56.1
1954	53.9	54.9	52.1
1955	51.8	52.5	50.6
1956	51.4	52.1	50.2
1957	53.1	54.0	51.5
1958	53.2	54.2	51.6
1959	54.0	55.1	52.2
1960	53.4	54.4	51.8
1961	51.8	52.5	50.6
1962	39.6	35.0	47.1
1963	39.3	34.8	46.8
1964	27.5	17.8	43.9
1965	26.3	16.8	42.1
1966	34.5	29.0	43.8
1967	34.1	28.1	44.0
1968	40.7	35.0	50.3
1969	54.8	55.1	54.2
1970	52.3	52.9	51.3
1971	31.3	21.3	48.0
1972	31.3	21.3	48.0
1973	34.1	25.1	49.1
1974	39.3	32.3	51.2
1975	32.1	21.2	50.2
1976	31.4	20.3	50.0
1977	30.6	19.2	49.8
1978	31.4	20.3	50.0
1979	30.0	19.1	48.3
1980	33.1	23.5	49.2
1981	4.7	− 14.2	36.4
1982	4.7	− 14.2	36.4
1983	15.8	3.5	36.4

Source: Charles R. Hulten and James W. Robertson, "The Taxation of High Technology Industries," *National Tax Journal*, vol. 37 (September 1985), p. 337.
a. These estimates refer only to the corporation income tax and only to equipment and structures used in the non-real estate part of the corporate sector. Furthermore, the estimates refer to the tax treatment of new investment put in place in each year and not to the *average* tax rate on all capital in place in a given year (hence the term *marginal*).

following these incentive programs, the incentives were often eroded. In some cases the incentives were explicitly removed (for example, the

statutory tax rate. They also capture the impact of inflation: inflation causes true depreciation costs to rise, but tax depreciation deductions are allowed only on the original cost of an investment. Taxable income is overstated on this account, and the marginal effective tax rate is increased.

suspensions of the investment tax credit in 1966 and 1969), and at other times the erosion was the result of inflation.

The most recent removal occurred in 1986. The tax reform act of that year treated investment incentives as undesirable devices that undid the optimal allocation of capital by the marketplace. This legislation removed overt incentives like the investment tax credit and most of the benefit of the accelerated cost recovery system (ACRS) of depreciation allowances, eliminated the favorable capital-gain rate differential, tightened the accounting rules so as to require capitalization rather than expensing of more business costs, reduced the generosity of savings incentives like individual retirement accounts (IRAs), and included various rules to reduce the benefit of tax shelter activities. The intent was to use the increased tax proceeds to lower (and compress) statutory tax rates.

Although the Tax Reform Act of 1986 succeeded in removing many incentives from the tax system, broadening the tax base, and reducing statutory tax rates, it failed to achieve a completely level playing field, even for a partial list of assets within the corporate sector (see table 2). Furthermore, owner-occupied housing retains its highly favorable tax treatment, the corporate tax continues to be unintegrated, intangible investments are still expensed, and many tax credits and savings incentives remain. The result is a variegated pattern of effective tax rates: some types of capital income are taxed heavily and others lightly, if at all.

We now turn to the question of whether this variation is desirable. More generally, what is the "optimal" role of incentives? This is, in effect, a question of the optimal structure of effective tax rates since we have defined incentives in terms of the variation in these rates. The notion of an optimal system of effective tax rates encompasses many issues: equity, efficiency, full employment, revenue sufficiency, and tax administration. No single model of optimality encompasses all of these issues, and in the following sections we deal with each separately.

Efficient Taxation with a Fixed Stock of Capital and No Externalities

The standard criterion for judging the efficiency of a tax system is Pareto optimality. The allocation of capital among competing uses is said to be Pareto optimal if there is no way to reallocate the capital and

Table 2. *Effective Corporate Tax Rates, by Asset Type*
Percent

Asset type	Before Tax Reform Act	After Tax Reform Act
Equipment		
Autos	2	40
Office/computing	2	36
Trucks, buses, and trailers	2	35
Aircraft	2	35
Construction machinery	2	28
Mining and oil field machinery	2	33
Service industry machinery	2	33
Tractors	2	32
Instruments	7	33
Other	2	32
General industrial	7	30
Metalworking machinery	1	28
Electric transmission	20	37
Communications	1	23
Other electrical	1	28
Furniture and fixtures	1	27
Special industrial	1	25
Agricultural	1	26
Fabricated metal products	14	33
Engines and turbines	28	40
Ships and boats	1	36
Railroad	22	22
Total	6	31
Structures		
Mining/oil and gas	11	12
Other	45	40
Industrial	41	37
Public utility	24	30
Commercial	38	34
Farm	38	34
Total	34	32
Total equipment and structures	25	32

Source: Jane G. Gravelle, *Tax Reform Act of 1986: Effective Corporate Tax Rates* (Congressional Research Service, 1987), p. 4.

labor input to make any person better off without making someone else worse off. As part of this definition, an allocation is efficient if there is no way to wring more output (and hence a higher before-tax rate of return) from a given total amount of capital. An inefficient allocation of inputs is undesirable because it implies that resources are wasted.

Thus, in the absence of externalities,[5] Pareto optimality requires an equal before-tax rate of return on all assets. When before-tax rates of return are equal, no reallocation of capital among alternative uses will increase total income. For example, if all capital earns 10 percent, a shift of one unit from one use to another does not change the return to that unit. If, on the other hand, capital earns 5 percent in one use and 15 percent in another, a reallocation of capital from the former to the latter increases income and the initial allocation is not Pareto optimal.

The imposition of a tax on capital causes the before- and after-tax rates of return to differ; indeed, the effective tax rate is defined as the difference in the two rates, expressed as a percentage of the before-tax rate of return. Since the process of arbitrage tends to drive after-tax rates of return into equality, there is no guarantee that before-tax rates of return will be equal. In other words, the invisible hand of the free market does not necessarily ensure an efficient allocation of resources when income is subject to taxation.

One further condition is needed: the effective tax rate must be equal across all types and uses of capital. The equality of effective tax rates, in conjunction with equal after-tax rates of return, implies that before-tax rates must be equal, and this implies that the allocation of capital is Pareto optimal. Conversely, a system of unequal effective tax rates results in an inefficient system of unequal before-tax rates of return.

The equality of effective tax rates is thus a characteristic of an efficient income tax system under the conditions of complete arbitrage, a fixed stock of capital, no externalities, and taxation of *all* capital. This is the source of the "level playing field" standard advocated by proponents of tax reform. In this framework there is no role for investment incentives.[6]

5. Externalities occur when the market fails to value fully a given form of economic activity. The effects of externalities are discussed below.

6. In the Haig-Simons definition of a pure income tax, the base of the income tax should be consumption plus change in net worth. This means that accrued income (for example, unrealized capital gains and implicit income from owner-occupied housing) should be taxed along with money income flows. It also implies that the tax base should not be eroded by investment incentives. Because all income is taxed in the Haig-Simons model, the effective tax rate on all capital income is equal to the statutory tax rate.

Efficient Taxation: The Consumption Tax

The preceding analysis has taken the total size of the capital stock as given. This might be a valid assumption if the size of the stock is determined independently of tax considerations. But, as we have argued, taxes can affect the total supply of capital. In this case the tax could produce an allocational inefficiency even though the total capital stock, whatever its size, was allocated efficiently among competing uses in any given year.

The Pareto-optimal size of the capital stock is determined, in simple intertemporal models, by the optimal allocation of income between current and future consumption. In general, income and optimal consumption streams do not exactly match, and income must be reallocated through net saving or dissaving. Under certain circumstances an intertemporal Pareto-optimal allocation of resources can be achieved if consumers trade current for future consumption (that is, save) at the market rate of return to capital.

A tax on income reduces the return to saving and thus, in general, alters the allocation of income between current and future consumption. If the before-tax allocation was optimal, the introduction of the tax will tend to yield an inefficient intertemporal allocation of income. It is not possible to say, a priori, whether saving will increase or decrease but only that a tax on the return to capital will, in general, result in a total capital stock that differs from its optimal size. There is a widespread presumption, however, that the size of the capital stock is too small under the income tax.

A tax on consumption does not impose a tax on the return to capital. It thus offers the possibility of eliminating the intertemporal inefficiency associated with the income tax. Indeed, it is possible to show that under certain circumstances a consumption tax is more efficient than an income tax of equal yield.

If one accepts the superiority of the consumption tax, then one is led to a tax system with a zero effective tax rate on capital income.[7] This, in turn, leads to the conclusion that investment incentives in a tax system

7. A consumption tax can be thought of as an income tax that excludes saving from the tax base. In the aggregate this is conceptually the same as deducting investment from income, which is the definition of expensing. It is not hard to show that expensing results in a zero marginal effective tax rate on capital income.

that is nominally based on income should be structured to achieve a zero effective tax rate. A consumption tax could be achieved by allowing accelerated depreciation equivalent to expensing (immediate write-off) for all types of capital.

Optimal Taxation

The two models described above present alternative views of efficient taxation. Both suggest that a system of equal effective tax rates is efficient, although they differ on the appropriate "level" of the playing field: under a Haig-Simons income tax, the effective tax rates would equal the statutory tax rate; under the consumption tax approach, the common effective tax rate would be zero. Both views have played prominent roles in the debate over tax reform, with the income tax view ascendant for the time being.

Both models are special cases of a more general approach known as *optimal commodity taxation*.[8] The optimal commodity tax model starts with the problem of raising a given amount of revenue from a tax on all inputs and outputs associated with the productive process of an economy. A uniform tax on all inputs and outputs raises no revenue since inputs are really negative outputs in the productive process and the value of outputs equals the negative value of inputs used in production. (This is known as "Walras's law.") As a result, a system of differential taxes is necessary to raise revenue, and a certain amount of inefficiency must be tolerated. The problem is to find a system of tax rates that minimizes inefficiency while raising the required revenue.

A number of such systems have been derived using special assumptions about the elasticities of supply and demand of the various commodities in the economy. For example, under certain conditions the

---

8. The literature on optimal taxation is enormous, with fundamental contributions by F. P. Ramsey, "A Contribution to the Theory of Taxation," *Economic Journal*, vol. 37 (March 1927), pp. 47–61; Paul A. Samuelson, unpublished memorandum for the U.S. Department of the Treasury, 1951; W. J. Gorlett and D. C. Hague, "Complementarity and the Excess Burden of Taxation," *Review of Economic Studies*, vol. 21, no. 54 (1953–54), pp. 21–30; Peter A. Diamond and James A. Mirrlees, "Optimal Taxation and Public Production: I—Production Efficiency," *American Economic Review*, vol. 61 (March 1971), pp. 8–27; and Diamond and Mirrlees, "Optimal Taxation and Public Production: II—Tax Rules," *American Economic Review*, vol. 61 (June 1971), pp. 267–78. An excellent summary is given in Anthony B. Atkinson and Joseph E. Stiglitz, *Lectures on Public Economics* (McGraw-Hill, 1980), chaps. 12–14.

optimal tax rates vary inversely with the elasticity of demand for various commodities. The implication of the inverse elasticity rule is that taxes should be levied primarily on those goods that are inelastic in demand.

A comprehensive income tax or a consumption tax can each be shown to be an optimal system if appropriate assumptions are made. However, neither has a claim to *general* validity on optimal tax grounds. This proposition can be demonstrated with a simplified version of the optimal commodity tax model in which there are three goods: consumption during a person's working years and consumption during a person's retirement years (both of which can be taxed) and leisure during the retirement years (which cannot be taxed). The results of this conventional model are nicely summarized by Michael Boskin and John Shoven:

Thus, a pure consumption tax is optimal *only* when working period and retirement consumption are equally good substitutes for retirement leisure. The optimal tax system in this stylized world taxes the weaker substitute for leisure during retirement more heavily than the closer substitute.[9]

Depending on the relationship between the taxed goods and the untaxed consumption of leisure, a consumption tax might be optimal or an income tax might be optimal, but in general the conditions under which either of these results occurs are sufficiently restrictive that neither a pure consumption nor income tax is likely to be optimal.

The policy debate over the relative merits of pure consumption versus income taxation must be viewed in light of the special restrictiveness of the conditions under which each is optimal. Complicating the relative optimality analysis of the two taxes is the fact that neither tax is pure (that is, general) when it is applied in the real world.

In general, then, the optimal tax structure requires different effective tax rates on different kinds of capital goods.[10] Given our definition of investment incentives as tax provisions that result in differential tax rates, we must conclude that there is, in principle, a role for investment incentives in an efficient tax structure. When an optimal tax rule dictates differential tax rates on different types of capital, the statutory rate could

9. Michael J. Boskin and John B. Shoven, "Issues in the Taxation of Capital Income in the United States," *American Economic Review*, vol. 70 (May 1980, *Papers and Proceedings, 1979*), p. 165.

10. For further discussion, see Alan J. Auerbach, "The Optimal Taxation of Heterogeneous Capital," *Quarterly Journal of Economics*, vol. 93 (November 1979), pp. 589–612.

be made to vary appropriately, or an investment incentive could be used to secure the required differential.

Thus, despite the level-playing-field analysis, investment incentives can, in theory, improve economic efficiency. The optimal structure of investment incentives generally depends, however, on the elasticities of supply and demand for thousands, if not millions, of goods. The practical problem of finding the optimal structure is virtually insurmountable.

Market Failure

The optimal tax framework discussed above assumes that markets function perfectly. We have not considered thus far any provision for external economies or diseconomies, involuntary unemployment, imperfect competition, or uncertainty about the future. Below we reexamine the role of investment incentives when some of these assumptions are violated.

Externalities

We have assumed in our discussion of optimal taxation that the before-tax rate of return and the social rate of return are the same. This implies that the market captures all the costs or benefits associated with a particular activity. This, in fact, is not always the case. For example, the market may fail to account for the pollution caused by steel mills or the benefit to the national defense of having a certain steel production capacity. When this occurs, the social rate of return differs from the before-tax rate of return.

The analysis of optimal commodity taxes can be extended to incorporate externalities where they exist. When the private and social returns differ, the optimal tax structure can make allowance for the difference. For example, if the optimal tax structure implied equal effective tax rates when externalities were absent, the emergence of an externality might require corrective incentives that would cause optimal effective tax rates to vary. This introduces yet another theoretical rationale for investment incentives, although in practice it is difficult to measure the extent of the externality.

Unemployment

The optimal tax model assumes full employment of resources. It is therefore not suited to the analysis of a tax policy designed to correct for underemployment of resources. Yet the traditional Keynesian argument for investment incentives is precisely that they stimulate economic activity during recessions.

The design of Keynesian investment incentives differs markedly from the design that would be imposed under the optimal tax literature. The Keynesian goal is to stimulate the growth of aggregate income, not minimize the inefficiency of taxation. The optimal Keynesian tax incentive is presumably one that achieves the maximum degree of stimulation per dollar of revenue loss. By this standard the investment tax credit would be preferable to a general tax cut as an efficient fiscal stimulus since it largely concentrates revenue cost on new investment decisions.

There is, however, the question of effectiveness. An economy in recession is characterized by low rates of capital utilization and by operating losses (and thus no taxable income). Both of these characteristics may cause investment incentives to be ineffective. The presence of low rates of utilization implies that expansion can be achieved without new investment spending, and the absence of taxable income would generally blunt the effect of tax breaks.

The effectiveness of tax incentives is a subject of much controversy. Some studies find that tax incentives have been rather ineffective in stimulating investment and that the desire to produce output is usually a more powerful determinant of investment spending.[11] This finding suggests a limited role for investment incentives, although evidence can be found to support the position that "taxes matter."[12]

11. See Peter K. Clark, "Investment in the 1970s: Theory, Performance, and Prediction," *Brookings Papers on Economic Activity, 1:1979*, pp. 73–113; Martin Feldstein, "Inflation, Tax Rules and Investment: Some Econometric Evidence," *Econometrica*, vol. 50 (July 1982), pp. 825–62; and Robert S. Chirinko and Robert Eisner, "Tax Policy and Investment in Major U.S. Macroeconomic Econometric Models," *Journal of Public Economics*, vol. 20 (March 1983), pp. 139–66.

12. Consider, for example, the intense concern about tax shelter activity that surfaced during the recent tax reform debate. If tax incentives were completely ineffective, it is hard to see how tax-sheltered investment could have grown to such proportions that it became a major target of tax reformers. The generous real estate incentives introduced by the Economic Recovery Tax Act of 1981 are reflected in the building boom of the mid-1980s.

Inadequate Economic Growth

The marketplace may fail to provide adequate economic growth, just as it may fail to provide for full employment of resources. The desire to promote growth with investment incentives has greatly influenced tax policy in the United States. The perception of inadequate growth, in fact, played a major role in the adoption of tax incentives in 1954, 1962, 1971, and 1981. Unfortunately, it is not always possible to sort out the causes of slow growth. For example, during the productivity slowdown of the 1970s, inadequate saving was identified as a culprit, as were the energy crises, the baby boom generation of workers, and a host of other factors. It is even difficult to define an optimal rate of growth, and thus an optimal structure of investment incentives is hard to identify.[13]

Equity Considerations

Horizontal equity requires that individuals who are equally well off should have equal tax burdens. Furthermore, vertical equity requires that tax burdens increase with the level of well-being. A major complaint about investment incentives is that they violate both principles.

During the debate over tax reform, much attention was paid to rich individuals and corporations who paid no income tax. This supposed violation of vertical equity was associated with the existence of tax shelters and liberal investment incentives. By implication, investment incentives are undesirable on equity grounds.

This line of argument is fairly simplistic: the absence of tax liability due to a tax shelter does not necessarily imply a higher after-tax income.[14]

---

13. Optimal economic growth is the subject of voluminous studies. See Edwin Burmeister and A. Rodney Dobell, *Mathematical Theories of Economic Growth* (Macmillan, 1970). According to a simplified version of the theory—the "golden rule" of economic growth—the optimal rate of saving is such that the rate of return to capital equals the rate of growth of the economy. But even this simple rule sheds little light on whether the actual rate of saving is adequate.

14. Consider, for example, individual *A* in the 50 percent tax bracket who owns $1,000,000 in tax-exempt municipal bonds yielding a 5 percent rate of return, and individual *B*, also in the 50 percent tax bracket, who owns $1,000,000 in taxable corporate bonds yielding a 10 percent rate of return. Does *A* enjoy a tax advantage over *B* because *A* pays no taxes? Both receive an after-tax income of $50,000 per year and are therefore equally well off. In this example the tax-favored investment was no better than the

Arbitrage tends to level after-tax rates of return on capital, and this means that investors in the same tax bracket tend to have the same after-tax income. Horizontal equity among recipients of capital income can hardly be said to be violated in this case.

The horizontal equity between recipients of capital and labor income is, however, another issue. If labor income is taxed at the statutory tax rate, and capital income is taxed at a lower effective tax rate because of investment incentives, there are clearly grounds for questioning the equity of the incentive system. This suggests the possibility of a clash between equity and efficiency objectives. These trade-offs may be analyzed formally, however, since the efficiency-oriented optimal tax model can incorporate progressive tax rules. Theoretically, an optimal tax formula can be derived that embodies equity considerations, and indeed investment incentives may be used to promote equity. For example, the tax code contains investment incentives for low-income housing that are surely related to the desire to improve the economic welfare of the poor.

The Political Economy of Taxation

The theoretical analysis above yields the conclusion that investment incentives may well be part of an efficient tax system. However, no general rule—like the optimality of a comprehensive income or consumption tax—emerges from the analysis to guide the formulation of tax policy, and we are left with the problem of determining the optimal structure of taxes and tax incentives. Unfortunately, this involves information about the economy and about societal values that is virtually impossible to obtain. Although investment incentives may be part of an optimally designed tax system, there is no credible a priori way to determine what the optimal structure actually is or to evaluate the actual incentives that have played so prominent a role in the tax system.

taxable investment. In general, arbitrage will tend to guide money to the investment with the highest after-tax rate of return. An important implication of arbitrage is that all investment in the same risk class earns the same net return regardless of the amount of taxes paid. In this case investment incentives do not necessarily violate equity principles. This analysis is complicated by a progressive tax rate structure, where different marginal tax rates can result in tax benefits to some tax brackets despite arbitrage. It is still true, however, that the absence of a direct tax liability does not mean that a tax consequence has been escaped. (These issues are discussed in greater detail in the paper by Alan J. Auerbach in this volume.)

Determination of the appropriate role for investment incentives thus centers on the process by which tax policy is formulated and implemented. But is this process likely to result in the enactment of investment incentives that are optimal under the theoretical economic criteria discussed earlier? The answer to this question lies in an examination of the political economy of taxation, a field that has received considerably less attention than the models reviewed in the preceding sections.

The process of tax legislation is inductive. The tax code is a continually evolving document, changed regularly by new legislation, regulations, and rulings by the Internal Revenue Service and the courts. The pressure for tax legislation occurs in response to new economic conditions, changes in societal values, and shifts in political power. Tax laws are the result of a complex interaction of Congress, the administration, and the public, and once passed they are frequently altered in significant and unexpected ways by the process of tax implementation and administration.

This uncertain inductive process has two potentially desirable features. First, decisions about tax burdens are made in accordance with democratic procedures. While the end result might not please a particular group, the perceived fairness of the entire process makes certain undesirable outcomes acceptable. This is very important in a tax system that is largely self-enforcing.

Second, the tax legislative process provides for feedback. Information about how the system is functioning is fed back into the process so changes can be made. This is a desirable feature since the consequences of any tax provision cannot be fully known at the time the provision is adopted. Over time, the process may even arrive at something akin to the optimal tax solution—that is, a tax system that is widely perceived to maximize social welfare.

This possibility is limited by special interest groups, which develop to ensure that their constituencies receive as much as possible of the valuable tax benefits produced by the incentives. Their influence becomes unduly strong for three reasons: First, it is extremely difficult for legislators to separate special pleading for provisions that are beneficial from an optimal tax standpoint from those that are detrimental. Second, the legislative representatives of the region or group promoting the investment incentive may find it advantageous to their constituency to support the interests of other constituencies in order to obtain support for their own proposals. Third, special interest groups receive far greater benefits from tax advantages than their share of any harm to the general welfare.[15] Indeed, it is precisely because of the diffuse nature of the general welfare loss that opposition to special interest provisions is often weak. The individual welfare loss from any one special provision is likely to be too small to generate a broad-based political reaction.

But, as the number of special interest provisions multiplies, a point is reached where the revenue loss becomes significant, and additional tax revenue must be sought from the general public. Furthermore, the perception of widespread tax avoidance becomes a political issue. At this point tax reform moves to the front of the political agenda.

As an example of this process, consider the granting of a tax credit for a certain type of machinery because its use will conserve energy. This credit benefits investors in this machinery by lowering their tax liability and raising the after-tax rate of return, at least temporarily. The lost tax revenue must be made up through additional taxes somewhere in the system, by increased government debt, or by reduced government spending. These costs, along with any welfare costs (or gains) due to a distortion in the allocation of resources, tend to be spread widely, and the portion of the costs borne by the recipients of the energy credit thus tends to be far less than the tax benefits gained.

Of course, legislators are not obliged to accept the energy conservation rationale for this investment incentive, but the diffuse nature of its costs makes it hard for them to resist the lobbying efforts of those whose potential gain is large, especially if they are organized and well financed.

Administrative problems caused by the adoption of investment incentives also militate against their desirability. There is generally tension between the economic result sought through an investment incentive and the administrability of the provision needed to achieve that result. Thus, assuming there could be agreement on an optimal investment incentive, concerns about its administration are likely to require it to be modified during the legislative process so that both taxpayers and revenue agents can understand it and apply it. And to the extent administrative concerns are not dealt with, the compliance process

15. As previously noted, the tax benefits of a provision to individual investors will tend to be temporary because the flow of investment to the favored activity will lower the net return until it is the same as in other, less-favored activities. What is initially a tax benefit is thus extinguished. As this happens, however, the allocation of resources is distorted, and a welfare loss is created. Furthermore, there is still a continuing loss of tax revenue.

becomes overburdened and does not achieve in practice the theoretical results envisioned by the legislation.

Yet another factor to consider in weighing the desirability of investment incentives is the precedential effect. The provision of one investment incentive seems to spawn numerous siblings and descendants. This is almost inevitable given the difficulty of identifying those incentives that will be beneficial and the strength of special interests.

Consider the history of the investment credit. The credit was originally envisioned as a reduction in tax equal to 15 percent of the cost of investment in new machinery and equipment beyond investment that would have been made in any event. (Current depreciation allowances were to be used as a proxy for expected investment.) By the time President John F. Kennedy made the proposal, the credit was 15 percent for new investment above depreciation, 6 percent for new investment above 50 percent of depreciation, and 10 percent for the first $5,000 of new investment. These changes were adopted to make the credit more widely available and hence more likely to be enacted. Then the House Ways and Means Committee converted it to a 7 percent across-the-board credit. This was done to make the credit easier to administer but at the cost of spending many tax dollars on investment that would have been made in any event. Moreover, the credit was extended to a modest amount of used property, despite its expressed goal of encouraging the purchase of new machinery. Finally, the Senate Finance Committee adopted a rule to reduce the tax basis of property for depreciation purposes by the amount of the credit. As finally enacted, the credit little resembled the investment incentive that had been developed on the economists' blackboard. Moreover, between enactment in 1962 and final repeal in 1986, the investment credit was suspended twice; the rates of credit were tinkered with regularly; the requirement for a basis reduction was ended and then a 50 percent of credit basis reduction was reinstated; and the amount of used property qualifying for the credit was frequently changed.

Also during its troubled twenty-four-year existence, the allowability and amount of the investment credit were constantly disputed during audits conducted by revenue agents. There were also numerous Internal Revenue Service rulings and court decisions dealing with arcane investment credit questions.

When the investment credit was enacted in 1962, the only credits in the Internal Revenue Code were the foreign tax credit, the dividend received credit, and the retirement income credit, none of which were investment incentives. After enactment, however, the credit was followed by a host of narrowly focused investment incentives—the residential energy credit, the qualified clinical testing expenses credit, the credit for producing fuel from a nonconventional source, the research credit, the credit for transferring securities to an employee stock ownership plan, the rehabilitation credit, the business energy property credit, the credit for expenses incurred in connection with work incentive programs, and the targeted jobs credit.

The message is clear: even if an investment incentive is proposed with the purest of motives, it rarely achieves its originally intended results. Moreover, the incentive is likely to produce compliance problems, tax shelters, revenue waste, perceptions of unfairness, an unstable environment for investment, and pressure for more incentives. The result is likely to be a periodic need for tax reform as the burden of investment incentives becomes too heavy and too costly for the system to bear.

Conclusion

Our analysis of the process by which investment incentives are adopted has focused on the role of special interest groups and on implementation problems. We have identified major costs to society associated with the use of such incentives. There may also be benefits. Whether one favors investment incentives depends on whether one believes the benefits outweigh the costs.

Economic theory cannot provide an a priori answer to this question, for exactly the same reason that it cannot provide an unambiguous answer to the optimal tax problem. Political economy strongly suggests, however, that the action of special interest groups will ultimately cause the societal costs of investment incentives to outweigh their benefits. The pursuit of tax incentives is an ongoing process that logically ends only when the perceived benefits and costs of incentives get sufficiently out of line that public opinion can be mobilized. The logical outcome of this dynamic process is the periodic curtailment of investment incentives through tax reform.

We conclude that those responsible for enacting tax legislation would be well advised to adopt a general rule that investment incentives should be avoided. Although investment incentives can theoretically be used to promote economic welfare, it is our view that such incentives are likely in practice ultimately to produce more harm than good.

Appendix

The marginal effective tax rate is a measure of the actual rate of income taxation as opposed to the statutory tax rate. It is the difference in the rate of return to the marginal investment before and after tax—an implicit measure of the actual amount of tax liability on income accruing to the asset—expressed as a percentage of the before-tax income earned by the asset.

An analytical expression for the effective tax rate can be derived from the Hall-Jorgenson user cost model.[16] The Hall-Jorgenson user cost is the cost associated with using (or renting) one unit of capital stock for one year (as opposed to the cost of buying that unit of stock). The user cost c per dollar of investment is equal to:

$$(1) \qquad c = (1 - uz - k)(r + d)/(1 - u),$$

where u is the statutory rate of taxation, z is the present value of tax depreciation deductions, k is the rate of the investment tax credit, r is the after-tax rate of return, and d is the true (economic) rate of depreciation.

The quantity c is the return to one unit of capital gross of taxes and depreciation costs. The before-tax income associated with the unit of capital, h, is thus

$$(2) \qquad h = c - d,$$

or the gross return less economic depreciation. The marginal effective tax rate, e, is defined as the difference between the before- and after-tax rates of return divided by the before-tax rate:

$$(3) \qquad e = (h - r)/h.$$

This definition is illustrated in figure 1. The curve DD denotes the rate of return to capital before taxes, h, as a function of the amount of capital, K. (Alternatively, DD is the demand for capital at each rate of return.) The curve DD' denotes the after-tax rate of return, r, for each K. If the

16. Robert E. Hall and Dale W. Jorgenson, "Tax Policy and Investment Behavior," *American Economic Review*, vol. 57 (June 1967), pp 391–414.

Figure 1. *The Supply of and Demand for Capital*

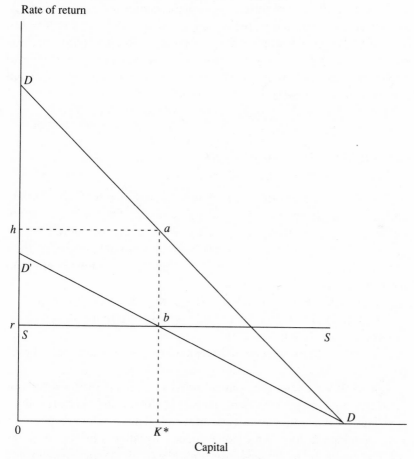

Rate of return

Capital

supply of capital, the curve *SS*, is perfectly elastic at a rate of return *r*, equilibrium occurs at *K**, where the after-tax rate of return to the investment on *DD'* is just equal to the amount that savers required on *SS* in order to make the investment.

The effective tax rate in figure 1 is the vertical distance *ab* divided by *aK**. Total tax liability is given by the rectangle *habr*, and total income before tax is *haK*0*.

Because of equation 1, the effective tax rate in equation 3 will change with variations in the present value of depreciation allowances, *z*, the rate of the investment tax credit, *k*, and the statutory tax rate, *u*. Accelerated depreciation leads to an increase in *z* and can be shown to reduce the effective tax rate e. Similarly, an increase in k or a reduction in u reduces e. When tax and economic depreciation are equal in present-value terms, $e = u$; that is, the effective and statutory rates of taxation are equal. When investments can be written off immediately, or "expensed," $z = 1$ and $e = 0$. In other words, expensing is equivalent to imposing a zero effective tax rate on investment income, even though the statutory rate is positive.

Comments by Jerome Kurtz

This paper is refreshing in its reminder that reality is frequently untidy and that intensely practical political and administrative problems cannot be ignored in formulating tax policies. When such considerations are ignored, carefully aimed tax incentives may completely miss their intended marks and rather than improve the economic and tax environment do serious damage to both.

Authors Charles Hulten and Robert Klayman make these basic points:

—Optimally, the tax system should impose different rates of tax on different types of capital income.

—We do not know enough to determine what those differences should be.

—Even if we knew, the political process, because of the enormous pressures on it to accommodate special pleaders, is unlikely to produce legislation that adequately carries out the ideal plan.

—Opening the door to providing special investment incentives in the tax law is likely to increase the unfairness of the tax system and consequently the disrespect in which it is held, requiring periodic reform to undo these mistakes.

History certainly provides no reason for doubting any of these statements.

Before the Tax Reform Act of 1986, the income tax system was widely viewed as a disgrace. The problems—high marginal rates, lack of horizontal and vertical equity, proliferation of tax shelters, and complexity—were, for the most part, the result of flawed attempts to provide investment incentives.

Rates were too high because the tax base had become too narrow, largely because of exclusions and credits intended to provide investment incentives.

The system was viewed as grossly unfair because of the lack of both horizontal and vertical equity. Those with similar incomes were paying vastly different amounts of tax, and many with very high incomes were paying less tax than factory workers. Again, these distortions were largely attributable to investment incentives that were more widely available to high-income taxpayers, thus diminishing vertical equity, and were unevenly available across income classes depending on the sources of income, thus distorting horizontal equity.

Hundreds of thousands of taxpayers, through tax shelters, had claimed billions of dollars of unintended and frequently bogus tax deductions. This discredited the system, created an administrative nightmare, and fostered a feeling of contempt for the tax system. Tax shelters are the result of investment incentives gone astray.

The tax system was viewed as overly and needlessly complex. Much of the complexity (although by no means all) is caused by targeted investment incentives and the frequently complicated rules required by attempts (usually unsuccessful) to keep them on the target. The decline in tax compliance in recent years is, in my view, largely attributable to these problems.

Although the 1986 act succeeded in simplifying the tax law in many areas, in others it failed. The act's attempts to retain some targeted investment incentives and at the same time prevent the worst abuses produced mind-numbing complexity. There are now at least eight different categories of interest expense, each governed by a different set of deduction rules depending on the use of the proceeds of the borrowing. The alternative minimum tax and the passive-loss rules are enormously complicated. And there are other such provisions. Without investment incentives neither the minimum tax nor the passive-loss restrictions would be needed, and the interest deduction rules could be greatly simplified.

Are such complicated rules required to prevent abuses of investment incentives in an income tax, or are they the result of political compromises? Is there a better way?

The paper apparently assumes that investment incentives (assuming adequate knowledge to determine proper targets and amounts of incentives) could be designed and implemented efficiently and fairly if only the political process would allow the theoreticians to have their way. I am not so sure.

The basic problem that has yet to be solved is how to deal with borrowing and interest deductions when providing selective investment

340 CHARLES R. HULTEN AND ROBERT A. KLAYMAN

incentives. If a tax deduction is provided as an incentive for a particular type of investment or savings, and distortion of the incentive is to be prevented, either the deduction must be reduced to the extent attributable to related borrowing or the related borrowing must be included in income. Similarly, interest expense should not be fully deductible where the borrowing is related to investments in assets from which the income is exempt, taxed at a preferential rate, or deferred. The meaning of the word *related* is at the heart of the problem of designing directed investment incentives.[17]

A few examples of the tax code's attempts to target investment incentives are instructive, as to both the variety of the problems and the responses. There has long been a provision in the code denying the interest deduction on loans "incurred or continued to purchase or carry" state and local bonds on which interest is exempt from income tax. It is obvious that this provision, depending as it does on tracing loan proceeds to bond purchases, is easily and widely avoided.

There are provisions to deny interest deductions on loans "incurred or continued to purchase or carry" life insurance policies where the "inside" buildup (that is, the increases in value attributable to investment earnings on premium payments in excess of current actuarial risks) is taxed currently only if the interest is incurred pursuant to a plan contemplating the systematic borrowing of the cash value increases. Furthermore, there is an exception to the disallowance if four of the first seven premiums are not financed.

In similar situations there are no restrictions on borrowings. The deduction for contributions to IRAs is provided to encourage saving for retirement. If a taxpayer borrows funds to contribute to an IRA, the policy goal is not realized but the tax deductions for both the interest on the loan and the contribution to the IRA were nevertheless provided. The same can be said for the tax deduction provided a taxpayer who withdraws funds from a savings account to put into an IRA—a tax deduction with no net savings.

The story of legislation dealing with tax shelters is a story of the difficulties of trying to provide targeted investment incentives while preventing their abuse. The attempts to limit the use of investment incentives to a taxpayer's investment have necessitated "at risk" rules of gradually expanding scope and increasing complexity to combat

17. See C. Eugene Steuerle, *Taxes, Loans, and Inflation: How the Nation's Wealth Becomes Misallocated* (Brookings, 1985).

taxpayers' moves to avoid each new limit. The 1986 act recognizes the failure of prior legislation to prevent abuse and takes a different approach. For the most part, it denies deductions for losses to passive investors in pass-through entities—subchapter S corporations, partnerships, and proprietorships. Deductions are denied, regardless of whether the invested funds are borrowed and whether the losses are real or paper. Real cash losses are not currently deductible except against income from the same kinds of investments.

This approach also does not appear to solve the problem of allowing investment incentives and preventing their abuse. First, the provision goes too far in denying losses for real current decreases in net worth incurred in business transactions. Such losses should be allowed under an income tax. Second, there is substantial movement under way to generate passive activity income so that it can be offset by passive losses. This is done by organizing large partnerships for ventures that otherwise would have been conducted in corporate form. The Treasury is now trying to deal with this new set of problems.[18]

These examples illustrate just a few of the difficulties encountered in trying to control and direct investment incentives under an income tax.

Many who advocate investment incentives start with a preference for a consumption tax rather than an income tax. Since under a consumption tax all investments are deducted from income, it would seem to follow, if one prefers a consumption tax, that deducting some investments is better than deducting none. The "half a loaf is better than none" position does not, however, work in this situation. Under a consumption tax, while all investments are deducted, all borrowing is taxed. Thus, only net investments are deducted, and net borrowings are added to income. The problem of how to deal with borrowing does not exist in a consumption tax as long as all investments are treated the same, that is, excluded from the tax base. In that situation all borrowing is taxed.

Similarly, the tracing of borrowing would not be a problem under a pure income tax since no investment would be deductible from income; only real economic declines would be taken into account. Therefore, no borrowing need be included in income. But the problem of borrowing is serious in a hybrid system, that is, an income tax that provides investment incentives. If investment incentives are allowed in full to the owner of

18. Congress addressed this problem in the Revenue Act of 1987, P.L. 100-203, secs. 10211, 10212.

the investment, the incentives will be misdirected and excessive where the investment is financed wholly or partially with borrowed funds.

Although this problem is addressed in the law in a variety of ways, a satisfactory solution has not been found. The code provisions are a series of ad hoc rules, frequently ineffective, invariably (and I am afraid inevitably) blunt instruments of enormous complexity.

I do not believe there is any satisfactory answer to this problem. Money is fungible, and taxpayers will generally find ways to avoid whatever standards the law uses to "relate" borrowing to the tax-favored activity. Trying to prevent these strategies results in enormous complexity and unsatisfactory results.

Hulten and Klayman argue against investment incentives because we do not know what they should be and even if we knew, the political process would not produce legislation carrying out the plan. I would add that even if we knew what ideal investment incentives were and had a receptive Congress, we wouldn't know how to design the incentives to prevent distortion, abuse, and complexity.

Comments by John B. Shoven

This paper addresses one of the most important matters of tax policy in the past decade, a period when the United States completely changed direction on investment and savings incentives. Between 1978 and 1981 strong savings and investment incentives were instituted. Capital gains tax rates were lowered, tax shelters for retirement saving were liberalized, and depreciation was sharply accelerated. Since 1982, and particularly since 1986, the direction of these changes has been completely reversed.

Authors Charles Hulten and Robert Klayman begin their assessment of the role of investment incentives in a hybrid income-consumption tax environment by reviewing optimal tax theory in some very simple models. In a static Harberger model (in which total factor supplies are fixed), the optimal tax is a flat factor tax, either on capital or labor or both. Deadweight loss occurs when the factor taxes are partial (that is, apply to different sectors at different rates). But any tax, as long as it is flat across sectors, would be efficient. The authors argue that there is no room for special investment incentives in such a model, although capital could be taxed at a different rate than labor. The static nature of the Harberger model probably makes it ill suited to address the optimal taxation of labor and capital income, however.

The authors then examine simple dynamic models. The most relevant one (although still very simple) has overlapping generations. In that model the second-best optimal tax system depends on the relative supply elasticities of factors of production. Since economists cannot agree on labor and capital supply elasticities, optimal tax considerations, Hulten and Klayman argue, cannot be very helpful in guiding tax policy.[19]

In their discussion of the political economy of taxation, the authors explain that the United States has a self-assessing income tax system and that the perception of fairness is important to sustain voluntary compliance. They do not discuss the responsibility of the economics profession to educate politicians and the public regarding taxation. What the public perceives as fair, however, may not be logically fair at all. This is true not only in the area of taxation, but also regarding such subjects as trade restrictions, minimum wages, and price controls. There is a question as to whether the profession should try to operate within the restrictions of what will be perceived as fair, or whether it should try to deliver its message to the public and the decisionmakers. Besides, if the ultimate problem is to preserve or restore compliance, then perhaps tax reform should have directly addressed compliance measures, such as withholding on interest and dividends, and new noncompliance penalty structures.

The authors argue that the 1981 act went too far in terms of investment incentives, at least in terms of striving for the perception of fairness, and that the direction of change was reversed because of that. The effectiveness of the incentives in stimulating growth is exceedingly difficult to assess, given that some of them were reversed within twelve months.

Finally, the authors suggest that investment incentives are more targeted than is optimal because of the power of special interests. A

19. The authors suggest that one might want to deviate from optimal tax considerations for income distribution or externality reasons. Of course, in a full-blown optimal tax framework, with social welfare weights on individuals or income classes, the income distribution issue would be part of the solution. The authors are not very specific about what kind of externality situation they have in mind. I can conceive of a model in which new technologies are embodied in new investments and in which those who first adopt the technology cannot capture the total social return from the experiment that they provide for society. But that process would require careful and probably complex modeling that is beyond the scope of this paper.

"partial level playing field" probably is more efficient than the special targeted incentives that tend to result from the political process, they claim.

While interesting and on an important topic, the paper misses a lot of the crucial issues. First, there is very little mention of why a separate corporate-level tax is desirable. The choice between a consumption tax and an income tax is discussed, but the real question is whether to have a second income tax at the corporate level and whether to rely on this second income tax for more revenue than in the recent past. In this regard the paper never tackles the incidence question of who bears the corporation income tax, and I don't see how one can talk about fairness without addressing this issue. Perhaps one can talk about the perception of fairness, which is what the authors do for the most part. The authors seem to assume that the corporate tax is borne by capital, even in the long run, since they argue that a higher corporation tax may be an indirect way to increase the progressivity of the tax system. The long-run models that I know of, however, tend to show that the tax is borne by labor.[20]

Once the issue of the desirability or existence of a second-level corporate tax is raised, then the paper could discuss the choice between collecting revenue at the personal or corporate level. For any given level of corporate tax collections, it could address the trade-off between low rates and investment incentives. And it could bring up the issue of whether the tax should apply only to equity financed investments or whether a corporate cash-flow tax (including payments to debtholders) would be superior.

Also given short shrift in the paper is the importance of the taxation of housing. The authors come out against targeted investment incentives, but certainly the imputed income of owner-occupied housing should not be and will not be taxed. The amount of capital in owner-occupied housing exceeds the amount of corporate equity, so the tax treatment of housing and the level-playing-field concept that they support leads one to a consumption tax. It could even lead one to support the 1981 package of investment incentives, which were, in the authors' opinion, somewhat equivalent to expensing. Certainly, efficiency without taxation of the return to housing (in the Harberger model) would suggest no taxation of

20. See, for example, Martin Feldstein, "Incidence of a Capital Income Tax in a Growing Economy with Variable Savings Rates," *Review of Economic Studies*, vol. 41 (October 1974), pp. 505–13.

corporate capital rather than two layers of taxation. I think the institutional fact that housing probably cannot be taxed changes the whole concept of a level playing field a great deal.

The models in the paper are all closed-economy models. Several times the paper discusses savings and investment incentives as if they are two sides of the same coin, but in an open model with capital mobility they are very different, as Slemrod's paper in this volume demonstrates. I believe a recent paper by Larry Summers argues that part of the country's trade deficit problem is due to the imbalance in savings and investment incentives in the tax law.[21] In real policy analysis, presumably one must be concerned with the location of investment and the competitive nature of tax investment incentives. The United States had a higher cost of corporate capital in 1986 than did the United Kingdom, Japan, and West Germany. A major contributing factor is that real interest rates do not appear to be equated around the world and appear to be particularly high in the United States.[22] However, in this international competition framework, it is probably unwise to raise the cost of investment by reducing tax incentives when the United States already has a higher cost of capital than its competitors.

In the real world there is some ambiguity as to what constitutes an investment incentive. For instance, depreciation that is more rapid than economic depreciation is considered a tax incentive. This ignores two facts. First, despite the superb study by Hulten and Wykoff,[23] the precise rates of economic depreciation are not known. Second, real physical investments are very risky, and yet the tax code permits only a fixed pattern of depreciation allowances. Because of this the government does not share in a lot of the riskiness of the firm.[24] One way to offset the lack of risk participation by the government is to allow more rapid write-offs.

The paper neglects two additional aspects of investment incentives. The first is their ability to offset the effects of inflation on a nonindexed

21. Lawrence H. Summers, "Tax Policy and International Competitiveness," National Bureau of Economic Research Working Paper 2007 (Cambridge, Mass.: NBER, August 1986).

22. B. Douglas Bernheim and John B. Shoven, "Taxation and the Cost of Capital: An International Comparison," in Charls E. Walker and Mark A. Bloomfield, eds., *The Consumption Tax: A Better Alternative?* (Ballinger, 1987), pp. 61–85.

23. Charles R. Hulten and Frank C. Wykoff, "The Measurement of Economic Depreciation," in Hulten, ed., *Depreciation, Inflation, and the Taxation of Income from Capital* (Washington, D.C.: Urban Institute, 1981), pp. 81–125.

24. Jeremy I. Bulow and Lawrence H. Summers, "The Taxation of Risky Assets," *Journal of Political Economy*, vol. 92 (February 1984), pp. 20–39.

corporation income tax. (Clearly, a major reason for the acceleration of depreciation deductions and the investment tax credit is the fact that inflation erodes the value of nominal depreciation deductions. The reduction in the rate of inflation in the past four years was probably crucial in allowing the reversal of policy toward investment incentives.) Second is the role of investment incentives in the complexity of the tax system. Targeted tax incentives are a major feature of most complicated tax shelter schemes, and an important reason for eliminating many of them was simplicity.

I suspect that the one lesson many readers will take from the paper is that not enough is known about elasticities to implement optimal tax theory. Although there is some truth to this position, the situation is not quite as bleak as the authors paint. At least in some applied general equilibrium models, the results are relatively robust to elasticity parameters. A direct personal consumption tax implemented by permitting a general deduction for saving improves efficiency for a wide set of elasticity specifications.[25] These specifications include a zero uncompensated savings elasticity as well as the type of high savings elasticities that Larry Summers has described.[26] Douglas Bernheim and I have discussed translating a matrix of priors regarding the variance and covariance of elasticity parameters to a posterior distribution of results. Some work along these lines has been done. My guess is that if one did this sort of exercise regarding the issues in this paper, a consumption tax would prove more efficient than the current hybrid tax system and that a pure single-level income tax system would probably improve efficiency.

25. Charles L. Ballard and others, *Computation of General Equilibrium for Tax Policy Analysis* (University of Chicago Press, 1985).

26. Lawrence H. Summers, "Capital Taxation and Accumulation in a Life Cycle Growth Model," *American Economic Review*, vol. 71 (September 1981), pp. 533–44.

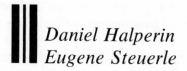

Daniel Halperin
Eugene Steuerle

Indexing the Tax System for Inflation

WITH even moderate rates of inflation, full taxation of nominal income from capital would impose extraordinarily high rates of tax on capital income. Without indexing of some type, therefore, an income tax often could be considered a tax on capital and not on income. In practice, however, all existing income taxes provide a substantial amount of indexing, albeit in an inexact and hidden way.

If an income tax system is likely to be indexed one way or the other, and if indexing already occurs under current law, then the question of whether indexing should occur is a bogus issue. The real question is whether an alternative system—in particular, explicit indexing—can be implemented so as to obtain a better measure of real income than the ad hoc adjustments provided by current law.

This paper shows how the need to avoid extraordinary rates of taxation on capital income strongly supports indexing. The paper then examines current law in the United States and shows how indexing is already applied in a very inexact manner. Although our focus is on the United States, similar tax provisions apply in most other countries. The remainder of the paper provides an overview of some practical difficulties of alternative methods of indexing.

Although we believe more formal methods of indexing would be superior to the ad hoc measures used under current law, we recognize that a final assessment requires a comparison of alternatives specified in greater detail than presented here. These alternatives must be compared on a variety of grounds, including the overall level of taxation, the extent of differential taxation of different sources of income, and the administrability of tax rules made necessary by each type of system. Although we discuss these issues briefly, we do not present a full-fledged alternative indexing scheme. Our goals here are more modest. We hope to convince researchers and policymakers that they cannot avoid the basic issues of

347

indexing: it is needed; it is already in use; and many of the difficulties of formal indexing are no different from the problems raised by the informal indexing under current law. Therefore, the development of a formal scheme would be a valuable, if not an essential, undertaking.

The Case for Indexing

In a modern developed economy, the net worth (assets less liabilities) of individuals is usually estimated to be about three to four times their total income and about twenty to twenty-five times the capital income generated from their net worth.[1] Suppose that net worth is exactly four times income and that the real rate of return on assets remains constant at 5 percent, no matter what the rate of inflation. Under these assumptions, if net worth equaled 400γ, income from capital would be 20γ (5 percent $\times$ 400γ) and total real income, including 80γ of labor income, would be 100γ.

What does inflation do to the tax base? If the inflation rate is 10 percent, then net inflationary gains of 40γ would equal 40 percent of real income in the economy (100γ) and twice real capital income (20γ).[2] If there were no difference between total income in the economy and taxable income and if all nominal income were subject to tax, the tax base would be expanded enormously. In this example inflationary gains (40γ) equal two-thirds of the total nominal income from capital (40γ + 20γ, or 60γ) and 29 percent of the total tax base (40γ + 100γ, or 140γ).

Full taxation of all nominal income on an accrual basis—what we label here as taxation of nominal Haig-Simons income—adds considerably to the tax base even at more modest rates of inflation. For instance, using the same assumptions as above except for an inflation rate of 5 percent, net inflationary gains (20γ) would still equal 20 percent of total real income and exactly equal the amount of real capital income.

1. In the United States, for instance, net worth of individuals was estimated at $12.0 trillion at the beginning of 1985, while personal income equaled $3.3 billion. See Board of Governors of the Federal Reserve System, *Balance Sheets for the U.S. Economy 1946–85* (The Board, October 1986). Data on individuals were furnished to the authors. See also U.S. Department of Commerce, Bureau of Economic Analysis, "Personal Income and Outlays: September, 1986," *News,* October 23, 1986.

2. In this example, we ignore losses incurred by holders of government debt. Here the gains of borrowers do not balance the losses of lenders within individual sector accounts.

In highly inflationary economies, inflationary income or gains will far exceed total real income: under our simplifying assumptions, the crossover point (where inflation gains equal real income) occurs when the inflation rate reaches 25 percent. Countries with high rates of inflation thus present especially strong cases for indexing of some type.

The case for indexing has become much stronger as rates of taxation and the levels of expected inflation have increased in the postwar era. Obviously at an expected inflation rate of 1 percent and a maximum income tax rate of 25 percent, or an inflation rate of 4 percent and a maximum income tax rate of 10 percent, the failure to index would add only modestly to the tax burden on capital income. Thus, while it still might be desirable to tax only the real income from capital in each case, the costs of adopting a new method of indexing might be assessed differently if either rates of tax or rate of inflation were low.

Changes in Net Worth in the Postwar Era

While these hypothetical examples demonstrate in a simple manner the relationship between inflationary changes in net worth and real income from capital, it is also useful to look at empirical data on actual changes in net worth during the postwar era in the United States. For this purpose, we turn to balance sheet calculations of assets, liabilities, and changes in value made by the Flow of Funds Section of the Federal Reserve Board.

The total change in nominal net worth derives from three sources: real saving, real gains in value, and inflationary gains in value. To facilitate our calculations, we have made a number of simplifying assumptions. First, because the savings figures are not reliable, we approximate net saving by net investment. One difficulty with this approach is that international flows can and do cause domestic saving and domestic investment to diverge. Second, we "look through the corporate veil," at least as far as investment is concerned, and assume that total investment of individuals includes investment they make as owners of corporations. Finally, since the Flow of Funds Section does not divide total changes in net worth into inflationary and real components, we assume that the inflationary component equals the inflation rate times the sum of the underlying value of net worth at the beginning of the year plus one-half the investment made during the year. The real component then equals the residual after these inflationary gains are

Figure 1. *Change in Net Worth, by Components, as a Percentage of Net National Product, 1948–85*
Percent of net national product

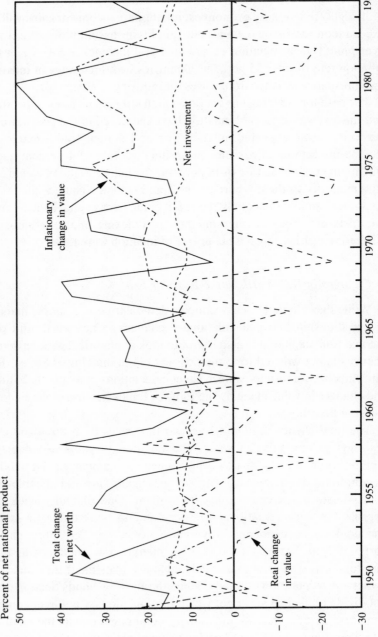

Sources: Authors' calculations based on Board of Governors of the Federal Reserve System, *Balance Sheets for the U.S. Economy 1946–85* (The Board, October 1986), and unpublished data for individuals; and U.S. Department of Commerce, Bureau of Economic Analysis.

subtracted from total gains. We recognize that a number of equally valid alternative assumptions could have been made, but we believe that they would not have changed the results significantly.

We next compare changes in net worth with total income in the economy, as measured by net national product (NNP). A common procedure in much previous research is to divide changes in net worth by a measure of net worth or assets in order to compute some rate of return or growth rate. Our purpose here, however, is to see how much the income tax base might be affected by including such nominal gains and losses in income subject to tax every year.

In figure 1, we show that from 1948 to 1985 total net worth increased on average by 25.9 percent of NNP.[3] Net worth grew at a 7.7 percent rate (similar to the NNP growth rate of 7.5 percent), but recall that net worth is about 3½ times the size of NNP. When separated into components, total change in net worth equaled the sum of (1) average net investment of 12.3 percent of NNP, (2) average inflationary gains in value of 16.1 percent of NNP, and (3) average real gains in value of − 2.6 percent of NPP.[4]

The reader is again cautioned that errors of measurement are inherent in these types of figures. For instance, measuring depreciation of existing assets accurately is difficult. To the extent that depreciation (capital losses on depreciable assets) is understated, net investment is overstated. If total change in value is still correct, then capital gains are understated.

Nonetheless, these empirical results support the case for indexing shown in the hypothetical examples presented above. If the 1948–85 era portends likely future changes in value of individual net worth, a tax on nominal Haig-Simons income would expand the tax base far beyond real economic income and would result in a large increase in the tax rate on capital. Capital income would face a much higher tax rate than labor income. As we shall show, however, this problem does not occur because the tax system has been and still is effectively indexed.[5]

---

3. There are various ways of taking these averages, but the results do not change greatly from one method to the next. Here we use an unweighted average of change in net worth divided by net national product.

4. One interesting aspect of these results is that apart from real investment there appear to be minimal positive real gains over time, due to such factors as the increased scarcity value of land and the scarcity of resources used to build the capital stock. Also, most real gains in one sector (for example, land in the 1970s, corporate stock in the 1980s) tend to be offset by real losses in another sector (corporate stock in the 1970s, land in the 1980s).

5. Another difficulty with the taxation of nominal Haig-Simons income on a mark-

Equal Treatment of Income from Capital

The impetus for taxing income on a Haig-Simons basis is not inflation but rather the many problems that arise when income—in particular, capital income—is taxed in an uneven manner. Tax advice becomes essential for each business or investment decision. Efforts to squeeze transactions into more favored categories in turn lead to enormous complexity in the rules and regulations and to frequent litigation.[6] From an economic standpoint, the uneven tax treatment of income from capital by favoring certain assets and firms causes major distortions in investment patterns; leads to many unnecessary mergers, leases, and divestitures; and explains much of the failure of investment and savings incentives. Equity issues also become much more pronounced when there are large variations in the way the individual income tax taxes capital income.[7] Elsewhere we have discussed how many recent economic reform movements—for a comprehensive income tax, for a flat tax, and for a consumption tax—have been driven by the desire to tax capital income more evenly.[8]

Ignoring practical problems of implementation, taxation of Haig-Simons income, *whether on a nominal or a real basis*, would solve most of these problems by taxing all capital income in an equal manner. The difficulty with taxing nominal income is that in an inflationary setting capital income would be taxed more heavily than labor income. In a sense, taxation of nominal Haig-Simons income represents the opposite end of the spectrum from a pure consumption tax, where equal taxation of capital income is achieved by exempting all capital income from tax. Both theoretically achieve the goal of equal treatment of capital income, but both abandon real income as the tax base.

---

to-market basis is that this procedure would introduce far too much variation in the tax base. As noted in figure 1, the total change in net worth has fluctuated between -2 percent and $+50$ percent of net national product. If the tax base were to vary by an equivalent amount from year to year, fiscal policy could be thrown into chaos. Federal expenditure and monetary policy would also be affected significantly by the fluctuations in expenditures and bond sales that would be induced. This problem can be dealt with in various ways, such as income averaging and loss limitations.

6. See, for example, Henry J. Aaron and Harvey Galper, *Assessing Tax Reform* (Brookings, 1985), p. 5.

7. See C. Eugene Steuerle, *Taxes, Loans, and Inflation: How the Nation's Wealth Becomes Misallocated* (Brookings, 1985).

8. Ibid., chap. 12.

In summary, indexing in an income tax system is required to avoid overtaxation of capital income. More formal indexing may lead to more even taxing of capital income, but equality can also be achieved in systems that have no indexing at all.

Indexing in the Current Tax System

A comparison of the amount of capital income subject to taxation with the amount of income generated in the economy demonstrates that the current tax system is largely indexed, that is, despite the absence of formal indexing, the inflation returns to capital are usually not taxed. Less than one-third of real capital income, for example, is actually subject to taxation at the individual level.[9] The portion of nominal capital income subject to tax would, of course, be smaller still. In addition, although individuals accrue net capital gains of at least 13 percent of NNP each year, their recognized capital gains are only a small fraction of that amount, averaging less than 3 percent of NNP.[10]

Hidden Forms of Indexing

These aggregate figures, of course, hide the intricacies of the story (see table 1). Interest receipts and short-term capital gains (gains not deferred over tax periods) are not indexed at all. They are subject to full taxation on both the real and the inflationary component of the income. Most capital income, however, is not taxed as interest or short-term capital gains. Furthermore, interest receipts are more than offset by interest payments. Taxpayers deduct 85 percent of interest payments, while about half of interest receipts are nontaxable because they flow to tax-exempt entities, are not reported, or are otherwise excluded from taxation.[11]

9. See Eugene Steuerle, "Is Income from Capital Subject to Individual Income Taxation?" *Public Finance Quarterly,* vol. 10 (July 1982), p. 283.

10. Average gains are derived from the data in figure 1 by subtracting net investment from total change in value of the net worth of individuals. Net realizations are estimated through U.S. Department of the Treasury, Internal Revenue Service, *Statistics of Income, Individual Income Tax Returns,* various years.

11. For figures on the taxation of interest payments and receipts, see Eugene Steuerle, "Tax Arbitrage, Inflation, and the Taxation of Interest Payments and Receipts," *Wayne Law Review,* vol. 30 (Spring 1984), pp. 991–1013.

Table 1. *Methods of Indexing under Tax Reform Act of 1986*

Category of income	Method of indexing
Interest receipts	Full taxation for recognized receipts; however, about half of receipts excluded from taxation, not reported, or received by tax-exempt entities
Interest payments	Full taxation; about 85 percent of payments deducted on returns
Capital gains recognized currently	Full taxation of gains without indexing
Capital gains recognized in future years	Partial or full indexing through deferral
Capital gains on assets held until death	Full indexing through exclusion
Depreciation	Deductions allowed currently are faster than decline in value
Inventories	Last-in, first-out (LIFO) option
Dividends	Full taxation; however, inflationary gains in value of underlying asset usually shown as capital gains, which can be deferred or excluded from taxation by holding the asset until death

Any income that is nontaxable, of course, is effectively indexed in the sense that inflation imposes no additional tax burden. Qualified pension plans can be put in this category. The treatment of pension contributions and earnings is equivalent to the nontaxation of capital income as long as the taxpayer's marginal tax rate at the time of receipt of benefits is not higher than when contributions were made to the plan. Returns from consumer durables and owner-occupied housing are also nontaxable. Unrealized capital gains at time of death are exempt from tax because the basis is "stepped up" to current market values.

Many assets are sold during the taxpayer's lifetime, but not in the same year that they are purchased. Gains on these assets are deferred from taxation. The longer the period of deferral, the lower the effective rate of taxation. As the deferral period is lengthened, the effective tax rate on the capital gains approaches zero (see table 2).

In the case of depreciable assets, the tax system adjusts to inflation in a different way. Depreciable assets are those for which losses are estimated through the use of depreciation schedules and are recognized currently, rather than deferred until the disposition of the assets. Thus depreciable assets essentially are on an accrual system, except that a depreciation schedule rather than the market is used to determine changes in value. The schedule, however, is not adjusted for inflation,

Table 2. *Effective Tax Rates on Real Capital Gains,*
by Length of Deferral, Pre- and Post- 1987 Laws[a]
Percent

| | Statutory rates | | | |
| | Pre-1987 law | | Post-1987 law | |
Period of deferral	50[b]	36[c]	28	33
1 day	90	65	51	60
1 month	90	65	50	59
6 months	36	27	50	59
1 year	35	25	50	58
5 years	31	22	44	52
10 years	26	18	37	45
20 years	19	13	28	33
40 years	11	8	17	20
Until death	0	0	0	0

a. Examples assume 4 percent inflation and 5 percent real rate of return. Under pre-1987 law, gains deferred for less than six months were not excluded, while gains deferred for six months or more received a 60 percent exclusion.
b. Top marginal rate.
c. Typical rate for taxpayer realizing capital gains.

and as the inflation rate increases, future deductions of a fixed magnitude become worth less in current dollars.

It should be noted, however, that depreciation allowances have been accelerated several times in the postwar era. Acceleration causes an overstatement of actual depreciation in the early years of the investment, resulting in an interest-free loan from the government. In addition, investment credits have been granted frequently for purchases of equipment.

These various preferences have often more than offset the effect of inflation on the value of the depreciation allowance. Using depreciation schedules contained in the Tax Reform Act of 1986, for instance, estimates of effective tax rates (at a predicted level of inflation of 4 percent) for corporate investment in equipment fall in the range of 37–38 percent.[12] This rate is slightly less than it would be in a fully

12. Jane Gravelle of the Congressional Research Service estimates a 38 percent tax rate for equipment, whereas Yolanda Henderson of the Federal Reserve Bank of Boston estimates a 37 percent rate. Their methods of estimation differ, and the reader should use caution in making comparisons. Estimates were furnished to authors. For further background, see Jane G. Gravelle, "Effective Tax Rates in the Major Tax Revision Plans: Updated Tables Including the Senate Finance Committee Proposal," Report 86-691E (Congressional Research Service, May 16, 1986); and Yolanda K. Henderson, "Lessons from Federal Reform of Business Taxes," Federal Reserve Bank of Boston, *New England Economic Review* (November–December 1986), pp. 9–25.

indexed system, in which returns from corporate capital would face a corporate rate of 34 percent plus an additional individual-level tax on dividends paid or capital gains realized.

The calculation of taxable income from sale of inventories also benefits from ad hoc indexing. Under last-in, first-out (LIFO) methods of inventory accounting, sellers of inventory are allowed to calculate gain from a sale as if the asset sold were the last one purchased. In a growing firm, purchases may grow faster than sales, so that each item sold is treated as if it were originally purchased by the seller in current dollars. Inflationary gains on remaining inventory are effectively deferred from tax until current sales begin to exceed current purchases. Because many firms do eventually decline in size and many other firms continue to make use of first-in, first-out (FIFO) methods, a portion of inflationary gains from sales of inventories remain taxed under current law.

Income can also be received in the form of dividends. Dividends, however, come from ownership of underlying assets. As long as the dividend rate is less than the real rate of return on the assets, there is no taxation of inflationary gains through the dividend tax by itself. Instead, the inflationary gains are reflected in the increased value of the underlying assets and may be taxed eventually as capital gains. Sometimes the dividend rate does exceed the real rate of return of a firm, but this process cannot continue indefinitely because the real value of the firm is being depleted. Some forms of dividends (generally dividends on preferred stock), however, are quite similar to payments of interest because the nominal basis of the asset cannot change. For these kinds of assets, dividend (interest) rates are overstated in the same way as are interest payments on bonds.

In summary, almost all forms of capital income receive some form of special treatment or ad hoc indexing under current law. The realization principle prevents current taxation of many capital gains, while various exclusions and deferrals prevent much tax from being imposed on the inflationary component of capital income. The major exception is interest income, but there taxable interest receipts are more than matched by the deduction of interest payments, so that net taxes on private interest income are actually negative. The other exception is short-term capital gains, which benefit neither from significant deferral nor from any form of exclusion at death. Most inflationary returns, however, are not received as either taxable interest receipts or taxable short-term capital gains.

Effect of Inflation on Current Methods of Indexing

The effect of inflation on the tax rate applying to specific investments may differ from its effect on the total rate of taxation imposed on all capital income. Yolanda Henderson estimates that under the 1986 act the total effective tax rate on corporate investment is 39 percent at 0 percent inflation, 42 percent at 4 percent inflation, and 44 percent at 8 percent inflation.[13] The aggregate changes appear small because of offsetting factors. For example, as inflation increases the effective tax rate on equity investments in depreciable assets, it increases the net loss to the government from deductions of interest payments less the inclusion of interest receipts. In addition, market rates of return on different assets may adjust in ways that prevent large overall changes in the taxes collected.

For different sources of income and different taxpayers, however, inflation can have widely different effects upon the rate of taxation. The full inclusion of the inflationary component often leads to very high rates of taxation on interest receipts and short-term capital gains. As an example, if the real interest rate is 5 percent and the inflation rate is 5 percent, nominal income is twice real income, thus doubling the effective rate on a taxpayer in the 33 percent bracket to 66 percent.

At the opposite end of the spectrum, the tax rate on vacant land and other nondepreciable assets remains zero, regardless of the rate of inflation, as long as the gains on these assets are not realized. The rate of tax for capital gains depends in part upon the period of deferral, although an increase in the rate of inflation generally increases the rate of tax on all realized capital gains.

Depreciable assets fall into a special category. Under the 1981 law known as ACRS (accelerated cost recovery system), many calculations showed negative rates of taxation on equipment at moderate rates of inflation; that is, the value of investment credit and acceleration more than offset the total tax eventually paid. At very high rates of inflation, however, those depreciation allowances were much less valuable and the tax rate turned positive. Under the 1986 law, the tax rate still varies significantly with the rate of inflation, but much less than it did.

The use of aggregate figures to assess the impact of inflation therefore hides large disparities that can lead to uneconomic activity. For example,

13. Estimates furnished by Yolanda Henderson.

when after-tax interest rates are very low or negative, borrowing to invest in assets with low or negative productivity may be encouraged significantly at the margin. If the real rate of interest is negative, an investor can still profit by borrowing to purchase an asset with a less negative after-tax rate of return. In such a case the investor may prefer an unproductive and relatively riskless asset (which is easier to leverage) to a more productive but risky investment. Most models used to estimate effective tax rates do not take into account this type of welfare loss because they assume an average effective rate across various types of assets and across time.

Alternative Methods of Indexing

This section explores the possibility of replacing the current partial and ad hoc methods of adjusting income from capital for inflation with full exact indexing. By exact indexing we mean an adjustment to the basis of all assets and an assumed increase in all outstanding indebtedness equal to the assumed rate of inflation multiplied by the prior basis. For example, if the basis of an asset were $1,000 and inflation were 4 percent, the inflation-adjusted basis would be $1,040. The Treasury Department recommended this approach in 1984, except in the case of debt instruments, where it proposed that the inflation adjustment be applied to interest rather than basis.[14]

As we have shown, the current system falls far short of full taxation of nominal income from capital. At least to the extent that these departures have been justified as a means of mitigating the effects of inflation, the system can be said to be indexed. Current law already indexes depreciation, inventories, and capital gains on an ad hoc basis. For these categories, exact indexing would make relatively modest changes in tax liability. Interest payments, however, are not indexed;

14. U.S. Department of the Treasury, *Tax Reform for Fairness, Simplicity, and Economic Growth: The Treasury Department Report to the President*, 3 vols. (Department of the Treasury, 1984) (hereinafter referred to as Treasury I). *The President's Tax Proposals to the Congress for Fairness, Growth, and Simplicity* (GPO, 1985) (hereinafter referred to as Treasury II) contained similar rules for indexing inventory and depreciable assets. Although Treasury II would not have allowed taxpayers to combine indexing with the preferential rate for capital gain, taxpayers could, in lieu of the preferential rate, index the basis of capital assets held for more than twelve months. Treasury II dropped the Treasury I proposal to index debt.

debtors can now fully deduct nominal interest payments (see table below). If the inflation rate is high, indexing by limiting the deduction to real interest could mean a large increase in tax liability. Much of the resistance to exact indexing can be laid to this factor, but other objections must also be considered.

Income category	Ad hoc indexation	Income measured annually
Depreciation	Yes	Yes
Inventories	Yes	Yes
Capital gain	Yes	No
Interest	No	Yes

Some opponents of indexing argue that it is too complicated. This criticism may be particularly justified either where there is no annual accounting for gains and losses or where there are frequent changes in the size of the investment—a money market checking account or a dividend reinvestment plan, for example. One suspects, however, that in the large majority of the latter cases, individuals deal with financial institutions that have access to the technology to implement indexing without undue difficulty.

Objections have been raised on the ground that indexing would provide different treatment for persons who appear to be similarly situated. This concern turns out to involve primarily the question of when gains and losses should be treated as realized. As such, it is not a problem peculiar to indexing. Any income tax system will struggle with the problem of realization; indexing only raises the issue in different circumstances. Indexing does not, however, change the nature of the problem or increase the difficulties imposed by the failure to recognize gains and losses as they accrue.

Finally, a number of issues arise because technical or political reasons may make it impossible to index fully all assets or liabilities on an exact basis. The 1984 Treasury I proposal for indexing debt tried to avoid some of the difficulties of exact indexing, but in turn raised several other problems, primarily the potential undertaxation of financial institutions.

The special treatment provided for mortgage interest also endangered interest indexing. Treasury I excluded mortgage interest from indexing, which would have given taxpayers an incentive to borrow against their homes on a fully deductible basis in order to buy bonds or make deposits, the interest on which would be partially excludable. Ultimately, this opportunity would have been considered too subject to abuse to be allowed. It should be possible to accommodate indexing to the special preference for housing. For example, homeowners could be required to take account of mortgage interest (or mortgage debt) in determining whether they have *net* interest income (or are net creditors) so as to make any indexing for interest (or debt) appropriate.

Some argue that either all assets should be indexed or none. Otherwise, for example, if capital gains and depreciation allowances were indexed while interest incurred on borrowing to purchase such assets remained fully deductible, a serious problem of arbitrage would be created. The income from the asset might be properly stated, but because nominal interest would be deductible, the expense associated with the acquisition of the asset with borrowed funds would be overstated. This situation could lead to excessive borrowing, or, as explained above, uneconomic investments in assets that could be more heavily mortgaged. However, before being discarded, partial indexing should be compared with other rules that have excluded nominal or real capital income from tax while allowing full deductibility of interest. The question should not be whether partial indexing provides opportunities for arbitrage, but whether it increases or reduces the arbitrage opportunities that would otherwise exist.

Indexing under an Accrual System

Indexing for inflation would be easier to implement if the tax system took account of accrued gains and losses. It is therefore useful to consider how indexing would work under such a regime. By showing that certain presumed problems with indexing will not arise under an accrual system, we can more easily isolate questions of realization from issues peculiar to indexing itself.

Under an accrual regime, the basis of assets on hand at the beginning of a taxable year would reflect their value at that time. If these assets remained on hand at the end of the year, taxable income would be measured by first increasing the basis to reflect the rate of inflation for the year and then comparing this new basis with the year-end value. In addition, periodic receipts such as interest, rents, or dividends would be included in income.

For example, assume that a taxpayer held a $1,000 bond that bore interest at 10 percent and that inflation for the year was 6 percent. The basis of the bond would be increased to $1,060 to reflect inflation. Since the real value of debt remains at $1,000, the creditor would have a $60 loss. Subtracting this loss from $100 of interest income, the lender would have net income of $40. Conversely, the debtor would have a net cost of $40. Restating the debt in real terms ($1,060) and then comparing it with the amount required to discharge it ($1,000) would produce a $60 gain, partially offsetting the $100 of interest expense.

Indexing assets held for only part of a year is more complex, requiring procedures for measuring inflation only for the period the asset is held.[15] This goal can be achieved in a variety of ways.

For depreciable assets, Treasury I would have denied an inflation adjustment in the year of acquisition and provided a pro-rata adjustment in the year of disposition. Treasury I suggested a different approach for nondepreciable assets.[16] These assets generally would be deemed to have been acquired at the midpoint of the quarter of acquisition and sold at the midpoint of the quarter in which disposition occurred.[17] This convention would overstate the period for which the asset was held in the event it actually was acquired at a later point in the quarter than the actual point of disposition. Treasury I, therefore, proposed a special rule to deal with relatively short-term holdings of less than two full quarters, where the distortion could be most pronounced.[18]

It would be simpler to assume that an asset was acquired at the

15. It is generally assumed that no indexing is needed for the cost of assets that are deducted immediately because their useful life does not extend beyond the taxable year. On the other hand, depreciation presumably would be claimed by first adjusting the basis for the year's inflation before applying the applicable rate for depreciation. It seems that there is a continuum here rather than a sharp dichotomy. To match costs against related receipts, the inflation adjustment ideally should reflect the period of investment. The expensed asset may be used for up to twelve months while presumably a portion of the depreciable asset is "disposed" of each day. However, it is probably not essential to be so precise.

16. Treasury I, vol. 2, pp. 158, 183.

17. Treasury I called for the IRS to publish tables of inflation-adjustment factors that would be applied to the original cost basis to determine the inflation-adjusted basis. A single adjustment factor would be applied depending upon the calendar quarter in which the asset was acquired and the calendar quarter in which the sale took place.

18. No adjustment would be permitted unless an asset was held for one full calendar quarter. Otherwise, for example, there would be an undue advantage for an asset purchased on March 31 and sold on April 1. Further, if an asset was held for only one full quarter, its basis would be adjusted for inflation in that quarter alone. For example, if an asset was purchased on March 31 and sold between July 1 and September 30, it would be adjusted for inflation between April 1 and June 30, rather than between February 15 and August 15. However, if the sale took place on October 1, then the taxpayer would get the benefit of inflation between February 15 and November 15.

362   DANIEL HALPERIN AND EUGENE STEUERLE

beginning of the quarter following the quarter of acquisition and disposed of at the end of the quarter preceding the quarter of disposition. This method would limit opportunity for manipulation while still closely approximating the degree of inflation during the period the asset was held.

The procedure would be complex, however, if numerous purchases and sales were made during the year, as in the case of inventory. Rather than adjusting the cost of each item, a possible approach would be to increase cost of goods sold by the inflation rate multiplied by average inventory during the year. Ideally a daily average would be used to prevent manipulation or distortion.[19]

Another example of numerous purchases and sales would be a money market checking account with a fluctuating daily balance. A single inflation adjustment could be made based upon the average daily balance. Presumably a financial institution already needs this information to credit interest (or to charge interest in the event of a revolving loan).[20] If this method is considered to be too inexact when inflation fluctuates widely during the year, the appropriate adjustment could be applied to the average balance for each quarter or month.

Inflation Adjustment and Realization

Since the tax system is based on realization, any indexing plan must decide when the inflation adjustment will be realized. It should not be surprising that indexing will be shown to be imperfect in a system based on realization. Seemingly like situations will receive unlike treatment in

19. Under Treasury I, taxpayers could use an indexed FIFO method. The Treasury suggested that taxpayers use "relatively simple computational methods" such as applying the percentage increase in the consumer price index to the FIFO cost of the number of units in the beginning inventory that does not exceed the number of units in the ending inventory. This method would in general increase the cost of goods sold by the cost of the opening inventory multiplied by the inflation rate. The Treasury rule would appear to be subject to substantial abuse if inventory on the first and last day of year were quite large relative to the average. The net profit under this approach would be similar to that determined under the LIFO method. However, indexed FIFO would allow a larger opening inventory in the next period than would LIFO. Moreover, indexed FIFO is intended to reflect actual cost of goods sold. LIFO might merely suggest that to the extent a company must use funds to replace inventory, it has not earned a true profit.

20. In fact, if the interest rate has not changed throughout the year, the nontaxable or nondeductible portion of the interest could be computed by applying a fraction to the total interest, the numerator being the inflation rate and the denominator being the nominal rate of interest.

the *timing* of gain or loss, just as they would in an unindexed system based on realization. The question, therefore, is whether indexing would provide an overall improvement in income measurement, rather than perfect income measurement—an impossibility in a realization-based system.

The general idea of indexing is to adjust the basis of an asset, so that when the cost is compared with the amount received in the year of disposition (or year of use of a depreciable asset), values would be stated in comparable real terms rather than nominal dollars. Thus it is usually assumed that the indexing adjustment for most capital assets would be left unrealized until the asset is sold or depreciated. Income flows from such capital assets—dividends, rents, or royalties—would therefore continue to be fully taxable.[21]

It is generally assumed, however, that indexing for debt instruments should result in a *current* adjustment to interest income and interest expense.[22] In other words, the inflation adjustment for debt would result in a realized loss for creditors, whose interest income would be partially exempt, and a realized gain for debtors, whose interest deduction would be reduced.

Some analysts have complained that this lack of symmetry (that is, interest is currently indexed, while the inflation adjustment to rental or royalty property would only be realized as the indexed basis is depreciated) would create an incentive to recharacterize fully taxable rents or royalties as partially excludable (and deductible) interest whenever the recipient is in a higher tax bracket than the payor and, conversely, to recharacterize partially deductible (and taxable) interest as fully deductible rents or royalties when the payor is in a higher bracket.[23] A difference between debt and other investments, explained below, justifies this discrepancy, however.[24] Moreover, those who deplore the potential

21. For example, assume a basis of $10,000 for property that is rented for $1,000 a year. If inflation were 4 percent, the basis of the property would increase to $10,400, resulting in $400 of additional depreciation over the life of the property. The rent of $1,000 would remain fully taxable.

22. In the case of a $10,000 bond paying $1,000 of interest, 4 percent inflation would mean that $400 of the interest payment would be neither deductible nor taxable. The $400 inflation adjustment would be immediately realized.

23. See Jerome Kurtz, "Comments on 'Indexing for Inflation and the Interest Deduction'," *Wayne Law Review,* vol. 30 (Spring 1984), p. 971; Myles H. Tannenbaum, letter to Secretary Donald T. Regan, reprinted in *Tax Notes,* vol. 26 (February 11, 1985), pp. 604–05.

24. See T. Nicolaus Tideman and Donald P. Tucker, "The Tax Treatment of

distortion caused by treating debt differently from other assets may fail to recognize that similar distortions can occur because of the differential timing of inflation gains and losses in an unindexed system.

PERIODIC RETURN AS CAPITAL REPAYMENT. For assets other than debt, it is generally assumed that current payments greater than the desired real rate of return are not needed to protect the asset holder against a decline in the value of the asset caused by inflation. All other things being equal, the nominal value of stock or real or personal property should increase at the rate of inflation. The amount of debt, however, ordinarily is fixed and does not rise in nominal terms to reflect a reduction in the real value of the currency. Because inflation will reduce the real amount that will be due on maturity, a creditor who anticipates inflation must recover a portion of his real outlay in other ways. Thus it is assumed that the nominal interest payment is not wholly interest. Rather, in addition to interest a debtor will be required to pay down a portion of the debt so that the remaining unpaid balance in real terms will not exceed the real value of the original nominal loan.[25]

Since repayments of principal are not deductible, the portion of "nominal" interest that is in reality a principal payment should not be deductible (or taxable); it should instead be treated as a reduction of the outstanding loan. Taxation of the full amount of interest would overstate the interest income of the lender and the interest deduction of the borrower.

While the stated distinction—that the nominal value of debt does not rise with inflation while the nominal value of other assets does—is generally true, it is not invariably so. Nonconvertible and nonparticipating preferred stock is an obvious example of an asset whose nominal value does not rise with inflation. If inflation is anticipated, the current cash flow must be intended to "repay" principal to the extent the value of the stock will be eroded by inflation. If so, the dividend should not be fully taxable. Other examples in which the nominal value of an owner's interest may not increase include real estate for which the tenant has a long-term lease or an option to buy at a price that may not fully reflect a

---

Business Profits under Inflationary Conditions," in Henry J. Aaron, ed., *Inflation and the Income Tax* (Brookings, 1976), pp. 33, 57–59.

25. In the example in footnote 22, 4 percent inflation means that a $10,000 debt has been reduced to approximately $9,600 in real terms. The creditor does not lose, however, because the debtor pays off $400 of the debt in the guise of interest. A debtor who desires to maintain the amount borrowed in real terms should borrow an additional $400. In that case, his net outlay ($600) would be equal to his deduction.

change in value caused by inflation.[26] In these cases the nominal value of the property may increase with inflation, but the benefit inures to the tenant or option holder rather than to the landlord.

Conversely, a lender could be protected against inflation by an automatic increase in the principal amount through use of an indexed bond, by the right to convert into an equity instrument, or by contracting for a share of any rise in value of the property (often referred to as an "equity kicker"). In these instances full taxation and deduction of the current interest payments and treatment of the indexing adjustment as unrealized may well be appropriate.

In the case of an indexed bond, the desired result should automatically follow from existing law. For example, if the real interest rate is 6 percent and the anticipated inflation rate is 4 percent, the parties may provide for an annual interest payment of 10 percent. Alternatively, the coupon rate could be 6 percent and the bond could be "indexed" so that the principal amount increases by the rate of inflation. If inflation of 4 percent ensues, indexing should result in current income of 6 percent in either case.

As noted above, indexing would result in the exclusion of that portion of the nominal interest equal to the rate of inflation divided by the interest rate. Thus, of the 10 percent interest, 6 percent would be taxable and deductible, but only 2 percent of the 6 percent payment would be so included in income and expense. In the case of the indexed bond, there also is a 4 percent increase in the principal amount. Under current law, the difference between the issue price and maturity value of a debt instrument—the so-called original issue discount—is taken into account currently. Extension of those rules would result in current inclusion and deduction of the inflation adjustment.

In the case of convertible debt, however, an increase in the nominal value of the underlying equity does not result in accrued interest, as would occur upon an increase in the maturity value of the bond itself. Exclusion of a portion of the nominal interest, therefore, could result in understatement of current income and expense whenever creditors obtain protection against inflation through convertibility rather than increased interest. Ideally, therefore, the line between full or only partial taxation of current flows should not place all debt on one side and all other assets on the other. The correct distinction is between assets that

26. See Michael J. McIntyre, "Comments on 'Indexing for Inflation and the Interest Deduction'," *Wayne Law Review*, vol. 30 (Spring 1984), pp. 979–81.

rise with inflation and those that do not; debt is not a wholly satisfactory proxy. No division would be perfect in a realization system, but further research is required to determine if a better line can be drawn than that which merely separates debt from other assets.

ANTICIPATED VERSUS UNANTICIPATED INFLATION. We have assumed that the interest rate on debt equals the sum of the desired real rate of interest and the anticipated rate of inflation. If no inflation or deflation is anticipated, it follows that the annual payment will be equal to the real rate of interest. In these circumstances no portion of the annual payment by the debtor is intended to be a payment of principal, even if there is unanticipated inflation and the debt declines in real terms.[27] The question then is whether the decline in the real amount of the debt should properly be considered an *unrealized* gain or loss.[28] If so, interest would be currently taxable and deductible to the extent the amount of nominal interest exceeded *anticipated* rather than *actual* inflation.[29] If no inflation is anticipated, there would be no effect on the treatment of interest even if inflation actually occurred. In that event the creditor's loss and the debtor's gain would be deferred until payment of the principal amount or disposition of the bond.

We conclude that even if using anticipated rather than actual inflation to determine the current treatment of interest income and expense is more consistent with notions of realization, distinguishing between anticipated and unanticipated inflation is neither practical nor essential to a sound system of indexing. Three examples may clarify our reasoning.

First, if no distinction is made between anticipated and unanticipated inflation, the impact of the basis adjustment for inflation for assets other than debt would not be felt until the asset is disposed of or depreciated. This practice is in accord with the current system of realization for such assets. A lessor with a long-term lease at a *fixed* rent would suffer a decline in value if a rise in interest rates or inflation caused rents generally to rise. But just as a loss caused by increased interest rates would be considered unrealized, so would a decline in real value due to an unanticipated increase in the rate of inflation.

27. Continuing with the above example, the outstanding debt remains at $10,000, but inflation gives the debtor the opportunity to discharge the debt with a payment of approximately $9,600.
28. McIntyre, "Comments," pp. 980–81.
29. See Roger E. Brinner, "Inflation and the Definition of Taxable Personal Income," in Aaron, ed., *Inflation and the Income Tax*, p. 149.

Second, a bondholder would suffer a similar decline in real value in the event of an unanticipated rise in interest rates due to a change in the rate of inflation. But the result of reducing interest income by the actual rate of inflation is to treat the loss as realized. Discharge of the debt at its nominal value would have no further tax consequences.

Consider a situation where inflation is not fully anticipated. Suppose the parties seek a 6 percent real rate of interest and anticipate 2 percent inflation. Hence the debt instrument bears an 8 percent rate of interest. The borrower in effect pays $60 in interest and a $20 principal payment on a $1,000 bond, reflecting that in real terms the obligation is expected to be equivalent to approximately $980 after one year. Assume, however, that actual inflation for the year is 4 percent, so the borrower will have to pay back only $960 in real terms. The $20 difference between the expected and the actual obligation would seem to be an unrealized gain and the current interest expense should be $60.[30] Limiting the interest deduction to $40 treats the gain as realized because the stated outstanding debt, by remaining at $1,000 (or $960 in real terms), reflects the actual obligation.

Suppose, however, that inflation turns out to be zero. The creditor can claim that current interest income is only $60 and that the additional $20 reduced the stated outstanding loan to $980. The creditor will be entitled to $1,000 when the loan is due, but would argue the $20 gain is unrealized. If, however, indexing were based on actual, rather than anticipated, inflation, $80 would be taxed currently.

Last, to appreciate the distinction between realized and unrealized gains more easily, it may help to assume that the parties had provided for 6 percent interest and an annual increase in the principal equal to 2 percent, the expected inflation. They believe this will keep the value of the outstanding obligation constant in real terms. Using the previous example, when inflation is higher (4 percent), the value of the obligation in fact declines, but the gain to the borrower would seem to be considered to be unrealized. Similarly, when there is no inflation, the value of the obligation increases in real terms. Here the lender's gain would seem to be unrealized.

This analysis suggests that the adjustment to interest expense should ideally reflect the anticipated rather than the actual inflation rate. Such

30. Increasing the liability for 4 percent inflation to $1,040 and disallowing only 2 percent interest would leave a stated debt of $1,020, which could be paid by transferring $1,000.

a rule, however, would require that one know the rate of anticipated inflation in each case, which is simply not possible.

On balance, therefore, we believe it is unwise to try to distinguish between anticipated and unanticipated inflation. Creditors would recognize gains currently when inflation was smaller than anticipated. Conversely, debtors would be forced, through disallowance of a deduction for a portion of interest paid, to recognize gains due to greater than anticipated inflation. The potential unfairness in not making the distinction is most apparent when a differently treated asset is juxtaposed to the debt. Suppose an investor who underestimates inflation has a long-term lease on property purchased with borrowed funds. As inflation rises, the real value of the lease goes down and his real debts are also reduced. For this taxpayer, rents would be fully taxable while some portion of the interest would be nondeductible even though it does not in fact pay down his debt. Thus the gain on the debt is realized currently, but the offsetting loss on the lease is spread over time. While the total net income is properly measured, too much income would be taxable in early years and too little later on.

Such anomalies, however, are inevitable as long as realization governs. For example, under existing law, parties who anticipate inflation can fully deduct interest (which is really in part a loan repayment) and postpone realization of the nominal gain on the property until sale. An indexed system would eliminate this advantage and on the whole seems likely to reduce, although not eliminate, the disparity of treatment between borrowing and assets purchased with the borrowed funds.

Inexact Indexing for Interest

One of the most controversial aspects of the Treasury Department's first tax reform proposal was its suggestion for inexact indexing of interest and debt instruments. This provision was not included in Treasury II.

Under Treasury I, interest was to be indexed for tax purposes by excluding a fractional amount of interest receipts from income and expense. The exclusion was based on the assumption that the real rate of interest was 6 percent and that all interest payments reflected a real interest component equal to 6 percent and an inflation component equal to the current rate of inflation. Thus, if inflation were 4 percent, 40 percent of all interest would be excluded.[31]

31. Treasury I would have applied the exclusion to net interest income or expense,

One problem with the inexact method is exactly that: it is inexact. As Treasury explained, its proposal would not have accounted for differences in real interest rates among loans. For example, assume that three $1,000 loans are made at different real rates of interest and that the parties correctly anticipate an inflation rate of 4 percent. The Treasury proposal would have produced the following results:

Real rate of interest	Assumed inflation rate	Nominal interest rate	Amount of interest (dollars)	Adjustment for inflation
4	4	8	80	32
6	4	10	100	40
8	4	12	120	48

As this example shows, Treasury's approach would have understated the effect of inflation for real rates of interest below 6 percent and overstated it at higher rates, although it still would have been far more accurate than current law under almost all circumstances.

Nominal rates of interest may also vary because of different assumptions over time about the rate of future inflation. For example, the three loans above could bear rates of interest of 8 percent, 10 percent, and 12 percent even if at the time the loans were made all aimed for a real interest rate of 6 percent. These variations would occur if the parties anticipated inflation of 2 percent, 4 percent, and 6 percent, respectively. The adjustments would differ again in the same manner as above, depending on the difference between the actual rates of inflation and the rate assumed in each case.

Another difficulty with Treasury's inexact method involves financial institutions that charge borrowers a higher rate of interest than they pay depositors. Because inexact indexing operates on interest, a bank would exclude a greater amount of interest receipts than it would lose as deductions for amounts paid to depositors. To the extent that the bank was lending borrowed funds, a net inflation adjustment was clearly unwarranted, and the excess adjustment allowed by Treasury I in many cases would have completely eliminated taxable income.

One way to deal with this problem would be to use an exact method for financial intermediaries but not for the depositor or borrower. This solution would, however, cause an erroneous adjustment for the economy as whole, which the inexact method would avoid.

---

excluding interest on a mortgage secured by the principal residence of the taxpayer and tax-exempt interest income. An individual would not have been subject to any disallowance with respect to the first $5,000 of net interest expense.

For example, assume a bank pays 6 percent interest on deposits but charges 10 percent on loans. Therefore, on a deposit of $1,000, it would generate $40 of profits before wages and other expenses. Under the exact method, assuming 4 percent inflation, the inflation adjustment would be $40 on a $1,000 loan, and the depositor would have $20 of taxable income and the borrower a $60 deduction. The treatment of the bank would be reciprocal in each case, so its profits would still be $40 before wages and other expenses. Under the inexact method, with 4 percent inflation, 40 percent of all interest would be neither deductible nor taxable. The depositor would be taxed on $36 and the borrower allowed a $60 deduction. The bank's treatment would again be reciprocal, so instead of its actual profit of $40, it would report only $24, or $16 less. This may be said to be compensated for by the fact that the depositor is taxed on $36, or $16 more than the $20 of real income. If exact indexing applied to the financial intermediary, it would correctly be taxed on $40. In this case, the erroneous underadjustment for the depositor would not be offset by overly favorable treatment of the bank.

The problem is not limited to financial institutions but affects anyone who is both a lender and a borrower. Assume an individual taxpayer has $100,000 in money market certificates that produce 10 percent interest and $100,000 of outstanding loans at 12 percent. The net interest expense is $2,000, but under Treasury's inexact method, some of the $2,000 would not be deductible, even though the individual obviously had not benefited from inflation.

Inexact indexing for interest could lead to other difficulties if exact indexing were applied to other payments. As the Treasury proposal noted:

> The variation between basis indexing and application of the fractional exclusion rate could in some cases be exploited by taxpayers if future variations could be known with sufficient certainty. Such exploitation seems to present the greatest likelihood of taxpayer manipulation in the case of pass-through entities holding a substantial proportion of interest-bearing assets. In such cases, partners would be precluded from increasing basis in their partnership interests faster than at the rate implied by the fractional exclusion rate applied to the partnership's interest receipts.[32]

For example, assume that a partnership's sole asset is a $10,000 bond bearing interest at 10 percent and that the inflation rate is 7 percent. A is

32. Treasury I, vol. 2, p. 200.

a 10 percent partner and his basis for his partnership interest is $1,000. The partnership earns $1,000 in interest, of which $100 is allocable to A. The fractional rule would result in an exclusion of $54 (7/13) of interest even though the more accurate adjustment would be $70. A's share of partnership income would be $46 and his basis for his partnership interest would be $1,046 (original basis plus share of partnership income) before the inflation adjustment. If the adjustment were $70 (as it would be under the Treasury proposal for adjusting capital assets), A's basis would be $1,116, or $16 more than his share of partnership assets. In such a case, A would have a potential $16 loss, which would compensate for the inadequate inflation adjustment. The Treasury suggested that A's inflation adjustment be limited to $54, which would make A's basis equal to his share of partnership assets. Otherwise the use of the partnership would create a potential asymmetry between basis (or exact) indexing on the income side and inexact indexing by the payor of interest. With inexact indexing it might make sense to pass through the partnership's adjustment to the partners rather than to make a separate determination at the partner level. This alternative might not work, however, where there is a difference between the partner's basis for his partnership interest and his share of the partnership's basis for its assets.

Given these difficulties of inexact indexing, it is appropriate to reconsider whether exact indexing for interest would in fact be more difficult to administer. On balance, it may well be easier to implement.

Indexing for All Assets Other than Debt

Some have noted that indexing for debt is less important than indexing for other assets. Because the treatment of the debtor and the creditor is reciprocal, the parties can in effect compensate for the lack of indexing for anticipated inflation.

For example, suppose the tax rate is 33 percent and the expected rate of inflation is 4 percent. If the real rate of interest is 3 percent before tax and 2 percent after tax, the nominal rate on the debt would rise to 9 percent (as opposed to 7 percent if there were indexing).[33] The after-tax real rate of return to the creditor would still be 2 percent [9(1 − 0.33) − 4], as would the cost to the borrower. Failure to index generates neither tax savings nor tax costs and thus has no effect on investment decisions.

33. The interest rate increases by anticipated inflation divided by the after-tax rate of return. Here this is 4 percent divided by (1 − 0.33) = 6 percent.

Of course, tax rates for lenders and borrowers are not always identical. Ordinarily borrowers are in a higher bracket. Thus the excessive deduction for interest when there is no indexing would lose more revenue than the extra inclusion would gain.[34] At the same time, low-bracket borrowers such as the government would not be compensated through a deduction for the interest rate necessary to compensate a higher-bracket lender for inflation.

As usual, therefore, it is much better to try to treat each taxpayer correctly than to rely on compensating errors. Across-the-board indexing is definitely preferable to indexing only assets other than debt.

Assume, however, that indexing for interest proves impractical and politically infeasible. Does that mean all indexing should be dropped? We believe the answer depends upon the alternative. It is true that indexing for assets while allowing full deduction for interest permits arbitrage, but ad hoc adjustments in lieu of indexing, such as accelerated depreciation, also allow arbitrage to occur.

Unlike exact indexing, accelerated depreciation does not vary with the rate of inflation. Because the protection declines as inflation rises, the amount of arbitrage is limited. Because exact indexing would vary with inflation, it would not have such a limit. But if a limit were found to be important to prevent an increase in arbitrage opportunity, one could certainly be set. For example, the indexing adjustment could be limited to a specified percentage regardless of the rate of inflation. Furthermore, it might be possible to limit indexing to net equity investments and thus reduce opportunities for arbitrage. In short, partial indexing is not necessarily worse than the alternatives. It depends upon the details.

We believe that full taxation of income from capital depends upon the development of a system to exclude all nominal gains from taxation. Thus the development of a system for full indexing is important. Whether such a system should ultimately be adopted depends upon how well it stacks up against the alternative. We believe we have shown that full indexing would be more accurate than the ad hoc adjustments that occur under current law and that a fair and administrable system for full indexing can be devised.

---

34. If this is so, indexing for interest should produce a revenue gain, but surprisingly Treasury I indicated a revenue loss from interest indexing due to the exclusions for mortgage interest and for individuals with a small amount of net interest and to the overgenerous treatment of financial intermediaries.

Comments by Mark Perlis

Halperin and Steuerle's paper is animated by the belief that indexing a hybrid income tax is inevitable. The authors contend that (1) indexing is essential to avoid overtaxation of capital income, (2) both the 1954 and 1986 Internal Revenue Codes contain numerous provisions that counteract the effects of inflation on nominal capital income, and (3) more direct methods of indexing may prove easier to administer and more accurate than the collection of indirect, de facto indexing provisions in current law.

Notwithstanding the theoretical appeal of direct indexing, the Tax Reform Act of 1986 included none of the proposals advanced in Treasury I for indexing depreciable assets, capital assets, indebtedness, and inventory. Halperin and Steuerle present a useful critique of the original Treasury proposals and offer valuable suggestions for redesigning indexing proposals. However, as the authors readily concede, their paper does not present a fully developed, comprehensive indexing system, although they suggest that a fairer, more administrable indexing system than current law could be attained. I would like to suggest that greater emphasis be given to certain inherent advantages of direct, comprehensive indexing proposals over the indirect, de facto inflation protection provisions in current law.

The theoretical case for indexing capital income in an income tax is well accepted by most tax scholars, although it has not been most effectively presented to policymakers. Full accrual taxation of nominal Haig-Simons income results in higher effective tax rates on capital income than on other income and, as Halperin and Steuerle demonstrate, can approach an exaction on the real capital stock at even modest rates of inflation. While most commentators, including the authors, usually advocate indexing as a means of achieving more neutral taxation of current capital and labor income, the case for indexing is actually much stronger if consideration is given to seeking neutral tax treatment of capital income from different types of assets.

A guiding principle of both Treasury I and II was the attainment of neutral taxation of different sources of capital income. For example, both Treasury proposals justified indexing of depreciable assets principally as a means of assuring a uniform, predetermined effective tax rate for different types of machinery and equipment with different patterns of economic depreciation. Indexing is necessary to assure neutrality across assets with different holding periods because, even at a constant rate, inflation is likely to have a different proportional effect on total nominal gain (or loss, in the case of depreciable assets) as holding periods vary. Thus the typical indirect adjustments for inflation—such as a uniform accelerated depreciation rate and a uniform exclusion percentage for capital gains—employed under unindexed tax systems do not achieve neutrality in the taxation of similar assets with different holding periods. The case for comprehensive indexing would be strengthened if such neutrality were considered to be an important objective.

Direct indexing of assets is also superior to a system of ad hoc, indirect inflation adjustments with respect to neutrality of taxation under conditions of fluctuating rather than static inflation. When the inflation rate is assumed to be fixed, comparisons of effective tax rates between an indexed and unindexed tax system do not reveal inherent benefits of the indexed system as the inflation rate varies over time. For example, Halperin and Steuerle cite initial estimates that the newly enacted incentive depreciation system will result in effective tax rates only slightly lower than a fully indexed accrual system that retains double taxation of distributed corporate earnings. These estimates hold only if a fixed inflation rate is assumed. If inflation rates fluctuate, an indexed depreciation system maintains a uniform target level of effective tax rates, whereas an unindexed, accelerated depreciation system ceases to provide equal incentives to all assets. Moreover, an indexed system preserves anticipated depreciation incentives for existing assets; under an unindexed depreciation system, fluctuating inflation creates windfalls for existing assets. Thus the chief virtue of direct indexing is that it adjusts tax liabilities for unanticipated changes in inflation, while de facto indexing measures do not.

In hindsight, the Treasury II proposal for an indexed, accelerated depreciation system lost out to a more accelerated, nominal depreciation system in part because of a failure to understand the effects of changing inflation, especially if inflation rates exceeded the prevailing assumed rate of 4 percent. The prevailing assumption of a fixed, 4 percent inflation rate meant that to attain equal incentives an indexed depreciation system would defer deductions while an accelerated system would allow recovery of only original nominal-cost basis. Thus, over the prevailing five-year budget period, an indexed depreciation system appeared to cost the government less revenue than a comparable nominal depreciation system with special incentives for investment. This apparent advantage was actually turned against indexing with the specter of reduced revenue outside the budget period. Fears of out-year revenue shortfalls were heightened by observations that higher inflation rates would increase depreciation allowances under an indexed system, but not under an unindexed one.

Unfortunately, naysayers failed to see or acknowledge that higher inflation rates would also increase the rate of growth of the tax base, as well as reduce the level of incentives in an unindexed system. In fact, assuming a permanent, fixed rate of inflation, indexed and unindexed depreciation systems with equal incentives probably produce roughly comparable revenue streams over the long run, although a definitive analysis requires consideration of capital stock growth rates and other factors. In the next legislative debate over indexing, effective presentation of the short- and long-run revenue and incentive trade-offs as inflation fluctuates would help the cause of direct indexing.

Legislative critics of Treasury's indexed depreciation system also questioned whether indexing of depreciable assets, but not interest expense, would in fact improve the measurement of income relative to an entirely unindexed system. The Treasury II proposals abandoned indexing of capital assets and indebtedness, and the indexed depreciation system became substantially more tied to incentives than an economic depreciation system would be. Thus the ever-present concern about leveraging assets with low effective tax rates was accentuated by the claim that higher inflation rates would tend to increase leveraging of indexed depreciable assets relative to an unindexed depreciation system. Halperin and Steuerle seem to accept this claim by noting that inflation limits the disparity between the treatment of interest and unindexed depreciable assets, whereas exact indexing of only depreciable assets would have no such limit. The authors somewhat offhandedly suggest that limiting indexing to net equity investments would reduce opportunities for arbitrage. Because the bias against leveraging runs so deep among policymakers, proponents of partial indexing should develop a fuller analysis of the consequences of leveraging indexed assets under conditions of fluctuating inflation.

Much of the Halperin-Steuerle paper is devoted to an enlightening examination of whether indexing indebtedness could be fairly implemented in a realization-based tax system. The authors' central point seems to be that an indexed system, such as Treasury I, that adjusts current interest flows, rather than assets and liabilities directly, will necessarily result in realization of the inflation adjustment in a manner that seems inconsistent with the realization rules generally applicable to assets and liabilities. If realization principles are to be maintained, indexing of current interest flows should reflect anticipated rather than actual inflation. Since such a theoretical result is unobtainable, indexing of current interest flows will create certain mismatches in the realization of income. Moreover, the authors correctly note that indexing of current interest flows raises other difficult problems concerning both the identification of interest and the treatment of financial intermediaries.

It becomes useful, therefore, to reconsider the premise that indexing of indebtedness would necessarily involve adjustments to current interest flows. Treasury I proposed its inexact inflation adjustment for current interest flows because of perceived administrative difficulties in determining taxpayers' principal balances and interest rates over the course of an annual accounting period. Those difficulties may have been overstated and certainly deserve further scrutiny by policy analysts. To the extent aggregate average principal balances and interest rates can be determined with tolerable accuracy, a more exact adjustment of current interest flows would be possible. To the extent individual loan balances and average interest rates can be determined, an accrual adjustment of assets and liabilities might be possible. While this latter prospect may seem fanciful today, the probable introduction of new allocation and tracing rules implementing various interest limitation rules (such as limitations on the deductibility of consumer interest, investment interest, and passive activity interest) may facilitate more exact interest indexing proposals. For now, the Halperin-Steuerle paper points the way toward a more complete examination of the vexing problems associated with indexing indebtedness.

Comments by Richard A. Musgrave

This paper deals with a proposition that almost everybody will support: an orderly income tax system requires protection from inflation. The paper makes three major points. First, indexing of capital income is needed because otherwise it will be taxed at a much higher rate than labor income, even with only a moderate rate of inflation. Second, the present system does in fact provide for substantial indexing but in an indirect and unsatisfactory sort of way (that is, by excluding capital income or deferring its taxation). Finally, exact indexing is difficult but has not yet proven impossible. However, the authors do not quite prove that it can be done.

Various illustrations are given to show that without indexing capital income under inflationary conditions is overtaxed relative to wage income. The authors then consider the postwar experience in the United States and conclude that the annual increase in net worth averaged about 25 percent of the increase in net national product. Out of these 25 percentage points, 17 points of the nominal increase in net worth, or as much as 70 percent, were inflationary gains. So if the nominal gains had been taxed at 20 percent, the real gains would have been taxed at 66 percent, and had the nominal gains been taxed at 30 percent, the real gains would have been taxed at about 100 percent. The authors note, however, that in reality such taxation of capital income did not apply since capital income, to a considerable degree, has been excluded from the tax base or deferred. Capital income is said to be "effectively indexed" for tax purposes.

With less than one-third of real capital income included in the tax base and with an even lower inclusion rate for nominal income, the authors note that indexing by exclusion and by deferral is quite extensive. However, it is not a satisfactory way of dealing with the problem, the authors conclude. Depending on the tax rate, the rate of inflation, and the holding period, deferral may well result in under- or overindexing.

The paper then examines how correct indexing may be introduced. I take it that such indexing is defined so as to apply the same rate of tax to real capital income as to wage income. It is also generally assumed that the treatment of wage income is indexed by an inflation adjustment of exemptions and rate brackets. By considering how correct indexing may be introduced, a distinction is then drawn between an income tax system that operates on an accrual basis and the more realistic case of a system based on realization.

The conclusion is that indexing for inflation in an accrual system would be relatively simple because the index could be applied to the value of the assets at the beginning of the period and then income flows in nominal terms could be taxed. Some people would gain and some would lose, but on the whole this procedure would be feasible. A minor difficulty would arise if the asset were held for only part of the tax period or if there were multiple transactions within the period; nonetheless, introduction of indexing into an accrual-based system would be relatively straightforward.

The problem is more difficult in a realization system. The question there is how to determine when the inflation adjustment is to be realized. If indexing is applied to the base value of an asset while income flows are fully taxed, then indexing becomes effective only with realization. But if indexing for debt instruments is applied through a current adjustment for interest income and expense, then debt instruments will be treated differently than other assets. This problem may be met, however, by limiting the adjustment only to the inflationary component in interest receipts and payments. That solution, however, raises the further problem of how to separate the inflationary from the real components of interest. The Treasury I plan suggested the use of a uniform real rate of return of 6 percent, but this proposal would disregard differentials in the real returns on various debt instruments.

Further difficulties—and the authors examine many of them—arise when actual and anticipated rates of inflation differ. The authors conclude that ideally anticipated rates should be used but that in practice the use of actual rates probably would not do too much harm. Under an exact system of indexing, mortgages should be treated like other debt, and the authors criticize Treasury I for excluding mortgage debt from indexing.

In all, the paper concludes that the possibility of fairly exact indexing has not been disproven and that indexing would be relatively simple for an accrual system. Moreover, the authors evidently believe that an acceptable solution could be found even for a realization system. They believe that finding a solution is important because otherwise capital income cannot be fully taxed, even with only a moderate degree of inflation. Indexing is needed not only to protect capital income against overtaxation but also to make it contribute its fair share. It is thus a merit of the paper that it looks at the problem of indexing not only as a specific problem of inflation adjustment, but also relates it to the general problem of how capital income should be included in the tax base.

A few brief comments may be added. I feel somewhat uncomfortable when the exclusion or deferral of capital income from the base is referred to or rationalized as indexing. Such exclusion did not come about as indexing, but rather as a way to keep capital income out of the tax base, even when there is no inflation. Exclusion goes back to an old debate and faulty definitions of what constitutes income and not to the problem of inflation adjustment. Inflation became an issue later, and thus some degree of exclusion served to play the role of indexing and perhaps offer an improvement. Depending on the degree of deferral, rate of tax, and rate of inflation, deferrals and exclusions might produce the same result as an accrual taxation system with proper indexing. But that would be a rare case.

While I think it is good to relate the problem of indexing to the general question of whether capital income should be excluded, I wish the authors had made a greater distinction between how to treat capital income in the tax base under noninflationary conditions and how to deal with indexing for inflation, a problem that should not be dealt with through exclusions.

The paper might have been more critical of the failure of the 1986 Tax Reform Act to deal with the indexing problem, as distinct from the rather heroic position taken in Treasury I. By failing to consider indexing while fully including realized gains, the reform leaves a situation that may not prove viable, even with relatively modest inflation rates, and it leaves the idea of taxing unrealized gains even more unthinkable.

One of the advantages of inflation—and there are not many—might indeed be that it makes a strong case for taxation on an accrual basis, which would be desirable even without inflation. Inclusion of unrealized gains in the tax base, as called for by the accretion concept, is of course much the larger part of the problem of how to tax capital gains. Only the minor part of the problem—the full taxation of realized gains—was tackled by the reform. Considering the political opposition to moving to an accrual basis, inflation might indeed help as borrowers would favor it and only lenders would oppose it. Thus it might not be impossible to obtain political support for moving to an accrual basis. In the spirit of a Haig-Simons income concept, that would surely be the best solution.

Finally, it should be noted that moving toward fuller indexation of the tax system would reduce the built-in flexibility of the system. While this would be most true of indexing bracket rates, even indexing of capital income would carry some costs. Thus indexing would make the government's inability to use discretionary tax changes as countercyclical instruments even more costly. Nevertheless, indexing of capital income is needed, not only to protect it against overtaxation, but also to avoid undertaxation. The argument, therefore, is as much for broadening the base as for indexing, especially if the focus is on the accrual route.

Comments by Arnold C. Harberger

In the face of a widespread belief that the adjustment of the income of business enterprises for inflation is enormously complicated, I shall present in this comment a very simple system that copes extremely well with the main problems that an indexing scheme for business income is supposed to entail. A summary of the system as it applies to various assets and obligations is in table 3.

The Basic Structure of the Scheme

The only inputs required to put the system into effect are the standard items that appear on the balance sheets and income statements of business firms. Three operations need to be performed:

1. All real assets would be written up by the inflationary adjustment percentage. The amount of this writeup would then be entered as an upward adjustment to profit on the income statement.

2. All real or indexed liabilities, and also capital and surplus (owners' equity) would be written up by the inflationary adjustment percentage. The amount of this writeup would be entered as a downward adjustment to profit (that is, as a loss item) on the income statement.

3. Depreciation would be calculated on the basis of the written-up values of physical assets, as determined in step 1 above.

With these three adjustments the indexing system can be regarded as complete. It *can* be made somewhat more complex, but it *need* not be. Indeed, one can argue that the three operations defined above fully accomplish the indexing of business income for tax purposes and that any further adjustments that might be contemplated (for example, separate adjustment percentages for assets and liabilities expressed in foreign currencies, or for specific commodities such as oil) could with equal force be advocated for a noninflationary system with changing relative prices.

Table 3. *Treatment of Various Business Assets and Obligations in a Business Income Tax, with and without Indexing*

Item	Without indexing	With indexing
Capital asset acquired during year	Asset must be kept separate from others in its class and depreciation calculated just for the revelant part of the year	Asset must be kept separate from others in its class and both inflation adjustment and depreciation calculated just for the relevant part of the year
Capital asset acquired before beginning of year	Asset may be mingled with others in its class, and common depreciation rate applied	Asset may be mingled with others in its class; inflation adjustment and common depreciation rate may then be applied for the class as a whole
Nonindexed obligation or receivable acquired before or during year	Interest and amortization must be calculated at the contractual rate	Same as without indexing
Indexed obligation or receivable acquired before or during year	Even when the system is not indexed, the firms involved must calculate the inflation adjustment as specified in the instrument of debt and then apply the contractual rate of interest	Same as without indexing
Inventory acquired during year	Net increase of increase of inventory is added to stock of inventory, valued at its cost	Same as without indexing
Inventory carried in stock at beginning of year	Stock is altered to reflect net depletion of inventory	Initial stock is adjusted upward for inflation, then treated the same as without indexing
Issue of new shares of stock during year	No change if stock dividend or stock split; if shares issued in exchange for cash or other assets, capital and surplus must be written up by the amount involved as of the date of the transaction	Same as without indexing, but in addition this new capital must be written up by the inflation adjustment for the relevant part of the year
Capital and surplus as of beginning of year	Nothing to be done	Written up by the inflation adjustment for the year
After-tax profits	Added to capital and surplus at end of year	Added to adjusted capital and surplus at end of year

Treatment of Inventories

Although it is easy to imagine that the treatment of inventories in an indexing scheme could become extremely complex, the system can be kept very simple. The key is to conduct inventory accounting on a last-in, first-out basis, which assumes that the bulk of the inventories "used" for any purpose will have been recently acquired (for accounting purposes, at least). Thus there would not in general be a need to take into account differences between the price level prevailing when inventories are acquired and that prevailing when they are used. The only exception occurs when inventories are depleted during a period and the business must use up some inventories that were acquired in earlier periods. The adjustment that automatically corrects for a difference in the price level in such cases is to write up the beginning inventory by the inflationary adjustment factor of the period. Any reduction in physical inventory holdings would thus be costed at prices reflecting the accumulated inflation (up to the current period).

Treatment of Assets and Obligations Expressed
in Foreign Currency

Within an indexing system, there are really three potentially sensible ways to treat assets and liabilities expressed in foreign currency.

First, if the national currency (say, the rupiah) is more or less closely linked to a major foreign currency (dollar, pound, yen), it is appropriate to treat foreign-currency assets and liabilities as if they were in domestic currency. Thus a nonindexed debt in foreign currency would, in this case, *not* be written up to reflect an ongoing inflation. The only current cost arising out of such an instrument of debt would be the interest that had to be paid on it.

Second, if a substantial domestic inflation is under way that is out of line with world inflation and creating a situation in which the exchange rate must be devalued periodically to avoid systemic calamity, foreign currency obligations and assets can be treated as if they were *real* obligations and assets. In this case, the rupiah value of a dollar debt would be written up in just the same way as an *indexed* rupiah obligation.

Third is an intermediate case in which the domestic inflation sometimes exceeds the world inflation and by relatively moderate amounts, requiring occasional but not regular currency devaluations. In these circumstances, one might contemplate an ad hoc special treatment of foreign currency debts and assets, writing them up by the percentage of the relevant devaluation in each case. The amount by which an asset is written up automatically becomes a positive adjustment to profits and the amount by which a liability is written up correspondingly becomes a negative adjustment to profits, just as in the case of the standard inflation adjustments treated earlier in this paper. The only difference is that the percentage of devaluation in a particular year would probably be different from the standard inflationary adjustment based on price-level movements.

One must be extremely careful not to extend the principle underlying the third case to assets and liabilities generally, which would be the sure road to making the indexing system unbearably complicated. In a nonindexed system with flexible exchange rates, obligations and assets expressed in different currencies are all going to change in value by different percentages. It is not the task of an indexing system to correct for the variations of the mark relative to the pound, the pound relative to the yen, or the yen relative to the dollar. One correction at most should be applied to all of these currencies.

Most foreign-currency assets and liabilities fall into the first category of treatment, which applies when the national currency is not inflating at a rate significantly different from other currencies, or into the second category, which occurs when there is a significant and systematic difference between the inflation rate of the country in question and those applying in the major world centers. The third category is anomalous to begin with, but gives rise to a plausible need for special adjustment. The peril is to extend the principle of a special adjustment so as to have separate adjustments for the different principal currencies—and even, ultimately, for differential movements in commodity prices. The key to simplicity in an indexing system is to recognize that inflation is a movement of the *general* price level. It therefore calls, in principle, for one adjustment, and one adjustment only. Multiplying the bases on which different adjustments are made is thus to be avoided at all cost.

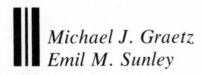

Michael J. Graetz
Emil M. Sunley

Minimum Taxes and Comprehensive Tax Reform

THE dramatic lowering of marginal tax rates, the near doubling of personal exemptions, and the expansion of the tax base may make the Tax Reform Act of 1986 the most sweeping federal tax legislation since the wartime Revenue Act of 1942, which converted the income tax to a mass tax. The 1986 act retains the individual and corporate taxes as the primary sources of federal revenue and, at least for the moment, reverses the trends of the early 1980s by shifting the burden of these taxes toward corporations and away from individuals. While determining corporate tax incidence is always controversial, the act also seems to shift a portion of the tax burden toward capital income and away from labor income.

A central feature of the 1986 legislation is the strengthened minimum tax for both individuals and corporations. The minimum tax was first added to the Internal Revenue Code in 1969 in the form of a 10 percent excise, or "add-on," tax on certain specified tax preference items granted to both individuals and corporations under existing tax law. Subsequent years produced frequent changes in the minimum tax rate, the structure and level of minimum tax exemptions, and the list of tax preference items subject to the minimum tax. In 1978 Congress enacted a so-called alternative minimum tax for individuals—payable only if the minimum tax computation produced a tax greater than that under the regular income computation—but also retained the add-on minimum tax for certain preferences involving deferrals of tax. In 1982 Congress repealed the add-on minimum tax for individuals and expanded the base of the individual alternative minimum tax. The 1986 legislation once again

The authors wish to thank Ken Timbers for undertaking the calculations of effective rates and Rita Cavanagh for research and editorial assistance.

Table 1. Number of Taxpayers Covered and Revenue Produced by Corporate and Individual Minimum Taxes, 1969–84

| Year | Corporate tax | | Individual tax | | | |
| | Number of taxpayers (thousands) | Amount (millions of dollars) | Add-on tax | | Alternative tax | |
			Number of taxpayers (thousands)	Amount (millions of dollars)	Number of taxpayers (thousands)	Amount (millions of dollars)
1969	0.7	3.1	n.a.	n.a.	...	...
1970	4.9	265.1	18.9	122.0	...	...
1971	5.1	179.1	24.4	169.5	...	...
1972	5.5	315.9	26.6	216.3	...	...
1973	5.3	335.1	26.4	182.3	...	...
1974	4.6	346.8	18.5	142.6	...	...
1975	4.3	156.7	20.2	144.1	...	...
1976	5.7	192.9	246.7	1,000.3	...	...
1977	10.6	163.3	399.5	1,322.9	...	...
1978	11.1	340.5	495.3	1,514.5	...	...
1979	10.7	433.6	74.4	309.2	153.2	865.9
1980	9.2	438.8	94.6	412.6	122.7	850.3
1981	8.0	524.9	125.7	565.6	137.1	1,261.3
1982	7.6	478.5	101.4	450.7	131.4	1,069.2
1983	n.a.	561.5	...	...	n.a.	2,530.2
1984	n.a.	n.a.	...	...	n.a.	1,908.7

Source: U.S. Internal Revenue Service, *Statistics of Income.*
n.a. Not available.

expanded the alternative minimum tax base for individuals and replaced the add-on corporate minimum tax with a new 20 percent alternative minimum tax. The list of corporate tax preferences subject to minimum tax was also expanded. Most dramatically, it now includes one-half of untaxed book income, that is, one-half of before-tax income reported to shareholders on a company's financial statements. (Appendix A provides a more detailed history of the minimum tax provisions.)

With the expanded tax base for the minimum tax and the reduced tax rate differential between the regular and minimum taxes, the minimum tax is estimated to increase individual tax receipts by $3.9 billion and corporate tax receipts by $5.3 billion in fiscal 1988, compared with actual annual collections of about $2 billion for individuals and $500 million for corporations under prior law. The minimum tax is now a big revenue raiser: if the corporate minimum tax were repealed, an increase of two to three percentage points in the corporate tax rate would be required to offset the revenue loss. Even these projections may understate the full revenue effect of the minimum tax. It not only raises revenue paid as minimum tax but also serves to increase the regular income tax paid by taxpayers who limit their use of preferences to avoid triggering the minimum tax (see table 1).

The Role of a Minimum Tax

Purists would view the enactment of minimum taxes as a sign that basic, comprehensive tax reform has failed or is unattainable. If the United States ever adopts a truly comprehensive income tax or a truly comprehensive consumption tax, a minimum tax with all its complexities would presumably not be needed. In fact, the November 1984 income tax proposals of the Treasury Department (Treasury I) would have repealed the minimum tax. The Treasury did suggest, however, that if its base-broadening proposals were not fully enacted, a minimum tax might still be necessary.

We do not view the enactment of a minimum tax as a sign of failure. Instead, it is an admission that the U.S. income tax involves trade-offs among competing objectives. Congress wants to use income tax provisions to encourage particular economic investments or activities and to promote certain societal goals. At the same time, it wants to ensure that the income tax burden is distributed generally in accordance with taxpayers' abilities to pay. A minimum tax is necessary because the ability of a few large, profitable companies or high-income families to pay little or no U.S. income tax is inherently unfair and undermines public confidence in the tax system by inducing widespread perceptions of tax inequity. A well-designed minimum tax should be able to ensure that no taxpayers with substantial economic income can reduce their tax liabilities to zero by combining tax-preferred exclusions, deductions, and credits. But this objective can be achieved only by incurring considerable complexity and by blunting the effectiveness of tax incentives. On balance, we favor minimum taxes for both individuals and corporations under the current income tax; the improvements in both the fairness of the distribution of the tax burden and the perception of tax fairness by the populace outweigh the costs.

As we discuss below, the 1986 minimum tax amendments played an important transitional role in facilitating the fundamental changes required by the 1986 act. Graetz has suggested elsewhere that a broad-based minimum tax might also serve more generally as a transition mechanism to move the tax system toward a broad-based, relatively flat-rate income tax.[1] Such a minimum tax, by reducing tax benefits of preferences, might wean taxpayers away from a preference-riddled tax base toward a more comprehensive tax base. As the gaps in tax bases and in rates between the regular and minimum tax narrow, one or the other tax might eventually be repealed. Sunley is skeptical that a minimum tax has such potential because of the inherent complexities and distortions it introduces into the system. Both authors agree that whether or not such a transitional role is ultimately fulfilled, a minimum tax is currently necessary to ensure that those with high economic incomes pay at least minimum income taxes.

After the enactment of the Tax Reform Act of 1986, Congress adopted legislation reauthorizing the environmental superfund, imposing taxes on corporations to fund environmental protective and cleanup activities. Under this law, a 0.12 percent tax is imposed on corporations' alternative minimum taxable income above $2 million. As a result, all corporations that earn or expect to earn more than $2 million must calculate alternative minimum taxable income, even if their regular income tax liability would

1. Michael J. Graetz, "The 1982 Minimum Tax Amendments as a First Step in the Transition to a 'Flat-Rate' Tax," *Southern California Law Review,* vol. 56 (January 1983), pp. 527–71.

always be large enough to avoid any minimum tax liability under the income tax.

We agree that this superfund legislation might increase the number of corporations faced with the complexities of the minimum tax without either the compensating gain in tax fairness or perceptions of tax fairness that accrue under the income tax. Moreover, this new environmental tax is not appropriate as a means to facilitate a transition to a more comprehensive broad-based, low-rate income tax. However, Congress's selection of the minimum tax base rather than the regular corporate income tax base for imposition of this relatively small environmental tax may reflect continuing congressional concern that corporate taxable income contains overly generous exclusions, deductions, or credits, even after the 1986 amendments.

Link to Comprehensive Income Taxation

In broad conceptual terms, the minimum tax has been closely linked to the goal of comprehensive income taxation. This linkage suggests that support for a comprehensive minimum tax depends heavily on the theoretical model against which it is measured. Realistically, the U.S. income tax has never been either a pure income-based or a consumption-based tax, but rather has been a hybrid that exempts to varying degrees many forms of consumption, savings, and investment. Given this hybrid character, the scholarly and political debate over the minimum tax often has mirrored underlying preferences for aligning the tax system more closely to the theoretical poles of income-based or consumption-based taxation.

Those who support the latter form of tax system necessarily consider the minimum tax to be a step in the wrong direction. The primary justification for substituting some type of consumption or expenditure tax for the present system is that an income-based tax distorts economic behavior by creating a preference for current over future consumption. The reason is that under an income tax both the amount of saving and the return on saving are subject to taxation. For those who prefer consumption taxes, current income tax preferences designed to create savings and investment incentives are desirable offsets to the distortions between current and future consumption created by income taxation. Therefore, proponents of consumption taxes would oppose any limitation—including a minimum tax—on the use of tax preferences, especially those related to investment activity, because such limitations reduce desired savings and investment incentives and the neutrality between current and future consumption.

Supporters of broad-based income taxation, on the other hand, tend to have less dispute with the goals of a minimum tax and instead focus their criticism on its effectiveness and appropriateness as a means of achieving its goals. The corporate minimum tax debate, even among supporters of broad-based income taxation, has also reflected disagreements over the appropriate role for a corporate tax in an income-based tax system. As we later explain, those who believe that the separate corporate tax should be eliminated and corporate income imputed fully to shareholders would also probably favor similar integration of the corporate and individual minimum taxes. By the same reasoning, proponents of corporate tax reductions on earnings distributed to shareholders as dividends would tend to support similar dividend relief for minimum tax purposes, although they might regard some corporate minimum tax as an essential antidote to the perceived unfairness that would result under such a regime if profitable corporations avoided all corporate-level tax simply by paying dividends.

Political support for a minimum tax appears to have waxed and waned with shifting short-term economic policy concerns and with the political primacy of different models of the tax system overall and the system of business taxation in particular. The conceptual link between minimum taxes and comprehensive taxation of economic income, perhaps as a consequence, has seemed at times tenuous as a political force and, with respect to the corporate minimum tax, remained attenuated until the adoption of the alternative corporate minimum tax in the 1986 act.

Basic Structure of U.S. Minimum Taxes

Taxpayers must pay the higher of their regular tax liability or their minimum tax liability. The minimum tax liability is 21 percent (20 percent in the case of corporations) of the taxpayer's alternative minimum taxable income (AMTI) reduced by the allowable exemption amount. The exemption amount is $40,000 for corporations and married taxpayers filing a joint return and $30,000 for single taxpayers. The exemption amount is reduced twenty-five cents for each dollar by which AMTI exceeds $150,000 ($112,500 for single taxpayers). In the income range

Table 2. *Tax Preferences for Alternative Minimum Tax under Tax Reform Act of 1986*

Preference	Individuals[a]	Corporations
Accelerated depreciation on real property	X	X
Accelerated depreciation on personal property	X	X
Expensing of intangible drilling costs above 65 percent of net oil and gas income	X	X
Amortization of certified pollution control facilities	X	X
Expensing of mining exploration and development costs	X	X
Expensing of circulation expenditures (for newspapers and magazines)	X	X[b]
Expensing of research and experimentation expenditures	X	. . .
Percentage depletion	X	X
Incentive stock options	X	. . .
Tax-exempt interest on private-activity bonds	X	X
Completed contract method of accounting	X	X
Installment method of accounting	X	X
Bad-debt reserve deductions for financial institutions	. . .	X
Net loss from passive trade or business activities	X	. . .
Losses from passive farming activities	X	X[c]
Charitable contributions of appreciated property	X	X
Capital construction funds for shipping companies	. . .	X
Special deduction for certain tax-exempt insurance providers	. . .	X
Untaxed reported profits	. . .	X

a. Itemized deductions allowed individuals: casualty, theft, and gambling losses to the extent of gambling winnings; charitable contributions; medical expenditures above 10 percent floor; investment interest to the extent of investment income; and qualified housing interest.
b. Applies only to personal holding companies.
c. Applies only to personal service corporations.

for which the exemption is being phased out, the marginal tax rate is 26.25 percent for individuals and 25 percent for corporations.

To compute AMTI, a taxpayer begins with taxable income and adds specified tax preferences. While some tax preferences exempt certain types of income from taxation, others defer income taxation until a later date. Both deferrals and exemptions are included in the corporate and individual lists of tax preferences that must be factored into AMTI.

The 1986 act makes several noteworthy additions to the lists of tax preferences (see table 2). For the first time, accelerated depreciation on machinery and equipment will be a preference for all taxpayers. Tax-exempt interest on private-activity state and local bonds issued after August 7, 1986, is included in income for minimum tax purposes. (Private-activity bonds principally benefit private rather than traditional governmental activities; industrial development and home mortgage bonds are examples.) This addition should finally permit resolution of the debate over whether it is constitutional for the federal government to tax interest on obligations of state and local governments. Under the minimum tax, the untaxed appreciation for charitable contributions of appreciated property is a new tax preference. Probably the most controversial addition to the list of tax preferences is the new "book-income" preference for corporations, which has the effect of basing some corporations' income tax liability on the amount of income reported to shareholders on financial statements.

To reinforce the inescapability of the minimum tax, net operating-loss carryovers and foreign tax credits can offset no more than 90 percent of AMTI. Thus companies with no economic profits over a period of several years and companies with only high-taxed, foreign-source income will still pay a minimum tax equal to 2 percent of the current year's income. Although the investment tax credit was repealed, corporations are allowed to offset up to 25 percent of the minimum tax by investment tax credits carried over from prior years (or earned on certain transition property).

If taxpayers pay minimum tax greater than their regular tax liability, the excess (except that attributable to income exclusion preferences such as tax-exempt interest) may be carried forward as a credit against any subsequent year's regular tax above the minimum tax.

Five Fundamental Design Issues

In designing a minimum tax, there are five fundamental issues: (1) Should the tax apply to both individuals and corporations? (2) Should the tax be an add-on or an alternative tax? (3) Should the list of tax preferences include both exemptions and deferrals? (4) What should be the rate of the minimum tax? (5) What special design issues does a corporate minimum tax raise?

The Case for a Corporate Minimum Tax

The case for a minimum tax on individuals is premised on a belief that persons with larger economic incomes should bear their fair share of the tax burden and at least pay some minimum amount of tax in all events. If they do not, the fairness of the tax system is eroded, and many think that tax compliance may be undermined as a result.

The case for a minimum tax on corporations is more complex and ultimately is related to one's view of the corporate income tax. In general, the desirability of an effective corporate income tax is due to two structural features of the U.S. income tax. First, in the absence of full integration of corporate and personal income taxes (under which all corporate income would be imputed to shareholders and taxed only at the shareholder level whether the income was distributed or not), the corporate tax is necessary to ensure taxation of undistributed income from corporations.[2] In this regard, a separate minimum tax on corporations is not a step toward integrating the corporate and individual income taxes. A corporate minimum tax would make the separation of individual and corporate taxes more rather than less complete, and its burden may fall on individual shareholders (or perhaps in some cases even customers or employees) who already pay their fair share of individual income taxes.

Second, the close linkage between the corporate and individual income taxes requires an effective corporate tax to ensure that the corporate tax does not become an escape hatch for individual taxpayers. Regardless of one's theoretical view of the appropriate role of business taxation and its relationship to individual taxation, practical considerations necessitate a close relationship between the two. This connection is due principally to the fact that businesses are given great flexibility as to both the legal form of business enterprise that they may select and the nature of the myriad business relationships into which they routinely enter. In terms of both rates and the structure of the tax base, it is essential that corporate or other business tax laws do not become an opportunity for tax avoidance through manipulation of income or deductions or shifting of income or deductions between businesses and their owners. Complementary corporate and individual minimum taxes may inhibit tax avoidance opportunities that would remain feasible if a minimum tax applied only to individuals.

Moreover, while there is considerable controversy over who pays the corporate tax, the Treasury Department's measure of economic income

2. On the subject of integration of the corporate and individual income taxes, see Alvin Warren, "The Relation and Integration of Individual and Corporate Income Taxes," *Harvard Law Review*, vol. 94 (February 1981), pp. 719–800; and Charles E. McLure, Jr., *Must Corporate Income Be Taxed Twice?* (Brookings, 1979).

used for the personal income tax distribution tables implicitly accepts the view that at least in the short run the corporate income tax is borne by stockholders.[3] While the long-run incidence of the corporate tax is also controversial, there seems to be some agreement that owners of capital bear the tax. To the extent that these conclusions are supportable, the corporate tax is the primary source of federal revenue from the taxation of capital.

Those who would eliminate any taxation of capital income in favor of a consumption or wage tax use this fact to demand an end to the corporate tax. The failure to eliminate the corporate tax by statutory means is only a spur to eliminate the corporate tax through tax planning, and for those with this view, any strengthening of the corporate tax—including a corporate minimum—is a step in the wrong direction. For those committed to taxation of income from both capital and labor, however, recognizing this significant role of the corporate tax argues for protecting it from erosion with a corporate minimum tax.

Finally, one of the major goals of the 1986 legislation was to narrow somewhat the wide disparity in effective tax rates across industries and among companies within the same industry. The Treasury Department has observed that these tax-induced distortions in the use of labor and capital and in consumer choices have severe costs in terms of lost productivity, lost production, and reduced consumer satisfaction.[4]

The great disparities among industries have largely been the result of accelerated depreciation and the investment tax credit, combined with favorable tax treatment of debt financing. Both the general and corporate minimum tax provisions of the 1986 law should reduce such cross-industry disparities.

Disparate tax rates among companies in the same industry result in part from variations in each company's history of gains and losses. This history depends, in turn, on whether the company has been able in the past to take advantage of accelerated depreciation and the investment credit. Several unintegrated companies may have the same combined taxable income as a single conglomerate but pay a higher corporate income tax. That is because the conglomerate may elect to file a consolidated return, which permits the tax losses of one subsidiary to

3. J. Gregory Ballentine, "Broadening Our Approach to Income Tax Reform," *American Journal of Tax Policy*, vol. 5 (Spring 1986), pp. 1–11.

4. U.S. Department of the Treasury, *Tax Reform for Fairness, Simplicity, and Economic Growth: The Treasury Department Report to the President* (Government Printing Office, 1984), vol. 1, pp. 1–5.

offset the tax gains of another. This disparate treatment may encourage economically inefficient mergers and acquisitions as well as economically inefficient transactions, such as leasing, among unaffiliated companies.

A corporate minimum tax may exacerbate unintended distortions across firms in the same industry. For example, if mineral depletion is a preference for the minimum tax, a stand-alone copper company may be subject to that tax. But if a similar copper company is owned by a diversified manufacturing corporation, the conglomerate may have sufficient regular tax liability to avoid the minimum tax.

Imposing a minimum tax on corporations may further encourage tax-induced mergers that serve no useful economic purpose. The pool of merger targets ought to expand to include not only those companies with unused tax preferences but also those companies whose full utilization of tax preferences available to them subjects them to the alternative minimum tax. Marriages between companies should not be made in the Internal Revenue Code. Just what net effect a corporate minimum tax will have on mergers is a controversial empirical question. The fact that many companies with unused investment tax credits have not been merger targets may suggest that a corporate minimum tax will provide little real impetus for mergers.

Variations in financing patterns among companies—especially in their balance of debt and equity financing—also have produced variations in their relative tax burdens. The U.S. corporate income tax traditionally has favored debt over equity financing: interest paid on indebtedness is deductible to the company, while dividends paid on equity are not. This preference has been exacerbated by an asymmetrical taxation of assets and loans that has resulted from the failure of Congress to adjust the income tax base for inflation.[5] Meanwhile, Congress, the Treasury Department, and the courts have repeatedly proved incapable of imposing clear rules to distinguish between debt and equity. A corporate minimum tax may redress to some extent the advantages of debt financing.

Finally, a minimum tax on corporations may be necessary to redress

5. Dale W. Jorgenson and Martin A. Sullivan, "Inflation and Corporate Capital Recovery," in Charles R. Hulten, ed., *Depreciation, Inflation, and the Taxation of Income from Capital* (Washington, D.C.: Urban Institute, 1981), pp. 171–237; Michael J. Graetz and Barbara McDowell, "Tax Reform 1985: The Quest for a Fairer, More Efficient and Simpler Income Tax," *Yale Law and Policy Review*, vol. 3 (Fall 1984), pp. 5–40; and Henry J. Aaron, ed., *Inflation and the Income Tax* (Brookings, 1976).

widespread perceptions of income tax unfairness. Average citizens—who have no well-formed theoretical view of the incidence of the corporate income tax, its economic function, or its conceptual linkage with the individual income tax—are often simply unable to understand why they should be subject to a significant income tax burden while large public corporations that pay dividends to shareholders and report profits on financial statements nevertheless pay no corporate income tax. A middle-income employee of a profitable corporation tends to resent a tax system that imposes a greater income tax burden on the employee than on the corporation. At the least, the existence of such circumstances undermines the confidence of the citizenry in the tax system and the institutions of government. Many observers seem to believe that such perceptions of unfairness also contribute significantly to tax noncompliance. The public's objections to income tax avoidance by large corporations undoubtedly supplied a substantial political impetus to the corporate minimum tax amendments of the 1986 act.

Add-On versus Alternative Minimum Tax

A minimum tax can be an add-on tax, such as the minimum tax that applied to corporations from 1969 through 1986, or it can be an alternative tax, such as the tax enacted for individuals in 1978 or for corporations in 1986. A pure add-on tax is essentially an excise tax on use of preferences. It reduces the value of those preferences without considering the taxpayer's total economic income. The corporate add-on minimum tax repealed by the 1986 act allowed a deduction for regular income taxes, as had prior versions of the individual add-on minimum tax. Such a deduction tends to focus the minimum tax on those corporations or individuals that would otherwise pay little or no regular tax.

An alternative minimum tax applies to a taxpayer's regular taxable income plus certain specified tax preferences. An alternative tax could be optional or mandatory. If it is optional, taxpayers would pay the lower of their regular tax or their alternative tax. If the alternative tax is mandatory, as it is currently for individuals and corporations, taxpayers are required to pay the greater of their regular tax or the alternative tax.

The case for a mandatory alternative tax is straightforward: without a minimum tax, taxpayers might be able to combine various tax preferences and reduce their tax to zero. However, taxpayers could not reduce their tax liability below zero—tax preferences generally are not refundable. There is nothing magical, however, about zero. Congress could decide that taxpayers can combine tax preferences to reduce their effective tax rate to no lower than, say, 20 percent.

An alternative minimum tax is more complicated than an add-on tax. An alternative tax requires running two tax systems in parallel: both the regular and the alternative tax system. It is very important to correlate the rules for those taxpayers who are subject to regular tax one year and to the alternative minimum tax another year. For example, the net operating-loss carryover allowed for the regular tax should be allowed for the minimum tax, but the carryover should be reduced to the extent that it is due to tax preferences. Coordinating the regular and minimum taxes is most significant and difficult when deferral preferences are involved.

Exemption versus Deferral Preferences

Tax preferences come in two types. They are either permanent forgiveness through tax credits or tax exemptions, such as the exclusion for interest on state and local bonds, or they are tax deferrals, such as accelerated depreciation. An extreme deferral, such as an immediate write-off of a capital expenditure, may under certain conditions be economically equivalent to an exemption of the income from the expensed asset.[6] Both exemptions and deferrals reduce taxes. In general, however, tax exemptions permanently reduce the tax, while tax deferrals affect only the timing of when the tax is paid.

Once a decision is made to include deferral preferences in the minimum tax base, a minimum tax, even with a low rate, can eliminate the full value of the preferences. For example, accelerated depreciation on real estate may be taxed under the alternative tax at a 20 percent rate in the first year. In the second year, the taxpayer may sell the building and then would be subject to full taxation under the regular tax. In such a case the minimum tax in effect imposes a "toll charge" greater than the value of the deferral benefit. As this example suggests, the potential for overtaxation from including deferral preferences in the minimum tax base is typically greatest when taxpayers are subject to minimum tax in some years and regular tax in others.

6. For the conditions required for this equivalence to hold, see Michael J. Graetz, "Expenditure Tax Design," in Joseph A. Pechman, ed., *What Should Be Taxed: Income or Expenditure?* (Brookings, 1980), pp. 161–295.

This problem could be alleviated with appropriate basis-adjustment rules. For example, the tax basis of an asset could be increased by the amount of minimum tax paid as a result of any deferral preference associated with the asset. Such rules were considered when the minimum tax was first enacted in 1969. To date, however, the judgment in the United States has been that a low-rate minimum tax does not impose a sufficient toll charge to warrant complicated basis-adjustment rules.

There are at least two other ways of handling deferral preferences under a minimum tax, both of which are allowed under current law. First, taxpayers may include any minimum tax preference item in making their regular tax computation. This option, which has long been available under the minimum tax, in effect permits taxpayers to forgo the preference. Taxpayers thus lose all benefit of the tax preference, but they avoid being whipsawed by the combination of regular and minimum taxes. This approach works quite well for taxpayers who are generally subject to the minimum tax each year, but creates extraordinary planning difficulties for those taxpayers who do not know which tax they will be subject to in which years.

A second approach is to permit taxpayers to claim a credit for minimum tax against their regular tax in a future year to the extent that the minimum tax exceeds the regular tax in the current year. In the example of the building mentioned above, this approach would allow the taxpayer in the second year to claim a credit against the regular tax to the extent that the minimum tax in the first year exceeded the regular tax in that year. (Beginning in 1970, the minimum tax contained a variation of this theme, namely, a provision that allowed certain regular tax payments from prior years to reduce minimum taxes in subsequent years. See Appendix A.)

The 1986 act provides such a minimum tax credit for both individuals and corporations but only for that portion of the minimum tax liability attributable to deferral preferences. There is no carryback for the minimum tax credit, which may make the relief inadequate in some cases. For example, a taxpayer may record in one year a large liability for financial reporting purposes (say, for expected product liability claims) but not recognize the liability for tax purposes until the next year (when the claims are paid). With the new book-income preference under the minimum tax, the taxpayer might be subject to regular tax in the first year when book income is reduced, but subject to minimum tax in the second year when book income is higher and regular taxable income is reduced (by the liability). The resulting minimum tax credit could not be carried back to apply to the regular tax paid in the first year. For such a taxpayer, relief from the minimum tax will depend upon when regular tax liability subsequently occurs.

The Minimum Tax Rate

The 1986 act significantly narrowed the distance between the regular and minimum tax rates for individuals. Under prior law, the top individual rate under the regular tax was 50 percent and the minimum tax rate was 20 percent. With this differential in rates, individuals could have $1.50 of preferences for every dollar of fully taxed income (0.20 × $2.50 = 0.50 × $1.00) without being subject to the alternative minimum tax. Under the 1986 law, the top individual rate is 28 percent (once taxable income rises above a 33 percent surcharge range) and the minimum tax rate is 21 percent (ignoring the phaseout of the $40,000 exemption, which produces a top minimum tax rate of 26.25 percent). Under the new rate differential, individuals at the margin will be able to have only 33.3 cents of preferences for every dollar of fully taxed income (0.21 × $1.33 = 0.28 × $1.00).

In the case of corporations, a dollar of fully taxed income generated 46 cents of tax under prior law. Since the regular tax was deductible for purposes of the add-on corporate tax, a dollar of fully taxed income at the margin supported 46 cents of preference income. Under the 1986 act, the regular corporate tax rate is 34 percent and the minimum tax rate is 20 percent. Corporations at the margin can have 70 cents of preferences for every dollar of fully taxed income (0.20 × $1.70 = 0.34 × $1.00).

Notwithstanding the close relationship of the individual and corporate minimum tax rates, it is very difficult to discern any coherent basis for (1) the relationship between dollars of fully taxed income and preferences unaffected by the minimum tax for individuals or corporations taken alone; (2) the disparities in the amount of preferences that can be protected by a dollar of fully taxed income of individuals versus that of corporations; or (3) the substantial reduction of this relationship for individuals coupled with an increase for corporations, although this latter phenomenon is related to the 1986 act's reversal of the historic relationship between the top individual and corporate regular tax rates. No doubt revenue considerations dominated the 1986 act's selection of minimum tax rates.

Determination of the rate (or rates) of the minimum tax should require a balancing of two competing considerations. On the one hand, because a minimum tax should be intended to apply to only a minority of taxpayers, the rate should be set sufficiently below the relevant regular rates of tax to avoid overly broad application. On the other hand, the rate should not be set so low that taxpayers can continue to avoid incurring any significant tax liability. When the minimum tax for individuals was originally proposed in 1969, Treasury thought an appropriate balance could be achieved by ensuring that taxpayers pay minimum tax equal to half the regular rate applied to taxable income plus preferences (economic income). The rate structure of the 1986 act suggests that Congress now regards such a 50 percent relationship as inadequate for both individuals and corporations.

Achieving additional minimum tax revenue might be accomplished either with higher rates or a broader minimum tax base. Adopting a higher minimum tax rate in lieu of broadening the base would permit substantial numbers of high-income taxpayers to avoid taxes by using preferences not included in the minimum tax base. A higher rate–narrower base approach will penalize some high-income taxpayers for use of particular preferences while others remain untouched. As a policy matter, a minimum tax should not be a device that favors some preferences over others but rather one that favors some minimal level of taxation over unlimited use of any preferences. The minimum tax base therefore should be as inclusive of preferences as is practical.

Special Design Issues of a Corporate Minimum Tax

In addition to the basic design issues applicable to both corporate and individual minimum taxes discussed above, two additional issues concerning a corporate minimum tax require special attention. These are the appropriate role, if any, of income reported on the company's books to shareholders, regulatory agencies, or creditors; and the ability to use losses from one line of business to offset gains from another.

THE BOOK-INCOME PREFERENCE. The new book-income preference for corporations is one of the most significant changes for the minimum tax enacted in 1986. Companies are required to increase AMTI by one-half of any excess of before-tax book income over minimum taxable income before the book-income preference. This new preference is aimed at ensuring that companies that report profits to shareholders pay at least a minimum amount of tax.

There are two sharply conflicting views over the appropriateness of using book income as a preference item. One point of view predicts that as reported profits for financial purposes become an element of each company's tax computation, the government will lose control of the tax base because it simply will not be able to prescribe practical rules for computing book income. In addition, this book-income tax will treat similarly situated companies differently depending on how each chooses to report book income; for example, oil and gas companies can choose between full-costs accounting versus accounting on the basis of successful efforts. Moreover, critics of the book-income preference believe it is likely that the preference will put pressure on financial accounting; for example, companies subject to the minimum tax will have an incentive to increase reserves to reduce book income.

The other point of view is that direct linkage of the minimum tax and book income is necessary if a corporate minimum tax is to reduce or eliminate instances where companies report high earnings to shareholders and pay little or no tax.[7] Without such linkage, the current legislation would not have redressed this important ground for the widespread perception among the populace that the income tax is unfair. Under this view, the Treasury Department should administer the book-income preference in a rough and ready fashion, generally allowing the chips to fall where financial statements place them. Suggestions that the book-income preference will unhinge financial accounting practices are regarded as greatly overstated. Large public companies—which, after all, are the source of the tax unfairness perception problem—seem far too wedded to the current practice of emphasizing short-term profit reports to engage routinely in manipulations that would understate book income substantially to avoid the minimum tax.

Moreover, reducing book income would mitigate the spectacle of companies reporting high earnings and paying little or no tax. Such manipulations by privately held companies would not seem to undercut significantly the function of the book-income preference. Indeed, the perception problem would be largely unaffected if the book-income preference were generally limited to publicly held companies. Some averaging device may be warranted to deal with those cases, such as the

7. See testimony of Michael J. Graetz in *Tax Reform Proposals: Minimum Tax Issue*, Hearings before the Senate Committee on Finance, 99 Cong. 1 sess. (GPO, 1986), pt. 26, pp. 2–96.

products liability expense example discussed above, where deductions occur earlier for book purposes than for tax purposes.

In 1990, the book-income preference will be replaced with a preference based on adjusted current earnings (ACE), which in turn is based on current earnings and profits (the tax concept most closely linked to economic income) but with significant adjustments that generally work to increase the minimum tax base. For example, in computing ACE, taxpayers must use depreciation allowed for earnings and profits purposes or book depreciation, whichever is slower in present value terms.

The scheduled shift to ACE is likely to be the subject of controversy and legislation in future years. Additional complex transition rules will be necessary because of timing differences between book income and earnings and profits. For example, a company may have written off a loss for financial reporting purposes in 1989 but recognized the loss for tax purposes, including its computation of earnings and profits, in 1990. In addition, companies that have had no practical reason to be concerned with earnings and profits—mutual financial institutions for example— will now have to make such determinations. Book reserves, to cover product liability, for example, would no longer have tax consequences, and accounting methods would generally be those used for tax purposes. Although there is disagreement on the merits of the book-income preference, we agree that a switch to adjusted current earnings after only three years makes little sense. The transition costs are likely to be quite high and, when all is said and done, Treasury's regulations under an ACE preference may be just as extensive and controversial as those required under a book-income preference.

TREATMENT OF LOSSES FROM UNRELATED INCOME. As we mentioned earlier, a minimum tax on corporations may encourage some tax-induced mergers that serve no useful economic purpose. If shifting tax losses or otherwise achieving tax savings in this manner were deemed a substantial problem, perhaps the corporate minimum tax could be applied line-of-business by line-of-business. In other words, regular corporate income tax rules that allow losses to be offset against unrelated income from a different line of business could be disallowed for minimum tax purposes.

Of course, if Congress really desired to prohibit corporations from shifting tax losses, a variety of other financial arrangements would also require scrutiny. Corporations today, for example, routinely shift tax benefits to one another through leasing arrangements. The basic issue involved in loss shifting concerns something of a trade-off between the advantages to the country that such free transferability of tax losses produces in terms of economic efficiency and the disadvantages that loss shifting produces in terms of citizens' perceptions about income tax unfairness.[8]

We might not have raised this issue in discussing corporate minimum tax design had it not been made virtually unavoidable by the 1986 act's treatment of "passive losses" of individuals. The 1986 act attempts to curtail individual investments in tax shelters by prohibiting individuals from offsetting losses or credits from "passive" trade or business activities against "active" or "portfolio" income under either the regular or minimum tax.

The new rules do not permanently disallow losses and credits from passive activities. Unused or suspended losses and credits from passive activities can be carried forward (but not back) indefinitely and can be used to offset passive income realized in a subsequent year. In essence, these passive-loss rules create a third alternative tax base for individuals. However, there seems to be no reason (other than revenue considerations) why this base should be subject to the regular tax rates rather than the minimum tax rate. In fact, the passive-loss rules originated in Senate bills for an alternative minimum tax. In these proposals the passive-loss rules were designed to create a minimum tax floor equal to salary plus certain investment income. The passive-loss rules enacted in 1986 represent a further movement toward a schedular tax, at least for individuals.

A historical antecedent of the passive-loss rules is the 1973 Treasury proposal for a limitation on artificial losses (LAL).[9] Under LAL, deductions would have been limited only to the extent losses were due to specific tax preferences. In contrast, the passive-loss rules also will apply even if the taxpayer has true economic losses. The LAL rule was to have been applied on a project-by-project basis, although the technicians were never able to define satisfactorily just what would constitute a separate project. The new passive-loss rules generally permit taxpayers to aggregate the income from all passive activities.

Given the separation of different kinds of economic income and losses

8. Alvin C. Warren, Jr., and Alan J. Auerbach, "Transferability of Tax Incentives and the Fiction of Safe Harbor Leasing," *Harvard Law Review*, vol. 95 (June 1982), pp. 1752–86.

9. See testimony of George P. Shultz in *General Tax Reform*, Hearings before the House Committee on Ways and Means, 93 Cong. 1 sess. (GPO, 1973), pp. 6873–99.

by the passive-loss rules of the 1986 act, we cannot help but wonder whether revenue concerns, perceptions-of-unfairness concerns, or merger concerns might not someday produce momentum for a separate "basket," or line-of-business, approach to corporate alternative minimum taxable income.

Simplification, Equity, and Efficiency

Though administrations and secretaries of the treasury come and go in Washington, the criteria for a good tax remain largely unchanged. They are simplicity, equity, and efficiency. How do minimum taxes stack up when measured against these criteria?

Simplification

Minimum taxes surely are not simple, particularly when deferral preferences are included in the tax base and the tax takes the form of an alternative tax. Minimum taxes make tax planning more difficult, particularly for those taxpayers who do not readily know whether they are going to be subject to the regular tax or to the minimum tax and for those taxpayers subject to the regular tax in some years and to the minimum tax in other years.

The minimum tax presents significant opportunities for tax planning. For example, a cash-basis individual who expects to be subject to the alternative minimum tax in the current year but not in the next year may reduce tax by: (1) accelerating income into the current year so that this income will be taxed at the alternative minimum tax rate of 21 percent, instead of potentially higher regular income rates in the next year; (2) deferring until the next year expenses that are not deductible for the alternative minimum tax, such as state and local income and property taxes; and (3) deferring until the next year expenses that are deductible for the alternative minimum tax, such as cash charitable gifts. Expenses paid in the current year might not yield as great a tax benefit, even in present value terms, as they would if deducted in the next year under the regular tax rates.

The scope of tax planning is more limited for corporations because most corporations are on the accrual method of accounting. The new book-income preference, however, may put some pressure on reported earnings, particularly for privately held companies. Some of these companies undoubtedly will provide book reserves for future liabilities in order to reduce current reported profits and thereby reduce the minimum tax on untaxed book income.

Only to the extent that a minimum tax reduces individual and corporate tendencies to use tax preferences and engage in tax planning can it be said to simplify. But no one advocates minimum taxes on grounds of simplification; minimum taxes are advocated primarily on equity grounds.

Equity

The traditional notions of equity that have informed much of the minimum tax debate have led to a view that the numerous exclusions, deductions, credits, and other allowances permitted by the tax code have created widespread violations of both horizontal and vertical equity. Horizontal equity has been violated because tax preferences allow taxpayers with equal economic incomes to pay different amounts of tax. Vertical equity has been violated because the relative tax burdens intended to apply to taxpayers with different levels of economic income under the regular income tax rate structure are not, in fact, imposed. High-economic-income taxpayers may reduce their effective tax rate disproportionately relative to low- or middle-income taxpayers. Those informed by these traditional equity norms tend to view the scenario of high-economic-income taxpayers with low or zero tax liability as an undesirable by-product of the provision of tax preferences and the minimum tax as a necessary measure to restore tax equity. Moreover, taxpayer perceptions of tax unfairness may be of independent concern in a tax system based on self-assessment.

In addition, if the tax system is in fact bifurcated into a system that imposes largely involuntary compliance on the majority of taxpayers through withholding on wages and third-party reporting of interest and dividend income yet allows high-income taxpayers who use tax preferences to play the "audit lottery," there is a serious inequity in the treatment of taxpayers of different income levels, quite apart from any perception of unfairness. Furthermore, if, as some commissioners of internal revenue believe, taxpayers respond to perceived unfairness by devising illegal ways to reduce their own tax liability, the basis for an effective and equitable tax system is undermined.

Low- or middle-income workers simply cannot understand why the corporation and its officers or the individual employer for whom they work pay less tax on a higher level of economic income than the workers pay on their salary. We accept the basic equity arguments for the minimum tax.

Economic Efficiency

Minimum taxes may rank low on simplification grounds and high on equity grounds, but what about economic efficiency? Any minimum tax blunts the incentive effects of tax preferences. If a business engages only a little in activities or investments specifically encouraged by tax subsidies, no minimum tax will be imposed. But if the business is good at these activities and specializes in them, it will have to pay the minimum tax, perhaps putting it at a competitive disadvantage. If only efficiency considerations were relevant, the minimum tax would not receive very high marks. On efficiency grounds alone, no one should care if ten companies each invest a little in a tax-preferred activity or one company invests a lot.

There clearly are economic efficiency costs in a tax world in which competing companies are subject to different depreciation systems and tax rates. These efficiency costs may be magnified if some companies are subject to the regular tax some years and to minimum tax other years. With the advent of the book-income preference, the corporate income tax can be viewed as involving three tax systems with three different depreciation rules and three different tax rates. Specifically, there is a regular tax with incentive (modified accelerated cost recovery system) depreciation and a 34 percent tax rate. There is an alternative minimum tax computation using specified nonincentive depreciation and a 20 percent tax rate. And there is a third tax on excess book income using even slower book-income depreciation and a 10 percent tax rate. Under prior law, corporations were subject to two marginal tax rates on an additional dollar of fully taxed income.[10]

In an attempt to get some sense of the potential efficiency costs that result from operating multiple tax regimes, we consider a world with a regular tax and a minimum tax, but to simplify the analysis, we assume

10. The marginal tax rate was 46 percent for corporations not subject to the add-on minimum tax and 39.1 percent for corporations subject to it $(0.46 - 0.46 \times 0.15)$ because the 46 cents of regular tax on the additional dollar of income reduced the add-on tax by 6.9 cents.

that the minimum tax does not contain a preference for untaxed book income. We also assume that companies are always subject to either the regular tax or the minimum tax, thereby ignoring any additional efficiency costs that might result from companies' shifting between the regular and minimum tax during a multiple-year period. We further assume a rate of economic depreciation equal to 11 percent a year, which corresponds to what Charles Hulten and Frank Wykoff estimated for furniture and fixtures,[11] and that all units of capital must earn a 6 percent after-tax real rate of return. The top marginal regular and minimum corporate tax rates (34 percent and 20 percent, respectively) are then applied, and effective tax rates are calculated under the two regimes.[12]

To compute the effective tax rates, we must first compute the real internal before-tax rate of return, given an after-tax real rate of return of 6 percent and an 11 percent rate of economic depreciation. The effective tax rate, e, is then calculated as $e = (r - R)/r$ (where r is the real internal before-tax rate of return and R is the required after-tax real rate of return, 6 percent in this case). In this example pertaining to furniture and fixtures, the effective tax rate is 23.5 percent if the company is subject to the regular tax and 18.9 percent if the company is subject to the alternative minimum tax. The effective tax rate on this capital income is lower under the alternative minimum tax—the slower depreciation allowed is more than offset by the lower tax rate.

The results may reverse when debt is introduced into the example because interest deductions are worth less at the lower marginal tax rate under the minimum tax. (The effective tax rate is still defined as $e = (r - R)/r$, but r is now the before-tax rate of return on equity.) We assume that one-third of the investment is financed by debt at a 10 percent rate of interest. In this case, the effective tax rate on the equity capital is -1.3 percent if the company is subject to the regular tax and 10.9 percent if the company is subject to the minimum tax. In the foregoing computations we have assumed that all units of capital must earn the same after-tax real rate of return. This assumption seems appropriate when considering allocative efficiency across industries;

11. Charles R. Hulten and Frank C. Wykoff, "The Measurement of Economic Depreciation," in Hulten, ed., *Depreciation, Inflation, and the Taxation of Income from Capital*, p. 95.

12. In making these computations, we follow the method of Jane G. Gravelle, "Which Effective Tax Rate? A Comment and Extension," *National Tax Journal*, vol. 38 (March 1985), pp. 103–08.

that is, at the margin, capital should earn the same after-tax rate of return, after adjusting for risk (which we ignore here). Two firms in the same industry—one subject to the regular tax and the other to the minimum tax—may have to have the same before-tax rate of return because they sell in the same product market. In such a case, the firm with the higher effective tax rate may get squeezed.

These computations should be regarded as preliminary and suggestive; we have just scratched the surface in our discussion of allocative efficiency in a world in which some firms are subject to the regular tax and others are subject to the minimum tax. Appendix B sets forth some estimates of regular and minimum effective tax rates for different industries.

Notwithstanding these general observations, a minimum tax may serve to improve allocative efficiency in certain situations. Consider tax-exempt bonds. The traditional analysis assumes that the yield differential between taxable and tax-exempt bonds is established by the marginal tax rate of the marginal investor. High-tax-bracket investors in tax-exempt bonds, therefore, are able to enjoy an inframarginal windfall that might be captured for the treasury if tax-exempt interest is included in the base of the minimum tax.

The above analysis suggests that the effect of the minimum tax on economic efficiency is quite complex. To the extent that a minimum tax serves to narrow differences in effective tax rates across industries, allocative efficiency should be improved. On the other hand, minimum taxes may introduce new economic inefficiencies among companies in the same industry. The effect of the minimum tax in inducing inefficient mergers and acquisitions is uncertain. As this first cut at analysis shows, the efficiency effects of both corporate and individual minimum taxes demand further study.

The Minimum Tax as a Transitional Tool

The corporate minimum tax provisions in 1986 played a special transitional function that helped make possible enactment of the Tax Reform Act. The basic thrust of both the corporate and individual revisions was to finance significant reductions in tax rates by expanding the income tax base through the elimination or restriction of a variety of exclusions from income, deductions, and tax credits. The corporate rate reduction from 46 percent to 34 percent was financed largely through repeal of the investment tax credit. This combination of changes, by itself, would have financed a major reduction in taxes on income from the existing capital stock by increasing taxes on income from new capital investments. Various suggestions were advanced throughout the legislative process to mitigate this effect—most notably the Treasury Department's proposal for a special recapture tax on prior ACRS depreciation deductions[13]—but ultimately Congress relied on the minimum tax (and, in the case of individuals, restrictions on deductions of passive losses) to impose taxes on income from pre-enactment capital investment. By so doing, the corporate minimum tax helped finance the corporate rate reduction while reducing the potential windfall gains from the change. Both the list of specified preferences subject to the 20 percent minimum tax rate and the preference imposing a 10 percent tax on the excess of book income over minimum taxable income played important roles in this regard. As mentioned earlier, without the revenue from the corporate minimum tax, a two- to three-point increase in the corporate tax rate would have been necessary.

Thorough evaluation of transitional problems generally and of the use of minimum taxes as devices to facilitate transition to a new tax regime is beyond the scope of this paper. Nevertheless, the 1986 act generally eschewed the prior congressional practice of routinely protecting pre-enactment transactions from the burden of legislative changes through so-called grandfather clauses, and the transitional role played by the minimum tax amendments is noteworthy.

The Minimum Tax in a Consumption Tax World

To this point, we have considered the minimum tax in an income tax world and not in the context of a consumption-based system of taxation, which would tax only consumption and exclude from the tax base all changes in net worth. As with the truly comprehensive income tax, to the extent that consumption were accurately measured and taxed, a minimum tax would be theoretically inappropriate and unnecessary.

A consumption-based tax system implemented in the form of an

13. *The President's Tax Proposals to the Congress for Fairness, Growth, and Simplicity* (GPO, 1985), pp. 192–96.

expenditure tax might, however, be as preference-riddled as the current tax system,[14] creating a divergence between economic consumption and taxable consumption analogous to the economic and taxable income dichotomy present under the current income tax. Many tax preferences of the types currently included in the minimum tax base for individuals could be transferred easily to an expenditure tax, and an individual minimum tax might be warranted for reasons similar to those under the income tax.

Nonetheless, a corporate minimum tax under an expenditure tax system should be unnecessary. The appropriate policy would be to repeal the corporate tax except perhaps as a withholding tax creditable against the shareholders' expenditure tax liability.[15] It would be theoretically inappropriate in a consumption tax system to tax business on production. An expenditure tax should be levied ultimately only at the shareholder level on distributed earnings when consumed. Many consumption tax proponents, however, urge that a cash-flow corporate tax should accompany consumption at the individual level. Such a corporate tax might well serve to induce the same sorts of perceptions of unfairness that have produced calls for a corporate minimum tax in the current income tax system.

In broad conceptual terms then, the minimum tax has been closely linked to the goal of comprehensive income taxation. An individual minimum tax probably has no place within an expenditure tax that is comprehensive, and repeal of the corporate tax should eliminate any theoretical or practical function for a corporate minimum tax. The role of corporate and individual minimum taxes within an expenditure tax that retains tax preferences is unclear.

Conclusion

On balance, we conclude that equity considerations justify both a corporate and individual minimum tax along the lines detailed in this paper, notwithstanding the additional complexities these taxes create for high-income taxpayers and corporations and despite uncertainties regarding the economic efficiency properties of such minimum taxes.

14. See Graetz, "Expenditure Tax Design."
15. Ibid., pp. 239–46.

The case for a minimum tax on corporations is somewhat weaker than the case for a minimum tax on individuals. However, an effective corporate minimum tax is a necessary counterpart to an effective individual minimum tax. A minimum tax should be an alternative tax, not an add-on one. An alternative tax is consistent with the goal of broad-based income tax, whereas an add-on tax is much closer to an excise tax on preferences. To be effective, a minimum tax must cast a wide net. A comprehensive list of tax preferences—both deferral and exemption preferences—should be included in the tax base for the minimum tax, but there is some disagreement about the wisdom of including a book-income preference.

The current relationship between minimum tax and regular tax rates seems quite haphazard. These relationships under the 1986 legislation are quite different for individuals and corporations and appear to have been set principally in response to revenue considerations. A principled relationship along the lines of the original minimum tax proposals (which would have imposed one-half the regular income tax rates on an expanded minimum tax base) merits fresh consideration.

Appendix A: Legislative History of U.S. Minimum Taxes

During the early 1960s, Senator Russell Long, Democrat of Louisiana, proposed an "optional simplified tax," which would have permitted taxpayers to elect either to compute taxable income in the normal manner and apply the regular tax rates or to apply a lower tax rate to an expanded base. The expanded tax base would have included many items excluded from gross income or deducted in arriving at taxable income.

Senator Long's proposal appears to have been the precursor of the 1968 individual minimum tax recommendations of the Johnson administration.[16] Under this proposal, an individual would have computed tax liability under the regular rules and also would have made a special tax computation by applying tax rates equal to one-half of the applicable regular income tax rates to an expanded tax base. The taxpayer would have been required to pay the larger of the two liabilities.

The expanded base under this minimum tax proposal would have

16. *Tax Reform Studies and Proposals, U.S. Treasury Department,* Committee Print, Joint Publication of the House Committee on Ways and Means and the Senate Committee on Finance, 91 Cong. 1 sess. (GPO, 1969), pt. 1.

been taxable income increased by four items of tax preference, all of
which were exemption preferences and two of which were included in
the list of preferences enacted by Congress only beginning in 1987:
(1) tax-exempt interest on state and local bonds, (2) the appreciation in
value of property donated to charity, (3) the excluded one-half of capital
gains, and (4) percentage depletion after the cost of the property had
been recovered. The Treasury's 1968 minimum tax proposal did not
include deferral preferences. With marginal tax rates up to 35 percent
under this minimum tax proposal, Treasury said that deferral preferences
could be included only if very complicated basis adjustment rules also
were provided.

The 1968 Treasury proposal was largely a backdoor means of increasing the maximum tax rate on capital gains to 35 percent. Stanley Surrey,
then the assistant secretary for tax policy, despaired that Congress would
ever repeal the 25 percent alternative tax rate on capital gains. If tax
preferences could not be attacked directly, reaching them through a
minimum tax seemed better than nothing.

To complement its minimum tax proposal, the Treasury proposed to
allocate itemized deductions between taxed and exempt income with
disallowance of deductions allocated to exempt income.

The Nixon administration proposed tax reform in 1969 that included
a limit on tax preferences and an allocation of deductions similar to that
proposed by the 1968 Treasury study. The version of the 1969 Tax
Reform Act passed by the House of Representatives adopted these
proposals, but modified the list of preference items.

The House version did not contain a corporate minimum tax. Nor did
the Treasury Department in either the Johnson or Nixon administration
propose one. The original focus of these minimum tax proposals was on
high-income individuals who paid little or no tax. It was argued that only
a few industries used major preference items that would be subject to a
corporate minimum tax. Whether the tax structure of tax-favored
industries should be altered was a question that Treasury and the House
said would be addressed separately. (The decision not to seek a minimum
tax for corporations predated the extensive depreciation revisions of
1971 and 1981 but came after the 1962 shift to guideline depreciation and
the enactment of the investment tax credit, which was repealed in the
1969 act.)

The Senate, however, had a different view, and the minimum tax
provision finally enacted bore little relation to either the Treasury or

House proposals. The Senate Finance Committee eliminated the House provisions and substituted what it labeled a minimum tax. This provision, however, really was an excise tax of 5 percent on certain preference items; that is, an add-on minimum tax. The proposal to allocate deductions was dropped, and to compensate for the lost revenues, the minimum tax was extended to corporations. On the Senate floor, the rate of the minimum tax was increased from 5 percent to 10 percent and a deduction was allowed for regular income taxes in an effort to link minimum tax liability in some way with varying burdens under the regular income tax.

The minimum tax enacted as part of the Tax Reform Act of 1969 followed the Senate bill. It applied to both corporations and individuals at a rate of 10 percent and was based on the amount by which certain tax preferences exceeded a statutory exemption amount ($30,000), plus the amount of regular taxes. The minimum tax was payable in addition to the regular income tax.

The Excise, Estate, and Gift Tax Adjustment Act of 1970 modified the minimum tax by allowing a deduction from the minimum tax base of the "unused regular tax carryover." The unused regular tax could be carried forward up to seven years. The Revenue Act of 1971 changed the minimum tax by expanding the list of tax preferences subject to the minimum tax.

The Tax Reform Act of 1976 increased the minimum tax rate from 10 percent to 15 percent, expanded and modified the list of tax preferences, and replaced the statutory exemption and deduction for regular taxes allowed individuals under prior law with an exemption equal to the greater of $10,000 or one-half of the regular tax liability. The new exemption for corporations was $10,000, or the regular tax liability, if greater. These changes significantly increased the number of taxpayers required to pay the minimum tax as well as the total amount of minimum tax collected.

The Tax Reduction and Simplification Act of 1977 modified the definition of tax preferences subject to the minimum tax. The Revenue Act of 1978 added an alternative minimum tax for individuals payable only if it exceeded the regular tax. The tax base for this new tax was generally the taxpayer's taxable income, plus certain itemized deductions and capital gains excluded from regular taxes. The tax rates were graduated up to 25 percent for alternative minimum taxable income over $100,000. This tax was paid if greater than the amount due under the regular tax and the add-on minimum tax. Certain adjustments were added to prevent the permanent loss of tax credits as a result of the operation of the alternative minimum tax. The add-on minimum tax for individuals was retained for deferral preferences. The list of tax preferences for both individuals and corporations was modified again.

The Economic Recovery Tax Act of 1981 lowered the top individual tax rate to 20 percent for alternative minimum taxable income over $60,000. Some of the tax preferences subject to the add-on minimum taxes were redefined.

The Tax Equity and Fiscal Responsibility Act of 1982 repealed the individual add-on minimum tax, and changed the alternative minimum rate to a flat 20 percent on alternative minimum taxable income above $40,000 for joint returns ($30,000 for individuals and $20,000 for married persons filing separately). The list of tax preferences subject to the individual alternative minimum tax was expanded to include the preferences previously subject to the add-on tax as well as certain new preference items. With the 1982 legislation, the minimum tax for individuals largely had come full circle to its initial conception as an alternative tax.

The 1982 act modified the corporate add-on minimum tax by cutting back certain corporate tax preferences by 15 percent so that only 85 percent of those items would be allowed to reduce regular taxable income. The Deficit Reduction Act of 1984 extended the 15 percent cutback to 21 percent for all listed preferences except depletion on certain mineral deposits.

The Tax Reform Act of 1986 replaced the corporate add-on minimum tax with a 20 percent alternative tax. The list of preferences was expanded to include tax-exempt interest on new, private-activity state and local bonds; accelerated depreciation on machinery and equipment; untaxed appreciation on charitable gifts; and untaxed book income.

In summary, Congress in 1969 first enacted 10 percent add-on minimum taxes for both individuals and corporations. Over the years, it frequently changed the tax rates, the level of the exemptions, and the items of tax preference. In 1978 Congress enacted an alternative minimum tax for individuals but retained the add-on minimum tax for certain deferral preferences. In 1982 Congress repealed the add-on minimum tax for individuals and expanded the individual alternative minimum tax. In 1986 Congress replaced the add-on minimum tax for corporations with an alternative minimum tax.

The legislative history suggests that minimum taxes have not been a stable area of the tax law. Inasmuch as the Tax Reform Act of 1986 increases their importance as revenue sources, Congress is likely to revisit these taxes frequently, and they surely will be amended again.

Appendix B: Effective Tax Rates

Minimum taxes are justified primarily on equity grounds, but these taxes do impose efficiency costs because competing companies can be subject to different depreciation systems and marginal tax rates, causing effective tax rates on the income from capital to vary across industries or across firms within an industry. To get a better idea of these efficiency costs, this appendix measures the effective tax rates for firms subject or not subject to the minimum tax (see table 3).

Economic theory suggests that investments occur at the margin until after-tax rates of return on alternative investments are equalized. In table 3, this market-forced after-tax rate of return is assumed to be 6 percent, and to compute effective tax rates, this required after-tax rate of return must be compared with internal before-tax rates of return. Assuming no debt financing, two reasons explain why these before-tax rates of return will not be equalized across all assets. First, different assets face different tax rules, not only in terms of capital-consumption allowances, but also in terms of tax rates depending on whether the asset is subject to the regular 34 percent corporate tax rate or the alternative minimum 20 percent corporate tax rate. Second, assets differ in terms of durability or rates of real economic depreciation.

To obtain the before-tax rate of return for any given capital asset, one must first compute the applicable rental cost of capital, which is what a firm would pay, or should impute to itself, for the use of a capital asset. This rental cost is directly analogous to the wages companies must pay their employees. This imputed price for the use of physical capital includes the required after-tax rate of return as determined by market forces, an amount to cover the necessary tax burden, and an amount for capital recovery. For computational convenience, a single number that represents the present value of a flow of depreciation deductions is

Table 3. *Effective Corporate Tax Rates under Regular and Alternative Minimum Tax, by Asset Class*[a]

Asset class	ACRS class (years)	ADR life (years)	Economic depreciation (percent)	Present value of depreciation (percent)		Rental price ratio (minimum/regular)	Effective tax rate	
				Regular tax	Minimum tax		Regular tax	Minimum tax
No debt finance								
Furniture and fixtures	7	10	11.00	78.97	67.13	0.976	23.5	18.9
Farm tractors	7	10	16.33	78.97	67.13	0.976	28.7	23.4
Agricultural machinery (except tractors)	7	10	9.71	78.97	67.13	0.976	22.1	17.7
Construction machinery (except tractors)	5	6	17.22	84.76	78.42	0.977	23.3	17.3
Trucks and truck trailers	5	5	25.37	84.76	81.65	0.970	29.1	19.3
Autos	5	5	33.33	84.76	81.65	0.970	34.0	23.1
Commercial aircraft	7	12	18.33	78.97	62.43	0.987	30.5	27.6
Ships and boats	10	18	7.50	71.47	51.07	0.979	24.8	21.6
Farm buildings	20	25	2.37	48.03	41.65	0.904	27.2	16.9
One-third of investment debt financed								
Furniture and fixtures	7	10	11.00	80.97	68.84	1.032	−1.3	10.9
Farm tractors	7	10	16.33	80.97	68.84	1.019	10.6	18.5
Agricultural machinery (except tractors)	7	10	9.71	80.97	68.84	1.037	−4.6	8.9
Construction machinery (except tractors)	5	6	17.22	86.28	79.68	1.018	−1.9	8.0
Trucks and truck trailers	5	5	25.37	86.28	82.75	1.001	11.1	11.5
Autos	5	5	33.33	86.28	82.75	0.995	21.0	17.7
Commercial aircraft	7	12	18.33	80.97	64.27	1.027	14.3	25.1
Ships and boats	10	18	7.50	73.98	53.10	1.048	2.3	15.8
Farm buildings	20	25	2.37	51.43	43.66	0.996	8.6	8.0

Source: Economic depreciation figures from Charles R. Hulten and Frank C. Wykoff, "The Measurement of Economic Depreciation," in Hulten, ed., *Depreciation, Inflation, and the Taxation of Income from Capital* (Washington, D.C.: Urban Institute, 1981), p. 95.

a. The following parameters are assumed: 34 percent regular tax rate; 20 percent alternative minimum tax rate; 6 percent required after-tax real rate of return on equity capital; 4 percent expected rate of inflation; and 10 percent interest rate on debt.

usually used. In a world of no debt finance, the formula for the rental cost of a dollar investment in physical capital is:

$$c = \frac{(R + d)(1 - uz)}{(1 - u)},$$

where c = the rental cost of capital,
  R = the required real after-tax rate of return,
  d = the rate of economic depreciation,
  u = the applicable tax rate,
  z = the present value of depreciation deductions.

In table 3, the present value of depreciation deductions differs depending on whether the asset is subject to the regular or alternative minimum corporate tax. For the regular corporate tax of 34 percent, the Tax Reform Act of 1986 assigns property placed in service after December 31, 1986, to a three-, five-, seven-, ten-, fifteen-, or twenty-year class. For the three-, five-, seven-, and ten-year property, a double declining-balance method is applied; and for fifteen- and twenty-year property, a 150 percent declining-balance method is applied, both using a half-year convention and switching to the straight-line method at a time to maximize the present value of depreciation deductions.

For the minimum corporate tax of 20 percent, the 150 percent declining-balance method is applied over the asset depreciation range (ADR) midpoint life, using a half-year convention and switching to the straight-line method as well.

The before-tax rate of return is computed by subtracting the real rate of economic depreciation from the rental cost of capital, and the effective tax rate is merely the before-tax rate of return less the after-tax rate of return as a percentage of the before-tax rate of return.

The formula for the rental cost of capital makes apparent that if assets could be immediately expensed, the present value of depreciation deductions would equal one, the rental cost of capital would equal the sum of the required after-tax rate of return and the rate of economic depreciation, and the effective tax rate would be zero. At the other extreme, if depreciation deductions are equal to true economic depreciation, the effective tax rate would be equal to the statutory tax rate.[17]

17. Paul A. Samuelson, "Tax Deductibility of Economic Depreciation to Insure Invariant Valuations," *Journal of Political Economy*, vol. 72 (December 1964), pp. 604–06.

When debt financing is introduced, the model changes in several respects. The return on equity is isolated so that the effective tax rate now becomes the before-tax rate of return on equity less the after-tax rate of return on equity as a percentage of the before-tax rate of return on equity. The rental cost of capital now becomes:

$$c = \frac{(R + d)(1 - f - uz)}{(1 - u)} + \frac{f[i(1 - u) - p + d]}{(1 - u)},$$

where c = the rental cost of capital,
   R = the required real after-tax rate of return on equity,
   d = the rate of economic depreciation,
   f = the debt finance percentage,
   u = the applicable tax rate,
   z = the present value of depreciation deductions,
   i = the nominal debt interest rate,
   p = the expected inflation rate.

The discount factor for z is still a nominal rate, but it is now a weighted average between the nominal return on debt and equity capital.[18] The discount rate is:

$$q = f[1 + i(1 - u)] + (1 - f)(1 + R)(1 + p) - 1,$$

where q = the discount rate,
   f = the debt finance percentage,
   i = the nominal debt interest rate,
   u = the applicable tax rate,
   R = the required real after-tax rate of return on equity,
   p = the expected inflation rate.

If there is no debt financing, the before-tax real rate of return, r, is $r = c - d$. When the possibility of debt is included, the before-tax rate of return becomes $r = [c - f(i - p) - d]/(1 - f)$.

Because interest is deductible, effective tax rates are reduced for both the regular and the minimum tax when debt is introduced. Since interest deductions are worth more at higher marginal tax rates, debt financing

18. It should be noted that any computation of effective tax rates will be sensitive to the precise discounting methods used to calculate the present value of depreciation deductions. In calculating the effective tax rates shown in Appendix B, the first year's depreciation was not discounted, the second year's depreciation was discounted one year, the third year's was discounted two years, etc.

plays a larger role in reducing the effective tax rate for assets or industries subject to the regular corporate tax than for those subject to the alternative minimum corporate tax. As Jane Gravelle has noted, tax subsidies available for an entire investment go toward reducing the tax on the equity part of that investment, and therefore leverage lowers the corporate effective tax rate.[19] In reading table 3, one should also note that the industries or assets whose effective tax rates stay high or even exceed the statutory tax rates are the ones whose capital-consumption-allowance provisions are unfavorable compared with their true economic depreciation.

Comments by Jane G. Gravelle

Graetz and Sunley tackle the new minimum tax on both general principles and on specific design details. Their paper is impressive. It contains a comprehensive treatment of the issues involved in evaluating both the basic concepts and the specific features of the new tax. They essentially come down on the side of a minimum tax in its alternative tax form, although they have some reservations about certain details.

Under prior law, the individual minimum tax was an alternative tax applied at a lower rate on an expanded base and paid if it exceeded regular tax. The 1986 reform increased the rate of 20 percent to 21 percent and expanded the list of preferences. Before the 1986 law, the minimum corporate tax was an add-on tax of 20 percent on preferences greater than an exemption or regular taxes paid, whichever was larger. The 1986 act converted the corporate tax to an alternative tax and also expanded the preference list, with an important addition, through 1989, of one-half of book income above minimum tax income. Net operating loss carryovers can offset only 90 percent of minimum taxable income, and the foreign tax credit can offset only 90 percent of the minimum tax. Minimum tax above regular tax, except that arising from exclusions, can be carried forward as a credit against future regular tax liability.

Graetz and Sunley support the minimum tax primarily on equity grounds, both vertical and horizontal, and they consider both real inequities and perceptions of inequities to be rationales. They suggest

19. Gravelle, "Which Effective Tax Rate?"

that the tax ranks low on simplification and will complicate tax planning. They also suggest that the tax ranks poorly on efficiency grounds and will cause differentials in tax burdens on assets depending on whether the minimum or regular tax applies; they present some calculations of these different effective tax rates for several types of assets. Graetz also argues that the tax can serve as a transition toward a broad-based, relatively flat, income tax by weaning taxpayers away from preferences.

They note that support for the minimum tax is less likely to be forthcoming from those who favor a consumption tax base and that support for the corporate minimum tax is less likely from those who argue that corporate source income is excessively taxed in the current income tax framework.

Graetz and Sunley address five fundamental design issues. The first is whether a corporate minimum tax is desirable. They note that the corporate minimum tax is not a step toward integration but argue that an effective corporate tax is required to prevent the use of the tax as an escape hatch and that the corporate tax is the primary tax on capital income. Finally, they discuss the disparity between taxes across industries and across firms within an industry. The corporate minimum tax, they suggest, reduces distortions across industries. It may, however, exacerbate differences within industries by differentially taxing those firms that are not integrated. It may also stimulate inefficient mergers and leasing to avoid the tax. At the same time, the tax may reduce the distortion between firms with different debt-equity ratios.

The second issue they address is the add-on versus the alternative tax. They favor the alternative tax as appropriate for the objective of providing some minimum level of taxation, even though it is more complex. The third, and closely related, issue involves complications with deferral preferences, which involve timing under an alternative minimum tax. Without adjustments, deferral preferences could involve loss of deductions. This problem can be dealt with in several ways: by providing a basis adjustment, by allowing the option of including the preference in the regular tax base, or by allowing a credit mechanism. The credit mechanism, which permits minimum tax above regular tax (except for exclusion items) to be carried forward to offset future regular taxes, is incorporated in the current minimum tax.

The fourth issue involves rate structures. The ratio of minimum to regular tax rates differs for both the individual and corporate systems, and these ratios changed from their previous levels. The authors suggest that there is no clear rationale for these relationships. Moreover, the setting of rates requires a balance between the desire to avoid overbroad application and yet to require a significant minimum level of taxation.

Finally, they consider some special design issues of the corporate tax. They discuss conflicting views on the book-income preference item, with some suggesting that it will cause the government to lose control over the tax base, will differentially tax firms with different accounting provisions, and will put pressure on financial accounting. Others do not consider these criticisms to be so serious and view the preference as necessary to eliminate situations in which companies with high reported earnings pay extremely low taxes and thus create a perception of unfairness.

Another issue involves the problems of combining unrelated activities, which may induce merger activity. The authors speculate on the possibility of adopting a "separate basket" approach to activities within a firm, particularly in the light of the precedent of the passive-loss restriction.

In commenting on the paper, I would like to set aside the issues of the general desirability of a consumption versus an income tax, the proper role of a separate corporate tax, and vertical equity. These arguments are clear, they depend on tax base and distributional objectives that are themselves subject to debate, and they could be applied to any item that primarily increases the tax on capital or corporate income. In addition, I have no disagreement on the simplicity issue—it seems clear that the minimum tax would make taxation more complex. I would like to discuss first the basic issues of equity and efficiency and expand the efficiency analysis of the corporate minimum tax somewhat. Then I would like to discuss an issue that Graetz and Sunley do not address—the time path of a minimum tax that relies heavily on deferral preferences.

Consider first the equity argument, which is the major rationale Graetz and Sunley advance for the minimum tax. There are several aspects of this issue—corporate versus individual, horizontal versus vertical, and real versus perceived. First, consider the issue of horizontal equity in corporate taxation. The basic argument is that differential tax rates applied to different assets and firms are inequitable. Yet this argument is inconsistent with economic theory, which indicates that individuals require equalized after-tax returns, net of risk, from corporate equities. After-tax returns will converge, and the differentials induced by uneven taxation will cause before-tax, rather than after-tax, returns to diverge. This problem is one of efficiency, not equity.

Are there circumstances where differential corporate tax rates do reflect inequities? Setting aside the deliberate rate graduation, one might make a case where preferences are allowed for some firms, but not others in the same industry. I can discern only one such preference covered by the minimum tax—percentage depletion on oil and gas, which does not loom very large in the corporate sector, restricted as it is to limited production of independents.

Another aspect of this equity argument is that the minimum tax could create inequities where none existed previously. If the economic analysis above is correct, then all firms earn the same after-tax rate of return. The minimum tax could, however, produce different tax rates for firms competing in the same market. If market competition forces these firms to earn the same before-tax returns (since they face the same wages and the same market prices), then after-tax returns will diverge. How such firms will coexist in the market is not clear, but it is a point worth further consideration.

What about horizontal inequities in the individual tax? Here, a better case for the minimum tax can be made. Nevertheless, if the individual tax rate is flat and one is concerned with items of capital income, the same analysis follows as in the corporate case—after-tax returns are equalized and before-tax returns diverge. To the extent, however, that tax rates are graduated or that items of consumption as well as capital income are preferred, horizontal inequities result. But such a case could be made much more easily under the previous tax system than under the new one where rates are much flatter and where rates tend to be quite flat among those individuals likely to be affected by the minimum tax. Moreover, many major items of preferential treatment such as capital gains and tax shelters have been addressed through other provisions of the tax law. Indeed, as a general observation, it would seem that the case for the minimum tax on equity grounds is considerably weaker in the context of the new tax system than under the old system. On the other hand, future alterations in the base and rate structure of the individual tax may change the evaluation of the individual minimum tax.

Nevertheless, if a case can be made for an individual minimum tax on equity grounds, one could then argue that a minimum tax is desirable to prevent individuals from using the corporation as an "escape hatch." It is not clear how important this possibility is, particularly given that corporate regular tax rates are higher than individual regular tax rates. The issue does bear more examination. However, if this is the major rationale for a corporate minimum tax, it is a rationale for applying it to small, closely held corporations, not to large, public ones. Moreover, this rationale weakens the case for differentiating preferences between the two systems, such as the book-income preference item in the corporate tax.

What about the perception problem? I do not disagree that perception of equity can be very important to a self-assessed tax. Moreover, the perception of unfair treatment can alter welfare as well as the reality. It seems important, however, to consider carefully the events that led to these perceptions, particularly when discussing the corporate minimum tax.

These perceptions arose in large degree from reports that large corporations paid little or no taxes. To some extent, the low taxes paid were likely the result of temporary factors, arising from a cyclical downturn; the cumulation of tax deferrals under the generous depreciation rules adopted in 1981, which will begin to reverse themselves; and safe harbor leasing. These rates would have begun to turn upward in any case because of natural tendencies. Moreover, the new law as well as other changes made since 1981 should mitigate these observed low tax rates. If the perception problem is paramount, however, it does create a case for the book-income preference. A similar argument can be made that the instances of lower rates among individuals will be reduced, particularly to the extent that instances associated with high-income individuals paying low taxes involved tax shelters and capital gains preferences. In sum, while an equity case can be made for the minimum tax, I believe the case is much weaker than that presented by Graetz and Sunley.

Graetz and Sunley touch on a number of issues of efficiency, all of which seem valid. One point they make is that differential tax burdens apply to different assets under the minimum versus the regular tax. In their analysis, they use an effective marginal tax rate measure that compares before- and after-tax returns on the equity share of capital. This marginal tax rate measure is confined to corporate-level taxes, incorporates debt finance, and is an analog to the average effective tax rate measures that divide profits taxes by before-tax return. Out of the growing stable of effective tax rates to use, this one seems quite appropriate to the analysis at hand.

I have expanded their analysis to a number of assets using the same basic assumptions, and present the calculated effective tax rates for the major categories of assets in the economy in table 4.[20] In some cases I find the variations in effective tax rates to be relatively small, particularly among many equipment assets. Variations in structures are more pronounced simply because the rate reductions loom large compared with the differences in the present value of depreciation. (Note that the harshness of the minimum tax for mining and exploration, which relates primarily to oil and gas drilling, may be overstated because of the difficulties in modeling the net income offset.)

The effects of the two taxes on distortions depend not only on the spread between the equity tax rates but also on the importance of the equity return in the price of capital, which also includes debt returns and depreciation rates. Moreover, small variations in discounting techniques can have significant effects on effective tax rate measures but much smaller effects on measures of the price of capital. Therefore, the third column of table 4 reports the ratio of the rental prices of capital (the sum of the before-tax return and the economic depreciation rate) under the two systems.

How important these distortions are depends on the substitutability of assets within firms, the substitutability of output across industries, and the frequency of application of the minimum tax. Table 5 contains some estimates by industry that might aid in assessing this issue. The first three columns show effective tax rates by industry after assets have been aggregated, as well as an aggregation of weighted rental capital price ratios.

The last two columns of table 5 estimate a steady-state average tax rate for each industry under each tax. In other words, it is the effective tax rate one would expect to observe in the long run, taking into account the accumulated tax depreciation deductions generated by the two systems. The formula for estimating this tax rate is:

$$\frac{u[r + d - fi - (d + g)z]}{[r - f(i - p)]},$$

where u is the statutory tax rate, r is the before-tax real rate of return, d

---

20. The numbers in this table differ from those for the same assets in the Graetz-Sunley paper because of certain computational differences. The major computational difference is the method of determining the present value of depreciation. In the Graetz-Sunley paper, depreciation is determined by employing discrete discounting, while the estimates in this comment are based on continuous time formulas. The effective tax rates on equity can be quite sensitive to the value of depreciation, particularly when the depreciation period is short.

Table 4. *Effective Marginal Tax Rates and Rental Price Ratios, by Asset*

Asset	Effective tax rate		Ratio of minimum to regular rental price
	Minimum tax	*Regular tax*	
Inventories	22	37	0.996
Autos	22	33	0.979
Office/computing equipment	20	27	0.985
Trucks, buses, and trailers	16	25	0.983
Aircraft	27	25	1.005
Construction machinery	12	14	0.995
Mining and oilfield machinery	24	23	1.005
Service industry machinery	20	23	0.991
Tractors	19	20	0.998
Instruments	24	22	1.007
Other equipment	21	20	1.004
General industrial equipment	20	18	1.007
Metal working machinery	15	14	1.003
Electric transmission equipment	25	30	0.982
Communications equipment	15	5	1.028
Other electrical equipment	18	14	1.010
Furniture and fixtures	14	13	1.004
Special industrial equipment	16	9	1.019
Agricultural equipment	12	10	1.006
Fabricated metal products	20	23	0.989
Engines and turbines	22	33	0.945
Ships and boats	18	14	1.016
Railroad equipment	10	3	1.025
Mining, oil, and gas	−3	−13	1.029
Other	22	34	0.926
Industrial structures	19	29	0.932
Public utility structures	13	17	0.976
Commercial structures	16	25	0.939
Farm structures	10	15	0.968

Source: Author's estimates.

is the economic depreciation rate, f is the share financed by debt, i is the nominal interest rate, g is the real growth rate, z is the value of depreciation, and p is the inflation rate. The measure of z is determined as a present value calculation, employing the nominal growth rate rather than the nominal discount rate.

These estimates suggest that most industries are unlikely to be subject to the minimum tax in the long run. Thus in the long run distortions are

Table 5. *Effective Tax Rates, by Industry and Rental Price Ratios*

Industry	Marginal effective tax rate		Ratio of minimum to regular rental price	Long-run average effective tax rate	
	Minimum tax	Regular tax		Minimum tax	Regular tax
Agriculture	15	23	0.979	18	27
Mining	15	20	0.968	21	30
Oil extraction	5	1	0.966	11	14
Construction	17	24	0.980	24	35
Manufacturing	19	29	0.985	22	33
Transportation	16	16	0.959	21	27
Communications	15	15	0.967	18	24
Electric and gas	15	20	0.965	18	26
Trade	18	30	0.985	21	33
Services	18	24	0.965	25	37

Source: Author's estimates.

not likely to be important, not only because they are small but also because the instances of the tax occurring should be limited. Of course, some preference items are missing from this calculation, as their inclusion would make the rates diverge more. Conversely, land is excluded, which tends to make these rates converge more than they actually would. Furthermore, in the case of oil and gas production, where rates are closest, the minimum tax burden is probably overstated because of failure to account for the net income exception. In addition, much oil and gas production is undertaken in integrated companies.

How does one square these findings with the estimate of corporate minimum tax revenue of $22.1 billion between 1987 and 1990, accounting for almost 20 percent of corporate tax increases? One answer is that this long-run equilibrium takes a long time—technically forty-one years—to be achieved. However, because equipment investment tends to dominate, that equilibrium will come close to being reached in a much shorter time, probably around eleven years. Until equilibrium is reached, however, the minimum tax may be much more likely to apply, and this is an important aspect of the tax.

Initially the alternative depreciation systems will apply only to new capital. The difference between depreciation allowances will grow and then decline, the inevitable pattern of deferral items. As an illustration, consider a typical equipment investment that falls into the seven-year regular class and the ten-year alternative class, with double- and 150 percent declining-balance depreciation, respectively. Using the half-year convention, the difference in depreciation in the first year will be about 7 percent of investment in that property. In the second year, the cumulated differential will be 7 percent of first-year property plus about 11 percent of previous-year (slightly smaller, given growth) investment. For this property, the peak will be reached in about four or five years, when cumulated differentials will reach about 25 percent of current-year investment, before declining to a steady state rate of about 9 percent by the eleventh year.

Of course, there are many classes of assets. Shorter-lived properties will peak earlier, while longer-lived ones will peak later. Structures will begin with negligible effects and grow very slowly over time, although they are not nearly as important as equipment because their depreciation levels and ratios of investment to capital stock are much lower. The effect of accounting provisions is also likely to peak early.

While a full analysis of the time path of these rates is beyond the scope of this discussion, it appears likely that the minimum tax will be most important in producing revenue and user costs in the next few years and then gradually decline in the frequency of application. Indeed, the annual minimum tax revenue estimates show such a decline beginning in the third year.

Such a result leads to several significant points to consider. First, the revenue gain from the minimum tax is likely to be short-lived. Second, the hope that the minimum tax will lead to a transition to a broader-base, lower-rate tax appears questionable. Unless this transition occurs very quickly, the minimum tax will begin to fade in importance. Finally, and most important for efficiency analysis, many firms may find themselves with the prospect of paying the minimum tax in the early years and the regular tax later. Because the minimum tax credit mechanism does not preserve the time value of tax payments, the tax burdens on new investments for such firms are likely to be higher than for firms paying solely either the regular or minimum tax and will be quite uncertain as well. These effects might cause firms to delay investments in the next few years and lead to a significant amount of complexity in tax and investment planning.

I would sum up these points by suggesting that the minimum tax has some flaws, but it is also not likely to be a very important element in the tax system in the long run, at least for businesses. The major costs and benefits will occur in the next few years. The benefit of the tax is that it may ameliorate the problem of perceived inequity while that problem is working out of its own accord. The cost is significant complexity and a possible depressing effect on investment in the short run.

Comments by Donald C. Lubick

The paper is an excellent summary and analysis of the considerations in design and implementation of a minimum tax. Nevertheless, after weighing these considerations, I conclude that optimally the minimum tax ought not to be a permanent part of the tax system.

I side with the view discussed by the authors that justifies the minimum tax as a step toward the ultimate, truly desired goal of a comprehensive income tax base.

If one accepts the notion that tax preferences are tax expenditures, justifiable only to the extent that an expenditure is justified, one is hard put to accept the minimum tax as a permanent state of affairs. It seems to me that a minimum tax reflects a politically expedient way to trim tax expenditures; the fairness and efficiency of such a tax is in great doubt. The minimum tax is a roundabout way to undermine citadels that cannot be stormed directly.

The paper points out the minimum tax can produce bizarre results, depending upon a business's form of organization, whether or not it is part of a conglomerate, or even the happenstance of an unrelated economic circumstance occurring. Because it magnifies the unevenness of the incentive effect, the checkered and illogical applicability of the minimum tax makes even more shaky the economic case for retaining in the regular tax base the preferences that are included in the minimum tax base.

From projections of the numbers of returns and taxpayers affected by it, the minimum tax has been so greatly extended that it has become a not uncommon way of life. Indeed, as the authors point out, when the passive loss rules are taken into account, we may have not two parallel tax systems but three. The difficulties that are going to exist not only for taxpayers in planning but for the Internal Revenue Service in trying to administer these various systems are an inherent source of instability. The authors point out the very serious deficiencies both in equity and efficiency in running several tax systems. Indeed, "parallel" is the wrong word; they may even be divergent tax systems.

So, since there is a compression of brackets between the regular and minimum tax systems and a much broader population subject to both of them, it seems to me the forces for change have been placed in motion. I have talked to lots of accountants and tax practitioners who are baffled by how to cope with these situations created by the new law. The minimum tax simply is not going to play too well in Peoria.

The adoption of a broad minimum tax, in the context of rate cuts, ought to lead to the next logical step of revising the preferences themselves. Certainly there is going to be a need for revenue. Section 291 of the tax code, which pertains to corporations, gives a percentage cutback (for the most part, 20 percent) to certain preferences. It seems to me that approach could be used both for corporations and for individuals. That, I recognize, moves in the direction of the add-on minimum tax. This is not the direction the authors prefer, but it is consistent with the direction in which I think the basic tax system ought to be going.

The 1986 act shows acceptance of the notion that low rates and a broad base go together. The minimum tax, I think, was essential to get that concept through the tax-writing committees. But it seems to me that the minimum tax cannot survive as a permanent broadly applicable part of our law. If it does, and people just push their assets around to preserve their tax-preference way of life by getting different combinations, then the minimum tax will have failed, but at the expense of great difficulties of planning. In either event, I think the agenda is still the same. We should get to work to eliminate the preferences now while people are conditioned to accept their elimination as the price of maintaining low marginal rates.

Conference Participants

with their affiliations at the time of the conference

Henry J. Aaron *Brookings Institution*
Krister Andersson *University of Lund, Sweden*
William D. Andrews *Harvard University Law School*
Alan J. Auerbach *University of Pennsylvania*
J. Gregory Ballentine *Peat Marwick Main & Co.*
B. Douglas Bernheim *Stanford University*
John Bossons *University of Toronto*
Barry Bosworth *Brookings Institution*
David F. Bradford *Princeton University*
E. Cary Brown *Massachusetts Institute of Technology*
Sheldon S. Cohen *Morgan, Lewis & Bockius*
Bruce F. Davie *House Committee on Ways and Means*
Larry L. Dildine *Price Waterhouse*
Don Fullerton *Department of the Treasury*
Harvey Galper *Brookings Institution*
Richard B. Goode *Brookings Institution*
Michael J. Graetz *Yale University Law School*
Edward M. Gramlich *Congressional Budget Office*
Jane G. Gravelle *Congressional Research Service*
Daniel Halperin *Georgetown University Law Center*
Arnold C. Harberger *University of Chicago*
Patric H. Hendershott *Ohio State University*
Frederick Hickman *Hopkins and Sutter*
Charles R. Hulten *University of Maryland*
Dale W. Jorgenson *Harvard University*
Louis Kaplow *Harvard University Law School*
Mervyn A. King *London School of Economics*

431

Robert A. Klayman *Caplin & Drysdale*
Stanley Koppelman *Boston University Law School*
Laurence J. Kotlikoff *Boston University*
Jerome Kurtz *Paul, Weiss, Rifkind, Wharton, & Garrison*
Donald C. Lubick *Hodgson, Russ, Andrews, Woods, & Goodyear*
Robert Lucke *Price Waterhouse*
Charles E. McLure, Jr. *Hoover Institution*
John H. Makin *American Enterprise Institute*
Rosemary D. Marcuss *Congressional Budget Office*
Peter Mieszkowski *Rice University*
Joseph J. Minarik *Urban Institute*
Alicia H. Munnell *Federal Reserve Bank of Boston*
Richard A. Musgrave *University of California, Santa Cruz*
Göran Normann *Federation of Swedish Industries, Stockholm*
Joseph A. Pechman *Brookings Institution*
Mark Perlis *Department of the Treasury*
James M. Poterba *Massachusetts Institute of Technology*
Myron S. Scholes *Stanford University*
David O. Sewell *Economic Council of Canada*
Eytan Sheshinski *Massachusetts Institute of Technology*
John B. Shoven *Stanford University*
Jonathan Skinner *University of Virginia*
Joel Slemrod *University of Minnesota*
David A. Starrett *Stanford University*
Eugene Steuerle *American Enterprise Institute*
Joseph E. Stiglitz *Princeton University*
Lawrence H. Summers *Harvard University*
Emil M. Sunley *Deloitte, Haskins & Sells*
Vito Tanzi *International Monetary Fund*
Eric Toder *Congressional Budget Office*
Alvin C. Warren *Harvard University Law School*
Randall D. Weiss *Joint Committee on Taxation*
John Whalley *University of Western Ontario*
Bernard Wolfman *Harvard Law School*
Mark A. Wolfson *Stanford University*

Name Index

Subject Index